Mapping Male Sexuality

Mapping Male Sexuality

Nineteenth-Century England

Edited by
Jay Losey and William D. Brewer

Madison • Teaneck
Fairleigh Dickinson University Press
London: Associated University Presses

Associated University Presses
440 Forsgate Drive
Cranbury, NJ 08512

Associated University Presses
16 Barter Street
London WC1A 2AH, England

Associated University Presses
P.O. Box 338, Port Credit
Mississauga, Ontario
Canada L5G 4L8

The paper used in this publication meets the requirements of the American National Standard for Permanence of Paper for Printed Library Materials Z39.48-1984.

Library of Congress Cataloging-in-Publication Data

Mapping male sexuality : nineteenth-century England / edited by Jay Losey and William D. Brewer.
    p. cm.
    Includes bibliographical references (p.) and index.
    ISBN 0-8386-3828-7 (alk. paper)
    1. English literature—Male authors—History and criticism. 2. Sex in literature. 3. Homosexuality and literature—England—History—19th century. 4. Men—England—Sexual behavior—History—19th century.
5. English literature—19th century—History and criticism. 6. Gay men's writings, English—History and criticism. 7. Gay men in literature. 8. Men in literature. I. Losey, Jay, 1955– II. Brewer, William D. (William Dean)
PR468.S48 M36   2000
820.9'353—dc21   99-053165

Contents

Part III: Late Victorian

Introduction

ELIZABETH DELL AND JAY LOSEY

SEVERAL CRITICS—AMONG THEM MICHEL FOUCAULT, LOUIS CROMP-
ton, Jonathan Dollimore, Elaine Showalter, Herbert Sussman, and
Jeffrey Weeks—have argued that the nineteenth century was a decisive period in the history of male sexuality. In his controversial
study *The History of Sexuality: An Introduction* (1978), Foucault
argues that instead of repressing sexuality nineteenth-century culture became so focused on sexuality that it assumed the basis for
identity. To respond to this privileging of sexuality, which threatened the public domain, discourses bent on normalizing society
sought to police sexual desire. As a result, the conception of homosexuality altered dramatically in the nineteenth century, thereby affecting English society as a whole. On homosexuality, Foucault
memorably asserts:

> We must not forget that the psychological, psychiatric, medical category
> of homosexuality was constituted from the moment it was character-
> ized—Westphal's famous article of 1870 on "contrary sexual sensa-
> tions" can stand as its date of birth—less by a type of sexual relations
> than by a certain quality of sexual sensibility, a certain way of inverting
> the masculine and the feminine in oneself. Homosexuality appeared as
> one of the forms of sexuality when it was transposed from the practice
> of sodomy onto a kind of interior androgyny, a hermaphrodism of the
> soul. The sodomite had been a temporary aberration; the homosexual
> was now a species.[1]

According to Robert Corber, "Whereas before then, the love that
dared not speak its name constituted either a sin or a crime, it became a distinct form of personhood during the course of that century."[2] We cite Foucault's theory and its subsequent significance for
studies in masculinity because the contributors to this collection
make two antithetical claims. Some of the contributors—André De-
Cuir, Christopher Lane, and Kathleen McDougall—argue that there
is a long history within nineteenth-century writing of resistance to
the restrictions on same-sex desire that gradually emerge and later

dominate medical and legal discourses by century's end. Other contributors—William Brewer, Richard Dellamora, and Jonathan
Gross—demonstrate a complexly related set of discourses beginning in the late eighteenth century that validate desire between men
in other terms (friendship, elegiac, classical, Christian, Jewish, aristocratic, bourgeois, working class). In our view, neither approach
invalidates Foucault's observation made with specific reference to
the new field of "sexuality." Indeed, both approaches indicate that
the various constructions of same-sex desire in nineteenth-century
Britain functioned with ambivalence and antagonism.

Briefly, we will summarize four recent investigations of nineteenth-century male sexuality, which begin with Foucault's rejection of the "repressive hypothesis" advanced by, among others,
Herbert Marcuse, Wilhelm Reich, and Steven Marcus.[3] In *Between
Men: English Literature and Male Homosocial Desire* (1985), Eve
Kosofsky Sedgwick employed the term "homosocial" to discuss
same-sex relations within the context of ostensible heterosexual experience. In *Masculine Desire: The Sexual Politics of Victorian
Aestheticism* (1990), Richard Dellamora examined the chiasmatic,
reciprocal discourses of masculine experience. Dellamora focused
on the experience in literature of "men who appear recognizably
'homosexual'" and those who are "engaged in the production of
revisionary masculine discourses" by "enlarg[ing] masculine capacities for relationships while respecting the boundaries of conventional middle-class patterns of career, including marriage."[4]
More recently, in *Victorian Masculinities: Manhood and Masculine
Poetics in Early Victorian Literature and Art* (1995), Herbert Sussman examined Victorian masculinites as complicated sites of self-
regulation revealed, for example, by the monk and the monastery.
James Eli Adams, in *Dandies and Desert Saints: Styles of Victorian
Manhood* (1995), interpreted "manliness" in relation to "models of
masculine identity: the gentleman, the prophet, the dandy, the
priest, and the soldier."[5] For Adams, these models provided a range
of middle-class male authors with a rhetoric that circulated in nineteenth-century England and that established self-disciplining features in relationships and behavior. These four critical works point
to a growing field of increasingly sophisticated readings on nineteenth-century masculinity: from the normative to the transgressive,
from the private and domestic to the public and political, and from
the effete and effeminate to the virile and manly. As with the previous studies cited above, this study examines how masculinity was
constituted as a social construction in the nineteenth century and

how writers of this period were able to express themselves given the cultural constraints of that construction.

Contemporary scholarship has done much to define nineteenth-century masculinity by providing the methodological means by which to map these boundaries.[6] The purpose of this study is to complicate and, in some cases, contest the exciting work already available in this field. Studies such as those included in this collection widen the range of what can be thought and felt about same-sex relations beyond the limits within which sociologically or psychoanalytically based discussions move. We have in mind the split between "same" and "other" in Craig Owens' and Lee Edelman's work;[7] the "heterosexual/homosexual" binary and the regulatory force of the concept of the closet in Eve Sedgwick's *Epistemology of the Closet* (1990) and Linda Dowling's *Hellenism and Homosexuality in Victorian Oxford* (1995); the focus on male-female triangulation and on mimetic models of desire in Sedgwick's *Between Men*; the structuring of analysis in terms of "effeminacy," understood in terms of a binary model of gender difference in Alan Sinfield's *The Wilde Century: Effeminacy, Oscar Wilde, and the Queer Moment* (1994) and Joseph Bristow's *Effeminate England: Homoerotic Writing After 1885* (1995); and, finally, the representation of same-sex relations in terms of a much reduced class typology. Produced in the last decade, these critical works have radically altered our perception of nineteenth-century masculinity; this study examines writers and forms of writing less frequently investigated while adapting and challenging some of the previously proposed theories.

Comprising fourteen essays, this collection interprets various facets of masculinity, including many forms of sexuality and eroticism, and the institutional and political structures that help shape that construction such as boys' public schools, class formations and divisions, nationalism, and imperialism. It also examines a range of writers and texts from the late eighteenth century to the early twentieth century; and it contextualizes shifting views of masculinity by analyzing pertinent social, economic, and political movements. Although contributors differ on their approaches to reading these nineteenth-century texts, the collection as a whole strongly points to the intricate, yet unavoidable, exchange between British culture and juridical power. Several of the essays, for example, explicitly or implicitly address same-sex desire and the shift from social prescriptions to legislative acts as a means by which to regulate desire. From the 1860s through the 1880s, a series of legislative acts attempted to prescribe acceptable and unacceptable behavior. The Contagious Diseases Acts of 1864, 1866, and 1869 forced female prostitutes in specified garrison towns to register with police and submit to medical examinations. The consequence, as Martha Vicinus and Judith Walkowitz have shown, was to institutionalize prostitution.[8] The original Criminal Law Amendment Act of 1871 outlawed demonstrations during labor disputes. The revised Criminal Law Amendment Act of 1885 ostensibly dealt with the abuse of young girls, raising the age of consent from 13 to 16; but, in conjunction with previous acts, it had the additional effect of outlawing same-sex relations, as Richard Dellamora, Alan Sinfield, Jonathan Dollimore, and others have shown. Thus while the former Contagious Diseases acts institutionalized heterosexual prostitution, the latter Criminal Law Amendment acts criminalized homosexuality.

Generally speaking, the concentration in this collection is on writers and literary texts with contributors drawing from many discursive forms, ultimately with an aim to show that sexual discourses in the nineteenth century were embedded in a variety of disciplines. What may interest readers are the discursive techniques that writers of different periods employed to discuss masculine identity and sexuality. How, for example, does Byron's struggle with transgressive desire, as recounted in Gross's essay, differ from Pater's and Wilde's, as represented in Losey's essay? What language does each writer employ to convey desire? What distinctions can we make about Byron's use of *double entendre* and innuendo alongside Pater's coded, delicate prose? Is Byron, according to Gross, freer to "speak out" than the Victorians were, including Pater and Wilde, who faced a legal system prepared to enforce the above cited Criminal Law Amendment Act (1885)? Is "speaking out" already circumscribed by British culture, whether by Regency social mores or late-Victorian statutes? And how did the shift from socially labeled "sodomite" to legally categorized homosexual to criminalized homosexual occur—through a series of dramatic ruptures or, gradually, over the course of a century?

Writers as diverse as William Beckford, John Addington Symonds, Walter Pater, Walt Whitman, and Gerard Manley Hopkins continued throughout the century to resist the cultural (legal, medical, social) restraints against same-sex relations. Instead, some writers sought to elevate for a Victorian culture the discussion of same-sex relations by reminding readers of the Graeco-Roman tradition and the classical educative process in which refined and cosmopolitan older men taught unsophisticated younger men. Other writers such as Charles Kingsley and Matthew Arnold upheld conservative cultural views regarding same-sex relations and argued that such an interpretation of the Graeco-Roman tradition was a perversion of classical education. Still others, like William Godwin, worried over power relations and the influence of the sophisticated mind of the older man over the unformed mind of a younger man. Indeed, what had been at the beginning of the nineteenth century a way of covertly discussing same-sex relations—of linking the older/younger man relationship with the classical tradition and the Graeco-Roman Empire with the British—was made the subject of medical and legal investigation by century's end. In his celebrated trial Wilde argued for the older/younger man relationship, but his eloquence held little sway with a court that was eager at that time to regulate behavior.

In addition to a discussion of same-sex relationships, this volume pays attention to the discursive constraints placed on masculine feeling, nurture, and creativity resulting from nineteenth-century capitalism, the Industrial Revolution, and the theory of separate spheres. The Victorian bourgeois ideal of the gentleman, for example, represented a male of enormous self-discipline who could harness his emotions and commit himself to a life of work and industry and of duty to family and country. Such ideals led writers to investigate the cultural disciplining of feeling. Mary Wollstonecraft's *Vindication of the Rights of Woman* (1792), with its indictment of nascent modern industrialism, argues against a society based on separate spheres, which keeps women in the home without the option of education or work. Laurence Sterne conveys, through the sentimental, culturally repressed narrator Yorick, in *A Sentimental Journey Through France and Italy* (1768), the competing demands of nature, individual sensations, and language: " 'tis so ordered, that from the want of languages, connections, and dependencies, and from the difference in education, customs and habits, we lie under so many impediments in communicating our sensations out of our own sphere, as often amount to a total impossibility."[9] In *Fleetwood: or, The New Man of Feeling* (1805), Godwin complicates the masculine ideal celebrated in Henry Mackenzie's *Man of Feeling* (1771). While both Harley and Fleetwood are hypersensitive and emotional individuals, Harley's altruism and sympathy for others contrast sharply with Fleetwood's misanthropy and egoism. Whereas Harley knows the "pain" of "confusion . . . too well to think of causing [it] in another," Fleetwood can only feel sympathy through pain.[10] He declares: "If the lash inflicted on me will, being inflicted on another, be attended with a similar effect, I then know that there is a being of the same species or genus with myself."[11] This Romantic-era man of feeling is solipsistic, morbid, and (in his treatment of his wife) sadistic; he anticipates later connoisseurs of their own sensations such as Byron's self-destructive Manfred and Percy Shelley's psychopathic Cenci.[12] In *Fleetwood* Godwin suggests that the sentimental man of feeling and the Marquis de Sade have more in common than one might suspect.

If some nineteenth-century writers found the theory of separate spheres a threat to self-expression, others found it empowering. John Ruskin's *Sesame and Lilies* (1865) expresses this opinion:

> The man's power is active, progressive, defensive. He is eminently the doer, the creator, the discoverer, the defender. His intellect is for speculation and invention; his energy for adventure, for war, and for conquest, wherever war is just, wherever conquest necessary. But the woman's power is for rule, not for battle—and her intellect is not for invention or creative, but for sweet ordering, arrangement, and decision. She sees the qualities of things, their claims and their places.[13]

Ruskin's text celebrates masculine invention in the workplace and feminine regulation in the home; woman's love of order keeps in check man's sense of adventure, and vice versa. This line of reasoning reveals an urge to produce controlled, mechanical relations between men and women. Thomas Carlyle notes in *Sartor Resartus* (1833–34) the consequences of the Industrial Revolution on the Victorian male, "Upwards of five hundred thousand two-legged animals without feathers lie round us, in horizontal position."[14] Carlyle's protagonist, a former university professor, is reduced to writing his autobiography on pieces of scratch paper. Teufelsdröckh's alienation mirrors the alienation of industrialized males, whose mechanized labor estranges them from their product.

In a pre-psychoanalytic analysis of Victorian child's play, George Eliot's *Mill on the Floss* (1860) investigates the prescribed boundaries for boys and girls by inverting the needs, desires, and abilities of a brother and sister. In the beginning of the novel, Maggie is assigned the intellectual and creative talents Tom lacks. Tomboyish and clever Maggie anxiously awaits the homecoming of her beloved brother Tom, who is returning from an academy for boys. Honest if dull, Tom lacks Maggie's curiosity and sensitivity, preferring ratting with his dog Yap to book learning. Ignoring the social and cultural divide that marks his son from the sons of professional men, Mr. Tulliver plans to send Tom to a clergyman for a classical education. Tulliver believes that his son needs to learn how to interpret the law in order to be successful at business. Tulliver blames the "puzzling" rhetoric of lawyers for involving him in a series of costly civil suits over property rights, suits that he little understands and thus loses, causing his family's undoing.[15] As his sister-in-law says, Tulliver would do well to "let the lawyers alone"; but Tulliver, convinced that he is in the right, intends to do battle with this emerging class of professionals.[16] For Tom's father, the law is like a "cockfight," where the winning lawyer is the bigger "rascal."[17]

Just as the law is beyond his father's comprehension, a gentleman's education is beyond Tom's capabilities; lacking the cultural literacy and aesthetic refinement of Philip Wakem, Tom cannot read the Greeks. More importantly, education separates Tom from a life at the mill, where he is happiest, and it strains his relationship with his doting sister Maggie. Maggie's disappointment that she is kept at home, apart from her brother and the exciting world of books, leads her to act out her frustrations on her wooden doll, "a Fetish which she punished for all her misfortunes."[18] In his absence, Maggie has neglected Tom's rabbits, and Tom responds by cruelly hurting his sister. Maggie's self-abuse and Tom's reproach of his sister, over whom he has been taught to feel a masculine superiority, overshadow the homecoming. It is a brutal reunion for Maggie made so by the social and familial expectations that Tom, as the male, should rule her and "punish her when she did wrong."[19] It is also brutal for Tom, who believes, like his father, that life should be a fair fight. An altercation with a country lad foreshadows Tom's growing alienation from life at the mill. Tom has a scuffle with his boyhood friend Bob Jakin, whom he admires for an acute ability to read nature. Their falling out—largely the result of Tom's determination to punish harshly those he sees in the wrong—is only a temporary win for the mill owner's son whose inheritance is slipping away. The fight in which Tom should be engaged will soon be lost, and the punishment inflicted upon the Tulliver family for misreading its own nature will be severe. *The Mill on the Floss* illustrates a complicated network of discursive forces in which Tom and Maggie are circumscribed by their provincial, narrow-minded family and by Victorian culture. They are circumscribed by the laws that separate the mill from the water; the system of education that separates the sons of mill owners from those of professional men; and the culture of gendered spheres that separates boy from girl.

With such severe prohibitions on the behavior of men and women, it is plausible to imagine widely different conceptions of masculinity and femininity both within genders and from gender to gender, a point Sigmund Freud emphasizes in his etiology of homosexuality in *Three Essays on the Theory of Sexuality* (1905). Although Freud opens his discussion of homosexuality by invoking the "separate spheres" concept, he rejects this concept in favor of a more complicated interpretation. Theorizing about the origins of homosexuality, Freud asserts that childhood with its polymor-phously perverse tendencies provides a clue: "psycho-analysis con-siders that a choice of an object independently of its sex—freedom to range equally over male and female objects—as it is found in childhood . . . is the original basis from which as a result of restric-tion in one direction or the other, both the normal and the inverted types develop."[20] Freud's psychological mapping of same-sex pas-sion provides a clue into male subjectivities. Indeed, Freud's lan-guage here threatens to subvert the "species" that medicine and especially the fledgling field of psychoanalysis was so intent upon categorizing. The boundaries that such late nineteenth-century medical-legal discourses were trying to draw between normative and transgressive desire show the strains of an imposed and arbi-trary structure.

In this collection, the essays on Romanticism concentrate on how men of this period forge relationships with other men through work, class, art, travel, family, politics, and education. William Brewer discovers that Godwin modernized an old form of male relation-ships, paternalism, in order to advance a theory about how to estab-lish, in the writer's mind, appropriate and productive relations between men. Primary to Godwin's paternalism, Brewer claims, is not the old feudalism in which the older man assumes power over, or takes away, the rights of the younger man. Nor is it Hellenism in which the older introduces the younger to both historical and sexual aestheticism. Instead, Godwin professes "disinterestedness" by which he means that these men maintain very precise boundaries, remaining emotionally and sexually uninvolved. As a counterpoint, Dellamora's essay on William Beckford shows one of Godwin's contemporaries preoccupied both with the ideal of an equal rela-tionship between a younger and an older man and the "confusion" that results when emotional and sexual attraction begin to unsettle prescribed social limits. The attraction to an ideal of friendship be-tween males whose objective relations are asymmetrical is, for both writers, a prime focus of investment, contemplation, and anxiety. Beckford, however, indicates that such friendships are of necessity invested and therefore, at the least, complex.

Like the essays on Godwin and Beckford, Binfield's essay on the Luddites, specifically the 1811–13 riots, and Greene's on Shelley's *Adonais* concentrate on masculinity, power relations, and creativ-ity. Binfield's and Greene's essays suggest that men of an artistic bent needed to find ways to manage their creativity in a society that, because of industrialism and the shift from individual work to mass

production, tended to *devalue* their artistry. The Luddite cloth mak-
ers and the poet of *Adonais* use communal strategies and forms of
male friendship to strengthen their subject positions as artistic
males. During the early nineteenth century, cloth production still
required that skilled labor produce the work by hand in a series of
steps whereby each laborer was responsible for a part of the process. For the Luddites, cloth making led to a bond between men of
equal class and of similar interests and skills, forging intense male
friendships and cohesive class relations. But it is precisely these
creative threads—the cloth, the friendships, the class formation—
which threatened to unravel the upper-class cloth manufacturer. Violence erupted when the Luddites united, dressing themselves in
their collectively produced cloth. In retaliation, capitalists stripped
the Luddites of their work through physical force and rhetorical
emasculation.

Greene's reading of Shelley's *Adonais* also stresses masculinity,
creativity, and rivalry. Like Godwin and Beckford who valorize the
older-younger man relationship, the poet of Shelley's *Adonais*
seeks a male community by wedding an older form to a younger
voice. The poet employs the elegy not only because it praises the
dead while elevating the living poet (and thereby enables the living
poet to compete with the dead), but because it provides a tradition
for an "intellectual and spiritual transcendence obtained through a
noble, collective, and historically masculine endeavor." Through
his style—his poetic desire to express the inexpressible—Shelley
opens up issues about masculine identity and emotional expression,
which were otherwise culturally repressed, in ways reminiscent of
Henry Mackenzie and Laurence Sterne. Shelley's efforts at freeing
himself, however, are recontained not only within the private world
of poetry but within an intellectually exclusive, coded elegiac tradition. While these two essays, by Binfield and Greene, suggest that
creativity, self-expression, and masculinity cut across the grain of
early nineteenth-century England, more work in this area would be
useful. Was it possible to exhibit these traits openly and earn social
value? Where precisely were the culturally prescribed boundaries
for creativity and masculinity?

Gross and Daffron, both of whom treat facets of Byron's life and
art, analyze masculine subjectivity by applying Foucault's work on
sexuality. As Daffron argues, Byron's deep secret, his sexual orientation, conflicts with socially normative views of English masculinity. His effort to employ types common to travel literature—the
Oriental scholar, the sentimentalist, and the self-styled Orientalist—collides with his own subjectivity, a collision that leads to self-

alienation. To what extent does Byron discover "subjectivity" in his travel literature and his late poetry? These works, according to Daffron, expose shifting notions of the self and, simultaneously, a resistance to representations of British masculinity that uphold Eurocentric imperialism. Gross also focuses on Byron's masculinity, but isolates the idea of "gayness," both as a *double entendre* ("gayness" as gaiety and sexuality) and as a gendered issue. His references to the recent work of Judith Butler, Diana Fuss, and Eve Sedgwick indicate that, whether homo- or heterosexual, male or female, constructions of sexuality are ever-changing. The discursive efforts to police sexuality, according to Gross, lead, in the case of Byron, to creativity and exploration. Satire as a form and Orientalism as a topic enable Byron to complicate "gayness" in *Don Juan*, not only to reach a willing, if gullible, reading public but also to explore his own sexuality. Gross offers a new and compelling reading of the narrator's complex subjectivity in the poem and may cause readers of this collection to reconsider the role of the narrator and narrative voice and voices in nineteenth-century British literature.

The essays devoted to Victorian masculinity, the largest of the three groupings, show remarkable affinities with the Romantic essays, thereby challenging one of the popular stereotypes of nineteenth-century gender studies. Just how violent was the rupture in attitudes towards homosexuality in or about 1870? As early as the eighteenth century, the emerging medical and legal discourses were focusing on sexuality, a focus that intensified in the Victorian period. A dominant urge in Victorian literature, confession as a topos is found in a variety of complementary fields and genres and can be traced to Romantic writers as diverse as Rousseau, Wordsworth, and De Quincey. In *The History of Sexuality*, Foucault perceptively locates the urge to confess in pre-nineteenth-century institutions such as law and religion. But he overdetermines, according to André DeCuir and Donald Hall, the *symptomatic* need to confess in the newly founded disciplines of psychoanalysis and medicine.[21] As Donald Hall contends in his analysis of Eliot's *Silas Marner* (1861), "sexist, racist, classist, increasingly (as language metamorphosed) homophobic, and strikingly xenophobic, the Victorians can be seen as both victims and perpetuators, formed by discourses that depended upon hierarchized binaries and plagued by anxieties that fueled oppressive actions toward others." To complicate Hall's view, Laura Fasick believes that the hierarchized binaries of "masculinity" and "manliness" have "constituted a separate identity from biological membership in the male sex." She asks, "Why else would comments such as 'He's a real man!' be used (by some people) as praise that differentiates one male not from women but from other, less worthy men?"

Richard Dellamora maps a relationship between two figures associated with Enlightenment and Victorian political life: William Beckford and Benjamin Disraeli. Both men could be highly idealistic about politics; both cherished an ideal of intimacy between elite males that could be put in service of social transformation through the instruments of representative government. But Beckford was deprived of his seat in Parliament as a result of a sexual scandal in 1785, involving an adolescent, which was fomented by his political opponents. At the start of his career, Disraeli's antagonists attempted to drive him from politics by means of anti-Semitic slurs that were colored with suggestions of sexual deviance. Forced to defend his Jewish heritage from the outset, Disraeli, in the Oriental romance *David Alroy* (1833), infuses the text with the androgynous attractions of David, a Jewish Alexander-figure; simultaneously, the text suggests Disraeli's conflicted feelings regarding Western stereotypes of Jews as revealed in the intense sympathy that exists between the young leader and his Jewish mentor, the rabbi Jabaster. Disraeli was attracted to Beckford because he was able to endure severe attacks from his enemies, and survive terrible personal injustice, and because he explored contradictions within political friendships with honesty. Disraeli's attraction to Judaism served as a switch point for the expression of intense anxieties about the loss of masculine agency in the face of the overbearing influence of British tradition and the law.

Whereas Dellamora focuses on politics, Losey focuses on the British public school system, arguing that the all-male setting created a context for mentor and pupil, the older/younger man relationship, the most celebrated example of which is that of Pater and Wilde. In *Mrs. Dalloway* (1925), Virginia Woolf offers Clarissa Dalloway's assessment of Hugh Whitbread: "The stable-boys had more life in them than Hugh, she said. He was a perfect specimen of the public school type, she said. No country but England could have produced him."[22] Losey explores how this "type" was constituted both by the educational system and by the public. Losey elaborates on Thomas Hughes's groundbreaking study of public school life, *Tom Brown's School Days* (1857), both an exposure of abuse and an affirmation of the public school "type." Through the character "Pater" Brooke, an older boy at Rugby, Pater acquired strategies to preserve his sexuality from public scrutiny. How instructive, for example, was "Pater" Brooke's admonition to his classmates?

You'll be all the better football players for learning to stand it, and to take your own parts, and fight it through. . . . Then there's fuddling about in the public-house, and drinking bad spirits, and punch, and such rot-gut stuff. That won't make good drop-kicks or chargers of you, take my word for it. You get plenty of good beer here [at Rugby house], and that's enough for you; and drinking isn't fine or manly, whatever some of you may think of it.[23]

Brooke calls upon his classmates to avoid strong drink and other licentious behavior and uphold the tradition of the wholesome British male. Why, then, did Wilde, Pater's pupil, misunderstand his mentor's admonitory injunctions and openly violate acknowledged institutional rules of decorum? Like Dellamora, Losey investigates masculine relationships that involve, in part, an educative process: the older man teaching the younger. Where they differ, however, is on the vexing issue of religion and the roles of Judaism and Christianity in Victorian culture, specifically how the two religious traditions influence attitudes and responses to masculinity.

Laura Fasick examines the issue of religious influence on an Anglican priest, Charles Kingsley, and argues that "manliness" (its modern cognate is masculinity) is an ever-changing construction in Victorian culture. Whereas homosexuality as an identity marker dates from the late nineteenth century, sodomitical practice is often separated from concerns about sexual identity. Fasick offers a cogent rebuttal to the "homosexual/heterosexual" binary that Eve Sedgwick and Linda Dowling employ in their works through her analysis of the homophobic tension at the heart of the Kingsley-Newman debate in the 1860s. What role might the practice of abstinence play in preserving masculinity? André DeCuir shifts the focus from theological to medical issues involving the categorization of homosexual identity as they emerge in the writings of Le Fanu. For DeCuir, Le Fanu challenges medical "authority" on issues of sexual orientation by criticizing "a medical establishment for seeking to 'cure,' deny, or suppress" homosexuality. Ironically, the medical establishment, according to DeCuir, practiced homosexuality while condemning it as an aberration. He shows how Le Fanu, about whom there is little biographical material, exposes this repressive practice in "Carmilla" and "Green Tea." What appear to be Gothic melodramas are, in part, criticisms of hypocritical medical practice.

Donald Hall also focuses on medical diagnoses of aberrant behavior—for example, masturbation—and expands his analysis of medicine to include Victorian socialization of children and, especially, the treatment of puberty. How do "parents, teachers, religious figures, medical professionals, and other authorities" respond to boys' and girls' developing bodies? How do they connect juvenile sexual urges to "the body politic"? Hall examines the paradox of shaming pubescent youths into silence and isolation, on the one hand, and of castigating youths for not being socially integrated, on the other. This symbolic site of conflict is played out, according to Hall, between Eppie and Silas Marner.

Like Hall, Denisoff focuses on a nascent national language, one that has the tendency to repress because it is controlled by institutions. He explains how the issue of sexuality is continuously fluid in Victorian conceptions of individuality and institutions; he stresses the highly unpredictable "formation and ongoing re-formation of sexual identities" and develops his idea in the parodies and satires of the Aesthetic Movement. In the work of Gilbert and Sullivan, for example, their comic depictions of the dandy-aesthete's gender and sexuality yielded a vague moral position. Were gay men born, as Showalter (who quotes Edward Carpenter) says, "with a high percentage of essential femininity" or were they "the most purely 'manly' . . . representatives of their sex"?[24] For Denisoff, the issue is never a binary, an either-or, because community and class make identity both unique and marginal—a clear rejection of Foucault's overemphasis on institutional authority and its decisive sway over individuals.

In the late-Victorian essays, however, our contributors acknowledge the powerful regulatory function of the Criminal Law Amendment Act (1885), particularly the Labouchère Amendment (Article 11) which made the act of "gross indecency" between men, whether in public or private, punishable by up to two years hard labor. After Wilde's conviction, late-Victorian writers moved from a private to a public realm, examining the influence of institutions—law, medicine, military, government, and business—to regulate individual life.[25] Whether the individual relied on silence or aesthetics to avoid committing to a course of action, as Lane demonstrates, or glorified the institution in order to reform it, as Pannapacker shows, late-Victorian attitudes towards same-sex desire were complicated, as McDougall cogently explains, by medical and scientific discourses. Why, asks McDougall, were Victorian attitudes swayed by such discourses? She answers, in part, that the phenomenon is a consequence of the disciplines themselves: "Because it was lent the glamor of objective truth—as is still the case today, to a certain extent—science [figures] as a primary discourse, a source of 'facts' from which views of self and society were elaborated. There is no such thing as a primary discourse, of course, and in fact there was 'a constant movement of commonplaces between discourses' in the late nineteenth century." For McDougall, the proponents of "scientific naturalism," a phrase that pervades late-Victorian literature, had the chiasmatic, self-defeating tendency to take for granted scientific "truths" that ultimately undermined credibility. She explores how that chiasmatic effect plays itself out in the writings of George Bernard Shaw. McDougall's essay on Shaw, an unlikely figure in a collection on same-sex relations, points to the pervasive yet unprovable nature of such discourses.

Both Pannapacker and Lane explore the self-professed failure in Whitman and James to clarify their discourses on same-sex relations. Pannapacker shrewdly avoids a direct confrontation with Whitman, who famously chided Symonds for reading the "Calamus" poems (1860) as celebrating same-sex passion.[26] Rather, he indirectly proves that Whitman succeeded in creating, and existing within, a working-class milieu; this milieu contained a multitude of competing and overlapping discourses that focus on the issue of power and control: "elitism and populism, conservatism and radicalism, effeminacy and manliness, submissiveness and dominance, refinement and primitivism, noblesse oblige and working-class 'comradeship.'" Such a celebration is reminiscent of Wilde's visit to Whitman in January 1882; in the course of the conversation, according to Richard Ellmann, Wilde praised "the American masses as superior to the masses in England and Europe," a sentiment that pleased Whitman.[27] Whitman's distaste for aestheticism, particularly its highly mannered and refined style, enabled him to avoid the antihomosexual attacks that Wilde endured. While Pannapacker stresses the nexus of power relations involving class, Lane stresses the nexus between same-sex desire and its failure in James's aesthetic novels, *Roderick Hudson* (1875) and *The Tragic Muse* (1889, 1890). He explores the tension between individuality and desire, and thus James's "difficulties with his characters' credibility and sexuality." James avoids, according to Lane (and James himself), a confrontation with same-sex passion and instead conflates the issue of unifying a central object for both novels with artistry and subjectivity. The aesthetic characters—Miriam Rooth, Gabriel Nash, Roderick Hudson—are unable to harmonize their art and lives; the "sexual dissimulation in [James's] fiction" is a consequence of his ongoing struggle to make aesthetic concerns complement everyday experience, particularly in the analysis of masculinity. It is precisely in this analysis of masculinity that Lane complicates any sure conclusion that James had, in the words of Lee Siegel, "to silence

himself."[28] Like McDougall, Lane employs a highly evolved critical language, but in this instance language associated with drama—
"masquerade," "role," "character," "staginess"—to convey the
complexity of James's discourse on same-sex relations.

Of the many dilemmas and conflicts to which we have just referred, we could develop, by way of example, the relation between
capital and sexual drives. Some of the contributors—for example,
Dellamora, Hall, Lane—argue that "surplus capital" was the principal driving force of masculine identity; they claim that it regulated institutions and individuals. Other contributors—for example,
Binfield, Gross, Denisoff, Pannapacker—indicate that capital was a
means to separate various sexual groups and to enable those groups
to negotiate among themselves. They claim that slumming, an act
requiring contact with other classes, reveals this negotiating tendency. As William Pannapacker notes, Edward Carpenter synthe-
sized masculine identities, intending "to blur the boundaries
between genders and classes and to foster cross-class sexual contact." Such gender-bending informs not only cross-class sensibilities but also sexual sensibilities; in the novel *Teleny* (1893),
celebrating same-sex passion, a group of both effeminate and
manly men participate in cruising.[29] Camille Des Grieux, the narrator and protagonist of *Teleny*, encounters some "night-walkers" late
one night. He describes one of the male prostitutes as a "workman," another as a "catamite," a third as a "soldier," and a fourth
group of prostitutes as transvestites, with "sickening faces of effete,
womanish men. . . ."[30] Des Grieux summarizes his experience as
follows:

> As I learnt later in life, every large city has its particular haunts—its
> square, its garden for such recreation [i.e., cruising]. And the police?
> Well, it winks at it, until some crying offence is committed; for it is not
> safe to stop the mouths of craters. Brothels of men-whores not being
> allowed, such trysting-places must be tolerated, or the whole is a mod-
> ern Sodom or Gomorrah.[31]

Certainly in the months following the Cleveland Street scandal
(1889–90), working-class radicals attempted to justify the activity
of the telegraph boys by claiming their victimization by a bohe-
mian, upper-class clientele. Wilde, who participated in the writing
and editing of *Teleny*, had been linked by Charles Whibley to the
Cleveland Street scandal in his *Scots Observer* review of *The Picture of Dorian Gray* on 5 July 1890.[32] The point we would stress is
the unofficial collaboration between male prostitutes and police
"until some crying offence is committed."

These conflicts of capital and sexual drives have a common denominator: power and its possession. As Foucault claimed, where
power exists so does resistance, which itself is frequently recontained.[33] This disciplining effect made its presence felt not only on
the body itself but also in "workplaces" as diverse as the church,
the military, the university, the factory, and even the criminal underworld. Another division—that between normative society and
the criminal underworld—becomes complicated by individuals
moving between different class systems, as Wilde demonstrates in
The Picture of Dorian Gray (1890; revised 1891). The image of the
real Dorian Gray remaining forever young and the portrait of Dorian Gray aging with each new sin conveys a major conclusion of
this collection: the emergence of a split subjectivity in the rhetoric
of masculinities. The generous plurality of this rhetoric is revealed
in the geographical, historical, anatomical, and psychological map-
pings of the following collection.

NOTES

1. Michel Foucault, *The History of Sexuality. Volume 1: An Introduction*, trans.
Robert Hurley (New York: Pantheon, 1978), 43.

2. Robert J. Corber, "Lesbian and Gay Studies in Today's Academy," *Academe* (September-October 1998), 47.

3. Steven Marcus, *The Other Victorians: A Study of Sexuality and Pornogra-
phy in Mid-Nineteenth Century England* (New York: Humanities Press, 1965); and
Peter Gay, *The Bourgeois Experience: Victoria to Freud*, 5 vols. (New York: Oxford University Press, 1984–97). See, especially, volume 2, *The Tender Passion*,
which focuses on the confessional impulses of such diverse Victorians as Charles
Kingsley and John Addington Symonds. For an extended analysis of Foucault's
continuing relevance for same-sex studies, see Richard Dellamora, "Victorian Homosexuality in the Prism of Foucault," *Victorian Studies* 38, no. 2 (Winter 1995),
265–72.

4. Dellamora, *Masculine Desire: The Sexual Politics of Victorian Aestheticism*
(Chapel Hill: University of North Carolina Press, 1990), 5.

5. James Eli Adams, *Dandies and Desert Saints: Styles of Victorian Manhood*
(Ithaca: Cornell University Press, 1995), 2.

6. Jeffrey Weeks, *Coming Out: Homosexual Politics in Britain from the Nineteenth Century to the Present*, 2nd ed. (London: Quartet Books, 1990); Brian
Reade, ed., *Sexual Heretics: Male Homosexuality in English Literature from
1850–1900* (London: Routledge & Kegan Paul, 1970); Jonathan Dollimore, *Sexual
Dissidence: Augustine to Wilde, Freud to Foucault* (Oxford: Clarendon Press,
1991); Louis Crompton, *Byron and Greek Love: Homophobia in Nineteenth-Century England* (Berkeley: University of California Press, 1985); and Alan Bray, *Homosexuality in Renaissance England* (London: Gay Men's Press, 1982).

7. Lee Edelman, *Homographesis: Essays in Gay Literary and Cultural Theory*
(New York: Routledge, 1994); and Craig Owens, "Outlaws: Gay Men in Femi-

nism," *Men in Feminism*, ed. Alice Jardine and Paul Smith (New York: Routledge, 1989).

8. Martha Vicinus, *Independent Women: Work and Community for Single Women, 1850–1920* (Chicago: University of Chicago Press, 1985), and Judith Walkowitz, *Prostitution and Victorian Society* (New York: Cambridge University Press, 1982).

9. Laurence Sterne, *A Sentimental Journey Through France and Italy*, ed. Ian Jack (New York: Oxford University Press, 1984), 9.

10. Henry Mackenzie, *The Man of Feeling*, ed. Brian Vickers (London: Oxford University Press, 1970), 85.

11. William Godwin, *Fleetwood: or, The New Man of Feeling* (1805; London: Richard Bentley, 1832), 179.

12. Of Fleetwood's relationship with his wife, Steven Bruhm writes that Mary Fleetwood's "pain is the means by which Fleetwood can carve out a subjectivity and identity for himself . . . [Fleetwood's] sentimentality . . . transfers the masochistic pleasure of appropriating another's pain into the sadistic pleasure of causing it." *Gothic Bodies: The Politics of Pain in Romantic Fiction* (Philadelphia: University of Pennsylvania Press, 1994), 118.

13. John Ruskin, "Of Queens' Gardens," *Sesame and Lilies* (New York: Chelsea House Publishers, 1983), 84; and Alfred Tennyson, *The Princess, The Poems of Tennyson*, ed. Christopher Ricks (London: Longman Group, 1969). Here is a characteristic statement by "the old king," a representative of the patriarchy: "Man for the field and woman for the hearth: / Man for the sword and for the needle she: / Man with the head and woman with the heart: / Man to command and woman to obey; / All else confusion" (5.437–41).

14. Thomas Carlyle, *Sartor Resartus* (New York: Oxford University Press, 1987), 18.

15. George Eliot, *The Mill on the Floss*, ed. Gordon S. Haight (Boston: Houghton Mifflin Company, 1961), 19. For a compelling reading of the discursive forces at play in George Eliot's *Adam Bede*, see Eve Kosofsky Sedgwick, *Between Men*, 134–48.

16. Ibid., 64.

17. Ibid., 138.

18. Ibid., 25.

19. Ibid., 36.

20. Sigmund Freud, *Three Essays on the Theory of Sexuality*, trans. James Strachey (New York: Basic Books, 1962), 12.

21. Foucault, *History of Sexuality*, 1:65–70.

22. Virginia Woolf, *Mrs. Dalloway* (New York: Harcourt, Brace, Jovanovich, 1953), 73.

23. Thomas Hughes, *Tom Brown's School Days* (New York: A. L. Burt, 1900), 116.

24. Elaine Showalter, *Sexual Anarchy: Gender and Culture at the Fin de Siècle* (New York: Penguin Books, 1990), 172–73.

25. Ed Cohen, *Talk on the Wilde Side: Toward a Genealogy of a Discourse on Male Sexualities* (New York: Routledge, 1993), 210–14.

26. Phyllis Grosskurth, "Introduction," *The Memoirs of John Addington Symonds: The Secret Homosexual Life of a Leading Nineteenth-Century Man of Letters* (New York: Random House, 1984), 20.

27. Richard Ellmann, *Oscar Wilde* (New York: Vintage Books, 1987), 170.

28. Lee Siegel, "The Gay Science: Queer Theory, Literature, and the Sexualiza-

tion of Everything," *The New Republic* 219, no. 19 (9 November 1998), 36. Siegel offers a scathing analysis of queer theory, hyperventilating about the pernicious influence of Foucault and singling out Sedgwick for scorn. The bluntness of Siegel's language reveals the deep fears still pervading contemporary society about gayness and gay studies. The contributors to this collection strive to debunk the following Siegelian claim: "Find the sex, and you will have found the seat of social and politicial authority. But authority is repression, and must be unmasked. And so the poststructuralists set out to make sex as indeterminate, as 'other,' as depleted, as they had made language" (32). Sexual discourses do more than one kind of work. Moreover, particular terms or places in these discourses can serve as switch points between various kinds of discourse. Our contributors strive to be forthright about the ways in which these points make such moves.

29. Alan Sinfield, *The Wilde Century: Effeminacy, Oscar Wilde and the Queer Moment* (New York: Columbia University Press, 1994), 39.

30. *Teleny: A Novel Attributed to Oscar Wilde*, ed. Winston Leyland (San Francisco: Gay Sunshine Press, 1984), 99–100.

31. Ibid., 99.

32. Oscar Wilde, *The Picture of Dorian Gray*, ed. Donald L. Lawler (New York: W. W. Norton, 1988), 346.

33. Foucault, *History of Sexuality*, 1:61–63.

Mapping Male Sexuality

Part I
Romantic

Industrial Gender: Manly Men and Cross-dressers in the Luddite Movement

KEVIN BINFIELD

Clothes stand for knowledge and language, art and love, time
and death—the creative, struggling state of man. While they
conceal only his unapplied, unrealized body they reveal all of
his and its possibilities. But to do this, they (like language) are
condemned to contingency, and consequently the idea of them
is something of a thorn and a goad.

—Anne Hollander, *Seeing Through Clothes*

DURING THE SPRING OF 1812, A SERIES OF LUDDITE RIOTS OCCURRED
in Cheshire, Lancashire, and Yorkshire's West Riding. In one of
these disturbances, on 14 April 1812, men wearing women's clothing and calling themselves "General Ludd's wives" led a crowd of
men, women, and boys on a rampage through the market area of
Stockport, destroying food shops, and resetting prices for bread and
potatoes. The event culminated in the destruction of steam-powered
looms in a factory owned by John Goodair.

The Stockport riot was only one of a number of incidents of gender inversion and the feminization of self-presentation in the Luddite risings, the period of machine-breaking and rioting in the
textile-producing regions of the English Midlands and North between 1811 and 1813. Through these incidents, I propose to examine the structure of Luddism and the relationship of working-class
masculine identity to class organization during the period of rapid
mechanization in the textile industry, especially among the cloth-
workers of Yorkshire's West Riding and southeastern Lancashire. I
shall treat the instances of feminized Luddite presentation along
with components of the manufacturing context—clothing, machines, gender, and worker friendships—in light of recent theories
of male relationships and popular protest. I shall contend that these
incidents might be interpreted as markers of what I shall define
below as a "homoindustrial" desire and of changes in working-

29

class gender thinking, especially concepts of masculinity and masculine heroism.

The incidents I shall consider include, primarily, male transvestism and, secondarily, women's participation in riots, neither of which has received much attention in recent studies of Luddism. E. P. Thompson barely mentions the episodes in *The Making of the English Working Class* (1963), although he considers the issue of women's participation in some detail in *Customs in Common* (1991).[1] Malcolm Thomis has treated the matter more extensively in his book, *The Luddites* (1970).[2] Thomis and Jennifer Grimmett have undertaken the most thorough consideration of women's participation and male transvestism in *Women in Protest, 1800–1850* (1982), but their remarks on Luddite cross-dressing are limited to a few paragraphs introducing their real focus—the Rebecca rioters.[3] In the most recent study of the Luddite risings, *Rebels against the Future* (1995), Kirkpatrick Sale nearly relegates Luddite transvestism to "folklore," writing that there is "only" one

> clear instance of men using this disguise in the Luddite years, though there are suggestions from both Nottingham and Huddersfield that at least some articles of women's clothing had been worn on raids previously; it was so striking that it would go on to be part of local folklore for generations afterward.[4]

Nevertheless, cross-dressing appears too frequently in accounts of Luddism, both in contemporary documents and in later histories, to dismiss it as Sale does.

Besides the accounts in newspapers of the period, pioneering Yorkshire historian, Frank Peel, recounts several instances of transvestism, such as the February 1812 Luddite attack on wagons carrying shearing frames on Hartshead Moor, carried out by shearmen, several of whom wore women's frocks.[5] Other accounts in Peel's *The Risings of the Luddites* (1968) and in D. F. E. Sykes's *Ben o' Bills, The Luddite* (1898) describe several occurrences of cross-dressing in the Spen and Colne valleys.[6] A "general rising," scheduled for Huddersfield 24 July 1814, was announced as "the marriage feast of Mrs. Ludd."[7] Even a cartoon from the period depicts "General Ludd" leading an attack in feminine attire, a handsome frock and a bonnet.[8]

Luddism, of course, encompassed more than just machine-wrecking and factory raids, the participants of which seem exclusively to have been male, with the exception of some collective rioting in Lancashire and Cheshire. Luddism was a movement based

THE LEADER OF THE LUDDITES

Pub.d May 1st by Messr.s Walker and Knight, Sweetings Alley Royal Exchange.

Contemporary cartoon depicting a Luddite in women's clothing. Working Class Movement Library, Salford.

on community standards and included the participation of women protesting against injustices beyond the imposition of machinery. Women were especially prominent in food riots and other forms of disturbance within the industrial cities and towns of Lancashire and Yorkshire.[9] Occasionally, a "Lady Ludd" would be carried in a chair at the head of a food riot, as, for example, in Leeds, on 18 August 1812.[10] Nevertheless, as Thompson and Thomis and Grimmett acknowledge, Luddism was primarily a male (if not entirely masculine) enterprise, and cannot be understood in any of its constituent forms without consideration of the predominantly male culture of the textile worker.

Prior to the institution of factory mechanization, industrial relations among men were characterized by a sort of manual directness, described in a variety of works by Peel, Thompson, Hammond and Hammond, Thomis, and Adrian Randall.[11] Excepting outwork among spinners and hand-loom weavers, some of whom were women, most labor in the textile trades was performed by men working in close proximity to each other.[12] This was especially true in small cloth-finishing shops in the West Riding, which typically employed three to four shearmen or croppers, the radically masculinist workers who were perhaps the most determined Luddites (and those most frequently reported to use women's attire). In the cropping shops, men shared labor with other men, working with a common purpose to produce and finish materials which bound them to each other within the trade. Even between trades, work in wool bound men to each other as it passed from spinners to weavers to fullers and ultimately to croppers, who, in the spirit of cooperation and artisan pride, accepted the material as if it were their own, improved upon it, and returned it to a master clothier or gentleman merchant to be cut and fashioned. Cloth was both simultaneously an object upon which men concentrated their purposes and medium of serial exchange between them. Through cloth, working men participated in each other's labor and advanced a common interest.

Cropping, however, was a special trade. Seriality negotiated cooperative labor participation and common interest to a much smaller degree for croppers than for spinners and weavers. Because of the organization of the West Riding woollen industry, cloth finishers were quite independent. Whereas spinners and weavers were typically under the thumb of master clothiers, croppers almost always were out-hired or retained by gentleman merchants who, having purchased new cloth in the Cloth Hall, depended upon them to craft a finished, salable product.[13] The solidarity in purpose and the closeness of identity in the trade appears in a number of sources, including George Walker's artistic rendering of croppers at work, Peel's descriptions of John Wood's Huddersfield workshop, and Randall's account of work in the West Riding woollen industry.[14]

In West Riding, the cropping trade was threatened by both gig-mills (which had been prohibited by legislation since the reign of Edward VI) and newer, more efficient shearing frames. The replacement of human labor by machines reduced the need for employing many croppers and permitted "colts"—unskilled and unapprenticed laborers—to compete with skilled artisans for work, thereby eliminating the particular type of common interest necessary to bind working man to working man. We find a recognition of this common interest and the threat posed by machinery and industrial reorganization in a March 1812 Luddite letter to "Mr Smith Shearing Frame Holder at Hill End Yorkshire," in which the writer defines the shearing frame as "Machinery hurtful to Comonality [sic]."[15]

The replacement of "Comonality" with a competitive, alienating labor structure might merit the name heteroindustrialism—labor based on adversarial difference. Heteroindustrialism forces each man to relate to a machine and its owner rather than to the other

Croppers at work, in George Walker, *The Costume of Yorkshire* (London: Bensley, 1814).

men involved in production. Men who formerly engaged in cooperative processes of production became, in the new heteroindustrial
system, hostile competitors for jobs. In contrast, the traditional system, by encouraging cooperative, non-adversarial labor rather than
competitive endeavor, was a system of manufacture in which the
mutual dependency upon each other's manual skills permitted a
special relationship among working-class men through both the
processes and the products of labor, in which each man had cause
to admire and treasure the work of his fellows.

What the Luddite writers sought was a return to what I call the
"homoindustrial" relationship of worker to worker. Homoindustri-
alism is a traditional system of labor based upon cooperation, trade
identity, and, in the case of the croppers, masculine solidarity. In
such a system, the slippery concept which Eve Kosofsky Sedgwick
has named "homosocial desire"[16] plays a central role, manifested
in "The Cropper's Song" sung by croppers in a Huddersfield tavern
just before a Luddite raid:

> Come, cropper lads of high renown,
> Who love to drink good ale that's brown,
> And strike each haughty tyrant down,
>   With hatchet, pike, and gun!
> Oh, the cropper lads for me,
> The gallant lads for me,
> Who with lusty stroke,
> The shear frames broke,
> The cropper lads for me![17]

The song suggests much about the nature of the relationships
among the croppers. The communal self-identification of the plural
"cropper lads," the self-praise, the professed opposition to the singular "haughty tyrant" who would interfere with the brotherhood,
and the fellow feeling implied in the self-reflexive drinking song all
combine to bear witness to an intense homosocial bonding among
the West Riding shearmen.

The croppers were among the most respected of all the textile
workers of the North, men whose work involved shearing off stray
threads from new cloth. Typically brawny men whose tools were
forty- to fifty-pound hand-held shears, four feet in length, and
whose labor involved using the shears in the delicate operation of
making new cloth into a smooth and salable product, they represent
the ideal of the hard-working hard-liver described by Martha Vicinus in *The Industrial Muse* (1974).[18] More than weaving or stock-

ing-making, the other trades from which Luddism emerged, shearing was on a small scale a cooperative endeavor, less, I believe, out of necessity than because of the exclusivity of the trade and the sense held by each cropper that the man working beside him was to be prized for his strength and delicate skill.[19] The Yorkshire Luddite attacks upon shearing frames were made possible by the same special type of cooperation that characterized cropping— that is, by a concerted expenditure of the physical strength of men "whose daily labors toughened their arms to steeliness."[20] None would seem to represent this masculine ideal better than George Mellor, the large, unmarried Huddersfield cropper—described by D. F. E. Sykes as "but twenty-two years of age, a bright handsome young fellow with flaxen hair"—who led several attacks, including the famous, failed attack on William Cartwright's mill at Rawfolds.[21]

Despite the prevailing masculine ideal, and despite Rictor Norton's observation that during the eighteenth and early nineteenth centuries "virility and effeminacy" were at opposite cultural poles,[22] some effeminate men did number among the masculinist Luddites, and an examination of the friendship of the "effeminate" John Booth, saddle-maker's apprentice, and George Mellor provides an insight into the intensity possible in Luddite friendships.[23] Booth's place in West Riding Luddism demands an examination of effeminacy within the movement, and, even though the records of Booth's effeminate presentation and his close friendship with Mellor ultimately cannot be interpreted as indisputable evidence of a homosexual (rather than homoindustrial or homosocial) relationship, the records do point to a complex gender dynamic underlying Luddite identity.

Booth has been described as "educated," "effeminate," given to "pale cheek flushes," and possessing "large, soft, woman's eyes."[24] Sykes records that Booth's sister, Faith, described him as "soft and easy," and Peel has no doubts that, lacking "firmness and resolution," Booth's "feeble will melted like wax before the fiery determination of Mellor."[25] Nevertheless, Booth's relationship with Mellor clearly had some reciprocity. Booth, intelligent and well-read, successfully educated Mellor in the proto-socialist theories of contemporary radicals.[26]

While it would be an error, given the absence of primary documentation, to ascribe a sexual (rather than merely gendered) component to the Booth-Mellor friendship, there are remarks in Sykes and Peel which at least provoke questions about the nature of the friendship.[27] For example, Booth's sister, Faith, dismissed a speculative explanation by Ben Bamforth (Mellor's friend and fellow-cropper) of John's late nights, to wit, that John was "doing a bit o' courting." She told him, "Ah! Ben, if I could think it were only that. For well I know if John were court—; were doing what you say, you'd be like enough to know of it," adding a few lines later, "If it's right for George, it's right for John."[28] And immediately before the Rawfolds raid, fearing his own death, Booth asked Ben to watch over his sister: "Do you like Faith, Ben? Women like power in a man, Ben, not wrecklings like me."[29] Given Booth's own assumed standard for women's preferences, it would seem likely that he would ask the most powerful man he knew, a master cloth-dresser with more than £100, his closest friend, Mellor. The fact that he did not suggests some impediment. Absent much primary documentation of the friendship, we might interpret Booth's reluctance within the forms of Luddite solidarity rather than insisting upon a sexual interest. Booth may have, in his mind, reserved Mellor for the purpose of continuing to advance the masculine interests which found at least a partial expression as the trade interests which both men embraced; in other words, Booth may have thought of Mellor as "married" to the masculine cause of the Luddites and incapable of devotion to Booth's sister, someone peripheral to that cause.

Even captured, dying from a wound received in the attack on Rawfolds Mill, which shattered his leg at the knee, and apparently tortured with *aqua fortis* (nitric acid) during an interrogation, Booth's loyalty to his friend Mellor ought to refute Peel's initial characterization of him as unmanly. Both before and after a surgeon amputated Booth's leg, Reverend Hammond Roberson questioned the wounded boy about the identity of his fellow Luddites, especially the leader:

> Well owd Roberson wouldn't let him die i' peace, but wer all th' time naggin' him to confess. Then when Booth knew his end were near, he called owd Roberson to stand ovver him, an' th' owd sinner's face lit up wi' glee, an' he stepped up to John as brisk as a bee. . . .
> "Can yo' keep a secret, sir?" whispered John.
> "I can, I can," said th' parson.
> "An' so can I," said John, wi' a smile, an he put his head back an' never spak' no more.[30]

Just like Booth's loyalty to Mellor, Mellor's grief over Booth's death was intense, much more intense than that felt by his companions or that felt by Mellor for the other dead Luddites—cropper Samuel Hartley and others buried in secret after the attack:

If there existed in George Mellor's dark, flinty heart a particle of feeling, it had been entirely monopolised by his dead friend, Booth, and
when he ascertained that he had been deprived of the melancholy satisfaction of following Booth's dead body to the grave [due to the secret
burial], his whole frame quivered with passion.[31]

His fellows attempted to calm him, claiming to "feel the loss of
poor Booth as well as thou does," and urging that "it behoves us to
consider the living as well as the dead."[32] But, clearly, Mellor's
grief, concentrated on Booth, was extraordinary.

Booth's death spurred Mellor to exact vengeance. After failing in
an attempt to kill Cartwright, Mellor turned his wrath to another
factory owner, William Horsfall, among the most recalcitrant of the
capitalists in the Spen and Colne valleys. After the Luddite attacks,
Horsfall not only had celebrated the deaths of the Rawfolds Luddites and extended congratulations to Cartwright on the defense of
his mill, but also had vowed to kill Luddites until his horse had to
"ride up to the saddle girths in Luddite blood."[33]

There is much about Horsfall's murder which reveals both Mellor's hatred and what appears to be a sexualized character to the
violent act. Reports indicate that Mellor had charged his pistols
with an excess of powder and double balls in each. Huddersfield
surgeon Rowland Houghton described the wounds that Mellor's
pistols inflicted in killing Horsfall:

> I found two wounds on the upper part of the left thigh, about three
> inches asunder; another on the lower part of the belly on the left side;
> another on the lower part of the scrotum. And two more on the right
> thigh, and a slight bruise, not a wound, on the lower part of the belly;
> one ball had been extracted from the right thigh; and I extracted one
> musket ball from the outside of the right thigh, near the hip joint.[34]

At least eight balls struck Horsfall, all of them in or near the groin.
It would appear that Mellor had intended to emasculate Horsfall in
vengeance for Booth's death; put another way, Mellor's sexualization of his attack on Horsfall suggests a special intensity in his relationship to Booth, an intensity which calls for a sexualized
vengeance. Horsfall had, by aiding Cartwright, interfered with a
masculine friendship set amid masculine interests. In Mellor's
mind, the appropriate response to such interference was to remove
Horsfall from the masculine circle, through emasculation.[35]

The friendship between the saddle-maker's apprentice, Booth,
and the cropper, Mellor, enables us to understand Luddism and homoindustrial desire as something more than trade-particular no-

tions, despite the trade solidarity of the croppers. A more complex dynamic was operating in Luddite relationships. Even more valued than simple masculinity and artisan skill was the vigorous promotion of each other's interests. Mellor and Booth demonstrate that the promotion can be characterized as passionate; if we cannot say that the friendship had a sexual character, Mellor's vengeance, at least, seems to have assumed such a character as the only method sufficient to express his sense of loss. Booth and Mellor recognized that men exerted themselves, risked their lives, and died to preserve a traditional economic system which afforded the enjoyment of the valued fellow feeling and co-involvement of both bodies and hearts through work. Defense of that system and of the friendships formed within it occasionally, as in Mellor's case, took on a sexualized and violent intensity.

To preserve the traditional system, the Luddites adopted a military-style organizational structure. Sedgwick writes that the military is the most homosocial of institutions, but the Luddite variation is worth noting. Ordinarily, military forces depend upon unit identity, typically men recognizing bonds to other men within an authoritarian structure. The Luddites, however, had for their leader a *fictional* general (or sometimes captain)—Ned Ludd. Of course, Ludd took many forms and was played by many persons in many places. The variability of Ludd's identity suggests the existence of real but deliberately unsettled roles and a social structure in which roles might pass from one man to another, simultaneously authoritarian and democratic, reconciling two contradictory masculine ideals—the wishes to command and to think for oneself.

Luddite tactics were also variable: witness the comment in a Luddite song, "General Ludd's Triumph," that "when in the work of destruction employed / He himself to no method confines, / By fire and by water he gets them destroyed / For the Elements aid his designs."[36] Furthermore, Luddite transvestism (and perhaps women's participation) suggests that variability extends even to matters of gender-presentation, despite the apparent clarity of a single masculine ideal. What should we make then of the intersection of masculinity, feminized presentation, militarism, and violence? While there have been some speculations on the nature of this intersection, none adequately explains its function in Luddism.

One ready explanation is that cross-dressing in Luddism resembles or derives from the practice of "rough music," the popular method of disapproving violations of community values, described by Thompson and linked to Luddism by Craig Calhoun.[37] Rough music typically includes a number of emblems of discordance, from the "music" of clanging pots and pans, punctuated at times by gun-fire, to unusual masks and costumes and transvestism.[38] Certainly there are elements of rough music in the Luddite risings, but simply to assert the appearance of such elements in Luddism (as Calhoun does) does not explain their function. A more thorough explanation would account for the appearance of rough music, and its cross-dressing element in particular, as a symbolic form expressive of group solidarity within the context of an inter-class trade dispute, rather than as a method of intra-class communal regulation, as Thompson conceives of rough music.

Although Sale devotes more attention to feminization in Luddism than most historians have done, his explanation, like Calhoun's, fails to account adequately for the male use of women's clothing within the unique context of protest and same-sex relations in the Luddite regions. Supplementing his description of the episodes with some borrowed theoretical speculation, Sale remarks,

> Natalie Zemon Davis makes an interesting case that such female dis-guises were "quite popular and widespread" in Europe not only because of the effective camouflage itself but for their suggestion of the "sexual power and energy of the unruly woman" and her role as the one to de-fend "community interests and standards" and "to tell the truth about unjust rule."[39]

Davis's argument, as it is used by Sale, requires a refutation and a qualification. First, despite its ready availability, as camouflage or disguise, women's clothing would seem to offer little protection; hoods or poachers' blacking certainly would seem to be as effec-tive, especially considering that the English criminal justice system seems never to have been any less ardent in the pursuit of female criminal suspects than of male suspects. Arrests of women rioters were not infrequent in the Luddite regions. In May 1812, a woman was arrested for participating in a raid on a Sheffield militia ar-mory.[40] In June 1812, by decision of the Lancaster Special Com-mission, a woman, Hannah Smith, was hanged along with seven men for participating in (perhaps instigating) the April 1812 Man-chester Exchange riots. Smith was convicted of felony theft and riot for stealing potatoes, haranguing the crowd, and selling at the low rate of one shilling per pound twenty pounds of butter from a cart that she apparently had commandeered. Delivering her sentence, Commission chief Sir Alexander Thomson said, "Sex is not enti-tled to any mitigation of punishment when the crime is of such a nature to deserve it."[41] In a study of late eighteenth-century Lanca-

shire food riots and the prosecution of the rioters, Alan Booth discovers that "no differentiation seems to have been made between
the sexes."[42] Clearly, any Luddite man hoping to use women's
clothing for disguise to escape pursuit by the authorities and legal
retribution should have expected to be disappointed.[43]

As for a qualification of Sale's explanation of the symbolic importance of the feminized image, the Luddites certainly had enough
"power and energy" in their hammers and axes and were suffi-
ciently versed in the poverty and distress of the textile regions at
that time "to tell the truth about unjust rule" without having to appropriate the image of "the unruly woman," even though the image
may have proven useful.[44] Furthermore, I believe that it is possible
to frame an explanation of the role of transvestism in the Yorkshire
Luddite risings by attending to the phenomenon of self-presentation
by members of that highly masculinist community.

In *The Luddites*, Malcolm Thomis does not assume a binary sex-
structure but rather finds in Luddism a gendered complementarity
with the potential for overlap, which we might read as a step toward
a very basic understanding of the role of cross-dressing in the
"symbolic culture" of reaction:[45]

> But food riots were inextricably bound up with Luddism in the public
> mind for several reasons; one was that informers suggested that there
> had been Luddite instigators in the fomenting of the troubles [food
> riots], and another was that the current terminology of Luddism came
> readily to the lips of those who were involved in protest movements of
> other kinds. . . . Ludd could evidently be expected to rectify wrongs
> beyond his usual fields of operation, and where there was an issue on
> which women were naturally and traditionally forward in pressing a
> popular demand, that for lower food prices, Ludd's female half assumed
> leadership of the popular movement.[46]

Thomis's argument, of course, relies upon an unexamined assumption (which nevertheless had already been established by E. P.
Thompson in his famous essay, "The Moral Economy of the English Crowd in the Eighteenth Century" [1971] and further developed in Davis's work on popular life in France) that "women were
naturally and traditionally forward in pressing" demands for lower
food prices. Despite the weaknesses inherent in an assumed natural
gender division in the working-class resistance, the concept of
"Ludd's female half" actually undermines the idea of a *natural*
gender division and affords the opportunity to acknowledge the role
of feminized presentation in Luddite factory raids.

In *Women in Protest, 1800–1850,* Thomis and Grimmett do ex-

amine the question of transvestism in both raids and riots, concluding their study with an observation in line with Thompson's moral
economy position echoed by Thomis in *The Luddites* (quoted
above). Thomis and Grimmett write, "Where women were themselves unable to uphold rights and standards because they lacked
the physical strength or stamina for nocturnal destruction, the next
best thing to a woman was a man in women's clothing."[47] The obvious strength of the interpretation offered by Thomis and Grimmett
is the intellectual foundation—Thompson's much-approved moral
economy theory. However, important weaknesses remain in, first,
the failure to examine the linked phenomena of transvestism and
Luddism in terms of Luddism's own internal dynamic—that is, as
a product of the unique positions of the affected trades themselves—and, second, the problematic assumption (which Thomis
had avoided in his earlier book) that feminine presentation denotes
the female or its surrogate.

The theory which most adequately explains the role of cross-
dressing in the Luddite riots appears in Sedgwick's *Between Men*
(1985). Sedgwick proposes a view of male-to-male relations informed by Claude Levi-Strauss' observation that in certain cultures
men use women as exchange media to negotiate male relationships—what Sedgwick, following Levi-Strauss, describes as "male
traffic in women."[48] In a chapter on Wycherley's *The Country Wife*
(1675), Sedgwick discusses the exchange value of the women in the
play:

> To misunderstand the kind of property women are or the kind of transac-
> tion in which alone their value is realizable means, for a man, to endan-
> ger his own position as a subject in the relationship of exchange: to be
> permanently feminized or objectified in relation to other men. On the
> other hand, success in making this transaction requires a willingness and
> ability to temporarily risk, or assume, a feminized status. Only the man
> who can proceed through that stage, *while* remaining in cognitive con-
> trol of the symbolic system that presides over sexual exchange, will be
> successful in achieving a relation of mastery to other men.[49]

Sedgwick's theory has the great advantages of avoiding sexual (and
sexual-orientational) essentialism and of focusing on a symbolic
system; however, because the theory develops out of a study of canonical literature by authors outside of the working classes, it remains to be seen whether it can apply to the simultaneously
symbolic, productive, and property status of women's clothing in
the context of the Luddite protests, in which the aim was not ex-

change of women and mastery over other men but rather preservation of an economic system which afforded amicable male relations against the domineering efforts of those persons who would change the social structure of manufacturing from one of brotherhood to unvarying hierarchy. How might homosocial desire surface in an available structure of meaning—in this case, the industrial tension of the Luddite risings, which had its own forms of representation, based largely upon a social and industrial reality?

Relations between working-class males at the time of the Luddite risings might be said to correspond to the "traffic" structure described by Sedgwick, but one important qualification obtains: such as we know of it, the homosocial traffic between male laborers in the North and Midlands was constructed around textile commodities and was governed, to a large degree, by the changing conditions of production. I have argued that under the traditional homoindustrial system of manufacture, cloth was a physical marker of the relation of one man to another through the work of their hands. Understood as a representational or symbolic system, the process of cloth manufacture, along with its "transactions," was metonymic. No textile worker sought to control or to monopolize the cloth by changing its significance (specifically by changing the process of manufacture to one in which all workers of a single trade can be replaced and "represented" by a machine lacking any of the unique characteristics which made a trade, as a self-regulatory entity, necessary). Under the traditional system, there had to be some points at which the trade convened to pass its collective judgment upon cloth articles. Those points were set through custom, trade practice, and, occasionally, resort to institutions based upon custom; in particular, the textile trades have a long history of participation in the common law system to resolve disputes about quality and usage.[50] In contrast, under the machinery system, by manufacturing an article of consistent (if usually inferior) quality, the machine imposes its stamp upon the article, thereby eliminating inconsistency and the need for continual trade self-regulation and convention. The stamp of the machine is effectively a metaphor replacing the negotiative, flexible consensus of trade and tradition.

Part of the Luddite response was to defend consensus and solidarity in the trade by adopting an emblem of the values of the traditional system. They could not, in their raids and riots, manifest an abstraction—the homoindustrial system by which men were bound to each other in common interest, "commonality." They could, however, represent the product of that labor system, cloth, by foregrounding it so that it stood in unfamiliar contrast to the wearer, drawing attention to the juxtaposition. The assumption of a "feminized status" through the male use of women's clothing served exactly that purpose, preserving in its own presentation the trade's values of common purpose and variability.[51] For the time that Luddite efforts occurred within the realm of variability and were directed at those machines which were obnoxious to the trade, the croppers enjoyed great success. (In fact, the Luddites were aware that the use of some frames could be varied so as not to offend the trade and they let those frames stand.) However, this element of Luddite resistance was contradicted by another element which ushered in effigy, militarism, and violence.

Metaphoric presentation is made possible by the workings of identity and binary, distinguishing and counterposing that which is against that which is not. Insofar as this binary applies, metaphoric presentation is constricting and violent. So it was in the Luddite counter-metaphoric reaction against the machine's stamp of consistency. The imposition of obnoxious machinery by the West Riding clothiers required practical, destructive action effected by the military-style organization described above. Subsuming all of masculine labor in the textile trades under the single marker of General Ludd, no matter how variable "the General" might be, advanced a symbolic and economic system in which adversity is the rule, in which only one superintending metaphor could predominate. Two instances of Luddite presentation bear witness to the increasing adversariness that accompanied the binarizing identity of metaphor. The first piece of evidence of the Luddite desire for a determinate rather than a variable mode of representation appears in a newspaper account from Leeds of one riot, in which "A *Man of Straw* was carried, representing the *renowned* General Ludd."[52] Second, in September 1812, a Geldhill Luddite, Charles Milnes, wrote a song that replaces the customs, practices, and fellow feeling of the trade with General Ludd's "Rules": "Tho' the bayonet is fixed they can do no good / As long as we keep up the Rules of General Ludd."[53] The fact that the Yorkshire Luddites would wish visually to represent General Ludd and to ascribe to him superintending "Rules" suggests that they had embraced the linked concepts of determinate representation and adversarial singularity.

Violence follows adversarial (metaphoric) representation. Personification of trade values led to personification of trade hostilities, especially in the murders and attempted murders of clothiers, many of whom had been just a few years before closely affiliated to the trade.[54] Although the Luddites assumed, at times, what Sedgwick calls a "feminized status," which I interpret within the unique context of Yorkshire Luddism as variability and expanded sensibilities, they did not achieve cognitive control over the newly metaphoric symbolic process by which standards for cloth manufacture were realized.[55] Put another way, in that their defense of the traditional system changed its focus from processes and labor to persons and hostility, the croppers failed to sustain the variable and negotiative standards which defined that system, permitted its characteristic solidarity, and took form in variable gender-presentation. Instead, by embracing the polarizing representational method of machinery manufacture, even though their method sought to affirm a homoindustrial solidarity, the Luddites let themselves be pulled into a contest of mastery over men which they were bound to lose.[56]

For many months between 1811 and 1813, forced to defend a homosocial/homoindustrial solidarity between workers against the alienation of heteroindustrialism, the Luddites embraced a doctrine of variability, which encompassed organization, naming, and clothing. The product of masculine labor, clothing, individually worn in collective endeavors, replaced work itself as the marker of the homoindustrial solidarity between workers. And the Luddite hero is a man wearing upon his body a (foregrounded, because unusual) feminine mark of masculine labor, doomed to fail, but nevertheless demonstrating an intense male sociability and expanded conception of masculinity.

NOTES

1. Thompson's discussion of Luddism appears in the chapter titled "The Army of Redressers" in *The Making of the English Working Class* (1963; reprint, New York: Vintage, 1966), 521–602. For his discussion of women's participation in riots during the period, see chapter 5, "The Moral Economy Reviewed," in *Customs in Common* (1991; reprint, Harmondsworth: Penguin, 1993), 259–351.

2. Thomis, *The Luddites: Machine-Breaking in Regency England* (Hamden: Archon, 1970), 21–23.

3. Thomis and Grimmett, *Women in Protest, 1800–1850* (New York: St. Martin's Press, 1982), 31.

4. Kirkpatrick Sale, *Rebels against the Future: The Luddites and Their War on the Industrial Revolution: Lessons for the Computer Age* (Reading: Addison-Wesley, 1995), 131.

5. Frank Peel, *Spen Valley: Past and Present* (Heckmondwike: Senior & Company, 1893), 245–46. The contemporary accounts mentioned above include the *Manchester Mercury* 21 April 1812; *Manchester Commerical Advertiser* 21 April 1812; *Leeds Mercury* 18 and 25 April 1812; General Grey to Home Office, 18 April 1812, Home Office Papers 42/122, Public Record Office (hereafter cited as "Home Office Papers"); the *Times* 17 April 1812; *Political Register* 25 April 1812; 14 March 1812 letter in E. C. Parsons, *Memorials and Correspondence*

(Leeds: T. Walker, 1849), 43. See also the accounts forwarded to Home Office Under-Secretary John Beckett by Huddersfield magistrate Joseph Radcliffe, 6 September 1812, Home Office Papers 42/127 and 42/128. Some of these events are discussed in Thomis, *Luddites*, 22; and Sale, *Rebels*, 131.

6. Peel, *The Risings of the Luddites*, 4th ed. (London: Cass, 1968); Sykes, *Ben o' Bill's, The Luddite* (London: Simpkin, Marshall & Company, 1898).

7. J. L. Hammond and Barbara Hammond, *The Skilled Labourer, 1760–1832* (1919; reprint, New York: Augustus M. Kelley, 1967), 317.

8. Contemporary accounts include the *Manchester Mercury* 21 April 1812; *Manchester Commercial Advertiser* 21 April 1812; *Leeds Mercury* 18 and 25 April 1812; Home Office Papers 42/122, General Grey to Home Office, 18 April 1812; the *Times* 17 April 1812; *Political Register* 25 April 1812; 14 March 1812 letter in Parsons, *Memorials* 43. See also the Radcliffe depositions in the Home Office Papers 40/1. Some events are discussed in Thomis, *Luddites*, 22; and Sale 131.

9. Although the prominence of women in food riots has been well-established, the extent of their roles is still disputed. John Bohstedt has argued convincingly against a "myth of feminine food riot" (Bohstedt, "Gender, Household, and Community Politics: Women in English Riots, 1790–1810," *Past and Present* 120 [August 1988], 90). Thompson, however, claims that there was never such a myth to demolish (Thompson, *Customs in Common*, 306).

10. *Leeds Mercury* 15 and 22 August 1812; Home Office Papers 42/125, General Maitland to Home Office, 22 August 1812; *Leeds Intelligencer* 24 August 1812; Parsons 74. Accounts of the Stockport and Middleton riots (above) also detail women's participation. See also Thomis and Grimmett 31. On women's roles in English protest generally, see Thomis and Grimmett, Thompson's chapter, "The Moral Economy Reviewed," in *Customs in Common*, and John Bohstedt's article "Gender, Household and Community Politics."

11. Adrian Randall, *Before the Luddites: Custom, Community, and Machinery in the English Woolen Industry, 1776–1809* (Cambridge: Cambridge University Press, 1991).

12. Ivy Pinchbeck, *Women Workers and the Industrial Revolution, 1750–1850* (1930; reprint, London: Cass, 1969), 162–65; see also Duncan Bythell, *The Sweated Trades: Outwork in Nineteenth Century Britain* (London: Batsford Academic, 1978), 40. A brief discussion appears in the first chapter of Thomis and Grimmett, *Women in Protest, 1800–1850*. Generally, before the 1830s and the total victory of machinery over handicraft, women's occupations in the textile trades of the North were limited to spinning and weaving, both of which were frequently out-sourced. I find no record of a woman working as a cloth-finisher or even a gig-mill operator. Perhaps these occupational tendencies might explain the participation of women in Lancashire and Cheshire riots, where Luddism resulted from the threat of steam-powered looms to the weavers, and the absence of women's participation in Yorkshire, the seat of the cloth-finishing trade.

13. Randall, *Before the Luddites*, 22–24; see also Pat Hudson, *Regions and Industries: A Perspective on the Industrial Revolution in Britain* (Cambridge: Cambridge University Press, 1989), 181.

14. Frank Peel, *The Risings of the Luddites*, 4th ed. (London: Cass, 1968), 9–15, 120–21; see also Randall, *Before the Luddites*, 110–18.

15. Home Office Papers 40/1.

16. Sedgwick uses the term "homosocial desire" to "hypothesize the potential unbrokenness of a continuum between" male-bonding and homosexuality, or, put another way, "between 'men-loving-men' and 'men-promoting-the interests-of-

men' " (Sedgwick, *Between Men: English Literature and Male Homosocial Desire* [New York: Columbia University Press, 1985], 1, 3).

17. Peel, *Risings*, 47–48.

18. Martha Vicinus, *The Industrial Muse: A Study of Nineteenth Century British Working-Class Literature* (New York: Barnes & Noble, 1974), 36.

19. Describing the practice of cropping, Robert Reid writes, "Some apprentices who had worked alongside the croppers had been known to collapse, their hands running with blood, after only a few hours of the work" (*Land of Lost Content: The Luddite Revolt, 1812* [London: Heineman, 1986], 43).

20. Sale, *Rebels*, 11.

21. D. F. E. Sykes, *History of the Colne Valley* (Slaithwaite: F. Walker, 1906), 308.

22. Rictor Norton, *Mother Clap's Molly House: The Gay Subculture in England 1700–1830* (London: Gay Men's Press, 1992), 143.

23. Norton remarks that masculinity and effeminacy do intersect in the working-class gay life of the time; however, for all the cross-dressing among the London mollies (members of the gay or bisexual working-class male community, which included bargemen, blacksmiths, butchers, and coal-heavers), "most of the men mentioned throughout [Norton's] study were neither effeminate nor particularly conspicuous in appearance and manner. In fact we are left with an overriding impression of vigorous and lusty bonhomie" (Norton, *Mother Clap's*, 299, 104).

24. Peel, *Risings*, 13; see also Sykes, *Ben o' Bill's*, 180.

25. Linda Dowling, discussing effeminacy in the Victorian period, during which Peel and Sykes write, treats it as a discourse "which had previously set rigid limits . . . on any positive cultural response to the notion of masculine love" (*Hellenism and Homosexuality in Victorian Oxford* [Ithaca: Cornell University Press, 1994], 66). Whether Dowling's observations on a discourse operating in the south of England, especially Oxford and London, bear upon histories written by Yorkshiremen is uncertain; nevertheless, it is clear that Peel and Sykes use the term as a pejorative and link it to social roles that are described almost as sexual roles— "melted like wax," "soft and easy."

26. Sykes, *Ben o' Bill's*, 149–51; see also Peel, *Risings*, 14. As for what Peel calls Booth's "indifferent success," Mellor came to embrace Booth's radical politics, eventually aligning himself with political reform, as can be seen in Mellor's 30 November 1812 letter to Thomas Ellis from York Castle (Radcliffe Manuscripts 126/127A, Leeds Municipal Archives; see also Home Office Papers 42/123).

27. It is precisely the absence of documentation that hinders gay revision of working-class friendships. Quite apart from formal and informal homophobia, most working-class men—gay, bisexual, or heterosexual—lacked the education or leisure to record their private lives. Most of our meager information on male sexual life (particularly for homosexual or bisexual men) during the period comes from relatively nonmarginal literature, correspondence, and journals, which tend to be written by men of letters—a problem which must be addressed by historians of sexuality. One of the few scholars treating gay working-class life is Norton, who, in his excellent study, *Mother Clap's Molly House: The Gay Subculture in England 1700–1830*, examines sodomy trial records, which often provide highly detailed descriptions of London's working-class molly subculture.

28. Sykes, *Ben o' Bill's*, 150–51.

29. Ibid., 180.

30. Ibid., 208; see also Peel, *Risings*, 101–2.

31. Peel, *Risings*, 121. Reverend Patrick Brontë, father of the novelist sisters,

describes having seen such secret burials (John Lock, *A Man of Sorrow* [New York: Nelson, 1965], 114; see also Sale, *Rebels*, 11). Brontë's daughter, Charlotte, also offers an account of the attack on Rawfolds in her novel, *Shirley*.

32. Peel, *Risings*, 121.

33. Ibid., 129; see also Sykes, *Ben o' Bill's*, 91–92.

34. Sykes, *Colne Valley*, 317.

35. In reading a draft of this essay, Elizabeth Dell noted a possible connection between Horsfall's remarks about riding "up to the saddle girths in Luddite blood" and Booth's occupation as a saddle-maker's apprentice. Perhaps Mellor inferred a connection, understanding Horsfall's remarks to signify a special hatred or a despising of young Booth.

36. Home Office Papers 42/119.

37. Craig Calhoun, *The Question of Class Struggle* (Chicago: University of Chicago Press, 1982), 261.

38. Thompson, *Customs*, 469.

39. Sale, 131n, quoting Natalie Zemon Davis, *Society and Culture in Early Modern Europe* (Stanford: Stanford University Press, 1975), 147–48.

40. Sale, *Rebels*, 130.

41. Thomis and Grimmett, *Women in Protest*, 43–44, and Reid, *Land of Lost Content*, 170. Reid cites as sources the 6 June 1812 *Manchester Mercury*; *Cowdroy's Manchester Exchange Herald* of 6 June 1812; Hammond and Hammond, *Skilled Labourer*, 294. For Thomson's words at sentencing, he, like Thomis and Grimmett, cites the 6 June 1812 *Leeds Mercury*. For primary sources on criminal proceedings engaged against Smith and other female rioters, see the May and June 1812 letters to Home Office Secretary Richard Ryder from John Lloyd of Stockport and William Robert Hay of Manchester (Home Office Papers 40/1).

42. Alan Booth, "Food Riots in the North-West of England, 1790–1801," *Past and Present* 77 (1977), 106.

43. Thomis and Grimmett arrive at the same conclusion: "Such penalties [as Hannah Smith and later female East Anglia agricultural rioters received] indicate the futility of a general belief in any female advantage before the law" (*Women in Protest*, 45).

44. Probably the best description of the distresses affecting the Luddites and their communities can be found in Thomis's *Luddites* (41–73).

45. The term "symbolic culture" comes from Calhoun, who argues throughout his book, *The Question of Class Struggle*, that traditional representational forms impart to each community its mode of protest when its values are threatened.

46. Thomis, *Luddites*, 22.

47. Thomis and Grimmett, *Women in Protest*, 146.

48. Sedgwick, *Between Men*, 13, 53.

49. Ibid., 50–51.

50. Adrian Randall, "The Shearmen and the Wiltshire Outrages of 1802: Trade Unionism and Industrial Violence," *Social History* 7 (1982), 287–301; see also J. D. Chambers, "The Worshipful Company of Framework Knitters (1657–1778)," *Economica* (November 1929), 324–25.

51. Carole Pateman, especially in interpreting the work of T. H. Green, has examined the relationship between the individual body and the alienation of that individual's labor, orienting her interpretation specifically toward the issue of gender and contracted labor. Nevertheless, some general observations are made possible by Pateman's focus on gender and body. Pateman quotes Green as arguing that "labour . . . is a commodity which attaches in a peculiar manner to the person of

man" (Pateman, *The Sexual Contract* [Stanford: Stanford University Press, 1988], 150). The attachment of labor to the individual person, and the "right" of inalienability necessitated by that attachment, was assailed by the imposition of the mechanized factory system, which made it possible to sell labor and body to a use which did not depend upon the unique body practice of an individual disciplined within a trade and participating communally within it. The Luddite use of women's clothing may have been a way of insisting on the attachment of labor, and, by extension, the attachment of the product of labor to the individual person, foregrounded by the masculine use of feminine clothing which makes clothing, the product of labor, a sign of that attachment. The use of feminine attire is an act which insists upon the inalienability of labor and reasserts the attachment of the masculine body to labor.

52. *Leeds Mercury* 25 April 1812.

53. The King v. Charles Milnes and William Blakeborough, 2 January 1813, Treasury Solicitor's Papers 11/813, Public Records Office.

54. Reid, *The Land of Lost Content*, 138.

55. The connection of variable gender-presentation to expansive social and political ideas, especially peaceful ones, is evident in a couple of instances of authorial feminization, as in an April 1812 letter sent by a peaceful, reform-minded Luddite to a "respectable manufacturer" in southeastern Lancashire (Home Office Papers 40/1):

Sir,
    Doubtless you are well acquainted with the Political History of America, if so you must confess that, it was ministerial tyranny that gave rise to that glorious spirit in which the British Colonies obtain'd their independence by force of arms, at a period, when we was ten times as strong as now!—if bands of husbandmen could do this, in spite of all the force our government was then able to employ—cannot such an action be accomplish'd here, now the military strength of the country is so reduced—Consider Sir, what a few troops there is at present in England,—remember that none can be call'd home; because that would be relinquishing the little we have gain'd to the fury of the enemy—little indeed to have coss'd so much money and such torrents of blood, yes British blood!—let me persuade you to quit your present post, lay by your sword, and become a friend to the oppress'd—for curs'd his the man that even lifts a straw against the sacred cause of Liberty.

—Eliza Ludd

56. Calhoun agrees with this conclusion (that Luddism failed to gain control over the new cognitive system) although on different grounds. Calhoun argues that

older popular symbolic culture. . . . may have given Luddism its charivari-like character, with men dressed in women's clothing or their own inside out. . . . but it limited it to traditional ritualized opposition—to a mode of rebellion grown ineffective with the increasing insulation of "the powerful" from "the people." Such rituals of reversal reveal a cultural order, but that cognitive system, whatever its merits, was not capable of analyzing the new and complex turns which society was taking, though it might well be capable of rejecting them. (Calhoun, *Question*, 261 n. 72).

Male Rivalry and Friendship in the Novels of William Godwin

WILLIAM D. BREWER

IN A PROVOCATIVE ANALYSIS OF WILLIAM GODWIN'S NOVEL *THINGS AS they are; or, the adventures of Caleb Williams* (1794), Alex Gold has argued that Caleb's paranoid feelings toward his master, Falkland, have their roots in homophobia:

> Caleb tells a story about omnipotent persecution; that story reveals his deep affection for another man and emphasizes the trauma of brutal rejection by that man. Traditional psychoanalytic theory would suggest that Caleb's avowedly "distempered" preoccupation with persecution might indicate a paranoid dissociation issuing from Caleb's attempts to repress the homosexual impulses which became threateningly powerful during his residence at [Falkland's] manor. . . . The fact that Caleb always sees Falkland as his omnipotent persecutor, even though Falkland's brother is actually the initial and fiercest avenging fury, again corresponds to the theory.[1]

Gold's Freudian analysis of Caleb's behavior is cited approvingly by Eve Kosofsky Sedgwick, who links *Caleb Williams* to a number of other "paranoid Gothic novels" which thematize homophobia,[2] and Eric Daffron argues that the Caleb-Falkland relationship is sexualized throughout the novel: "Falkland registers the intimate probing of a man who has become all too familiar in an increasingly claustrophobic atmosphere as a threat to the very sanctity of his manhood. . . . Caleb adopts the language of sodomitical penetration when he explains that Falkland hired Gines to pursue him 'in [his] rear.' "[3] In a new historicist reading of the novel, Robert J. Corber contends that Godwin makes Falkland "a sodomite" and deploys homophobia to "discourage the sort of male bonding that helped sustain aristocratic hegemony."[4] According to Corber, Godwin's "novel renders middle-class men [like Caleb] who rely on patronage rather than on their own industry and talent vulnerable to stigmatization as sodomites."[5]

49

Caleb Williams is, however, just one of the novels in which Godwin explores the dynamics of masculine relationships, and not all
of his male protagonists' attitudes toward same-sex friendships are
homophobic. For example, his penultimate novel, *Cloudesley: A
Tale* (1830), presents a misanthropic male character, Borromeo,
who is taught how to love by a virtuous young man. In this essay I
argue that while Godwin frequently portrays pathological and apparently homophobic conflicts between male characters, his fiction
is also concerned with the need for men to establish non-competi-
tive friendships with each other in order to counteract their tendencies toward antisocial behavior. Male characters who are unable to
form close same-sex friendships in his novels usually fail to establish stable, relatively unconflicted masculine identities. Moreover,
as he explores and develops his conception of a supportive and intimate relationship between men, Godwin moves from a model of
friendship based on equality to a model based on paternalism, in
which one friend takes precedence over the other.

The theme of male bonding recurs throughout Godwin's fiction.
Caleb Williams declares that "the greatest aggravation" of Falkland's relentless persecution of him is that he is "cut off from the
friendship of mankind": "I can safely affirm, that poverty and hunger, that endless wanderings, that a blasted character and the curses
that clung to my name, were all of them slight misfortunes compared to this. I endeavoured to sustain myself by the sense of my
integrity, but the voice of no man upon earth echoed to the voice of
my conscience."[6] In *St. Leon: A Tale of the Sixteenth Century*
(1799), the eponymous narrator also mourns his friendlessness. A
stranger gives him the philosopher's stone and the elixir of life on
the condition that he never tell anyone his secret, and this separates
St. Leon from the rest of humanity. He belatedly discovers that
what he really wants is a perfect friendship with another man (in
this case, with his son, who, because of St. Leon's perpetual youth,
does not recognize him as his father): "I looked into him, and saw
a man; I saw expansive powers of intellect and true sensibility of
heart. To be esteemed and loved and protected by such a man; to
have him to take one by the hand, to enquire into one's sorrows, to
interest himself in one's anxieties, to exult in one's good fortune
and one's joys; this and this only deserves the name of existence."[7]
The title character of *Mandeville: A Tale of the Seventeenth Century
in England* (1817) declares that he became mentally unbalanced because he had no friend to guide him:

> The true definition of a friend is, he to whom I can bear to speak, and
> whom I can bear to hear! But where am I to look for the qualities of a

genuine friend? In the man whose assistance I want. . . . Were I but once convinced of his ability and his sincerity, did I but know the soundness of his judgment, and the frankness of his nature, were I assured of his love for me, and that it was his love that spoke, . . . could I meet with a man of sufficient purity of heart, and fervour of spirit, to dare on all occasions to tell me all the truth that my welfare required, I could not be impatient if I would. Had I encountered such a friend at my greatest need, I should never have gone mad.[8]

Orphaned at the age of three, Mandeville longs for a loving mentor who will be the father figure that he has never had.

A number of Godwin's male characters establish relationships with women as well as men, but they tend to feel constricted or emasculated by these relationships, particularly if they are with wives whose opinions differ from their own. Because men and women in his novels are educated separately and operate in different spheres, they have a difficult time communicating with each other, or even co-existing in a domestic setting. Thus the title character of Godwin's *St. Leon*, although devoted to his wife, Marguerite, cannot be contented with the "pastoral simplicity" of life with her and their children.[9] According to the stranger who offers St. Leon the philosopher's stone and the elixir vitae, his love for his wife is unmanly: "Feeble and effeminate mortal! You are neither a knight nor a Frenchman! . . . Was ever gallant action achieved by him who was incapable of separating himself from a woman? . . . In vain might honour, worth, and immortal renown proffer their favours to him who has made himself the basest of all sublunary things—the puppet of a woman."[10] St. Leon's chivalric ideology comes into conflict with Marguerite's dedication to the "domestic and private affections"[11] and his decision to accept the stranger's gifts and keep them secret from her amounts "to a divorce of the heart."[12] In *Fleetwood: or, The New Man of Feeling* (1805; rpt. 1832), the protagonist marries a much younger woman and their marriage is nearly destroyed by their constant misunderstandings. Like St. Leon, Fleetwood comes to regard his relationship with his wife as emasculating and enslaving: "Lately the most independent man alive, I was become a mere appendage to that tender and charming trifle, a pretty woman. I adored my wife; but I had cultivated high ideas of the prerogatives of my sex, and I did not altogether relish the being thus reduced to a cipher."[13] Fleetwood cannot reconcile his wife's "decisive partiality for visits, and assemblies, and crowds"[14] with his own "thoughts, and projects, and inventions, for fame and for usefulness."[15] Far from enhancing the masculine self, marriage prevents its full realization.[16]

In contrast to St. Leon and Fleetwood, Mandeville is unmarried. The only woman he has any affection for is his sister: "Henrietta was father, and mother, and every thing to me in one."[17] Unfortunately, however, Mandeville and Henrietta are raised apart, and when he needs a confidant, he turns to another man, a schemer named Mallison: "I secretly stood in awe of [Henrietta's] judgment. I knew she had an independent mind, and an instinctive discernment of right and truth, which . . . made me tremble lest she could discover the extent of my infirmities. But Mallison was so implicit, bowed so completely to all my judgments, and drank in all my suggestions, that it was a pleasure to talk to so accommodating a pupil."[18] Mandeville refuses to believe that his sister or any other woman is capable of understanding him and forgiving his "infirmities."

The title character of Godwin's last novel, *Deloraine* (1833), believes that women are inferior to men: "All ages and nations have recognised the practical inferiority of the female sex. They are not admitted among our legislators: in representative governments they have not even a direct voice in the choice of our representatives. Every path of society is open to the male; an infinite majority is shut upon the female."[19] From Deloraine's point of view, his brief marriage to Emilia is successful because she never opposes him. When they disagree, she is willing to "confess her error the instant she [is] aware of it."[20] As Marilyn Butler and Mark Philp observe, although this relationship is

> Idyllically happy in Deloraine's telling of it, [it] seems more involuted, less frank, and less equal to the properly suspicious reader. . . . Emilia remains noncommittally silent on her feelings at leaving behind her one-year-old child for two years in order to accompany her husband. . . . We cannot tell whether the companionate marriage that Deloraine celebrates so warmly was ever for her that passionate unity, the dissolution of their two identities in one crucible. . . . Emilia is not endowed with a distinct selfhood or a voice in the matter of her marriage.[21]

Deloraine's second marriage ends, however, in disaster: maddened by jealousy, he murders the man whom he suspects of having an affair with his wife, and she dies cursing him.

For a man to find his true antitype, Godwin's fiction suggests, he must turn to another man. The characters of his male protagonists are typically formed in single-sex institutions such as public schools and the military, and when they marry they are frequently unable either to understand or communicate with their wives. Even

Fleetwood, one of Godwin's most misanthropic characters, ideal-izes masculine friendship. For him, only a male friend, "the brother of [his] heart," can be "a part of himself."[22] He describes his ef-forts to form a relationship with another man:

> I met with men, who seemed willing to bestow their friendship upon me; but their temper, their manners and their habits, were so discordant from mine, that it was impossible the flame should be lighted in my breast. I met with men, to whom I could willingly have sworn an eternal partnership of soul; but they thought of me with no corresponding senti-ment; they were engaged in other pursuits, they were occupied with other views, and had not leisure to distinguish and to love me.[23]

Fleetwood's misanthropy is partly caused by his inability to form "an eternal partnership of soul" with another man who would "dis-tinguish" and "love" him. His description of this kind of spiritual union anticipates, in some ways, Percy Bysshe Shelley's famous essay "On Love" (written in 1818). According to Shelley, "the in-visible and unattainable point to which Love tends" is "The discov-ery of its antitype: the meeting with an understanding capable of clearly estimating the deductions of our own, an imagination which should enter into and seize upon the subtle and delicate peculiarities which we have delighted to cherish and unfold in secret, with a frame whose nerves, like the chords of two exquisite lyres strung to the accompaniment of one delightful voice, vibrate with the vibra-tions of our own."[24] But while Shelley discusses love in a general, philosophical way, Fleetwood dwells on homosocial love. His early experiences with two promiscuous Parisian coquettes and his tem-pestuous relationship with his flirtatious young wife have rendered him incapable of imagining a positive, open, and healthy relation-ship with a woman.

In Fleetwood's opinion, friendship, "in the sense in which [he feels] the want of it," must be an exclusive and almost obsessional partnership between two like-minded individuals:

> [it is] a sentiment that can grasp but one individual in its embrace. The person who entertains this sentiment must see in his friend a creature of a species by itself, must respect and be attached to him above all the world, and be deeply convinced that the loss of him would be a calamity which nothing earthly could repair. By long habit, he must have made his friend a part of himself; must be incapable of any pleasure in public, in reading, in travelling, of which he does not make his friend, at least in idea, a partaker, or of passing a day or an hour in the conceptions of which the thought of his friend does not mingle itself.[25]

Unfortunately for Fleetwood, his search for this kind of friend ends in failure. He experiences "the heart-breaking delusions and disappointments of a pretended friendship" and becomes a confirmed misanthropist.[26] The only positive relationships he is able to establish with other men are paternal rather than fraternal in nature: with his father, M. Ruffigny (his father's friend), and Macneil, who persuades Fleetwood to marry his daughter. But following the death of Macneil, his final mentor, Fleetwood is unable to find anyone who can provide him with moral guidance or emotional support. His homosocial impulses are frustrated, and, as a result, he becomes homophobic, marrying a woman who is ill-suited to him and becoming violently jealous of any man who associates with her.

Fleetwood's misanthropy begins during his years at Oxford University, and Mandeville's pathological hatred for Clifford begins while he is attending a public school. Left largely on their own, the pupils in these all-male educational institutions persecute and tyrannize over each other. In *Enquiry Concerning Political Justice* (1798 ed.), Godwin contends that "the characters of men are determined in all their most essential circumstances by education."[27] Fleetwood and Mandeville's educations teach them to hate and fear other males. Godwin's unhappy years as a boarder at Hoxton Academy provide a background for the portrait of Winchester College in *Mandeville*. At Hoxton, Godwin's "fellow students 'almost with one voice, pronounced [him] to be the most self-conceited, self-sufficient animal that ever lived,' " and "He seems to have suffered deeply from [their] persecution . . . and found it necessary to defend his beliefs as a means of upholding the integrity of his personality."[28] In fact, Godwin's experience fits a certain pattern: a proud student, filled with an elevated sense of his intellectual or social preeminence, comes to a school in which his pretensions are mercilessly exposed and flouted by his malicious peers. Godwin's son-in-law, Percy Bysshe Shelley, had an even worse time at Eton. Known as "Mad Shelley," "He was quickly recognized as an exceptional Latin scholar, and a remarkable non-conformist, and the bullying from fellow-pupils was extremely severe."[29] As Crompton notes, "At Eton it was the custom for masters to lock boys into dormitories at eight o'clock and leave them unattended: the authorities took no responsibility for their behavior 'after school.' "[30] In this laissez-faire atmosphere, Shelley was subjected to constant practical jokes and became so enraged that, on one occasion, he was "provoked . . . into striking a penknife through the hand of one of his tormentors and pinning it to the desk."[31] In *Fleetwood*, Godwin suggests that this type of persecution occurred at Oxford as well. A minor character, Withers, comes to Oxford full of literary aspirations; he has composed "a tragedy founded on the story of the Fifth Labour of Hercules [the removal of manure from the Augean stable]."[32] His fellow students devise an elaborate practical joke in which his manuscript is universally mocked, and he is thoroughly humiliated. As a result of this malicious treatment, Withers is thrown into a deep depression and commits suicide.

Fleetwood, Withers, and Mandeville are, like their real-life counterparts, Godwin and Shelley, hypersensitive and proud individuals who are completely unprepared for the torments visited upon pretentious or nonconformist boys in an all-male school. Social humiliation in this kind of environment has an especially traumatic effect on Mandeville because he comes from a wealthy and aristocratic family and expects to be treated with the deference due to his rank. In *Mandeville*, the tensions at Winchester College are intensified by politics: the Presbyterian Mandeville finds himself in an awkward position in a school in which the students are virtually all royalists, devoted to the memory of the executed Charles I. For Mandeville, an orphan raised in isolation, the pressures are intense in this psychologically and politically charged environment. His fellow pupils haze him as a matter of course:

> The elder boys . . . had felt the weight of the yoke upon their own necks; and they were resolved to retaliate their sufferings at the expence of the first victim they met. . . . I, as a new comer, was exposed to a thousand ridiculous questions. The inquiries were wanton, and the inquirers had small care of the answers they received. All that I experienced in this sort was frolicsome; it had little consideration for the feelings of the person to whom it was addressed.[33]

His real tormenter, however, is Mallison, who taunts him for being a Presbyterian aristocrat, "a *prig*, a *frump*, [and] a *fogram*."[34] Mandeville is mortified by this treatment:

> I was pointed and sneered at, as I passed. A significant winking of the eye, or a contemptuous shooting of the lip, the various mows and gibes of a school-boy's prolific and wanton malice, pursued me . . . here, within the walls of Winchester College, I was treated as nothing, a flouting-stock and a make-game, a monstrous and abortive birth, created for no other end than to be the scoff of my fellows, their sport, and their joy, when they stood in need of an object to spend their brutal and unthinking mirth upon.[35]

Mandeville declares of Clifford that "they who admired my competitor, should never turn a glance of passing approbation upon me."[36] Because he is an orphan, he lacks the parental guidance and support necessary to help him overcome his feelings of confusion and alienation.

In this environment Clifford is preeminent, and it is not surprising that Mandeville begins to hate the leader of a school that seems to be designed to crush his spirit. The friend he ultimately selects appears to reflect his "monstrous and abortive" self-image: Waller is "an abortive specimen of manhood" who is "deformed in his person."[37] He can dominate Waller because there is "nothing commanding or masculine in his turn of mind."[38] When Waller betrays him by telling their fellow students that Mandeville is the owner of a book lampooning Charles I, Mandeville finds himself utterly friendless. Although Clifford tries to spare his feelings, Mandeville blames him for his disgrace and social failure at Winchester. Despite the fact that Mallison, not Clifford, is the instigator of his torments, Mandeville will not stoop to hate a lesser boy: he is determined to despise Clifford because when he is compared to his rival he is revealed to be the inferior person, despite his higher rank.

At Oxford University, Mandeville is even more solitary and alienated than he was at Winchester. He is attracted to his only friend there, a fanatical royalist named Lisle, because Lisle resembles him in his misanthropy and ability to hate:

> [W]e loved by sympathy. We spent whole evenings together in silence: but, if thus we did not amuse each other, at least we had a mutual understanding, and did not the one torment the other by ill-applied attentions and civilities. We found a social pleasure in looking in each other's faces, and silently whispering to our own hearts, Thank God, I have a companion, that hates the world as much as I do![39]

While he desperately needs male companionship, Mandeville fears "attentions and civilities" from another man; thus his gloomy communions with Lisle suit him. In fact, Mandeville and Lisle consider establishing "a misanthropical club, where the knot that [binds] the members together, and the feature that they [hold] in common, should be a disappointed and embittered spirit." But they "never [add] a third member to [their] society" because they cannot be entirely convinced "of the eligibility of any stranger."[40]

Unfortunately for Mandeville, Lisle learns from Mallison of Mandeville's disgrace at Winchester and of his subsequent desertion of Colonel Penruddock, the leader of a group of royalists against Cromwell. Mallison also tells these stories to a number of other Oxonians, and Mandeville finds himself even more of an outcast in Oxford than he was at Winchester. This proves too much for him, and he runs away from Oxford, vowing to escape the "tyranny of [man's] eye."[41] He goes temporarily insane and his psychosis is, not surprisingly, characterized by extreme homophobia. When two laborers attempt to restrain him, he fights them, screaming that "Man shall never have power over me!"[42] Torn between his craving for a male friend and his conviction that men hate him and seek to control him, Mandeville ends up in an insane asylum where "the violence, the cords, the harsh language, [and] the blows" are not calculated to resolve his psychosexual conflicts.[43]

Unlike Mandeville, Fleetwood is assimilated into his new environment. His "understanding [is] brutified," and he becomes "an artificial personage, formed after a wretched and contemptible model."[44] Instead of establishing his own masculine identity and becoming the "New Man of Feeling" that his rural Welsh boyhood has prepared him to be, Fleetwood is "seduced" into imitating the behavior of his dissipated and sadistic fellow students.[45] His university experience teaches him that "Youth . . . is the minister of cruelty."[46] According to Fleetwood, the main goal of the pupils in these institutions is to "preserve the good opinion and esteem" of their peers:

> The great disadvantage to which young men in a populous place of education are exposed, is the freedom they enjoy from the established restraints of decorum and shame. They constitute a little empire of their own, and are governed by the laws of a morality of their own devising. . . . The principles by which [each student] is regulated are voted by an assembly that is prompted by turbulence, high spirits, convivial good-humour, and a factitious sense of generosity and honour; and, provided these principles are obeyed, he looks down with contempt on the sense of mankind in general.[47]

Essentially free of supervision by their "academical superiors," these students amuse themselves by tormenting each other.[48] Thus Fleetwood's misanthropy, like Mandeville's homophobia, stems from his dysfunctional relationships with other pupils in all-male schools. Although these protagonists recognize the importance of establishing same-sex friendships, they fail to find male companions who can offer them unconditional love and support. They are particularly unlucky in their dealings with young men. Mandeville chooses the treacherous Mallison as a confidant, and Mallison uses his position as Mandeville's adviser to engineer his former classmate's ruin. Similarly, Fleetwood allows the Iago-like Gifford to

manage his affairs, and Gifford responds by destroying Fleetwood's marriage and then hiring assassins to kill him.

There is, however, a kind of male relationship in Godwin's fiction which is nearly always presented in a positive way: that between a young man and a father figure, or a leader and his loyal
follower. Godwin himself played a paternal role in the lives of a
number of young men, including his stepson, Charles Clairmont,
his son, William Godwin Junior, and his future son-in-law, Percy
Bysshe Shelley. He also made it a practice to befriend troubled
youths who sought his guidance. In 1803, a student named Thomas
Turner wrote to ask for Godwin's help: "Last September an intimacy took place between me and two young men whom I proudly
designed to guide to knowledge and virtue. Instead of this they are
dragging me to ignorance and vice. . . . A violent affection for one
of these youths reduces me to the most abject slavery."[49] According
to William St. Clair, Turner became "an honorary member of the
Godwin family." He married an heiress, became a lawyer, and "for
the rest of his life . . . regard[ed] Godwin as his rescuer and adopted
father."[50] Godwin's relationship with another young man, Patrick
Patrickson, ended less happily. He helped to find money for Patrickson's tuition at Cambridge University, and, when Patrickson
was ridiculed by his snobbish fellow students as a "Barber's
Clerk," Godwin suggested that he console himself by reading Sen-
eca.[51] Despite his mentor's efforts, however, Patrickson committed
suicide by shooting himself.

Cloudesley reflects Godwin's fascination with and endorsement
of paternal/filial masculine friendships. In this novel, the misanthropic title character is taught how to love selflessly by his adoptive son, Julian. While still a "beginning tradesman," Cloudesley is
hoodwinked by an "adventurer" who persuades him "to become
his security" for two hundred pounds and then runs away.[52] He is
thrown in jail for debt and begins to regard "his brothers . . . as
worthy only of his hatred, and engaged in a general conspiracy
against him."[53] Disillusioned, he vows to become an opportunist.
Lord Alton, Cloudesley's master, is killed in a duel and his widow
dies two weeks later, after having given birth to a boy. In exchange
for an annuity of five hundred pounds, Cloudesley agrees to help
the dead man's brother defraud Lord Alton's son of his title and
estates by convincing the authorities that the infant died a few hours
after birth. His master's brother then returns to England to claim
the inheritance, and Cloudesley is left to dispose of the child.
Cloudesley's first impulse is to give the infant to some "poor person, in consideration of a comparatively trifling sum to be paid for

its future support."[54] But when the baby smiles at him and reminds him of his former master, he is moved and decides "that the orphan boy should never lose the advantage of his watchful care, or be removed from his sight."[55] Cloudesley's feelings for his ward exceed "the sentiments of a father" because they are "mingled [with] a mysterious sense of [Julian's] dignity of birth, and a recollection that the name he had an hereditary right to bear, removed him far from the plebeian herd."[56] He and his Greek wife take the orphan to Lombardy in order to raise him in a "divine and paradisaical climate."[57]

Julian is spared the schoolboy persecutions that Fleetwood witnesses and Mandeville experiences. His adoptive father carefully supervises the boy's socialization:

Cloudesley wished him to associate with other boys, and from the trials of animal strength, the collision of the passions of that age, and the competition and characteristic dexterity of childish wit, practically to prepare himself for the more serious intercourses and rivalship of mature age. He found the peasant children of Lombardy admirably adapted to his wish in that respect. They were animated and well tempered. . . . They were for the most part sympathetic and generous. Yet they had an earnestness in their pursuits, and a quickness in their desires, which gave to their sports all the advantages of emulation, at the same time that they seldom degenerated into anger and the fierceness of muscular contention.[58]

Cloudesley also provides Julian with a sympathetic seventeen-year-old tutor. Like the governor in Rousseau's *Émile*, Guiseppe adapts his methods to his pupil's needs and makes learning enjoyable:

Guiseppe watched the variations of Julian, even as an experienced navigator watches the variations of the needle. When excursion and sport was the order of the day, Guiseppe appeared to think of nothing but excursion and sport. And yet even in the wildest of their sallies, an apt quotation from the poets, a hint for science, or an observation on nature and the general system of things, would come in, and, instead of throwing a damp on their gaiety, would give to the feast of gaiety a zest unknown before.[59]

When Guiseppe ceases to be brotherly and turns into a "pedagogue," Cloudesley separates his ward from his tutor and enrolls him in the Florentine College.[60]

As Lord Alton, Julian would have, of course, received a much different education in England than he does in Italy. It is possible

that a British public school or university would have transformed
him into a misanthrope like Fleetwood or a homophobe like Mandeville. Unlike Fleetwood and Mandeville, Julian is extroverted and
uninhibited with other men, and he becomes passionately involved
with an Italian youth named Francesco:

> His mind was fresh from the histories of Achilles and Patroclus, Orestes
> and Pylades, Damon and Pythias; and he persuaded himself that there
> could be no true felicity but in the ardours of a romantic friendship,
> where neither party should have the smallest reserve from the other,
> pleasure should only be pleasure in proportion as it was participated,
> and on both sides they should be prepared for the most unbounded sacri-
> fices for each other's preservation and advantage. . . . By collision they
> raised the first sparks of friendship into a brilliant and mighty flame,
> and walked about amidst the groves and on the banks of the Arno, re-
> garding the rest of the world as if it were not, and swearing that they
> would build a temple of attachment and love, in comparison of which
> all the examples of antiquity should fade into nothing.[61]

This "romantic friendship" is clearly homoerotic and possibly homosexual. Inspired by the close male friendships celebrated in
Greek literature, it is suggestively described as "a brilliant and
mighty flame . . . raised . . . By collision." Instead of responding to
his attachment to Francesco with the "homosexual panic" that poi-
sons the same-sex relationships of several of Godwin's other male
characters, Julian frankly declares his passion for his friend and accompanies him on an excursion to Verona.[62] They also visit nearby
Sirmione, the birthplace of Catullus, who, in addition to his poems
addressed to Lesbia, wrote passionate verses to a boy named Juven-
tius. Julian subsequently demonstrates his willingness to make an
"unbounded sacrifice" for Francesco's "preservation" by risking
his life to save "the brother of his soul" from drowning.[63]

But Julian's friendship with Francesco, like most fraternal relationships in Godwin's fiction, is deeply flawed. Francesco and his
companions begin to undermine Julian's moral principles: "They
perpetually trod as it were on the brink of what was indecorum or
guilt . . . They dabbled with the arguments of vice, and found out
that such as trampled upon the censure of the world had much that
might be said on their side of the question."[64] When Cloudesley
leaves his ward to attempt to persuade his co-conspirator to restore
Julian's inheritance to him, he makes the mistake of leaving the
young man in the care of Borromeo, whose experiences as the slave
of Algerian pirates have left him profoundly homophobic. Borromeo has "scarcely the idea of any other intercourse in use between

man and man, except that of absolute command on the one hand, and instant submission on the other" and has "no conception [of] the sweet intercourse between human beings arrived at maturity on the one hand, and those who are still in their nonage on the other, the delicious emotions that arise between the parent and his off-spring, and their mutual endearments."[65] Repulsed by Borromeo's sternness and misanthropy, Julian seeks the companionship of Francesco and his friend's disreputable associates. Among these young men is St. Elmo, the attractive and Byronic chief of a band of robbers who operate throughout the Apennines.

Unaware of St. Elmo's occupation, Julian joins his friend in the mountains. St. Elmo and his band observe "an appropriate code of morality":

> They glossed over their actions, and endeavoured to turn what was arbi-trary and lawless, into justice and merit. . . . They gave out, that they abstracted from the rich, and imparted to the poor. They spared the means of the needy, and would allow no violence to be committed against the weaker sex; but they robbed the opulent man and the oppres-sor, and willingly made spoil of monasteries, of pampered monks and luxurious prelates.[66]

This code is not, however, observed by all of the banditti. One of the thieves, Corrado, attempts to rape some women whom he has robbed, and St. Elmo angrily orders him to leave his band. Corrado lingers near the encampment of his former companions, feeling "something like the melancholy of a lover, who has taken an eter-nal farewel of the mistress of his affections."[67] As a sexual preda-tor, he threatens St. Elmo's system of ethics, which prohibits rape, and his tenuous control over his fellow brigands. When Cloudesley arrives in search of his ward, Corrado agrees to guide him, thinking that Cloudesley is an officer of the government sent to discover the bandits' location. But he misjudges the location of St. Elmo's camp, leading Julian's adoptive father into an ambush led by Francesco. Seeing Corrado, Francesco orders his men to fire; Cor-rado is killed, and Cloudesley is mortally wounded.

Thus Julian's repudiation of Borromeo's patriarchal tyranny ends in the death of the man he most loves. While his fraternal friends prove to be criminals and nearly lead him to the scaffold, Cloudes-ley dedicates himself unselfishly to his ward: "His thoughts by day and by night, from the infancy of Julian to the death of his protec-tor, were how to premote [sic] the interests and the welfare of his pupil."[68] The narrator echoes Catullus's famous lament, "now &

forever, my brother, hail & farewell"[69] in his eulogy of Cloudesley, addressing the dead man as a guardian rather than a brother: "most devoted of guardians, hail, and farewel!"[70] In *Cloudesley*, guardians are more worthy of honor and respect than "brothers." Even the unprepossessing Borromeo proves to be a better friend to Julian than the irresponsible Francesco or the Byronic St. Elmo. When he witnesses Julian's grief over the death of his adoptive father, Borromeo undergoes a transformation:

> Here was Julian, undrilled to the hardships of existence, . . . now suddenly thrust out upon the world without guide, overseer, or ruler. . . . Now, he was like a youth, shipwrecked on a foreign shore, surrounded with strange faces, and persons utterly indifferent whether the first step he took might not lead to irretrievable destruction. . . . This situation awed Borromeo. . . . The ruggedness of his nature, which had been accustomed to regard no man's feelings, now gave place to a timidity altogether new.[71]

But despite his newfound sensitivity, Borromeo is incapable of expressing the sympathy he feels, and Julian leaves him to rejoin his transgressive friends in the Apennines.

In contrast to Borromeo, St. Elmo is extremely sympathetic, and Julian begins to consider the robber chieftain as a surrogate father:

> [T]he friendly yearnings of his heart to his protector rose to a degree which has rarely been paralleled. . . . He would have encountered any peril, and even had laid down his life, for his friend. . . . He required something to look up to, something to cherish with even a filial affection, something to regard with mysterious reverence, and to contemplate as too high to be comprehended, and considered as governed by impulses of the most exalted kind, which he was unable to unravel.[72]

Julian even condones St. Elmo's criminal activities: "he began to question whether the saws of morality which he had hitherto listened to, were any thing more than the prejudices of weak minds."[73] In fact, Julian finds "a perverse pleasure in attaching himself to St Elmo the rather because he [is] an outlaw."[74] The absence of a father figure impels him to form a filial relationship with a man who is implicated in his guardian's death and whose ethics and lifestyle violate society's norms.

But Julian's friendship with St. Elmo ends in disaster. When they are attacked by government forces, Julian springs to the defense "of the man he so profoundly love[s]."[75] They are captured, and Julian is "suddenly treated as the vilest of criminals, shut up in a dungeon, and destined to the scaffold." He belatedly realizes that Borromeo's restrictions were "planned in a spirit of kindness" and regrets his association with his "alluring but pernicious friends."[76] After being released from prison through the intervention of Lord Danvers, who reveals to the authorities that the "prisoner under sentence of death in the castle of Palermo" is an English aristocrat, the young man returns to Florence and is embraced by his forsaken guardian[77]:

> It was a striking spectacle to view the workings of Borromeo's mind, as they expressed themselves in his countenance, or, perhaps more strictly speaking, in the action of his body and limbs. He drew Julian towards him with all the energy of affection; he then motioned him to retreat, that he might more carefully peruse the nobility of his air, and the beauty of his physiognomy. He laughed . . . To his laughter succeeded a gush of tears; but they were tears of joy, the melting of the heart. He embraced him with the utmost fervour.[78]

Unlike St. Elmo, who dedicates his life to a long and futile struggle against patriarchal forces, Borromeo preaches universal love:

> [T]he true system for governing the world, for fashioning the tender spirits of youth, for smoothing the pillow of age, is love. . . . The one thing that most exalts and illustrates man is disinterested affection. . . . There is no joy like the joy of a generous sentiment, to go about doing good, to make it our meat and our drink to promote the happiness of others, and diffuse confidence and love to every one within the reach of our influence.[79]

In *Cloudesley*, the most self-sacrificing and "disinterested" same-sex love is either paternal or filial; fraternal love is associated with unlawful behavior and is described as "alluring but pernicious." The morose and misanthropic Borromeo proves to be a more reliable friend than the sympathetic and attractive outlaw.

In Godwin's late collection of essays, *Thoughts on Man, His Nature, Productions and Discoveries. Interspersed with Some Particulars Respecting the Author* (1831), he contends that "The great model of the affection of love in human beings, is the sentiment which subsists between parents and children."[80] According to him, the best friendships are those in which "there is neither interested intention nor rivalry."[81] Because individuals who are equal in age, rank, or talents tend to compete with one another, their love for one another can turn quickly into envy or even hatred, as is the case with Mandeville and Clifford. But since relationships between parents and children, "the creator and his creature,"[82] and leaders and

followers are between "unequals,"[83] they are likely to be non-com-
petitive and mutually beneficial. According to this theory, Caleb's
relationship with Falkland becomes dysfunctional because he dis-
obeys and passes judgment on his master, acting like an equal
rather than a subordinate.

Like his character Julian, Godwin believes that "the truest and
most exalted ideas on the subject of friendship [were] conceived
[by the] ancients":

> Among the most celebrated instances are the friendship of Achilles and
> Patroclus, Orestes and Pylades, Æneas and Achates, Cyrus and Araspes,
> Alexander and Hephæstion, Scipio and Lælius. In each of these parties
> are, the true hero, the man of lofty ambition, the magnificent personage
> in whom is concentred every thing that the historian or the poet was able
> to realise of excellence, and the modest and unpretending individual in
> whom his confidence was reposed.[84]

Even the greatest man, Godwin writes, needs a friend who will
allow him to be himself, to "be as a man merely to a man."[85] These
unequal friendships are also necessary for "a man of science" who
"wishes occasionally to forget the severity of his investigations"
in the company of a "modest and unassuming friend."[86] Godwin
suggests that in order for a hero or a philosopher to realize his potential he must have a self-effacing male friend who can provide
him with the unconditional emotional support he needs. Cloudesley's relationship with his ward, Julian, is unequal in two ways: as
Julian's adoptive father, Cloudesley is his superior, but he is beneath him in social class. There is no rivalry between them because
Julian defers to the man whom he believes is his father, and Cloudesley devotes himself to the youth who is the rightful heir of the estate and title of Lord Danvers. Thus their association is symbiotic
and ennobling, free of the conflicts which characterize more
"equal" friendships.

In Godwin's final novel, *Deloraine*, he depicts a male character
who has a special knack for forming fraternal relationships. William benefits from both the "unequivocal sympathy" of Bouverie
and the almost obsessional devotion of Travers, who is presented as
his antitype[87]:

> Neither of the two had ever met with an individual of his own sex, with
> whom his ideas so thoroughly accorded. They were like twins, whom
> some strange event had separated, and cast on opposite sides of the
> globe, and who, when they met, then for the first time felt a kind of

repose and entire contentment, as if half of himself had been torn away from each, and was now restored, so that he became perfect, equal to any encounter, and armed against every assault of nature or fortune.[88]

But while William and Travers are both young men, they are unequals, and thus their friendship fits the pattern described in *Thoughts on Man*. Travers is William's superior in rank and wealth: he is "the one best provided with worldly means to effect whatever he purposed."[89] His love for William is, however, far from domineering: "the first want of his heart was to love; and, when this want was emphatically gratified, he would become a mere child."[90] Although this relationship is brought to an abrupt and tragic end by Deloraine's impulsive murder of William, it suggests that a positive and close friendship between unequal men of the same age is possible, particularly if the men are capable of loving each other in a noncompetitive, childlike way.

In general, same-sex friendships in Godwin's fiction are presented as desirable but incredibly difficult to establish and maintain. As many of his characters recognize, friendship between members of the same sex is important as a guard against the tendency of conflicted individuals to brood over their passions and commit misdirected acts of violence. Moreover, because women in Godwin's novels receive "feminine" educations and are limited to the domestic sphere, they often are unable to act as the male characters' counselors or confidantes. Godwin had a more sympathetic attitude toward same-sex love than many of his contemporaries, but he believed that intimate male relationships should be between unequals[91]: " 'There is no limit, none,' to the fervour with which the stronger goes forward to protect the weak; while in return the less powerful would encounter a thousand deaths rather than injury should befall the being to whom in generosity and affection he owes so much."[92] His experience with Thomas Turner had taught him that while intimacy between youths can degenerate into "ignorance and vice," the guidance of a wise older man is likely to transform a young man in a positive way. On one hand, he believed that fraternal relationships tend to engender same-sex passion and become problematized as a result; on the other, paternal relationships tend to be desexualized and thus much less liable to inspire paranoia or transgressive desire. According to him, the most beneficial and enduring male friendships are those which are modeled after the relationship between parents and children.

NOTES

1. Alex Gold Jr., "It's Only Love: The Politics of Passion in Godwin's *Caleb Williams*," *Texas Studies in Literature and Language* 19, no. 2 (Summer 1977): 149–50.

2. Eve Kosofsky Sedgwick, *Between Men: English Literature and Male Homosocial Desire* (New York: Columbia University Press, 1985), 116.

3. Eric Daffron, " 'Magnetical Sympathy': Strategies of Power and Resistance in Godwin's *Caleb Williams*," *Criticism* 37, no. 2 (Spring 1995): 225; quoting William Godwin, *Caleb Williams*, ed. David McCracken (New York: Norton, 1977), 305.

4. Robert J. Corber, "Representing the 'Unspeakable': William Godwin and the Politics of Homophobia," *Journal of the History of Sexuality* 1, no. 1 (1990), 88, 96.

5. Ibid., 99.

6. Godwin, *Caleb Williams*, 308.

7. William Godwin, *St. Leon: A Tale of the Sixteenth Century*, ed. Pamela Clemit (Oxford: Oxford University Press, 1994), 448.

8. William Godwin, *Mandeville: A Tale of the Seventeenth Century in England*, vol. 6 of *Collected Novels and Memoirs of William Godwin*, ed. Pamela Clemit (London: Pickering & Chatto, 1992), 145.

9. Godwin, *St. Leon*, 177.

10. Ibid., 126.

11. Ibid., xxxiv.

12. Godwin, Ibid., 177.

13. William Godwin, *Fleetwood: or, the New Man of Feeling* (London: Richard Bentley, 1832), 271.

14. Ibid., 270.

15. Ibid., 273.

16. For an excellent discussion of Fleetwood's psychological conflicts and his dysfunctional relationship with his wife, see Steven Bruhm, *Gothic Bodies: The Politics of Pain in Romantic Fiction* (Philadelphia: University of Pennsylvania Press, 1994), 107–19.

17. Godwin, *Mandeville*, 63.

18. Ibid., 244.

19. William Godwin, *Deloraine*, vol. 8 of *Collected Novels and Memoirs of William Godwin*, ed. Maurice Hindle (London: Pickering & Chatto, 1992), 30.

20. Godwin, *Deloraine*, 23.

21. Marilyn Butler and Mark Philp, Introduction, vol. 1 of *Collected Novels and Memoirs of William Godwin*, ed. Mark Philp (London: Pickering & Chatto, 1992), 39–40.

22. Godwin, *Fleetwood*, 177.

23. Ibid., 178.

24. Percy Bysshe Shelley, *Shelley's Poetry and Prose*, ed. Donald H. Reiman and Sharon B. Powers (New York: Norton, 1977), 474.

25. Godwin, *Fleetwood*, 177.

26. Ibid., 181.

27. William Godwin, *Political and Philosophical Writings of William Godwin*, vol. 4, ed. Mark Philp (London: Pickering & Chatto, 1993), 24.

28. Peter H. Marshall, *William Godwin* (New Haven: Yale University Press, 1984), 44.

29. Richard Holmes, *Shelley: The Pursuit* (London: Penguin, 1974), 19.

30. Louis Crompton, *Byron and Greek Love: Homophobia in 19th-Century England* (Berkeley: University of California Press, 1985), 79.

31. Holmes, *Shelley,* 20.

32. Godwin, *Fleetwood,* 23.

33. Godwin, *Mandeville,* 78–79.

34. Ibid., 92.

35. Ibid., 92–93.

36. Ibid., 91.

37. Ibid., 96.

38. Ibid., 97.

39. Ibid., 127.

40. Ibid., 132.

41. Ibid., 142.

42. Ibid., 143.

43. Ibid., 144.

44. Godwin, *Fleetwood,* 22.

45. Ibid., 38.

46. Ibid., 38.

47. Ibid., 40.

48. Ibid.

49. William St. Clair, *The Godwins and the Shelleys: A Biography of a Family* (New York: Norton, 1989), 300.

50. Ibid., 302.

51. Ibid., 302.

52. William Godwin, *Cloudesley,* vol. 7 of *Collected Novels and Memoirs of William Godwin,* ed. Maurice Hindle (London: Pickering & Chatto, 1992), 72.

53. Ibid., 73.

54. Ibid., 119.

55. Ibid., 120.

56. Ibid., 123.

57. Ibid., 124.

58. Ibid., 143.

59. Ibid., 144.

60. Ibid., 148.

61. Ibid., 169.

62. Sedgwick defines "homosexual panic" in *Epistemology of the Closet* (Berkeley: University of California Press, 1990): "Because the paths of male entitlement, especially in the nineteenth century, required certain intense male bonds that were not readily distinguishable from the most reprobated bonds, an endemic and ineradicable state of what I am calling male homosexual panic became the normal condition of male heterosexual entitlement" (185).

63. Godwin, *Cloudesley,* 178.

64. Ibid., 164–65.

65. Ibid., 205.

66. Ibid., 216.

67. Ibid., 230.

68. Ibid., 240.

69. Gaius Valerius Catullus, *The Poems of Catullus,* trans. Charles Martin (Baltimore: Johns Hopkins University Press, 1990), 138.

70. Godwin, *Cloudesley,* 240.

71. Ibid., 241.
72. Ibid., 268.
73. Ibid., 268.
74. Ibid., 269.
75. Ibid., 270.
76. Ibid., 272.
77. Ibid., 283.
78. Ibid., 289.
79. Ibid., 289–90.
80. Godwin, *Political and Philosophical Writings*, 6.187.
81. Ibid., 6.194.
82. Ibid., 6.193.
83. Ibid., 6.195.
84. Ibid., 6.193–94.
85. Ibid., 6.194.
86. Ibid., 6.195–96.
87. Godwin, *Deloraine*, 66.
88. Ibid., 174.
89. Ibid.
90. Ibid., 173.
91. Louis Crompton, *Byron and Greek Love: Homophobia in 19th-Century England* (Berkeley: University of California Press, 1985), 158–59.
92. Godwin, *Political and Philosophical Writings*, 6.196.

Disorienting the Self: The Figure of the White European Man in Byron's *Oriental Tales* and Travels

Eric Daffron

> To the degree that "Romanticism" shapes the new discourses on America, Egypt, southern Africa, Polynesia, or Italy, *they* shape *it*. (Romantics are certainly known for stationing themselves round Europe's peripheries—the Hellespont, the Alps, the Pyrenees, Italy, Russia, Egypt.) Romanticism *consists*, among other things, of shifts in relations between Europe and other parts of the world.
>
> —Mary Louise Pratt, *Imperial Eyes:*
> *Travel Writing and Transculturation*

INTRODUCTION

WHEN ROMANTIC TRAVELERS CROSS GEOGRAPHIC BORDERS INTO foreign lands, they step foot on new psychic terrain. Traveling provides the occasion for remaking the self in ways that differ from the humdrum experiences of day-to-day life in the homeland, but not without unforeseen consequences. If treading foreign turf and charting exotic itineraries offer new possibilities for orienting the self, they do so at the risk of disorienting the traveler. As I shall argue, divergent ways of thinking and practicing the self come into conflict; confrontation with non-European peoples takes its toll on the white European.[1]

Just such a traveler, Lord Byron toured the Orient—the Near East of Greece, Albania, and Turkey—between 1809 and 1811. According to twentieth-century critics, he launched his tour for the sake of liberation—both sexual and political. To liberate his repressed homosexuality, as Crompton argues, Byron left the moral and legal constraints in England for the perceived freedom in foreign lands. In fact, he wrote to his lawyer from the East about a grave secret and confessed to Lady Caroline Lamb upon his return about having indulged in sodomy while on tour.[2] Not only did he seek to liberate his libido, but, as Christensen argues, Byron also hoped to liberate the Greeks. Like other Philhellenists, he believed that if Greece could only be freed from the oppressive tyranny of the Ottoman Empire, ancient Greek culture, and in particular its eros, would flourish once again.[3]

By focusing on Byron's goals of liberation, these critics locate his tour within the emergent discourse of modern subjectivity: one in which the self was essentially a secret buried deep in the soul, the secret was repressed sexuality, and the greatest secret of them all was homosexuality.[4] This explanation makes sense to critics perhaps because the discourse of modern subjectivity had so much pervaded early nineteenth-century culture and has so much taken root in our own century that its assumptions now appear as matter of fact. However, while this critical focus can account for the principal contours of Byron's tour, it cannot account for other practices detailed in his letters and papers written from and about the Near East. If placed in the context of European travel accounts to non-European lands, as I do in section two of this essay, these letters and papers tell a different story. When Byron activates subject positions taken from those travel accounts—the Oriental scholar, the sentimental traveler, and the self-styled Oriental—he often assumes agencies without repressed desires. In contrast to a model of repression and liberation—which reduces the self to a secret that, in turn, gives that self coherence and identity—these subject positions multiply and diversify Byron's subjectivity. At crucial moments in his travel writings, these forms of selfhood coalesce and collide and, in so doing, expose the contradictions composing the white European man in the Near East. While these contradictions typically enable the constitution of his subjectivity, at rare moments they put that subjectivity at risk.

After he left the Near East for England, Byron published a series of *Oriental Tales* (1813–14). Like his travel papers, Byron's *Tales* explore the possibilities of subjectivity. In these *Tales*, according to some twentieth-century critics, he contributes to the creation of the modern self: a self whose psychic and corporeal features constitute sex and race, which in turn provide the natural foundation for gender and ethnicity. In "The Corsair," as Elfenbein argues, Byron creates a male character with secrets so mysterious and passions so intense that readers read them as veritable signs of the poet's subjectivity. In contrast, female characters briefly acquire such intense subjectivity and typically serve as domestic complements to virile heroes.[5] Rearticulating these gender differences in racial terms, as Meyer argues in an essay on "The Giaour," Byron turns his protagonist into a "Hegelian sovereign subject": a white European man who liberates a dark-skinned woman from her oppressor and thereby affirms his racial superiority.[6]

By invoking the paradigm of repression and liberation as well as the systems of sex and gender, race and ethnicity, that such a paradigm supports, these critics have drawn our attention to the role that these *Tales* played in producing modern subjectivity and in making it convincing to contemporary readers. In other *Tales*, however, ones that I analyze in section three of this essay, the poet questions the cultural belief in a self with a psychic core as well as the cultural logics of sex and gender, race and ethnicity. With a woman passing as a man and a European passing as a non-European, these poems denaturalize categories such as masculinity and whiteness. But they do so without troubling the conventional definitions of those categories. Because the definitional integrity of white European masculinity remains intact, Byron's poems, unlike his travel papers, fail to destabilize that complex category and the power relations that it supports. In short, Byron's *Tales* encounter cultural beliefs that, finally, they cannot overturn.

In his travel papers and his poems, Byron turns the Near East into a terrain for exotic travel and scholarly pursuits, for fulfilling fantasies of marginal and alternative subjectivities. In making the Orient fulfill Occidental goals and dreams, Byron's texts promote modern Orientalism: the modern disciplines and fantasies that advance and affirm the imperial quests of white European men. But like all discursive events, his texts make their differences known. In his *Tales* he alters the threads that compose the white European man; in his travel papers he nearly unravels them. In the latter case, the Orient became more than something to write home about.

TRAVELING PERFORMANCES: BYRON'S LETTERS AND PAPERS

When in several letters he dubs himself "a citizen of the world,"[7] Byron places his ramblings in the Near East within the tradition of the Grand Tour.[8] While increasingly diverse groups of people sought foreign wonders, young men of means, such as Byron, still featured in debates about the tour. Proponents of the Grand Tour argued that it gave young men the opportunity to learn about foreign customs, compare them with English ones, and return more informed and polished. Opponents, however, worried that young travelers might adopt foreign manners at the expense of English cultural integrity.[9] Articulating the first half of this debate, Byron gives his mother a satisfactory report toward the end of his tour: "I am so convinced of the advantages of looking at mankind instead of reading about them . . . I see and have conversed with French, Italians, Germans, Danes, Greeks, Turks, Armenians . . . and without losing sight of my own, I can judge of the countries and manners of others."[10] Articulating the other half, he claims upon his return to England: "I believe I shall turn Mussulman [Moslem] in the end."[11] Thus, on the one hand, Byron occupies the position of the citizen of the world who can put himself in anyone's shoes but still wear his own. On the other, he assumes the role of the traveler who seeks to become a citizen of only *one* culture.

Although the discourse of the Grand Tour can account for some of the features of Byron's travels, that discourse cannot account for many of the contradictions that his travel papers raise. This is the case because Byron's itinerary differed starkly from the jaunts to France and Italy that the Grand Tourist typically made. For this reason, accounts of travel to non-European lands provide the best context for reading his travel papers. In this context, Byron's papers present three subject positions: the Oriental scholar, the sentimental traveler, and the self-styled Oriental. In adopting these positions, he alternates among positions that, respectively, hold him radically apart from the foreign culture, place him in supposed reciprocity with it, and assimilate him to it. Divergent in motives and practices, these subject positions at times converge and at other times collide in his letters and papers. In so doing, they expose the contradictions that usually enable but sometimes disable the white European traveler.

Oriental scholarship provided the discursive material for the first subject position that Byron assumed. Whether the Oriental scholar made people his object of study, he sought to observe and collect specimens, to order and classify them. Exemplifying these aims in his *Journey through Albania* (1813), John Cam Hobhouse produces out of the confusing religious, ethnic, and linguistic makeup of Albania a natural portrait of "Scythian Albanians," a litany of homogenized bodily features: "Their chests are full and broad, and their necks long. Their faces are of a long oval shape, with prominent cheek bones, and a flat but raised forehead."[12] In addition to mastering the Orient as an object of knowledge, Hobhouse frequently notes the "wild and savage appearance" of the Albanians.[13] In so doing, he, like other Orientalists, invests a seemingly natural description of Albanian bodies with a cultural assessment—one that invariably reaffirms the superiority of the West to the East.[14]

As an Oriental scholar, Byron adopts the same twofold strategy:

assembling Oriental artifacts and then evaluating their cultural significance. For instance, in notes written in Athens and later appended to *Childe Harold's Pilgrimage* (1812–18), he refutes those who believe that the Greeks "will never be better" "because they are very bad."[15] As evidence of their potential, Byron makes a list of Romaic authors and offers "some specimens of the Romaic," along with English translations for "the scholar only."[16] These literary artifacts, essentially products of European knowledge and mastery, serve as veritable "specimens" of Oriental culture for British consumption and study.[17] Based on such evidence, Byron can assert: "The Greeks will never be independent . . . but they may be subjects without being slaves. Our colonies are not independent, but they are free and industrious, and such may Greece be hereafter."[18] Or, conversely, he can assert: "we are deplorably in want of information on the subject of the Greeks, . . . nor is there any probability of our being better acquainted, till our intercourse becomes more intimate or their independence confirmed."[19] Thus, Byron's scholarship justifies Western intervention, which in turn promotes Oriental study. By articulating this circular logic—one whereby knowledge begets power, which begets more knowledge—Byron accustoms literate Britons to the aims of imperial power and knowledge in the form of scholarly endnotes to entertaining reading.[20]

Not all of Byron's experiences in the Near East held native culture under a panoptic gaze. As a sentimental traveler, he gave a more personal touch to his accounts of the Orient. By drawing on sentimental discourse, travel accounts like Byron's represented cross-cultural contact as reciprocal by delivering condescending testimonies of the relative validity of native customs. Witness Hobhouse, who in his *Journey to Albania* records the sight of a man's arm hanging from a tree but cautions his reader from concluding that "the Turks" are "a cruel, savage people." For "a stranger passing through Temple-Bar fifty years ago, might have concluded the English to be of the same character."[21] Though Hobhouse seems to liken the Turks to the English, he elsewhere notes their "ferocity" and here implies that now, fifty years later, England has adopted more civilized practices.[22] Thus, this relativism—the strategy that Hobhouse and others deployed in an effort to balance their culture with another—promotes European superiority and even promotes it at times under the guise of cultural reciprocity.[23]

In his role as a sentimental traveler, Byron utilized this strategy extensively. On one occasion, he tells a correspondent that he sees but little difference between "ourselves and the Turks": "we have foreskins and they none, . . . they have long dresses and we short,

and . . . we talk much and they little.—In England the vices in fashion are whoring & drinking, in Turkey, Sodomy & smoking, we
prefer a girl and a bottle, they a pipe and pathic."[24] Although this
rhythmic list of analogous practices balances the cultures of England and Turkey, it does so without acknowledging the cultural
mobility and knowledge that enables the Englishman to make such
statements. On another occasion, Byron's use of this strategy indicates how relativism could in fact promote imperialist motives. In
a note to *Childe Harold*, Byron compares Irish Catholics to the
Greeks. Just as the Irish enjoy limited religious freedom and few
political rights, the Greeks, "a kind of Eastern Irish papists," have
their own college, pay taxes, serve in the military, but have no independence.[25] "And shall we then emancipate our Irish Helots?"
Byron asks facetiously. "Mahomet forbid! We should then be bad
Mussulmans, and worse Christians; at present we unite the best of
both—jesuitical faith, and something not much inferior to Turkish
toleration."[26] The biting satire cannot be ignored: the British Empire comes off as badly as the Ottoman. Despite the apparent reciprocity, Byron nevertheless fails to advocate the decolonization of
Ireland and elsewhere promotes an European-sponsored Greek revolution. By refusing to question British imperial pursuits, whether in
the Celtic peripheries or in the Near East, Byron compels his British
readers to accept imperialism as a matter of fact and to assume their
place within the Empire.

As long as he remained a sentimental traveler, Byron could only
enjoy a superficial reciprocity with the natives. When on other occasions he styled himself as an Oriental, however, he went one
more step in an attempt to merge with native culture. Like other
Romantic men and Enlightened ones before them, he sought to re-
juvenate the ancient splendor of the Near East. In Near Eastern culture, European men found aesthetic possibilities and sexual
fantasies more congenial to their taste than the crass materialism
and bigotry that they perceived in modern Europe.[27] This was no
less the case for men-loving men. As a case in point, William Beckford lived out his Oriental fantasies at Fonthill, where he kept a
harem of boys with nicknames taken from London's sodomitical
subculture. Linking his sexual aesthetic to his interior decor and
exposing the consumer impulse driving both, he remarked: "it's
cruel to hear talk of fair boys and dark Jade vases and not to buy
them."[28] In Beckford's Oriental tale, Vathek, a thinly veiled stand-
in for the author himself, leads fifty naked boys to the edge of a
chasm, where "the spectators" admire "the suppleness and grace of
their delicate limbs." When the Giaour's "mouth waters," Vathek

entices each boy to the chasm with a jewel and then pushes him into the gulf, "where the Giaour . . . incessantly repeated, 'More! more!' "[29] In this scene, the Orient provides the setting and the material for staging a thrilling fantasy of liberated libidos. If some less fantastic version of this scene had been realized on English soil, the players, like other sodomites in early nineteenth-century England, might have found their necks in the noose.[30] But in the Near East, this fantasy conforms to a central feature of the discourse of Orientalism: the powerful Occidental who exploits the passive Oriental for sexual benefit.[31] Thus, although on domestic soil British culture marginalized sodomitical practices, on foreign soil British culture absorbed their challenge to customs and laws.

Like Beckford, addressed as "Vathek" in Canto I of *Childe Harold*, Byron styled himself as an Oriental.[32] Trumpeting his sexual prowess in one letter, Byron boasts of having committed "above two hundred pl & opt Cs"—a Latin abbreviation for the phrase "complete intercourse to one's heart's desire" from the *Satyricon* A.D. 54–65), a homoerotic text by Petronius.[33] As the allusion to the *Satyricon* makes clear, Byron modeled his sexual practices after ancient Greek pederasty. The pederastic relation involved ideally an Athenian male citizen and an adolescent boy of citizen status but more generally a citizen and any male youth without full citizen status, including prostitutes and slaves.[34] This relation clearly formed the contours of Byron's lengthier romances with adolescents, such as Nicolo Giraud in Athens.[35] By teaching Byron Italian, as a letter reveals, Giraud enters into a pedagogic relation with him only to reverse the ancient custom of elder teacher and younger pupil. Yet because Giraud calls his pupil "Padrone" [master] and "amico" [lover], serves as Byron's dragoman, and merits mention in an early draft of Byron's will,[36] their relation also follows, at least in structure, the paradigm of classical pederasty. Moreover, Byron claims that, in conjugating the verb "to embrace" in Greek, he will eventually arrive at "the pl opt C."[37] If he had arrived at the intended goal in England, moral and legal definitions of masculinity would have turned him, like other sodomites, into a virtual outlaw. But when sexual practices such as his entailed the exploitation of Near Eastern men, those practices, however contrary to other cultural norms, could promote the interests of British imperialism, for which exploitation had become something of a hallmark.

While it is possible to isolate each of these three subject positions—the Oriental scholar, the sentimental traveler, and the self-styled Oriental—they typically appear in various combinations in Byron's letters and papers. When they do so, they often coalesce.

In a letter to Charles Skinner Matthews from Falmouth, for example, Byron articulates the aspirations of one strategy—the self-stylized Oriental—in the vocabulary of another—the Oriental scholar. As Byron writes: "We are surrounded by Hyacinths & other flowers of the most fragrant [na]ture, & I have some intention of culling a handsome Bouquet to compare with the exotics we expect to meet in Asia. —One specimen I shall certainly carry off."[38] Alluding to Apollo's accidental murder of the beautiful Hyacinth, Byron places his sexual exploits within the tradition of ancient Greek eros. But in calling his potential lovers horticultural "specimens," he draws on the modern discourse of botany. As "specimens," the "exotic" boys of Falmouth become comparable to those in "Asia" and, moreover, analogous to "specimens" of plants and to the "specimens" of Romaic literature appearing in the notes to *Childe Harold*. In other words, Byron fits boys into a comparative analysis of pederasty; elevated to a "science," pederasty assumes (facetiously, of course) the status of a comparative discipline, such as natural history and philology.

When, much later in Byron's tour, these "specimens" turn into "antiques,"[39] they become archaeological objects of study. While Byron shows no qualms about collecting these antiques and giving them that designation, he berates Lord Elgin in *Childe Harold* and other poems for plundering the Acropolis of its antiques.[40] However, "it is difficult on the face of it," as Christensen muses, "to assess the ethical and political difference between [Byron's] enterprise and the despised Lord Elgin's."[41] Indeed, once Oriental disciplines, such as botany and archaeology, supply the terms for describing an adolescent boy, he appears as one among many objects of imperial exploitation. By virtue of his vocabulary, Byron consolidates into one imperial agency the diverse aims and motives otherwise divided among two roles—the self-stylized Oriental and the Oriental scholar. As a result, his sexual practices, illegal on English soil, serve the interests of Orientalism.

While in those letters Byron's scholarly pose converges with his Oriental style, in a note to *Childe Harold*, two different strategies—the scholarly and the sentimental—come into contradiction. At the beginning of a note, he compares the Albanians to Highlanders "in dress, figure, and manner of living" and notes their "predatory" "habits."[42] Like Hobhouse's, Byron's bit of natural history produces the Albanians as radically other and aligns them with Britain's Celtic subjects. Although he gains cultural authority in posing as an Oriental scholar, he does so by appearing impersonal, even derogatory. Therefore, immediately after these brief scholarly gestures, he turns to "[his] own experience"[43] and to the authority of his own heart. In a highly sentimental account of leaving his two Albanian servants, he offers signs of their amiability and loyalty—evidence that serves as a supplement to his natural history. While Basili took his wages "with an awkward show of regret at my intended departure," Dervish "dashed [his wages] to the ground; and clasping his hands, which he raised to his forehead, rushed out of the room weeping bitterly."[44] In true sentimental fashion, everyone present was brought to tears, "sympathiz[ing] with the unaffected and unexpected sorrow of this barbarian."[45] In fact, Dervish's "present feelings, contrasted with his native ferocity, improved [Byron's] opinion of the human heart."[46] According to this account, both master and servant bare their souls and attest to their inner depths. In so doing, they reveal their common denominator. Thus, it would appear that Byron closes his note by making the scholarly sentimental, turning the stereotype of a "predatory" Albanian into a description of a "feeling" servant.

Although the note appears to overturn the scholarly for the sentimental, the terms and assumptions of Byron's scholarly pose in the first part of the note nevertheless permeate the second part. Throughout the second part of the note, Byron calls his servants "my Albanians" and "barbarian[s]"—in short, his possessions like any other—and refers to their "native ferocity."[47] In this way, he reasserts his cultural superiority and thereby compensates for a sentimental strategy which had placed him, discursively at least, on equal footing with his servants. This contradiction between scholarly and sentimental poses enables the white European to share intimate feelings with his cultural other without losing his cultural integrity; it simultaneously exposes the diverse textual strategies and surreptitious maneuvers necessary to constitute his agency.

Not all contradictions, however, benefit the white European man. In Byron's account of Eustathius Georgious, another adolescent lover, the collision of all three subject positions—the Oriental scholar, the sentimental traveler, and the self-stylized Oriental—proves almost too difficult to bear. As Byron relates to Hobhouse, he has his own Oriental entourage of men, both servants and lover: "my Tartar, Albanians, Buffalo, Fletcher and this amiable [boy] prancing by my side."[48] Eustathius, the "prancing" boy, merits a description that mingles classical with modern aesthetic terms: "The next morning I found the dear soul upon horseback clothed very sprucely in Greek Garments, with those ambrosial curls hanging down his amiable back, and . . . a *parasol* in his hand to save his complexion from the heat."[49] With obedient men at his beck

and call and a "prancing," beautiful boy at his side, Byron orches-
trates an Oriental fantasy.

But human confrontation puts considerable strain on Byron's
Oriental style. No longer able to suffer Eustathius, Byron brings his
fantasy to a momentary close and ushers the adolescent back to his
father: "Our *parting* was vastly pathetic, as many kisses as would
have sufficed for a boarding school, and embraces enough to have
ruined the character of a county in England, besides tears (not on
my part) and expressions of 'Tenerezza' to a vast amount."[50] In
staging their departure as a melodrama, Byron replaces his role as
self-stylized Oriental with his role as sentimental traveler. To en-
hance this sentimental strategy, he makes quantitative comparisons
between his home country and this foreign land: they kiss "as many
kisses" as boys do in boarding schools; they "embrace enough" to
ruin an English county.

Yet where does Byron stand in this sentimental exchange? Although he compares his Greek encounter with English experiences,
he removes himself from the experience altogether when he insists
that only Eustathius sheds tears. Like the Oriental scholar, whose
safe distance enables impersonal evaluations, Byron momentarily
marks his difference from, rather than his reciprocity with, Greek
culture. This difference hinges on a contrast between proper British
mores—male friendship—and scandalous behavior—male eros.
Eustathius marks this difference both in his profuse tears and in the
"effeminate" parasol[51] which he holds "to [Byron's] utter astonishment and the great abomination of Fletcher."[52] For all his cultivation of an Oriental style, Byron ironically registers unease with a
sign of effeminacy—a sign which, according to the cultural logic
of the early nineteenth century, referred, in turn, to illicit sexual
practices. Indeed, only after Byron replaces the parasol with "a
green shade" does he resume his Oriental fantasy.[53]

On earlier occasions, the contradiction that this letter stages—the
one between the sexuality of the self-styled Orientalist and the imperialism of the Oriental scholar—constituted a coherent, albeit
multiple, agency. Here, however, Byron's inability to integrate the
sexual with the imperial, the self-styled Orientalist with the Oriental scholar, disconcerts and even threatens to decompose the self.
Granted, Byron possesses the discursive means to reconstitute himself; once his thrilling Oriental fantasy breaks down into a nearly
unbearable sentimental exchange, he assumes the safe, impersonal
distance characteristic of the Oriental scholar. Yet if imperialism
and the agencies it produces were securely wrought, Byron would
have no need for recourse to these discursive tactics. Indeed, pre-

cisely because he must retreat to the pose of the Oriental scholar, he exposes the weak points of imperial ideology.

At those points, the incompatible, at times unbearable discursive threads comprising the self momentarily disable the agency of a European traveler like Byron. Tired, financially drained, and suffering from venereal disease, Byron returns to England with " '[f]our ancient Athenian Skulls['] dug out of Sarcophagi, a 'phial of Attic Hemlock,' [']four live Tortoises[,]' a Greyhound . . . two live Greek Servants."[54] Whether we read this list as souvenirs of a "citizen of the world," as "specimens" of the Oriental scholar, or as accoutrements of an Oriental style, we must assess the ethics of listing antiquities, animals, and persons—things living and dead—in the same breath. But we must also account for the final item on the list: "myself."[55] To what degree has the self become a tourist's souvenir or a scholar's specimen? Which sentimental acts have led to a parallel list of Greek servants and English master? What Oriental style has turned the self into one among many aesthetic objects? The questions that we can pose from reading Byron's simple list signal the central lesson, if there is one, of the Oriental experience: despite the diligent efforts at orienting the self—on foreign turf, to new experiences, in relation to customary modes of travel writing—the traveler's subjectivity may nevertheless undergo a radical disorientation.

LITERARY PERFORMANCES: "LARA" AND "THE SIEGE OF CORINTH"

Not long after he left Turkey, Greece, and Albania for England, Byron began to publish a series of *Oriental Tales*. In "Lara" and "The Siege of Corinth," two of these *Tales*, Byron creates characters with features of sex and gender as well as race and ethnicity. According to Romantic discourse, sex provided the natural foundation for gender, and race provided the natural foundation for ethnicity. Moreover, a psychic core supposedly contributed to that natural foundation. While Romantic discourses built the natural edifice of personal identity, Byron dismantled it. In so doing, he imagined different features of sex and gender as well as race and ethnicity in unexpected combinations. Although Byron denaturalized the features of personal identity, he left untroubled the categorical integrity of masculinity and whiteness. As a result, these *Tales* fail to disorient the white, European man.

The *Tales* invoke and then alter the dominant model of subjectivity in the Romantic period. In the previous century, the state had gradually incorporated into a set of institutions the Christian imperative to examine the self and to confess sins. Understood as a sexual secret buried in the depths of the soul, the self became the target of strategies designed to produce the truth of the self and eventually to liberate its desire.[56] This model of subjectivity became so pervasive in Romantic culture that it shaped a debate soon after the publication of Byron's *Tales*. In a review of "The Corsair" and "The Bride of Abydos" for the *Edinburgh Review*, Francis Jeffrey celebrates a new stage of civilization: one in which people seek to liberate the passions that they formerly "repressed." In conjunction with this new social stage, according to Jeffrey, poetry like Byron's features characters with "all the anatomy of their throbbing bosoms laid open to our gaze."[57] In response to Jeffrey, George Ellis argues in his review of "The Corsair" and "Lara" for the *Quarterly Review* that poetry has no business "attempting to analyze [the] nature and origin" of passions. Instead, it should reveal the "effects" of the "secret sensibility which lurks within our bosoms": "its visible symptoms" on "the whole animated frame" of the body.[58] While Jeffrey and Ellis disagree about the proper province of poetry, they do agree on one matter: the self has at its origin a secret psychic core whose effects appear on the body or in its actions.

Jeffrey and Ellis took this model of subjectivity so much for granted that they failed to notice a curious feature of "Lara": it is never precisely clear if Lara has a secret psychic core; and if he does, it is never revealed to the public. When Lara returns from years of exile, the community assumes that he has something to confess:

> That brow in furrow'd lines had fix'd at last,
> And spake of passions, but of passion past;
>
> . . . .
> All these seem'd his and something more beneath
> Than glance could well reveal, or accent breathe.[59]

Subscribing to Romantic theories of physiognomy, the community assumes, like the physiognomist Johan Caspar Lavater, that "each state of the human mind, and of internal sensation, has its peculiar expression in the face."[60] Because Lara's face fails to reveal precisely what is lodged in his psyche, members of the community pry him for information but without success. In fact, "[h]is silence formed a theme for others' prate— / They guess'd—they gazed— they fain would know his fate."[61] Ironically, for all their desire to penetrate his secret, for all their attempts to make him confess, the poem never states with any certainty that Lara actually has anything significant to reveal. Indeed, though they assume that "his breast had buried" a fatal secret,[62] nearly every passage about that secret contains language of supposition: "some deep feeling" only "seem'd" to reside in his breast.[63]

As the spokesperson for the community, the narrator typically espouses the view that the self harbors a secret whose traces might appear fleetingly on the face. Yet at a crucial moment toward the end of Canto I, the narrator appears to diverge from the community's consensus about what constitutes a self. When Lara leaves Otho's festival after a heated confrontation with Ezzelin, Lara smiles:

> Could this mean peace? the calmness of the good?
> Or guilt grown old in desperate hardihood?
> Alas! too like in confidence are each
> For man to trust to mortal look or speech;
> From deeds, and deeds alone, may he discern
> Truths which it wrings the unpracticed heart to learn.[64]

After a litany of questions, ones apparently posed by the guests at the party, the narrator debunks any assumption that physiognomy or confession, "looks" or "speech," could possibly reveal the self. For only actions, what the narrator calls "deeds," constitute the truth of the self.

Whether a secret to be revealed or confessed or an action to be performed, the truth of Lara's self is never precisely revealed. After his death, "[t]hey found the scatter'd dints of many a scar / Which were not planted there in recent war."[65] Scars would surely attest to the truth of the self. But these signifiers fail to correspond to any fixed signified: they could just as easily refer to "his guilt" as to "his glory," to a secret as to an action.[66] In short, this poem is torn between the belief in a self that is psychologically deep, on the one hand, and a self that is socially variable, on the other.

Although Lara remains a mystery, the identity of Kaled, his male page, is revealed at long last: Kaled is really a woman. Yet, more than Lara's identity, Kaled's resists the assumptions that customarily gave the self coherence during the period. In Enlightenment and Romantic discourses, psychological depth constituted one layer of the foundation of gender difference. Attributing psychological depth first to women and then to men, literature, among other discourses in the eighteenth and early nineteenth centuries, produced women with tender, domestic feelings to complement the political, economic nature of men. About the same time, scientists discovered the sperm and the egg, isolated separate reproductive organs for the two sexes, and assigned them different names. Upon this natural foundation—both psychic and corporeal—emerged modern gender difference: the complex economic and ideological process whereby the public was separated from the private sphere, the social roles of men from those of women.[67] Mary Wollstonecraft, a vociferous critic of this division of spheres, glossed the ideology supporting it: "man was made to reason, woman to feel."[68] Among other reforms, she "earnestly wish[ed] to see the distinction of sex confounded in society."[69] With the character of Kaled, "Lara" made imaginative steps in that direction.

Although Kaled's ethnic and class features—she is a page from foreign parts—shape the specific contours which her identity assumes, the poem focuses on her sex and gender. At the end of Canto I, the narrator of that poem remarks that, despite all appearances to the contrary, Kaled is suspiciously feminine:

> Of higher birth he seemed, and better days,
> Nor mark of vulgar toil that hand betrays,
> So femininely white it might bespeak
> Another sex, when matched with that smooth cheek,
> But for his garb. . . .[70]

At first glance, it would seem that Kaled simply breaks the seamless connection between sex and gender: although Kaled's body is female, her clothes are masculine. Thus, the body "speaks" the truth; its outer garments tell a lie. Yet the situation is more complex, because even the body dissembles: "something in his gaze, / More wild and high than woman's eye betrays."[71] What the narrator sees in those wild eyes is "[a] latent fierceness that far more became / His fiery climate than his tender frame."[72] Thus, the narrator attributes to Kaled a masculine psychic core which is both consonant with the body's sex (wild eyes) and dissonant with it (smooth skin). Moreover, the psyche and the body variously support and conflict with Kaled's gender: although Kaled wears masculine clothing, she resists the cultural expectations of masculinity by refusing to engage in "the frolics of the page."[73] In other words, the features that should testify to the truth of the self—psychic, corporeal, and social—are so ambiguous and conflicted that to say Kaled is a woman passing as a man fails to capture the complexity of that character.

The subsequent revelation of Kaled's "true" identity only complicates matters. After witnessing the death of Lara, Kaled

> But strove to stand and gaze, but reel'd and fell,
> Scarce breathing more than that he lov'd so well.
> Than that *he* lov'd! Oh! never yet beneath
> The breast of man such trusty love may breathe![74]

Although still appearing as a boy, Kaled reveals a passion that, it is implied, only women possess. Any discrepancy among psyche, sex, and gender immediately disappears, however:

> That trying moment hath at once reveal'd
> The secret long and yet but half-conceal'd;
> In baring to revive that lifeless breast,
> Its grief seem'd ended, but the sex confest.[75]

Once the body "confesses" its sex, psyche and sex line up and confirm Kaled's identity. Moreover, henceforth the narrator refers to Kaled by feminine pronouns—linguistic markers of gender. But when a serf later spies a mysterious horseman dumping the body of Ezzelin into the river, the narrator suggests that the murderer is none other than Kaled. If so, Kaled's stereotypically masculine action confirms the masculine psyche earlier attributed to her. How can we reconcile a psyche that harbors both feminine love and masculine ferocity? Indeed, at every level—psyche, sex, and gender— Kaled confuses masculine and feminine traits. In disrupting the seamless features of the self that dominant discourses weave, this enigmatic page exposes masculinity as a constructed rather than an essential category—one that theoretically anyone, even a biological woman, can inhabit.

While "Lara" persistently disables any one verifiable marker of the self, "The Siege of Corinth" stages a debate between one character subscribing to the social construction of ethnicity and other characters insisting on the natural markers and psychic features of race. In staging this debate, Byron tried and tested the Enlightenment epistemology of race and ethnicity. During the Enlightenment, scientists included moral and mental qualities as well as skin color and physiognomy among the features that constituted "race." In *Systema Naturae* (1758), for example, Linnaeus explained that Europeans are "[f]air," "gentle," and "[g]overned by laws," while Asiatics are "[s]ooty," "haughty," and "[g]overned by opinions."[76] For scientists who subscribed to the theory according to which God created the three to five races that scientists variously identified, race supplied the natural, original cause of ethnic customs and manners.[77] In "Of National Characters,"(1748), for instance, David Hume explains that "[s]uch a uniform and constant difference could not happen" between "the negroes" and "the whites" "if nature had not made an original distinction betwixt these breeds of men." Once he gives this explanation, he can justify Western views of their cultural superiority: "the negroes, and in general all the other species of men [are] naturally inferior to the whites."[78]

It is the very foundational assumption of Hume's theory—that race supplies the natural origin of ethnicity—that is troubled in "The Siege of Corinth."[79] In the poem, Alp's function as a military commander provides the occasion for a debate over his ethnic status. Exiled from his birthplace, Venice, Alp assumes a Moslem name and bears arms against the Venetians. Moreover, he adopts Moslem customs: "[t]he turban girt his shaven brow," and "[h]is trembling hands refused to sign / The cross he deemed no more divine."[80] Although Alp has abandoned all traces of his European, Christian background and, for all intents and purposes, has become a Moslem Turk, his fellow Turks accept him only with difficulty. On the one hand:

> They followed him, for he was brave,
> And great the spoil he got and gave;
> They crouched to him, for he had skill
> To warp and wield the vulgar will.[81]

On the other hand:

> But still his Christian origin
> With them was little less than sin.
> They envied even the faithless fame
> He earned beneath a Moslem name.[82]

Thus, while they respect Alp's courage and skill, they still regard Alp as a Christian and resent his attempts to pass as Moslem. In other words, despite his valiant deeds on their behalf, they recognize his racial origin and Christian soul as true signs of his selfhood. On the battlefront, a similar inconsistency between nature and culture appears:

> Their leader's nervous arm is bare,
> Swifter to smite, and never to spare—
> . . . .
> Many a loftier turban may wear,—
> Alp is but known by the white arm bare.[83]

Alp uses his arm to perform many courageous acts, but its white skin, a naturalized marker of race, gives him away. Despite all his attempts to sever the link between race and ethnicity, between soul and religion, his troops resent those efforts and uphold the primacy of psychic depth and corporeal signs.

While according to contemporary discourses the soul and the body should ideally provide the natural foundation of gender and ethnicity, "Lara" and "The Siege of Corinth" question, weaken, and at times dismantle that very foundation. By dramatizing women passing as men and Europeans passing as non-Europeans, these poems denaturalize such categories as masculinity and whiteness, but without challenging the fundamental definitions of those categories. Indeed, the poems still feature gender conventions—passionate femininity and virile masculinity—as well as ethnic stereotypes: the singular, "brave" white man among the mass of "vulgar" dark men. As a result, "Lara" and "The Siege of Corinth" supplied readers with a repertoire for imagining an alternative makeup for the self but saved them from a disorientation like Byron's.

CONCLUDING PERFORMANCES

In one of the juiciest tidbits of Byronic miscellany, Lady Byron records a conversation that Lady Caroline Lamb supposedly had with Lord Byron. According to Lamb's account of that tête-à-tête, Byron "confessed" "that from his boyhood he had been in the practice of unnatural crime." Indeed, he had "practiced it unrestrictedly in Turkey."[84] In baring his soul, Byron stages a modern secular version of the confession: he made sex the truth of his self, turns the truth into a secret, and posits the secret in the depths of his soul. In so doing, Byron confirms claims made later by his twentieth-century critics: he typically assumed what was in the process of becoming the dominant mode of selfhood.

In assuming that form of subjectivity, however, Byron makes a crucial displacement. At the conclusion of his conversation with Lady Caroline Lamb, he "threaten[s] [her] in the most terrific manner, reminding her of Caleb Williams, and saying that now she knew his secret, he would persecute her like Falkland."[85] In those final words, he invokes William Godwin's *Caleb Williams*—a novel that dramatizes the potentially mutual blackmail of two men engaged in a highly manipulative, thrillingly sexual power relation.[86] In making this allusion, he invests an existing discourse with new meanings in order to shape and understand his own practices. He even styles Lamb, a biological woman, after Caleb, a male character. Thus, while at the beginning of the passage subjectivity seems to originate from the depths of the soul, at the end it appears to come from outside the self. In other words, this conversation denaturalizes subjectivity. But this conversation, like "Lara" and "The Siege of Corinth," fails to disrupt the conventional assumption about what constitutes personal identity: the self is in essence a secret to be confessed.

In this case, that failure had unfortunate consequences. Rather than evading or ironizing the so-called truth of his self, Byron confessed it and thereby became subject to the paranoid fears that men-loving men had in a nation where sodomy was a criminal act. This moment of paranoia resembles one moment during his typically confident months in the Near East, where, the majority of the time, Byron practiced sodomy "unrestrictedly"; where, for the most part, his exploitation of young men could be absorbed into the discourse of Orientalism without threat to his subjectivity. But even on Near Eastern soil, Byron's sexual practices on one occasion conflicted with the norms of English propriety. At that time, his usual ability to pose creatively and to shift successfully among three positions failed. While Byron eventually recovered from that moment of discomposure in Greece, he suffered from a relapse in England.

For Byron, the easiest way to resolve the contradiction between an imperial discourse that made use of his marginal sexuality and a moral discourse that condemned it was to go into exile—a decision made easier once Lady Caroline Lamb, playing the role of Caleb Williams, began to spread rumors about his sexual secrets. Byron's need to resolve this conflict exposes the weak points of any hegemonic formation. The success of Western imperialism depended, among other concerns, upon orienting the white European man: constructing his masculinity and whiteness as stable features and placing him in positions superior to women and dark-skinned peoples. Yet Byron's travel writings dramatize the disorientation of that very self: moments when the diverse threads of discourses and features composing white European masculinity meet only to diverge and even scatter. While disorientation does not by itself overturn the domination and exploitation of women and non-European peoples, it does question the stable construction of white European masculinity often taken for granted in discourses of sexuality and empire. Once exposed for all its instability, white European masculinity can be put to the test by resistant voices seeking to alter the sexual and imperial imperatives grounding that subjectivity. If nothing else, disorientation prompts the activation of different discourses, potentially less exploitative ones. The result is nothing less than a re-orientation of the self.[87]

NOTES

1. Throughout this essay, I have depended extensively upon the discussions of agency in Judith Butler, *Bodies That Matter: On the Discursive Limits of "Sex"* (New York: Routledge, 1993); Michel Foucault, *The History of Sexuality. Vol. I: An Introduction*, trans. Robert Hurley (New York: Vintage, 1990); Elspeth Probyn, *Sexing the Self: Gendered Positions in Cultural Studies* (London: Routledge, 1993).

2. Louis Crompton, *Byron and Greek Love: Homophobia in Nineteenth-Century England* (Berkeley: University of California Press, 1985), 124–28, 199. Although I reject Crompton's unacknowledged dependence on what Foucault would call the "repressive hypothesis," any essay on Byron's sexuality, including my own, has benefited from Crompton's work. And while I complicate and supplement Christensen's account of the "repressive hypothesis," certain features of what Christensen calls Byron's "strength"—an "ethos of invention," "symbolic mobility," and "performative aristocracy"—comprise and have greatly influenced my version of Byron. See Jerome Christensen, *Lord Byron's Strength: Romantic Writing and Commercial Society* (Baltimore: Johns Hopkins University Press, 1993), xiii–xxv, 3–31.

3. See William St. Clair, *That Greece Might Still Be Free: The Philhellenes in the War of Independence* (London: Oxford University Press, 1972), 1–22.

4. Eve Kosofsky Sedgwick, *Epistemology of the Closet* (Berkeley: University of California Press, 1990), 73.

5. Andrew Elfenbein, *Byron and the Victorians* (Cambridge: Cambridge University Press, 1995), 13–28.

6. Eric Meyer, " 'I Know Thee Not, I Loathe Thy Race': Romantic Orientalism in the Eye of the Other," *ELH* 58 (1991): 657–99. By looking at *Tales* other than "The Corsair," I do not in any way reject the general validity of Elfenbein's thesis: Byron's poetry fostered modern subjectivity. In addition to Elfenbein, Christensen, and Meyer—whose criticism has most influenced my own—I have also benefited from criticism on the *Tales* by Jerome J. McGann, *Fiery Dust: Byron's Poetic Development* (Chicago: University of Chicago Press, 1968); Peter J. Manning, *Byron and His Fictions* (Detroit: Wayne State University Press, 1978); Marilyn Butler, "The Orientalism of Byron's Giaour," *Bryon and the Limits of Fiction*, ed. Bernard Beatty and Vincent Newey (Liverpool: Liverpool University Press, 1988).

7. Lord George Gordon Byron, *Byron's Letters and Journals*, vol. 1, ed. Leslie A. Marchand (Cambridge: Harvard University Press, 1973), 248.

8. For a discussion of the homoerotics of the Tour, see G. S. Rousseau, "The Pursuit of Homosexuality in the Eighteenth Century: Utterly Confused Category and/or Rich Repository," *'Tis Nature's Fault: Unauthorized Sexuality During the Enlightenment*, ed. Robert Parks Maccubbin (New York: Cambridge University Press, 1987), 156–68.

9. Jeremy Black, *The British Abroad: The Grand Tour in the Eighteenth Century* (New York: St. Martin's Press, 1992), 1–85, 213–37, 287–305.

10. Byron, *Letters and Journals*, 2 : 34–35.

11. Ibid., 2: 94.

12. J. C. Hobhouse, *A Journey through Albania and Other Provinces of Turkey in Europe and Asia, to Constantinople, During the Years 1809 and 1810* (Philadelphia: M. Carey, 1817), 120.

13. Ibid., 25.

14. For the general information in this paragraph, I have benefited from Edward W. Said, *Orientalism* (New York: Vintage, 1978), 113–66; see also Pratt, 15–68.

15. Lord George Gordon Byron, *The Complete Poetical Works*, ed. Jerome J. McGann (Oxford: Clarendon Press, 1981), l. 201.

16. Ibid., ll. 212, 217.

17. Ibid., l. 196.

18. Ibid., l. 201.

19. Ibid., l. 204.

20. Byron's view here in the notes to *Childe Harold* conflicts, of course, with sentiments expressed in stanza 76 of Canto II: Greece should secure its own freedom without foreign aid.

21. Hobhouse, *Journey,* 56–57.

22. Ibid., 112.

23. For the general information in this paragraph, I have benefited from Pratt, 69–107.

24. Byron, *Letters and Journals*, 1 : 238.

25. Byron, *Poetical Works*, l. 211.

26. Ibid., l. 211.

27. Said, 113–23, 166–97.

28. Quoted in Rictor Norton, *Mother Clap's Molly House: The Gay Subculture in England 1700–1830* (London: Gay Men's Press, 1992), 224.

29. William Beckford, *Vathek. Three Gothic Novels*, ed. E. F. Bleiler (New York: Dover, 1966), 127.

30. Norton, *Mother Clap's,* 132.

31. In this and other discussions of male sexuality, I have benefited from Norton and Ed Cohen, *Talk on the Wilde Side: Toward a Genealogy of a Discourse on Male Sexualities* (New York: Routledge, 1993). For a discussion of Winckelmann's revision of Hellenism, see Richard Dellamora, *Masculine Desire: The Sexual Politics of Victorian Aesthetics* (Chapel Hill: University of North Carolina Press, 1990), 109–16.

32. Byron, *Poetical Works*, l. 275.

33. Byron, *Letters and Journals*, 2 : 23; 1 : 207.

34. David M. Halperin, *One Hundred Years of Homosexuality: And Other Essays on Greek Love* (New York: Routledge, 1990), 24–38, 55–58, 88–104.

35. In this way, Byron's romances resembled early modern relations between aristocratic rakes and younger boys whose asymmetrical structure was in the process of transforming throughout the eighteenth and nineteenth centuries to relations more symmetrical in class and age. For this point, see Randolph Trumbach, "London's Sapphists: From Three Sexes to Four Genders in the Making of Modern Culture," *Body Guards: The Cultural Politics of Gender Ambiguity*, ed. Julia Epstein and Kristina Straub (New York: Routledge, 1991), 112–15.

36. Byron, *Letters and Journals*, 2 : 12, 29, 71.

37. Ibid., 2 : 14; 1 : 207.

38. Ibid., 1 : 207.

39. Ibid., 2 : 27.

40. For a discussion of Lord Elgin's marbles, see William St. Clair, *Lord Elgin and the Marbles* (London: Oxford University Press, 1967), esp. 187–202.
41. Christensen, *Lord Byron's Strength,* 62.
42. Byron, *Poetical Works*, ll. 192–93.
43. Ibid., l. 193.
44. Ibid., l. 194.
45. Ibid.
46. Ibid.
47. Ibid.
48. Byron, *Letters and Journals*, 2 : 7.
49. Ibid., 2 : 6.
50. Ibid.
51. Ibid., 2 : 7.
52. Ibid., 2 : 6.
53. Ibid., 2 : 7.
54. Ibid., 2 : 59.
55. Ibid.
56. Michel Foucault, "Sexuality and Solitude," *On Signs*, ed. Marshall Blonsky (Baltimore: Johns Hopkins University Press, 1985), 365–72; *The History of Sexuality,* 17–73.
57. Quoted in Andrew Rutherford, ed., *Byron: The Critical Heritage* (New York: Barnes & Noble, 1970), 54–55, 58–59.
58. Ibid., 66–67.
59. Byron, *Poetical Works*, ll. 67–68, 77–78.
60. Johan Lavater, *Essays on Physiognomy*, trans. Thomas Holcroft (London: William Tegg, 1869), 96.
61. Byron, *Poetical Works*, ll. 293–94.
62. Ibid., l. 285.
63. Ibid., ll. 77, 83.
64. Ibid., ll. 504–9.
65. Ibid., ll. 542–43.
66. Ibid., l. 546.
67. Nancy Armstrong, *Desire and Domestic Fiction: A Political History of the Novel* (New York: Oxford University Press, 1987), 3–27; Thomas Laqueur, *Making Sex: Body and Gender from the Greeks to Freud* (Cambridge: Harvard University Press, 1990), 149–243; Michael McKeon, "Historicizing Patriarchy: The Emergence of Gender Difference in England, 1660–1760," *Eighteenth-Century Studies* 28 (1995): 300–315.
68. Mary Wollstonecraft, *Vindication of the Rights of Woman*, ed. Miriam Brody (London: Penguin, 1985), 154.
69. Ibid., 147.
70. Byron, *Poetical Works*, ll. 574–77.
71. Ibid., l. 580.
72. Ibid., ll. 580–81.
73. Ibid., l. 543.
74. Ibid., ll. 510–13.
75. Ibid., ll. 514–17.
76. Quoted in Pratt, *Imperial Eyes,* 32.
77. Nicholas Hudson, "From 'Nation' to 'Race': The Origin of Racial Classification in Eighteenth-Century Thought," *Eighteenth-Century Studies* 29 (1996): 247–64; Philip D. Curtin, *The Image of Africa: British Ideas and Action, 1780–1850* (Madison: University of Wisconsin Press, 1964), 28–57.

78. David Hume, *Selected Essays*, ed. Stephen Copley and Andrew Edgar (Oxford: Oxford University Press, 1993), 360.

79. For a useful contrast to Byron's depiction of Alp, see the analysis of T. E. Lawrence, who imitates a foreign culture in order to become master of rather than subject to it, in Kaja Siverman, *Male Subjectivity at the Margins* (New York: Routledge, 1992).

80. Byron, *Poetical Works*, ll. 75, 493–94.

81. Ibid., ll. 265–68.

82. Ibid., ll. 269–72.

83. Ibid., ll. 776–77, 784–85.

84. Quoted in Crompton, *Byron and Greek Love*, 199.

85. Ibid.

86. For such a reading, see my essay, " 'Magnetical Sympathy': Strategies of Power and Resistance in Godwin's *Caleb Williams*," *Criticism* 37 (1995): 113–22.

87. For invaluable suggestions on this essay, I thank Anne B. McGrail, Anne Graziano, Julia Miller, Anna Geronimo, James R. Keller, William Brewer, Jay Losey, and Elizabeth Dell.

"One Half What I Should Say": Byron's Gay Narrator in *Don Juan*

JONATHAN GROSS

> Man is least himself when he talks in his own person. Give him
> a mask and he will tell you the truth
>
> — Oscar Wilde

> His voice and accent are particularly clear and harmonious, but
> somewhat effeminate . . . he is too gay, too flippant for a poet
>
> — Lady Blessington on Lord Byron

CRITICS WHO DISCUSS BYRON'S NARRATIVE METHOD IN *DON JUAN* (1819–24) note its debt to John Hookham Frere's *The Monks and the Giants* (1817), Luigi Pulci's *Morgante Maggiore* (1817), and Ariosto's *Orlando Furioso* (1516).[1] Although historically accurate, such observations distract critics from explaining what is original about *Don Juan*. The following essay argues that Byron makes use of a gay narrator in his mock-epic. If persuasive, my argument explains several aspects of the poem that have confused modern critics. Recognizing the closeted nature of the narrator's sexuality can explain his digressive style and "conversational facility," one of the poem's most debated features.[2] Focusing attention on the gay narrator of *Don Juan* also sheds new light on the poem's comic puns and use of a conversational vernacular.[3] In an influential study, titled *Don Juan in Context*, Jerome McGann referred to "the notorious lack of form in *Don Juan*."[4] I hope to show how *double entendres* provide a homoerotic thematics to the poem which serves as a unifying device in what is, only at first blush, a "versified Aurora Borealis."[5]

My argument has certain implications for the editing and abridgment of this poem. To focus critical attention on a "gay" voice in Byron's poem exposes the extent to which editions of *Don Juan* have privileged heterosexual plot over homoerotic digression. In the same way that "learned men" expurgate the young Juan's clas-

91

sical texts,[6] the editors of the Oxford and Norton anthology censor
the poem,[7] omitting even the stanzas that call attention to censorship.[8] The Oxford anthology omits stanzas 2–4, 8–9, 11–12,
20–53; 67–68, 86–89, 95–100 to name only the first hundred,[9]
while the Norton anthology also omits biographical and misogynist
digressions crucial to any understanding of the narrator's tone,[10]
while retaining the heterosexual plot.[11] Yet readers cannot hope to
understand the poem's irony without considering the narrator's
ironic relationship to the very legend of Don Juan (and heterosexuality) he both narrates and subverts.

Finally, Byron's use of a gay narrator in *Don Juan* provides new
evidence for the aristocratic nature of his liberalism. The poem's
politics change throughout the 17 cantos, moving from an aristocratic liberalism expressed through a repressed narrator (cantos
1–5), to a more democratic form that denies any substantial "difference" between Byron and his narrator (cantos 6–17). To be sure,
the narrator attenuates the aristocratic nature of his liberalism as the
poem develops; however, it never entirely disappears. Leigh Hunt
and William Hazlitt had their doubts about the sincerity of Byron's
liberalism itself (aristocratic or otherwise),[12] and Andrew Rutherford and Leslie Marchand echo Byron's contemporaries by portraying him as ambivalently disposed toward revolutionary and
democratic ideas.[13] Byron used a gay narrator in his mock epic to
show the relationship between the poet's liberal beliefs and an aristocratic form of sexual practice,[14] what readers of Plato's *Symposium* (after 386 B.C.) might term the higher sodomy.[15] One can
extend the argument about Byron's gay narrator to his support for
Greek independence and see how this last adventure of his life reflects not a democratic but a personal and an aristocratic version of
Philhellenism.[16]

Having explained how my argument might influence subsequent
readings of Byron's poem, I need to clarify my title. Although one
might refer to Byron's narrator as bisexual, I describe him as
"gay"[17] because his gay identity informs a whole cluster of signifiers, including the poem's liberal politics. The term "gay" has several advantages over "homosexual," another term I might have
used: "gay" is not an etymological hybrid; it is not used by doctors
to describe a pathology; and it is used most often by gay people to
define themselves. The word has obvious advantages over terms
like "sodomite," "third sex," or other abusive epithets popular in
early nineteenth-century English society.[18] Though it might be
scorned as a neologism by some academics, the word "gay" more

accurately connotes a way of life than does the word "homosexual," which only (and imperfectly) describes a sexual orientation.[19]

Byron's gay narrator clearly derives from his "gayness" (defined here in Lady Blessington's sense of "cheerfulness" or "flippancy") by his freedom from heterosexual constraints: specifically the constraints of fatherhood, and the strained seriousness of such paternal and patriarchal figures as Lambro and Lord Henry.[20] Whereas a restrained and prudent Byron can only allow his gaze to fall upon beautiful women, Byron's gay narrator surveys both sexes with an eroticized eye. To him, Juan and Haidée,[21] Gulbeyaz and the Sultan,[22] and Baba and Catherine[23] are equally intriguing, though he gravitates more toward men than women, as the details in his description of each gender show.[24] The narrator, who once loved women passionately, finds himself transformed into a casual and almost mechanical misogynist. Throughout the poem, the narrator suggests more than he reveals about his present sexual appetite, and it is precisely the suggestiveness of this poem that accounts for the charges it incurred in angry reviews. A writer for *Bon-Ton* magazine referred to the "vulgar jargon" of the poem, its tendency to make "vice familiar with the public mind."[25] In using this "jargon," the narrator assumes a mysterious sexual identity connected with such "vice," as Jerome Christensen and Andrew Elfenbein have argued. The narrator's use of a "vulgar jargon" deserves more attention than it has received, however, because, once uncovered, the narrator clearly subverts the very legend of Don Juan he pretends to narrate.[26]

BYRONIC SILENCE AND THE DEATH OF
CHARLES SKINNER MATTHEWS

On the eve of his departure for the Morea in 1809, Byron wrote a letter to Charles Skinner Matthews. He described his flirtatious attention to a young man from Falmouth, adopting the coded language that would later characterize his narrator's digressions in *Don Juan*. The letter of 1809 alludes to Petronius' *Satyricon* (A.D. 54–65), declaring Byron's intention to pursue "Plen. and optabil. Coit.," or full intercourse to one's heart's content.[27] Matthews congratulated Byron on the "splendid success of his first efforts in *the mysterious*, that style in which more is meant than meets the Eye." Louis Crompton in *Byron and Greek Love* notes that "this letter unequivocally reveals the homosexual bond in the Cambridge circle."[28]

Critics before and after Crompton have speculated on Byron's sexuality.[29] In 1951, Doris Langley Moore suggested that the poet had homosexual experiences at Harrow[30]; in 1973, Harold Bloom introduced him as "fundamentally homosexual" in a popular undergraduate textbook[31]; and, in 1985, Cecil Lang speculated that his homoerotic experience in Albania provided an important clue to explicating the ninth (and for him, central) canto of *Don Juan*. Cecil Lang's essay, which appeared the same year as *Byron and Greek Love*, is unique in relating Byron's homoeroticism to the poetry itself. Most major studies of Byron's poetry which were written before Crompton's book appeared were far more decorous. Jerome McGann, Andrew Rutherford, and Robert Gleckner did not discuss the influence of homoeroticism on his most lascivious of poems at all.[32] Even recently, critics have not always chosen to follow Crompton's lead. Susan Wolfson's important essay on cross-dressing, for example, concentrates only on Byron's heterosexual politics in *Don Juan*, relegating Byron's homoeroticism to the status of a "more privately coded issue."[33] Yet Judith Butler's *Gender Trouble* and *Bodies that Matter* show how the tendency to treat any writer's homoeroticism as "private" may perpetuate the notion that heterosexuality alone is culturally intelligible.[34] By subtly manipulating a closeted sexual identity, Byron's narrator achieves his most striking effects.

I am certainly not the first to discuss Byron's narrator in *Don Juan*. William Marshall found a "myriad of speakers" in the poem,[35] while George Ridenour states that Byron's narrator is "self-consistent."[36] More recently, Nancy Benson has taken a psychological approach, describing the contrast between Byron and his narrator as an alternation of opposite tendencies that suggest the epistemological schema of Piaget.[37] Less theoretical is Andrew Parker's account of the narrator's "oblique style," which he connects with "rogue literature."[38] Following Paul de Man, Kim Michasiw sees Byron's narrator as aesthetically inconsistent and "effaced."[39] But whereas Michasiw views the narrator as a "sculpted voice" performed by some rhetorical sleight-of-hand, I argue that he is a fully fledged persona whose use of *double entendre* clearly differentiates him from Byron.[40]

The reluctance of most critics to make the poet's homosocial desire intelligible in his verse curiously reflects Byron's own practice. A poem in the *Morning Chronicle* of 1814 may be the first to rebuke Byron for this trait. It accuses him of subduing his "tuneful voice" and not publicly lamenting the death of his friend Matthews, who drowned in the Cam River in 1811.[41] Ruthra attributes Byron's silence to his sincere grief, but hints that there may also be an element of social snobbery attending his silence: Byron is unwilling to remember someone beneath his social station.

In fact, Byron's silence is most likely a result of his reluctance to exhibit his feelings for a member of his own gender in public, as the retitling of numerous elegies he wrote suggests. Below is a poem that has not been reprinted before (I believe), one that sheds considerable light on how Byron's complex relationship to other men was understood by his contemporaries.

To the Memory of
CHARLES SKINNER MATTHEWS, Esq.
SOMETIME FELLOW OF DOWNING COLLEGE, CAMBRIDGE,
DROWNED IN THE CAM, AUGUST, 1811

Why all our praises to the *titled* crew?
MATTHEWS, who never cringed, I sing to you!
Why all our art the *living* must engross?
Matthews, there are who yet do weep thy loss,—
There are who loath the lies by flatt'ry bred,
But pay their willing homage to the dead!
To him, alas! our sighs who may not hear
Nor heed the load of anguish that we bear,
To him—whom numerous Byron hath not sung—
For grief sincere subdued his tuneful tongue!
Yet we who loved not less, will strive in song,
Not him to honour—but our tears prolong.
Who loved him living will lament him dead,
And heep unheeded praises on his head!
His was the soul erect—the manly mind—
With learning's lore,—and wit—and taste refin'd;
And fair sincerity's ennobling charm.
A head so cool, and yet a heart so warm!
    Cambridge, farewell! my sorrow has not pow'rs
To tell thee, Granta, why I hate thy tow'rs!
And thee, ungrateful Cam! whose waters flow
Accursed ay—sad source of all my woe!
Damn'd be thy sedgy current, and thy stream
Of grief and hate the everlasting theme!
    In vain do suns and waning moons decline—
Untired my tears—unceasing sorrow mine.
With him I saw my dearest joys depart—
A frightful chasm still left within my heart;
In vain the hours and days each other urge,
For each revolving year I'll chant his dirge;
His virtue and our grief will still rehearse,

And pour the poor vain tribute of a verse!
Ah! who shall speak the hopes for ever gone—
The parent's heavy heart, and friends undone?
For thee the choaking sob, the big tears roll,
Side-piercing grief,—and pangs that reach the soul!
But hold,—no more!—let sorrow be but sad—
We must not think on't so—'twill make us mad.
Yet there is comfort—we shall meet again—
Byron!—there *is* a heav'n!—Amen, Amen!
4 Dec. 1814   RUTHRA

The phrase "numerous Byron" implicitly accuses Byron of libertinism and callousness, as if he has so many lovers he cannot spare
the time to lament those who have died. The speaker uses an italicized phrase ("*titled* crew") to distinguish himself from Byron,
whose social title prevented him from singing of Matthew's death;
Ruthra suggests that there is something unintelligible, "untitled" or
unentitled, about the love of one man for another.[42]
    Arthur describes Matthews as one "who never cringed" in the
face of social titles, precisely to expose the ingenue Byron as one
who has. Neither Arthur nor Byron is entirely comfortable displaying his feelings for another male in verse, however. Ultimately,
even Arthur conforms "cring[ingly]" to the conventions of the
Morning Chronicle by rearranging the letters of his own name before appending it to his poem as "Ruthra." Arthur publishes his
poem in the *Morning Chronicle* by adopting a literary mask that
must be "read through" (or even read backwards) to be understood.
Where Byron's "tuneful" voice is silenced by grief, Ruthra's name
is rearranged because he knows that certain forms of same-sex love
are unreadable in Regency society. No one "heed[s] the load of anguish that we bear," Ruthra complains. There is no one to "heep
unheeded praises on his head." That the mourners of Matthews
form a community of grievers is underscored by the first-person
plural of the poem, which refers not only to the men who knew
Matthews well, but to all men who have lost other men they loved
and found that love "unintelligible" in a heterosexual society.
    The poet's lament for Matthews subtly criticizes social institu-
tions like Cambridge and the *Morning Chronicle,* which encourage
and then frustrate the expression of homosocial desire. The poet
connects the river that drowned his friend with an institution that
supported loving relationships between men in their youth, only to
leave them vulnerable to a society that "drown[s]" them in a
muddy bog of compulsory heterosexuality when they grow up. The

poet's "choaking sob" of remembrance reminds the reader of the stifling weeds of the Cam River where Matthews "choak[ed]": Arthur's "choaking" elegy reflects the nurturing and punishing Cam River that inspires it. The alternation between restriction and release ("choaking sob[s]" and "roll[ing] tears") reflects the poet's own difficulty speaking out, first signaled in the anagram that forms his name.[43] The speaker imagines a better place ("there *is* a heaven") where all three men might meet unconstricted in their expressions of mutual regard, unhampered by social constraints.[44]

Like the "Byron" depicted in "Ruthra' "s poem, the bachelor narrator of *Don Juan* has a similar inability to "speak out." Despite the fact that he was living in Venice, a city attractive to English tourists for its relaxed laws governing sodomy,[45] Byron transferred some of his own English inhibitions to his Spanish-born narrator. This "moderate Presbyterian" misogynist is curiously silent about his education, his own love affairs, and his particular interest in the beauty of the young Don Juan. We learn he is an avid reader of English preachers who once resided in England, which might explain his scruples concerning how a prudent English public will receive his "moral" tale. From the very outset of the poem, he struggles to achieve a transvaluation of values that will validate not only his own sexual preference, but the heroism of his effeminate protagonist. His wry perspective on matrimony is redolent of an outsider (or gay man) mocking an institution that would make of man and woman a "moral centaur," one in which *"Wedlock* and a *Padlock"* mean the same.[46] Nevertheless, this cautious narrator has also imbibed enough of the cultural prejudices of the country Byron left behind to continue to narrate his story in a cautious style. It is worth noting in this regard that the very stanza about marriage quoted above (5 : 158) was removed by John Murray in the first edition of the poem.[47]

While some critics have argued that "the most challenging figure to analyze . . . in Byron's work is the narrator," I do not agree with the conclusion that often follows from this assertion, namely that the narrator of *Don Juan* can be read as " 'Byron himself.' "[48] I would distinguish Byron's gay narrator, with his preoccupations about truth, constancy, and sexual education, from Byron, who advertises his heterosexuality through a deliberate and unconvincing bravado.[49] By distinguishing himself from his narrator, Byron displaces his gay identity onto another: the dialectic that occurs in this poem between Byron's homo- and heterosexual selves provides a new context for explaining the theme of metaphysical doubt and the digressive method that have puzzled critics for some time.[50]

The Gay Narrator of *Don Juan*

What *do* we know about the narrator? In the unpublished preface to his poem which parodies Wordsworth's "The Thorn," Byron asks his readers to imagine that his narrator is "a Spanish gentleman in a village in the Sierra Morena on the road between Monasterio and Seville." The narrator describes two men who have decamped from their horses, and a reader of *Childe Harold's Pilgrimage* immediately recalls Byron and Hobhouse's tour of Europe and the Morea through this gesture and others. Byron deliberately distinguishes himself from "Our friend the storyteller."[51] Whereas the Byron figure in the preface watches the movements of a "tall peasant girl, whose whole soul is in her eyes and her heart in the dance,"[52] the storyteller does not.[53] He sits "*at some distance*" (my emphasis) with a small elderly audience, narrating his tale to a group of like-minded gentlemen, "without being much moved by the musical hilarity at the other end of the village green."[54] Like Socrates, who joined in his company's decision to banish flute girls from the symposium described in Plato's dialogue, Byron's gay narrator prefers the company of men.

References to the peculiar interests of Byron's narrator continue in the poem itself. He imagines a heterosexual script, complete with a "mistress in some soft abode," and then deliberately departs from it. His text is Horace, but he quotes the Roman writer only to depart from him. There is nothing "straight" about the narrative we are about to hear.

> Most epic poets plunge in "medias res,"
> (Horace makes this the heroic turnpike road)
> And then your hero tells, whene'er you please,
> What went before—by way of episode,
> While seated after dinner at his ease,
> Beside his mistress in some soft abode,
> Palace, or garden, paradise, or cavern,
> Which serves the happy couple for a tavern.
>
> That is the usual method, but not mine—
> My way is to begin with the beginning;
> The regularity of my design
> Forbids all wandering as the worst of sinning,
> And therefore I shall open with a line
> (Although it cost me half an hour in spinning)
> Narrating somewhat of Don Juan's father,
> And also of his mother, if you'd rather.[55]

In these stanzas, Byron's narrator uses double entendres and coded language ("usual method, but not mine"; "regularity of my design"; "wandering as the worst of sinning") to show how his narrative practice differs from conventional, "straight" narratives. Jerome McGann argues that Byron was writing in a Horatian style,[56] but the narrator insists that he is not following Horace at all: "that is the usual method, but not mine." Horace's "heroic turnpike road" is a heterosexual Ur-text, complete with domestic trappings and a "mistress in some soft abode," but the narrator notes that there are more "pathways" to the heart than Horace's.[57] He describes "Love" as

> that great opener of the heart and all
> The ways that lead there, be they near or far,
> Above, below, by turnpikes great or small.[58]

The enjambment of "the heart and all / The ways that lead there" introduces the comic *double entendre,* and yet conceals it through the line break. This passage, juxtaposed as it is with the narrator's apostrophe to Catherine's genitalia, makes us think of canals as material turnpikes to the heart.

Another instance of the narrator's dangerously allusive style occurs when he states his intention to speak of "Don Juan's father, / And also of his mother, if you'd rather."[59] Don Juan's decision to narrate of "Don Juan's father, / And also of his mother, if you'd rather" shows that he can only control his greater interest in the affairs of men with a struggle. The phrase, "And also of his mother" might not seem like such an afterthought if enjambment did not call attention to it, and if he did not go on to make more pointed remarks about his relationship to Jóse. The narrator knew Jóse "well," "very well," and proceeds to describe his friendship with Jóse in his own version of code: "a better cavalier never mounted horse, / Or, being mounted, e'er got down again."[60] When Don Juan and Lord Henry discuss horses again later in the poem, they also do so with many *double entendres* about "riding" and "mounting."

> Of coursers also spake they: Henry rid
> Well, like most Englishmen, and loved the races;
> And Juan, like a true-born Andalusian,
> Could back a horse, as despots ride a Russian.[61]

The narrator sets up this allusion to horses through a charged reference to the sexual history of "Constantinople" one line earlier,

"Where people always did as they were bid, / Or did what they should not with foreign graces."[62] My point is not that Juan is gay,[63] but that the narrator's descriptions of him ("back a horse") betrays the narrator's own sexual imagination. He clearly derives pleasure from placing his hero in sexually suggestive positions: on horses, in dresses, naked on Greek shores, with yellow stockings in Russian courts, and fully dressed in English ones.

By stressing that these seemingly gratuitous *double entendres* are repeated in *Don Juan*, sometimes eight cantos apart, I also want to underscore that they are intentional, not unplanned, haphazard, and undisciplined as some critics have assumed.[64] By decoding the poem's language, one finds thematic links between two passages that would otherwise seem like non sequiturs. Both examples quoted above speak twice, as it were, and address the reader on two levels: the level of plot and the level of homoerotic discourse.

Cecil Lang's ground-breaking article, "Narcissus Jilted," underscores how Byron's complex relationship with the Ali Pasha in Albania can illuminate the homoerotic content of *Don Juan*. Lang shows how Pacha's flirtation with the young poet was transmuted into unusual biographical correspondences in Byron's *Don Juan*, where Catherine the Great's tyrannical behavior recalls Ali Pacha's.[65] Without insisting on specific correspondences, I argue that Byron's erotic experiences in Albania and Venice clearly affected *Don Juan* in some way, though critics have been more concerned with literary than cultural influences. To consider the argument another way, Byron's poem must be *at least* as erotic and worldly as his letters to his own mother, yet the decorous criticism of Byron's poem lags far behind the erotic adventures detailed in his thirteen-volume correspondence.[66]

This way of reading the poem differs fundamentally from Susan Wolfson's otherwise fine analysis, which sees Byron agitating a sense of sexual dislocation only to generate "a series of defensive maneuvers" that "reinscribe sexual orthodoxy."[67] Wolfson argues that Byron's poem "does not, finally, escape the roles fashioned and maintained by his culture."[68] I argue that Byron uses his narrator's voice to surreptitiously challenge Regency sexual mores. He is able to do this not "despite an aristocratic allegiance," as Wolfson argues, but because of it.[69] As an aristocrat editing *The Liberal*, Byron was free from the risk of being imprisoned for sedition, as were Leigh and John Hunt in 1812.[70] Byron's decision to exchange the cautious Tory John Murray for the radical John Hunt as publisher of cantos 6 through 17 of *Don Juan* conceals the fact that the poem became more tame precisely as the publisher became more radical: to state the point perhaps too simply, the aristocratic liberalism of cantos 1–5 is more sexually subversive than the democratic liberalism of cantos 6–17.[71]

In the early cantos of the poem, the narrator reveals his prurient interest in Juan more often by what he leaves out than by what he includes. He spends "half an hour in spinning" (1 : 7 : 54) lines that ultimately tell us very little about Jóse. The narrator's disrupted syntax, as well as his use of an extended hyphen after the phrase "that's to come," indicates the difficulty he has beginning his narrative: Jóse "who / Begot—but that's to come———Well, to renew" (1 : 9). Later in the same canto, the narrator asserts that Jose and his wife were an "ill-assorted pair" but avoids saying more because "scandal's my aversion" (1 : 51). The narrator's possible involvement in the scandal he describes makes it difficult for him to cast the first stone. In canto 1, then, the begetting of Juan has two different enunciations, as the play on "mounted" and "being mounted" suggests.[72] The narrator's carnal knowledge of Jóse's father might explain why he knows as much as he does about the son—a fact that goes otherwise unexplained. It also might explain the slightly effeminate nature of Juan, who may have inherited his father's complicated sexual desire.

> I knew his father well, and have some skill
> In character—but it would not be fair
> From sire to son to augur good or ill.[73]

Not only the narrator's reticence, but his bisexuality (which now inclines toward a gay orientation), leaves him confused about how to begin his narrative. "My way is to begin with the beginning," he says, but he finds that this is easier said than done. No sooner does he begin this narrative than he imagines an "atrocious" (14 : 97) reader as perverse as himself, one not content with conventional beginnings and endings; a *hypocrite lecteur* who can read between the lines of his poem but who cannot openly confess his understanding of the narrator's *double entendres*. The result of this stammering narrative is a reader's guide that lacks the courage of its own convictions. "Firstly, begin with the beginning," the narrator playfully instructs his reader,

> (though
> That clause is hard); and secondly, proceed;
> Thirdly, commence not with the end—or, sinning
> In this sort, end at least with the beginning.[74]

At first glance, these lines would seem to have only a literal meaning, functioning as a series of textual instructions, as in *Ars Poetica*
(20 B.C.): the poet should invent "in such a way that the beginning,
middle, and end are all appropriate with each other," Horace
states.[75] Departing from Horace, even as he invokes him, the narrator makes up his own rules, becoming, in effect, his "*own* Aris-
totle"[76]: "Begin with the beginning . . . and secondly, proceed." A
second look at these comments, however, reveals a series of meton-
ymies ("Beginning"; "proceed"; "commence"; "end"; "sinning /
In this sort") that connect ways of reading with sexual acts. In this
sense, an epic poem is analogous to the human body, which may be
seduced or read from the front or back. As in other sections of the
poem, the ostensibly heterosexual plot is undermined by suggestions that the anatomy the narrator has in mind is male—its "front"
is hard, and entry at its "end" is prohibited. "Commence not with
the end—or, sinning / In this sort, end at least with the beginning."[77] The ranking of love in a *scala d'amore* reinforces the lessons of Plato's *Symposium*, mentioned earlier:

> The noblest kind of Love is Love Platonical,
> To end or to begin with; the next grand
> Is that which may be christen'd Love Canonical,
> Because the clergy take the thing in hand;
> The third sort to be noted in our Chronicle
> As flourishing in every Christian land,
> Is, when chaste Matrons to their other ties
> Adds what may be call'd *Marriage in Disguise*.[78]

Clearly, the use of phrases like "sinning in this sort," "To end or
to begin with," "take the thing in hand" and "*marriage in disguise*" invite supplemental readings, as does a phrase like "that
clause is hard."[79]

To uncover the nature of Juan's sexuality spells the end of the
narrator's coded style and hence the end of the poem itself. The
episode that precipitates this crisis is the hero's encounter with the
Duchess Fitz-Fulke. Most critics fail to note that the poem ends precisely at this moment of sexual self-discovery.[80] Byron's "Memor-
and" on the Murray manuscript reveals the price of decoding the
narrator's style. Structurally, he suggests a link between "The
Shade of the / Friar /" and "The D[ea]th of J[uan]."[81] That the appearance of Fitz-Fulke should spell the "death of Juan" is only natural, for Juan's death is not literal, but figurative: the death of the
legendary figure of Juan as an uncomplicated heterosexual. Juan

has worn dresses before in the manner of a masquerade, but his encounter with the "Shade of the / Friar" is the first time that his homoerotic desire is made plain to him in the form of an *anagnorisis*. Her hooded veil, her doubling presence, makes him grow pale and necessarily spells his death as a literary legend because it reveals him as attracted to men, even if the man is only a woman dressed as a man. This accounts, in part, for the "wan and worn" look the young man displays at the breakfast table the morning after his adventure with the Duchess Fitz-Fulke. What Juan displays is the shock of recognition.[82]

BEGINNINGS AND ENDINGS

The poem's injunction to "end at least with the beginning" is realized in Juan's discovery of his own homoeroticism, much as Byron realized he found Caroline Lamb more attractive when she wore a page's outfit. With this rich play on "beginning" and "ending" in mind, we might consider in what other senses the poem "end[s]" with the beginning. Edward Said notes that "Literature is full of the lore of beginnings despite the tyranny of starting a work *in medias res*, a convention that burdens the beginning with the pretense that it is not one."[83] In canto 1, concern with beginning his poem leads him to cite Horace to clarify his method. In canto 4, he brings up the subject of beginnings again, telling the reader that there is "Nothing so difficult as a beginning": the point is ironic because the poem is in its fourth canto, far from the beginning, and yet the episodic nature of the work demands that every canto be a new beginning. Byron's narrator chooses canto 12 to return to the very place where Virgil and Milton's epics end, and Homer's *Iliad* and *Odyssey* are half-over. "Now I will begin my poem," he says

> —'Tis
> Perhaps a little strange, if not quite new,
> That from the first of Cantos up to this
> I've not begun what we have to go through.[84]

What Byron has to "go through" is the details of his own erotic life, a subject alluded to teasingly by his gay narrator who only tells the reader "one half" of what he should. Lady Melbourne, Byron's closest confidante during his years of fame in England, heard all of his confessions about extramarital affairs and was privy even to the information regarding his relationship with Augusta Leigh. Yet

104   PART ONE: ROMANTIC

even Lady Melbourne did not know about Byron's close relationships with other men.

The subject of beginnings and endings takes on additional resonance given the "beginning" of Byron's erotic life. Byron's relationships with Edleston, Matthews, Wingfield, and especially John Clare were clearly erotic. Byron's relationship with Clare was more intensely meaningful to him than the servitude that he felt characterized his relationship with Teresa Guiccioli, which he deplored in letters to Hobhouse. A chance encounter with John Clare stopped him dead in his tracks on a road in Italy when he met his young Harrow friend after seven years. Phyllis Grosskurth notes that these were "the five most impassioned minutes of his life,"[85] and suggests that Byron was even more affected than Clare, who calmly rode on. She makes effective use of this episode as a preface for her biography, showing the power that "beginnings" had on Byron even as he approached the end of his life.[86] Until late in his life, however, he did not acknowledge his affection for these men in print; his lyric poem to Loukas, which gave meaning to his political activity in Greece, is an exception which shows how Byron's literary strategies changed during this period in his life.

Recently, theorists have argued that homosexuality precedes heterosexuality historically.[87] For Freud, the bisexuality of children precedes the heterosexuality of adults, which is based upon the repression of homosexual desire.[88] If we apply Freud's insight to Byron's poem, we can see that the beginning of this poem is not hetero- but homosexual. Homosexuality is not an aberration or wandering away from the norm, but the "regular" design. "Regular" though it may be, same-sex love was a capital offense in Regency England, punishable by public hanging or the pillory.[89] William Beckford's exile and Lord Castlereagh's suicide were potent reminders to Byron of the danger of being publically exposed as a sodomite. In order to speak of "common things in the *proper way*," as his epigraph from Horace commands, the narrator resorts to the popular genre of the pantomime with its "Principal Boys" and "Breeches Parts." "We have all seen him in the pantomime," the narrator says of Don Juan, "Sent to the devil, somewhat ere his time."[90] In the eighteenth century, as Peter Graham has shown, pantomimes were not dumb shows but a concatenation of ballet, dancing, and burlesque.[91] They appealed to a broad audience, in part, by playing havoc with gender roles. The narrator thus uses the theatrical conventions of the pantomime to please his audience's "common" tastes, and satisfy his own more polymorphously perverse predilections at the same time.

Juan's relationship to the pantomime would seem to make the effeminacy of the narrator irrelevant, and Juan's own cross-dressing, to use Susan Wolfson's term, self-explanatory. In fact, it is Byron's narrator who exposes and theatricalizes Juan. He performs the function of the pantomime's *corago,* or stage manager, who both encourages and conceals his spectators' view of his titillating hero, making visible this "beauteous Boy."[92] In eighteenth-century theater and popular entertainments, a principal boy's costume spoke for itself. In Byron's poem it takes a gay narrator to dress and undress his travestied hero. Byron absolves himself of responsibility for his *corago's* sexual prurience by constructing a narrator more transgressive than himself.

In a shrewd stage adaptation of the first 2 cantos of *Don Juan,* entitled "Don Juan's Earliest Scrape," Carole Benson directed Byron's narrator or "corago" to speak in his own person, delivering his words in such an arch manner that he makes his difference in style and sexuality plain from the outset. The narrator underscores the importance of his sexual orientation because he seems to orchestrate the action on stage for his own particular erotic satisfaction. Thus Juan and Alfonso fight in an extended sequence, grappling with one another until Juan is partially disrobed. As they tumble upon a red silk bed occupied by Juan and Julia only minutes before, the narrator winks knowingly to the audience, underscoring how interchangeable hetero- and homosexual love can be. The narrator's knowing smiles to the audience make it complicit in the drama they see. Through this scene, the narrator quickly establishes a knowing relationship between himself and the audience that continues throughout the length of the play.

Clearly these directorial decisions are only one way of interpreting Byron's poem or of adapting it to the stage. There are countless others. But "Don Juan's Earliest Scrape" succeeds in part because the director correctly reads the dramatic significance of the narrator's *double entendres.* The narrator is convincing as a character in this play precisely because he is not Byron, a perspective which a close reading of the poem itself supports. The narrator becomes more interesting to us as the differences between author and speaker are underscored.[93]

One example of the heightened interest which these differences can produce occurs when the narrator remarks on inconstancy between heterosexual lovers. These remarks have additional resonance if we read them as emanating not from Byron, but from a narrator reflecting on his own inconstancy to a particular gender. Fittingly, the reflections take place during a Venetian carnival, when a masked "creature" appears before the narrator's eyes in the midst of his sermon on "constancy."

> I hate inconstancy—I loathe, detest,
> Abhor, condemn, abjure the mortal made
> Of such quicksilver clay that in his breast
> No permanent foundations can be laid;
> Love, constant love, has been my constant guest,
> And yet last night, being at a masquerade,
> I saw the prettiest creature, fresh from Milan,
> Which gave me some sensations like a villain.
>
> But soon Philosophy came to my aid,
> And whisper'd, 'think of every sacred tie!'
> 'I will, my dear Philosophy!' I said,
> 'But then her teeth, and then, Oh heaven! her eye!
> I'll just inquire if she be wife or maid,
> Or neither—out of curiosity.'
> 'Stop!' cried Philosophy, with air so Grecian,
> (Though she was masqued then as a fair Venetian.)[94]

The possibility that the object of the narrator's curiosity could be neither "wife [n]or maid" alerts us to the fact that the sexual identity of the narrator's object choice remains unspecified, even as the gender of the creature is supposedly unmasked ("*she* be wife or maid"). The play on fair Philosophy as a character in Boethius' *Consolation of Philosophy* (524 A.D.) only adds to the confusion, since the "Grecian" "air" of the "Venetian" also suggests Plato's homoerotic dialogue, the *Symposium*,[95] in which several interlocutors, such as Pausanias, view heterosexuality as an inferior practice.[96]

Unable to speak as directly about homoeroticism as Plato, Byron's narrator makes use of what Sedgwick calls the "epistemology of the closet" to both infer and deflect interest in his homosexuality.[97] In canto 1, the narrator withholds information about himself even as he criticizes Inez's method of educating Juan.

> For my part I say nothing—nothing—but
> *This* I will say—my reasons are my own—
> That if I had an only son to put
> To school (as God be praised that I have none)
> 'Tis not with Donna Inez I would shut
> Him up to learn his catechism alone,
> No—no—I'd send him out betimes to college,
> For there it was I pick'd up my own knowledge.

> For there one learns—'tis not for me to boast,
> Though I acquired—but I pass over *that,*
> As well as all the Greek I since have lost:
> I say that there's the place—but *'Verbum sat,'*
> I think I pick'd up too, as well as most,
> Knowledge of matters—but no matter *what*—
> I never married—but, I think, I know
> That sons should not be educated so.[98]

The narrator both reveals and conceals—passes over—"all the Greek I since have lost," and tells the reader that *"Verbum sat,"* or "a word to the wise is sufficient."

In this canto, as in the next, Byron used the "Greek language" as a metaphor for homoeroticism or what Crompton calls "Greek love." The narrator picked up "knowledge of matters—but no matter *what*— / I never married."[99] Louis Crompton (and indeed canto 1 of *Don Juan* itself) shows how Byron was exposed to "foreign" forms of sexuality, through his reading of Greek and Roman literature as a schoolboy. Lady Byron complained to Harriet Beecher Stowe that "there was everything in the classical course of the schools to develop an unhealthy growth of passion, and no moral influence of any kind to restrain it."[100] Byron's vast library included many Greek and Roman authors; in *Don Juan* itself he connects the knowledge of these languages with other forms of instruction.[101] At the end of his preface to *History*, Winckelmann confessed that he would have "been able to say more if I had written for the Greeks, and not in a modern tongue, which imposes on me certain restrictions."[102] Byron's narrator feels a similar "restriction," using precisely this word to account for the chastity of his muse.[103]

In one sense, then, the narrator's failure to articulate truths may come from the fact that he does not know English very well: "Much English I cannot pretend to speak," he says,[104] even though he has learned the language from its "preachers" ("Barrow, South, Tillotson") and studies them "every week." This apparent paradox can only be explained if the reader allows that the narrator equates "English" with sexual repression, in the same way that he uses the word "language" as a metonymy for sexual performance. The narrator prefers a "strange tongue" to "English" as he confesses when narrating the Haidée episode.

> 'Tis pleasing to be school'd in a strange tongue
> By female lips and eyes—that is, I mean. . . .[105]

In this passage, the enjambment of "By female lips and eyes," clarifies the sexual object choice too late, as do the stumbling qualifications, "that is, I mean." Though the narrator is probably ironic in suggesting that he knows little of heterosexuality ("learn'd the little that I know by this"), his interest in women, unlike Byron's, is nevertheless chaste, in part, because it has "passed" away. "As for the ladies," the narrator continues,

> I have nought to say,
> A wanderer from the British world of fashion,
> Where I, like other 'dogs, have had my day,'
> Like other men too, may have had my passion—
> But that, like other things, has pass'd away,
> And all her fools whom I *could* lay the lash on,
> Foes, friends, men, women, now are nought to me
> But dreams of what has been, no more to be.[106]

The undermining of experience ("may have had my passion") is underscored by the final line of the stanza which suggests that the heterosexual experience of the narrator may in fact be as much of a prevarication as sexual identity itself, "*dreams* of what has been, no more to be" (emphasis added). It is not that the narrator's sexual experience with women has come to an end but that his heterosexual self, like his homosexuality, is not stable, as selfhood itself is unstable. The narrator does what he accuses Robert Southey of doing (and hence the dedication to him), of "struggling convulsively to deceive others without the power of lying to himself."[107]

The first two cantos are the most suggestive and immoral of the entire poem. After writing 180 octaves of *Don Juan*, Byron wondered whether "the poem was not—at least as far as it has yet gone—too free for these 'very modest days.' "[108] When his friends and publisher indicated that it would be "*impossible to publish this*" kind of verse in England, Byron lost his nerve and produced the more tepid third and fourth cantos.[109] By separating his discussion of the poem's composition from the poem's form, Andrew Rutherford sometimes loses sight of this change in the poem's tone, and discusses the poem's narration as if it were a unified whole.[110] Yet the narrator calls attention to a fundamental difference between the first two cantos and those that follow:

> Here I might enter on a chaste description,
> Having withstood temptation in my youth,
> But hear that several people take exception
> At the first two books having too much truth;

Therefore I'll make Don Juan leave the ship soon,
Because the publisher declares, in sooth,
Through needles' eyes it easier for the camel is
To pass, than those two cantos into families.[111]

The difficult syntax of the next-to-last line of this quotation reinforces or performs the narrator's point. The poem cannot "pass" into families, because its secret code (and not just the stanzas about Lady Byron) is visible to Byron's friends—Hobhouse, Scrope Davies, and others, who have urged him to refrain from publication. In another sense, the poem cannot reproduce itself into cantos 3 and 4 ("families" of cantos) without being altered significantly: it is not "reproductive" because the outlook the narrator presents is discernibly gay.

Shelley noted the poem's change from a homoerotic to a more heterosexual outlook. Disapproving of the cynicism evident in cantos 1 and 2 of *Don Juan*,[112] Shelley changed his assessment about cantos 3, 4, and 5, noting that the poem now seemed "pregnant with immortality."[113] The metaphor of pregnancy is apt and corresponds with Byron's change in lifestyle. Where Shelley once described Byron's visits to men who lack the "gait and physiognomy" of man in a letter to Thomas Love Peacock on 17 or 18 December 1818,[114] three years later he noted that Byron had "got rid of all those melancholy and degrading habits which he indulged at Venice"[115] and lived as an "altered man" serving as *cavalier servente* in Ravenna to "one woman," Teresa Guiccioli, whom he had met in April 1819.[116] Byron did ultimately compose cantos 3, 4, and 5 in ways that conformed to English notions of propriety.[117] He recognized early on that there was something about the narrator's allusive style—what Byron referred to as "*that there* sort of writing"—that did not accord well with "family values."[118] As the poem developed, however, Byron deliberately muted his outrageous narrator by assuming his identity, by denying that there was any difference between his hetero- and homosexual selves. Yet a careful reader can still discern that the whole poem is written against "straight" life: against stifling marriages like Julia's[119]; polygamous ones like Gulbeyaz's[120]; and sexless ones like Adeline's.[121]

When Teresa Guiccioli put a ban on the writing of *Don Juan* on 6 July 1821,[122] she did so (according to Byron) because it stripped the illusion of sentiment from life.[123] To press further on this explanation, one might say that the poem effectively took Byron out of the closet. In this poem, Teresa found her straight lover transformed into a gay narrator commenting cynically on heterosexuality. Her

banning of the poem performs the same work as the pillory in England. It shames the "outed" Byron into silence, punishing him for
his audacious wit and tracing the source of his humor to an animus
against women. When I say that Byron was against women, I do not
mean to deny his own statements to the contrary. "I have been their
martyr," he wrote to his publisher. "My whole life has been sacrificed *to* them & *by* them."[124] Byron was against women because he
blamed them for the repressions that were forced upon him. Perhaps
he blamed them for his need to travel abroad for two years: to pretend to feelings for Caroline Lamb which he no longer possessed in
order to flatter her vanity and her mother's[125]; to propose marriage
to Annabella in order to reform his character[126]; and to remain in
Italy as a fan carrier for Teresa Guiccioli long after he had set his
mind on a political adventure in Greece. Byron may well have been
wedded to a notion of his own career and literary strength, as Jerome Christensen suggests, but he was also wedded to perhaps the
greatest myth of all: the myth of his uncomplicated heterosexuality.
It was of only limited satisfaction to him to write in the style and
mores of a society that was too repressive to be vital, a place Byron
referred to as the " 'tight little island.' "[127]

In Greece, by contrast, he could pursue his attraction to young
men unhampered; his death in the cause of Greek independence
was really the death of his own sexual liberty—a battle he first
fought when he left England for two years in 1809.[128] One might
say that he died less in the service of nationalism than for the idea
of same-sex love. Because *Don Juan* only hinted at these frustrations, the poem became less and less satisfying to Byron, who
seemed more interested in shocking his audience after a while than
in delighting it. It was his memoirs and letters, rather than his poem,
that he felt to be his most sincere bequest to posterity.

In *Don Juan*, by contrast, the narrator's sexuality is based, in
part, upon a lie. One sign of this is that he continually protests too
much about his heterosexual adventures.

> I love the sex, and sometimes would reverse
> The tyrant's wish, 'that mankind only had
> One neck, which he with one fell stroke might pierce:'
> My wish is quite as wide, but not so bad,
> And much more tender on the whole than fierce;
> It being (not *now*, but only while a lad)
> That Womankind had but one rosy mouth,
> To kiss them all at once from North to South.[129]

This stanza, written after Teresa's ban on the poem, reflects the strategy of heterosexual masquerade which the poem increasingly adopted. On the one hand, the narrator has an endless store of desire for women which he would like to discharge through one passionate kiss. On the other, the narrator wishes that all womankind "had but one rosy mouth" so he could claim the credit for kissing them all without the tedium of prosecuting the act. The strange mixture of violence and tenderness in this passage, where kissing is implicitly compared with cutting off the necks of all of mankind, exposes Byron's discomfort with compulsory heterosexuality. "It is true from early habit, one must make love mechanically as one swims," he wrote Lady Melbourne on 10 September 1812. "I was once very fond of both, but now as I never swim unless I tumble into the water, I don't make love till almost obliged."[130] My reading of this passage does not depend upon a sexual reading of the term "make love." To make love is as much to profess as to engage in any explicit physical act. Professing heterosexual love involves Byron in the act of writing pseudo-poems and living a sort of pseudo-life: a poem to Edleston is disguised as a poem to "Thyrza" and represented to his own wife as a poem written for another woman.[131]

Unlike the obliging Byron, the gay narrator of *Don Juan* has refused women on more than one occasion, and will not "make love mechanically as one swims."[132] He describes Gulbeyaz's reaction when Juan similarly resists her advances and tells her "love is for the free."

> A tigress robb'd of young, a lioness,
> Or any interesting beast of prey,
> Are similes at hand for the distress
> Of ladies who cannot have their own way;
> But though my turn will not be served with less,
> These don't express one half what I should say:
> For what is stealing young ones, few or many,
> To cutting short their hopes of having any?[133]

Juan, who has cut short Gulbeyaz's hopes for having children, captures the sympathy of his narrator, who has presumably been in a similar situation. Pederasty, or "stealing young ones a few or many," is not nearly so bad as "cutting short their hopes of having any" by refusing the obligatory sexual performance. The ultimate revenge on women is adopting a lifestyle that denies them the opportunity to procreate. A "purposeless" sexuality matches the poem's praise of other nonteleological activities (the "great end of traveling—which is driving"[134]) and its narrative strategy which feigns to have no other purpose than "to giggle and make giggle."[135]

In one sense, *Don Juan* is Byron's riddle of futurity, "happily" hiding what it pretends to reveal.[136] In pointed digressions, Byron's narrator compares his sexuality to "hieroglyphics on Egyptian stones, / The pleasant riddles of Futurity— / Guessing at what shall happily be hid, / As the real purpose of a Pyramid."[137] Although Leslie Marchand argues that "the poem is . . . one in which the author 'speaks out' in his own person on whatever most concerns him at the moment," precisely the opposite conclusion is warranted.[138] Byron's complex relationship to his narrator shows him constantly silencing his own speech. Even behind the mask he adopts, Byron was reluctant to "speak out." Instead, the narrator builds his pyramid of a poem by hiding its homoerotic message in "riddles of futurity."

By the end of the poem, the narrator has kept up his screen but Byron fails to achieve "the fierce, Caravaggio style" he claimed Don Juan exhibited. The narrator shamelessly refers to Juan as a "beauteous Boy"[139] and lavishes more time in "painting" him than on Donna Julia, Haidée, Gulbeyaz, or Catherine. But the narrator's topic still requires "the due restriction" of "proper courtesy"[140]: "Ne'er doubt / *This*—when I speak, I *don't hint*, but *speak out*."[141] Clearly the statement is ironic, as the italicized words and pun on "doubt" suggest.

Contrast this with Byron's last love poem addressed to his Greek servant boy, Loukas Chalandritsanos, entitled "Love and Death." Written a year after *Don Juan* had been substantially completed on 6 May 1823, the poem repeats themes mentioned in "On This Day I Complete My Thirty-Sixth Year"—specifically the fear of no longer being a love object: "Tread those reviving passions down, / Unworthy manhood!" Byron wrote on his birthday. The poem to Loukas goes further than that poem to articulate the other half of what could not be said by Byron's gay, but closeted, narrator:

> yet thou lov'st me not,
> And never wilt! Love dwells not in our will.
> Nor can I blame thee, though it be my lot
> To strongly, wrongly, vainly love thee still. [142]

At the end of his life, Byron finally answered the anonymous critic of the *Morning Chronicle*, Arthur, who both rebuked and forgave him for "cringing" and not singing of Charles Skinner Matthews' death.[143] "To me he was much," Byron said of Matthews, "to Hobhouse every thing. . . . I did not love so much as I honoured him."[144] In 1824, he writes a poem that is unabashedly homoerotic—perhaps because he is now truly in love—and sings of his unrequited love without fear of "speaking out." To do so, Byron overcame the aristocratic scruples of one who could only express his love for a member of his own social class.

By dividing his consciousness in *Don Juan*, Byron both conformed to society's demand for heterosexual masquerade and gained "symbolic capital" by alluding to a more dangerous, subversive self behind this heterosexual persona.[145] When Horace Walpole complained to Horace Mann in 1742 that "balls and masquerades supply the place of politics," he anticipated the great theme of Byron's poem, where masquerade is inseparable from political life in Turkey, Russia, and England.[146] In a masquerade, according to Terry Castle, "the true self remained elusive and inaccessible—illegible—within its fantastical encasements . . . one was obliged to impersonate a being opposite, in some essential feature, to oneself."[147] Byron's poem, set in the eighteenth century, continues this tradition; it achieves the same illegibility. By impersonating a being "opposite, in some essential feature" from himself as conventionally understood, Byron managed to explode the legend of Don Juan that he had participated in creating. In doing so, he remained true not to the lyric voice of his poem to Loukas Chalandritsanos, but to the theatrical metaphor with which he begins *Don Juan*: "We all have seen him in the pantomime / Sent to the devil, somewhat ere his time" (1 : 1). Byron avoids the limitations of Wordsworthian sincerity by using the "pantomime" as his model for staging a self. What the poem loses in sincerity, it gains in artistic richness.

Yet the implications of my argument go beyond a reading of *Don Juan* and affect our understanding of Byron's life as well. To understand the delicate relationship between the poet's bisexuality and his political activities, for example, a reader of Byron's life must be fully attentive to the precise reasons why Teresa Guiccioli and *cavalier serventissmo* were not sufficient for Byron in Italy. In a letter to John Hobhouse, Byron was very articulate about his dissatisfaction with libertine conventions in Italy. "But I feel & I feel it bitterly —that a man should not consume his life at the side and on the bosom—of a woman—and a stranger—that even the recompense and it is much—is not enough—and that this Cicisbean existence is to be condemned."[148] The hyphens in this passage achieve a kind of crescendo ("the bosom—of a woman—and a stranger"), just as the first caesura calls attention to the gender choice ("bosom—of a woman") as one of the aspects of conventional libertinism that he condemns. That Byron ended his life substituting the bosom of Loukas for that of Teresa gives added resonance to this passage. Such letters suggest that it was not even libertinism, but conventionalized forms of sexuality that troubled him. When seen in this light, fighting for Greek independence became as much a battle for sexual self-expression as it was for Greek nationalism. The battle was more personal than political, more aristocratic (a defense of the intellectual traditions at Harrow) than nationalistic. Byron fought for his own freedom from sexual enslavement in Italy ("this Cicisbean existence"), as he had fought a similar battle to free himself from Caroline Lamb in his letters to Lady Melbourne in England.[149] His own hero continues the battle in verse, resisting the sexual tyranny of Gulbeyaz, Catherine, and even the Duchess Fitz-Fulke. Byron may well have "felt life was slipping past him" and hence sought a military adventure by way of compensation, as William St. Clair argues, but there were also more specific, erotic motives for his Greek adventure.[150]

If Byron's ambivalent attitude toward Teresa motivated him, in part, to his discomfort with sexual restrictions in England, his pilgrimage to Greece (1809–11) played a role in his extended stay there, as Leslie Marchand has argued.[151] Byron expressed his discomfort with heterosexual norms in England through the misanthropy of his most famous protagonist, Childe Harold. The Childe's numerous ejaculations of political protest in cantos 1 and 2 receive some of their force from Byron's dissatisfaction with his country's restricted view of human sexuality, most clearly alluded to in the passage on William Beckford's exile.[152] This tendency to transmute and disguise erotic frustration through political ejaculation becomes more apparent in the creation of such effeminate heroes as Selim and Conrad, who live out the lifestyle that Childe Harold only gestures toward, and which they can only sketch before disappearing from the poem entirely. The frustration expressed by Childe Harold and the heroes of his Eastern tales is not only political, then, as Daniel Watkins has ably argued, but erotic, as his most recent study of Wordsworth, Coleridge, and Keats suggests.[153] In my view, the early poems and tales are proleptic of the sexual dissatisfaction shown by his gay narrator in *Don Juan*. A reading sensitive to Byron's eros as a political trope thus adds a new dimension to our understanding of the Byronic hero. Peter Thorslev defined this hero as a concatenation of previous literary types and formulas, such as the Child of Nature, the Gothic Villain, the Hero of Sensibility, or the Noble Outlaw.[154] By paying closer attention to Byron's sexuality, his erotic liberalism in his early verse, one can see what is unique about him and how it was necessary for him to be transformed into the gay narrator of Byron's greatest comic poem. This final subject necessarily lies outside the scope of this essay, but I hope my reading of *Don Juan* will suggest further work that might be done on these poems.

The use of a gay narrator in *Don Juan* indicates Byron's intention to subvert increasingly restrictive modes of speech in England while outwardly conforming to heterosexual conventions. The true burlesque of *Don Juan* redounds upon the myth of *Don Juan* itself: not simply because Juan is more "pursued than pursuing" (as many have rightly argued), but because the narrator's erotic relationship to his male hero differs radically from any treatment of the Don Juan legend that preceded it.

NOTES

1. In his influential study, *Don Juan in Context, (DJC)* for example, Jerome McGann echoes the work of Elizabeth Boyd and M. K. Joseph in speaking of a "theoretical stylistic norm" based on the Italian poets (*DJC* 98) which Byron consciously imitated. See Lindsay Waters, "The 'Desultory Rhyme' of *Don Juan,* 429–42.

2. Byron, *Don Juan,* (Cambridge University Press, 1992), 15 : 20 : 155.

3. Critics have relied on external, rather than internal, evidence to elucidate the poem's style, comparing it to Horace's *Ars Poetica* (McGann, *DJC* 109, 111) or to "improvisations" in De Staël's *Corinne* (Ridenour, *The Style of Don Juan,* 162–66; Waters 431).

4. Virginia Woolf praised *Don Juan*'s "elastic shape, adding that it will hold whatever you choose to put into it" (Frank Jordan, *The English Romantic Poets,* 537), while Jerome McGann underscores "the notorious lack of form in *Don Juan*" (114). Yet George Ridenour has shown how Byron's apparent digressions develop the poem's thematic concerns (*The Style of Don Juan* 162–66), and even Horace argued that a poem must be unified or "self-consistent" (443, 461). I hope to build on Ridenour's insight in this essay.

5. Byron, *Don Juan* 7 : 2.

6. Ibid., 1 : 44.

7. The Oxford edition omits both stanzas (44–45), while the Norton edition omits the second (45). After introducing Byron as "fundamentally homosexual" (285), for example, the Oxford edition omits precisely those passages of the poem that would support this interpretation, namely those in which the gay narrator's persona is developed (34–36).

8. Byron, *Don Juan* 1 : 44–45.

9. *Byron: The Oxford Authors*, ed. Jerome J. McGann (New York: Oxford University Press, 1986), 378–403.

10. M.A. Abrams, et al. *The Norton Anthology of English Literature.* Vol 2, 6th

ed. (New York: Norton, 1993), stanzas 2–4; 14–21; 30–31; 34–36; 45–51; 66–68; 73–74; 80–85; 87–89; 95–102; 108–12.

11. Ibid., stanzas 103–7; 113–17.

12. Leigh Hunt, *Lord Byron & Some of His Contemporaries*, 35; and William Hazlitt (Rutherford, *Byron: The Critical Heritage*, 131).

13. Andrew Rutherford, *Byron: A Critical Study*, 182–197; Leslie Marchand, *Byron: A Portrait*, 321.

14. For a further discussion of this matter, see my essay "Byron and *The Liberal*: Periodical as Political Posture," *Philological Quarterly* 72 (Fall 1993): 471–85.

15. "The noblest kind of love is love Platonical," the narrator states, "To end or to begin with" (9 : 76). By Platonic love, I think Byron means something more than idealized love. Compare this passage with my discussion of the *topos* of "ends" and "beginnings" later in this essay.

16. As a young man, Byron cultivated male friendships as a literary *topos*, which reflects his aristocratic orientation. Louis Crompton shows that Byron was aware of homosexual acts between young boys at Harrow, and that his cultural education, based in Greek and Roman literature, validated such erotic longings (Crompton, *Byron & Greek Love*, 80). Byron penned his "List of Historical Writers Whose Works I Have Perused" when he was 19. Crompton also cites Byron's interest in the Nisus and Euryalus episode in Book 9 of the *Aeneid*, which found its way into *Hours of Idleness* in what Byron called a "paraphrase" of the episode (Crompton, *Byron & Greek Love*, 96–97). Byron's reading seems to me less significant than the lived experiences and cultural conditioning that clearly affected the creation of *Don Juan*'s gay narrator.

17. Jeffrey Weeks (*Sex, Politics & Society*, 108–17) and John Boswell (*Christianity, Social Tolerance, and Homosexuality* 44) distinguish between gay and homosexual in important ways.

18. John Boswell points out some difficulties in terminology. Homosexual, composed of a Greek prefix and a Latin root, means "of one sex" (as "homogeneous," "of one kind"). "But what is a 'homosexual person?' ", Boswell asks. There is no magical number of sexual experiences with the same sex that makes one a homosexual. Both the quality and intensity of those relationships are what matter. In Byron's case, it is less important that he slept with a number of Venetian prostitutes than the fact that he described his love for John Edleston as a "violent, though pure" passion and penned the last poem of his life to a young Greek boy. I am using the word "gay" in this essay, then, in order to evoke a lifestyle that is the narrator's own and that is not limited to a form of sexual practice.

19. Eve Sedgwick, *Epistemology of the Closet* (Los Angeles: University of California Press, 1990), 158.

20. His philosophy and playful digressions owe less to the eighteenth-century omniscient narrator of Fielding's novels (Marchand, "Narrator and Narration" 28), or Greek skeptics like Pyrrho (Terence Hoagwood, *Byron's Dialectic*, 16), than to a specific form of sexual practice.

21. Byron, *Don Juan* 2 : 105–20.

22. Ibid., 5 : 97.

23. Ibid., 9 : 53–66.

24. Ibid., 2 : 105–20.

25. Donald Reiman, ed., *The Romantics Reviewed: Contemporary Reviews of British Romantic Writers*, 5 vols. (New York: Garland Publishing, 1972), 1843.

26. Jerome Christensen and Andrew Elfenbein argue that Byron makes use of

homosexual allusions in his work to create a more marketable "mysterious style"—what Elfenbein calls "the shady side of the sword." For Elfenbein, "being *perceived* as homosexual could function as positive symbolic capital" (*Byron and the Victorians,* 207). A keen reader of homoeroticism in Byron's poem, Christensen shows how the Duchess Fitz-Fulke's name can be read as a homonym (*Lord Byron's Strength,* 342). My interest in this essay is not limited to Byron's literary strategies. The literary and the biographical were too closely connected in Byron's career for us to avoid defining the nature of his narrator because we might risk essentializing Byron's sexuality. Even Elfenbein and Christensen, who seem intent on avoiding "essentialist assumptions" (Elfenbein 206) about Byron, fall back on such assumptions when analyzing Byron's sexual practice (Elfenbein 206; Christensen 376).

27. Leslie Marchand, ed. , *Byron's Letters and Journals,* 12 vols. (Cambridge: Harvard University Press, 1973–82), 22 June [1809] 1 : 207; hereafter cited as *BLJ.*

28. Crompton, *Byron and Greek Love,* 129.

29. Jerome Christensen describes this as a literary strategy rather than part of a gay identity (*Lord Byron's Strength,* 60) and faults Crompton for not distinguishing between gay and homosexual. Yet Christensen separates the literary and the personal more rigidly than Byron did, seeing Byron as motivated by his career rather than his physical drives. The same critics who object to essentializing Byron are the first to fall back on essentialism when they make arguments about what Byron would or would not do in a given sexual encounter (see Christensen 376).

30. Doris Langley Moore, *The Late Lord Byron: Posthumous Dramas* (Philadelphia: Lippincott's, 1957), 243.

31. Harold Bloom and Lionel Trilling, eds., *Romantic Poetry and Prose* (New York: Oxford University Press, 1973), 285.

32. Peter Manning's Freudian study, *Byron & His Fictions,* comes the closest to unmasking Byron's sexual imagination, but does not find his homoeroticism as compelling or important as I do. Even critics who have focused specifically on Byron's narrator have avoided coming to terms with his sexuality.

33. Susan Wolfson, " 'Their She Condition': Cross-Dressing and the Politics of Gender in *Don Juan*" in *Recent Romantic Revisionary Poetry Criticism,* eds. by Gene Ruoff and Karl Kroeben (New Brunswick: Rutgers University Press, 1993), 268.

34. Judith Butler, *Gender Trouble: Feminism and the Subversion of Identity* (New York: Routledge, 1990), 148.

35. William Marshall, *The Structure of Byron's Major Poems,* 176.

36. George Ridenour, "The Mode of Byron's *Don Juan*" *PMLA* 79, no. 4 (September 1964): 443. I am in fundamental agreement with Ridenour's position as expressed in *The Style of Don Juan,* though I would add that this speaker changes after cantos 1 and 2. My purpose in this essay is to focus on what I consider to be a neglected topic: the narrator's sexual orientation.

37. Nancy Benson, "Hero & Narrator in Byron's *Don Juan,*" 38.

38. David Parker, "The Narrator of *Don Juan,*" 49.

39. Kim Michasiw, "The Social Other," 37.

40. Ibid., 39.

41. *Morning Chronicle,* 6 December 1814.

42. Sedgwick traces the roots of this unintelligibility in Billy Budd and Dorian Gray, noting its origin in "St. Paul's . . . denomination of sodomy as the crime whose name is not be uttered" and Lord Alfred Douglas's "epochal public utterance, in 1894, 'I *am* the Love that dare not speak its name' " (*Epistemology of the Closet* 74).

43. Byron did not want to call attention to his passionate friendships with young men. His poems to John Edleston and others were concealed and redirected toward women. Arthur invites Byron to consider the fact that there is a "heaven" in store for him, a place where he can lament his loss in love without sinning against social propriety. Matthews, to use Judith Butler's phrase, is not a body that matters. On the use of cryptograms in *Don Juan*, see Cecil Lang ("Narcissus Jilted: Byron, *Don Juan,* & The Biographical Imperative," 165).

44. One might say that the intense lament about growing up that appears so regularly in Byron's poetry is informed by a reluctance to leave the world at Harrow, where homosocial contact was allowed a freer range than at Cambridge, where it was concealed by means of coded exchanges.

45. David Greenberg, *The Construction of Homosexuality* (Chicago: University of Chicago Press, 1988), 310.

46. Byron, *Don Juan*, 5 : 158.

47. Marchand, *Byron: A Portrait*, 335.

48. Elfenbein, *Byron and the Victorians* 44. McGann also equates Byron with the narrator (*"Don Juan" in Context,* 66).

49. A biographical reading of the narrator is tempting, especially when we consider that Lady Blessington found Byron's "voice and accent . . . somewhat effeminate . . . [H]e is too gay, too flippant for a poet" (Lovell 350), she observed. Blessington hints at the constellation of characteristics we associate with the word "gay" long before its twentieth-century use became current. The *OED* records 1935 as the first year in which the word "gay" was used to describe a "homosexual." The citation is from N. Ersine's *Underworld and Prison Slang (OED* 6 : 409).

50. Hoagwood, *Byron's Dialectic:* 15, 152.

51. Marchand, *BLJ*, 39.

52. Ibid., 38.

53. Michasiw does not distinguish between the storyteller and the Byron figure.

54. Marchand, *BLJ*, 39.

55. Byron, *Don Juan*, 1 : 6–7.

56. McGann's influential *Don Juan in Context* argues that the poem follows the "rhetorical rules of decorum" and that Cantos 1 and 2 imitate "the Horatian plain style" (73). Such an interpretation leaves unexplained the "intermixture of ribaldry and blasphemy" which the *Edinburgh Magazine* noted even in cantos 3, 4, and 5 (review of August 1821; Rutherford, *Byron: The Critical Heritage*, 260), and which Murray called "outrageously shocking" (Marchand, *Portrait*, 390).

57. Byron, *Don Juan*, 1 : 6.

58. Ibid., 9 : 30.

59. Ibid., 1 : 7

60. Ibid., 1 : 9.

61. Ibid., 13 : 23.

62. Ibid., 13 : 23.

63. One could be forgiven for making this assumption, since many other characters in the poem comment on his effeminacy. Julia's maid, Antonia, wonders at Julia's "taste" (1 : 172) in choosing such a young boy with girlish features and a high voice; the Sultan ogles him (5 : 156); and the diplomats "[t]hought . . . / That they as easily might *do* the youngster . . ." (11 : 35).

64. George Ridenour shows how seemingly random digressions are united by thematic links in a fine discussion of the use of the "fall" as a metaphor for spiritual, metaphysical, and poetic flights (22–23). McGann's stress on the random na-

ture of the poem's composition—"the 'unplanned' manner [which] persists, even to an extremity" (67)—distracts him (I believe) from appreciating the aesthetic achievement of the final result (66).

65. Lang, "Narcissus Jilted," 160.
66. 12 November 1809; 1 : 227–228.
67. Wolfson, " 'Their She Condition,' " 286.
68. Ibid., 284.
69. Ibid., 267.
70. John Hunt was, in fact, prosecuted for publishing *The Vision of Judgment,* and Byron offered him legal aid as well as a promise to stand trial in an English court if necessary (Marchand, *Portrait,* 393).
71. See Elfenbein for a fine discussion of the "radical aristocratic ethos" and "homosexual performativity" of the poem (46); Marchand, *Portrait,* 396; Mc-Gann, *Complete Poetical Works,* 5 : 714.
72. Byron, *Don Juan,* 1 : 9.
73. Ibid., 1 : 51.
74. Ibid., 13 : 73.
75. Horace, *Ars Poetica, Critical Theory Since Plato,* ed. Hazard Adams (New York: Harcourt, Brace, Jovanovich, 1992), 70.
76. Byron, *Don Juan,* 1 : 204.
77. Ibid., 13 : 73.
78. Ibid., 9 : 76.
79. In his use of the phrase, "that clause is hard," Byron probably also had in mind Dante's reaction to the "hard" truth of the inscription on the gates of Hell, *"Dinanzi a me non fuor cose create / Se non etterne, e io etterna duro. / Lasciate ogni speranza, voi ch'intrate"* (3 : 7–9) [Before me nothing but eternal things / Were made, and I endure eternally. / Abandon every hope, who enter here (Dante, *Inferno* (3 : 7–9)]. Dante turns to his guide, Virgil, and states, *"Maestro, is senso lor m'e duro"* [its meaning is hard to understand / accept] which plays off of the other cognate of the word, *"io etterna duro"* [eternal I endure]. Byron saw a copy of Dante's *Inferno* on Teresa Guiccioli's desk in 1819. They read together a passage that occurs only two cantos later in the poem: "what was already a favorite passage of Byron's, and what seemed to parallel their own situation so closely, the episode of Paolo and Francesca," Leslie Marchand observes. "Byron later wrote his own translation of it" (*Portrait* 305).
80. Lang locates the moment of "sexual awareness" in Canto 9 and makes a compelling case ("Narcissus Jilted," 166). Juan's response to his encounter with the Duchess Fitz-Fulke is much more dramatic than his reaction to Catherine, however, which seems blasé and jaded. For this reason, I see canto 17 rather than canto 9 as the moment of Juan's *anagnorisis.*
81. McGann, *Complete Poetical Works,* 5 : 761.
82. 17 : 14 : 108 and 17 : 14. What makes the encounter with the Duchess Fitz-Fulke particularly striking is the extent to which Juan has resisted the truth of his own effeminacy before this point. Everyone seems to notice it but him. As early as canto 1, Antonia rebukes Julia for preferring the "half-girlish face" of Juan to a "stout cavalier" (1 : 171–172); the narrator notes that he "blasphemed an octave higher" than Don Alfonso (1 : 184); Haidée, "tall beyond her sex" (4 : 43) protects him from her father's wrath (4 : 42); Baba dresses him as a young girl and Juan must inform him "I'm not a lady" (5 : 73); Dudu accepts him as "Juan, or Juanna" (6 : 57) in part because his "Gender still was Epicene" (6 : 58); Gulbeyaz *must* ask him, "Christian cast thou love?" when he appears before her in feminine attire and

his sentimental response (he "burst[s] into tears" [5 : 117]) indicates that he cannot. In Russia, Catherine clearly enjoys playing a dominant role with the young man (*his* sexual prowess is not specified), before exhausting him so much that she must pack him off to England.

83. Edward Said, *Beginnings: Intentions & Method* (New York: Columbia Univ. Press, 1985), 43.

84. Byron, *Don Juan*, 12 : 54.

85. Phyllis Grosskurth, *Byron: The Flawed Angel* (New York: Houghton-Mifflin, 1997), 1.

86. Prologue 1–3.

87. Diana Fuss, *Inside Out: Lesbian Theories, Gay Theories* (New York, Routledge, 1991), 4.

88. Jonathan Dollimore, *Sexual Dissidence: Augustine to Wilde, Freud to Foucault* (Oxford: Clarendon Press, 1991), 176.

89. Crompton, *Byron & Greek Love,* 14.

90. Byron, *Don Juan*, 1 : 1.

91. Peter Graham, *Don Juan and Regency England* (Charlottesville: University of Virginia Press, 1990), 80.

92. Byron, *Don Juan*, 9 : 53.

93. "Don Juan's Earliest Scrape" appeared as act 2 of "One Fatal Swoon," Jermyn Street Theater, 4 December 1996. The play was adapted for the stage by Carole Bremson and directed by Mary Elliott Nelson.

94. McGann, *Complete Poetical Works*, 2 : 209–10.

95. Alexander Nehemas and Paul Woodruff, eds. *Plato: The Symposium* (Indianapolis: Hackett Publishing Co. , 1989), 191 E–92.

96. John Boswell, *Christianity, Social Tolerance, and Homosexuality* (Chicago: University of Chicago Press, 1980), 48.

97. The expurgated textbooks of Don Juan which once contained the homoerotic verse of Ovid and Sappho are the master trope for the narrator's pantomime in canto 1.

98. Byron, *Don Juan*, 1 : 52–53.

99. Ibid., 1 : 53.

100. Harriet Beecher Stowe, *Lady Byron Vindicated* (London: Sampson Low, 1870), 164.

101. Crompton, 93.

102. Ibid., 87.

103. Byron, *Don Juan*, 14 : 13, and 11 : 88.

104. Ibid., 2 : 165.

105. Ibid., 2 : 164.

106. Ibid., 2 : 166. Just as Julia stands in the way of Juan's wrestling with Alfonso, so does Haidée disrupt the sword fight between Juan and Lambro. In both cases, the conflicts "between men," to use Eve Sedgwick's phrase, seem even more erotically charged than do Juan's affairs with women.

107. T. G. Steffan, E. Steffan, and W. W. Pratt, eds., *Lord Byron; Don Juan* (London: Penguin, 1957), 40.

108. 19 September 1818; 6 : 67.

109. Marchand, *Portrait*, 292.

110. Rutherford, *Byron, A Critical Study*, 123–42.

111. Byron, *Don Juan*, 4 : 97

112. Jones 2 : 42; Rutherford, *Byron: The Critical Heritage,* 160.

113. Jones 2 : 330.

114. Ibid., 2 : 58
115. August [10?], 1821; Shelley, *Letters*, 2 : 330.
116. Marchand, *Portrait*, 298.
117. Cantos 1 and 2 were written between 3 July and 6 September 1818, while cantos 3, 4, and 5 were written between 17 September 1819 and 26 December 1820. My argument is that having met Teresa Guiccioli in April 1819, Byron responded to her influence, as well as the suggestions of his friends, when he composed cantos 3–17 of the poem; 7 February 1820; *BLJ* 7 : 82, 35.
118. 26 October 1819; 6 : 232.
119. Byron, *Don Juan*, 1 : 99.
120. Ibid., 6 : 24–25.
121. Ibid., 14 : 69.
122. Ibid., 8 : 147.
123. Leslie Marchand notes that she read the first 2 stanzas in a French translation and excerpts in the Milan Gazzetta (5 and 6 July 1821; *Portrait,* 344).
124. Marchand, *BLJ*, 10 October 1819; Byron, *Don Juan* 6 : 257.
125. Marchand, *BLJ*, 4 November 1812; Byron, *Don Juan* 2 : 239.
126. Marchand, *BLJ*, 20 September 1814; Byron, *Don Juan* 4 : 178.
127. Byron, *Don Juan*, 5 : 136.
128. Leslie Marchand points out that the phrase comes from a song by Charles Dibdin, "The Snug Little Island," in a musical play called *The British Raft* (1797) (5 : 136).
129. Byron, *Don Juan*, 6 : 27.
130. 2 : 193; Jerome Christensen (64–65) has shown how two other letters connect swimming and homoeroticism in less "mechanical" ways. In the first letter addressed to Hobhouse, Byron describes Signore Nicolo as a "bad . . . hand in the water" (23 August 1810; 2 : 14); in the second, to John Murray, he recounts Shelley's refusal to allow Byron to "save him" from drowning during a stormy day (15 May 1819; 6 : 126).
131. Grosskurth, *Byron: The Flawed Angel,* 223.
132. Marchand, *BLJ*, 10 September 1812; Byron, *Don Juan* 2 : 193.
133. Byron, *Don Juan*, 5 : 132.
134. Ibid., 10 : 72 : 576.
135. Marchand, *BLJ*, 12 August 1819; 6 : 208.
136. The narrator "establishes" his gay identity by comparing himself to other figures involved in homoerotic relationships whose sexuality is ambiguous: Socrates' erotic friendship with Alcibiades; Tiresias' bisexual experience; his own friendship with a monk who has gone to seed (14:81). He tells us that "[s]ome truths are better kept behind a screen, / Especially when they would look like lies; / I therefore deal in generalities" (14 : 80).
137. Byron, *Don Juan*, 8 : 137.
138. Leslie Marchand, "Narrator and Narration in *Don Juan*," *Keats-Shelley Journal* 25 (1976): 35.
139. Byron, *Don Juan*, 9 : 53.
140. Ibid., 11 : 88.
141. Ibid.
142. Marchand, *Byron: A Portrait,* 451.
143. See Karl Kroeber's stimulating discussion of this poem in *Ecological Literary Criticism: Romantic Imagining and the Biology of Mind* (New York: Columbia University Press, 1994): 4–5.
144. Marchand, *BLJ*, 7 September 1811; Byron, *Don Juan*, 2 : 93.

145. Elfenbein, *Byron & The Victorians*, 207.

146. Horace Walpole, *Horace Walpole's Correspondence*, 1 : 343.

147. Terry Castle, *Masquerade & Civilization: The Carnivalesque in Eighteenth Century English Culture & Fiction* (Stanford: Stanford Univ. Press, 1986), 4–5.

148. Leslie Marchand, *Byron's Letters & Journals*, 23 August 1819; 6 : 214.

149. Gross, "Byron & the Liberals," 115–18.

150. William St. Clair, *Lord Elgin & the Marbles* (Oxford: Oxford Univ. Press, 1973), 151.

151. Marchand, *Byron's Letters & Journals*, 1 : 233n; Lang, "Narcissus Jilted," 146.

152. *Childe Harold's Pilgrimage*, 1 : 22; see Christensen, *Lord Byron's Strength*, 66.

153. Watkins questions whether romanticism's "masculine identity" "appropriates and subordinates feminity." His concern with violence and sexual power, as well as his focus on Wordsworth, Coleridge, and Keats, differs from my own (xii).

154. Peter Thorslev, *The Byronic Hero* (Minneapolis: University of Minnesota Press, 1982).

Writing Between Life and Death:
Postmetaphysics and the Psychosexual
Dynamics of Elegy in Shelley's *Adonais*

FREDERICK GREENE

PERCY SHELLEY'S *ADONAIS* (1821), AS BOTH ARTWORK AND HISTORI-
cal document, may be profitably examined by those interested in
understanding the social complex of masculine subjectivity and its
component sexuality in early nineteenth-century England. But this
exquisitely accomplished pastoral elegy is not necessarily representative of the cultural experience and norms of masculine subjectivity during the period in which it was written. Because of its
idiosyncrasy and particularity, it instructively testifies to reconfigurations and contestations of masculinity occurring contemporane-
ously, as well as to the concerns and cultural anxieties framing such
phenomena. This essay is, among other things, a demonstration of
that thesis.[1]

In methodology, I proceed along queer theoretical lines for a variety of reasons. Preeminent among these is my belief that the pastoral elegy is a queer kind; a hybrid, syncretic form, the pastoral
elegy anticipates queer theoretical analyses through its own deconstructive dynamics, allegorical plurality, and (often subversive) critical capacity and tradition. Moreover, the homoeroticism of the
elegy tradition (latent or otherwise) and my focus on the experi-
ence/representation of masculine sexuality encourage such an approach. Finally, I am influenced by the poem itself: in *Adonais*, the
widespread characterization of Shelley as a poetical, philosophical,
and political radical suggests that the choice of pastoral for Keats's
eulogy serves a purpose other than the traditional obsequy. The
conventional form of the pastoral elegy affords Shelley—a writer
intimate with its history and critical capability—the ideal venue for
articulating a new theory of language, revising Platonic metaphysics, and reanimating a model of masculinity and same-sex relations
that was increasingly under attack.

Published a generation after Wordsworth's redefinition and redirection of poetry in his "Preface" to *Lyrical Ballads*, Percy Shelley's "*Adonais*, An elegy on the Death of John Keats, Author of Endymion, Hyperion, etc." rejects the stylistic prescriptions of that work. Shelley's poem does not use the "real language of men," nor is it sparing with convention, metrically simple, or easily digestible by nonclassically educated readers. Preoccupied with more abstract political and philosophical matters than challenging Augustan poetic convention and inaccessibility, Shelley's "highly wrought piece of art" uses Keats's funereal lament to consider the nature of life, language, death, and immortality.[2] An ambitious goal, perhaps, but hardly an indecorous one, insofar as the pastoral elegy had long been the canonical mode of mourning, whereby a (typically male) poet laments the untimely loss of a fellow (and typically male) poet and countenances, albeit vicariously, his own mortality. As such, the tradition affords a splendid array of formulas, figures, and responses that have been found transhistorically useful for mitigating grief and producing consolation. But Shelley's poem goes one step further: in the process of engaging the tradition and contributing to its historical development, *Adonais* explores the poetics and the putative consolation of pastoral elegy while inscribing a specific account of masculine subjectivity and sexuality.

Given the widespread attention to *Adonais'* Platonism, Jerrold Hogle's account of Shelley's personal, philosophic, and professional (poetic) radicalism is an investigation of that intellectual appropriation requiring our attention. After all, one may justifiably question how radical a political program based on neo-Platonic idealism or on Shelley's insistent privileging of the "One" and the "Power" could be. In *Shelley's Process*, Hogle makes a compelling argument that, despite the vocabulary of Platonism, Shelley's appropriation of it results in radical alteration of its philosophical and political message. Because I am persuaded by Hogle's study and because the interpretation of masculine sexuality that we distill from *Adonais* depends on understanding Shelley's reconceptualization of life, death, language, and immortality, I want to rehearse Hogle's claims about Shelley's poetry and neo-Platonism as support for my arguments concerning *Adonais'* work of mourning.[3]

According to Hogle, Shelley's writing is characterized by the "carrying forward" motion of the mind (and of the ideas and language that constitute it), the shift between mental positions or states of mind. This dynamic that he first calls "transpositional drive," is later renamed "transference."[4] This transference, then, forms a "decentered" center "for Shelleyan thought. . . . [I]t is a primordial, preconscious shift, intimated in the movement of perception, feeling, and language, always already becoming a different enactment of itself at another time and in conjunction with other elements."[5]

Transference, as used by Hogle (and distinguished from Freud's sense), describes Shelley's conception of the relationship between ourselves and others and his understanding of the structure of the mind and perception. It also explains Shelley's style wherein "verbal figures are continually dissolving and thus questioning their structures before any one of them has a chance to seem complete."[6] In other words, Shelley postulates that difference is the basis of cognition, that we only perceive an object or thought when it is no longer present to us or when our attention has shifted or been transferred to some other object or thought. "[E]ach basic thought is still a motion between at least two 'externalities.' It is a drive toward a counterpart rising ahead of it and a hearkening back to a different one receding in its wake."[7]

The consequences of this theory of subjectivity and language are many and profound: Shelley would have it that "a person is especially multiple, and not just because 'he' or 'she' is a succession of differentiations worked out by language as each word passes toward a future and looks back to a past," but because a person "is a self-interpreting and interpretable figure in bodily form, something far more social than individual."[8] For Shelley, the self always presupposes its others and thus, "as a fabrication defined only in its own terms [the self] is really an illusion, a willed perversion of its own defining process. It is the 'Mammon of the world.' "[9] In his literary work, Hogle insists, Shelley's poetic persona makes " 'voice' not the achievement of a unique persona, but the intentional losing of it within the onslaught of tropic possibilities emerging in the language he employs."[10] What energizes and characterizes Shelley's poetry in Hogle's judgment, therefore, is his philosophical refusal of rigidity and hierarchy (whether of class, or self, or figure), his analytical fascination with the desire for subjection to tyranny, and his vision of self-surpassing empathy.

To reread *Adonais* after Hogle is to encounter a markedly different text than it may have seemed before: for example, "Spirit," also called the soul, the "One," or an "energy," may be reinterpreted as a force of becoming, not being, and redefined by its movement, extension, crossings, and interpenetrations instead of by its permanence, purity, or "undifferentiated unity." Such claims concerning Shelley's neo-Platonism change the relationship between *Adonais* and the elegiacal tradition and enable a reconceptualization of the poem's account of masculine subjectivity.[11]

"Midst others of less note, came one frail Form," is Shelley's third-person introduction of his mourning persona.[12] "Companion-less" and pursued by his poetic progeny, with withering cheek and "branded and ensanguined brow," the poet has lost confidence in reproductive immortalization.[13] The meditative stanzas on his son's grave in a Roman cemetery imply that the condition for the confident assertion made a few stanzas earlier has not been met: "And many more, whose names on Earth are dark / But whose transmitted effluence cannot die / *So long* as fire outlives the parent spark."[14] Earlier, Urania's impotence with respect to her son, Adonais, mirrors the poetic persona's uncertainty about obtaining immortality through one's children.[15]

Instead, Shelley's *Adonais* puts faith in the immortalizing power of poetry in its least transcendental but most compelling version. According to this conception, it is the transhistorical community of poets and readers, the linkage of artistic endeavor and consciousness through songs, poems, and narratives that approximates immortality itself.[16] Indeed, writing in *A Defence of Poetry* a few months earlier in 1821, Shelley first articulated his notion of the "'great poem' created by many successive authors 'like the co-operating thought of one great mind.'"[17] One benefit of being in such a literary community is that those capable of fashioning such immortalizing machines are themselves eligible to be praised, honored, and memorialized. In *Adonais*, this anticipated reward is never far from Shelley's mind.

Shelley's gambit to achieve membership in the immortal ranks of poets is typical of the tradition and indicative of the individual: with characteristic hubris, he claims it. And, in *Adonais*, as in other famous pastoral elegies, Shelley supports his claim to immortalization by manifesting his ability to immortalize. After all, it is Shelley who places Keats among the immortal, enabling him to reciprocate, as the last lines of the poem so plainly indicate:

> The soul of Adonais, like a star,
> Beacons from the abode where the Eternal are.[18]

Indeed, Shelley's confidence is apparent as early as stanza one; he apostrophizes:

> And thou, sad Hour, selected from all years
> To mourn our loss, rouse thy obscure compeers,
> And teach them thine own sorrow, say: with me
> Died Adonais; till the Future dares

> Forget the Past, his fate and fame shall be
> An echo and a light unto eternity![19]

First, note the pronouncement upon Keats's fate and fame (ll. 8–9). By the conclusion, Keats becomes the echo and the light, a star that "Beacons from the abode where the Eternal are." Earlier in the stanza (ll. 6–7), Shelley offers a remarkable display of poetic power, ego, and control, due primarily to the lines' wonderful ambiguity: "[S]ay: with me / died Adonais" means that the personified hour—the first mourner, time—is asked to bear the ignominy of coincidence with Keats's demise. Or reading over the colon and breaking more naturally at the line ending, the hour appears to be learning to speak Adonais' death—"Died Adonais"—along with the poet. Or "with me died Adonais" makes the poet the agent of death. It is as if Keats, to be an immortal poet, relies fundamentally on the figural death of Adonais, a death for which Shelley is ultimately responsible. In this first stanza, Shelley demonstrates with exquisite subtlety the ambivalent relationship of love and rivalry that often exists between the dead friend or beloved and the live commemorating artist.[20]

Shelley's relationship to Keats, because severed by death, leaves in its wake an accumulation of affect (grief, relief, disbelief, rage, etc.) that needs to be processed and expressed by the survivor. As is often the case, the lost object of attachment is subject to an additional distortion of memory, both as a defensive distancing of the self from mortality and as a manifestation of a temporary triumph. In *Adonais*, Shelley exercises his anxiety of influence through Urania's description of Keats as an immature poet with great potential:

> "Oh gentle child, beautiful as thou wert,
> Why didst thou leave the trodden paths of men
> Too soon, and with *weak hands though mighty heart*
> Dare the unpastured dragon in his den?
> *Defenseless* as thou wert. . . .
>
> . . . .
> Or hadst thou *waited the full cycle*, when
> Thy spirit should have filled its crescent sphere,
> The monsters of life's waste had fled from thee like deer."[21]

These apparently sympathetic evocations of Keats's physical weakness and tender age, coupled with the mention of potentially greater but prematurely deceased poets—Sidney, Chatterton, and Lucan—function as backhanded compliments. As part of the defensively articulated work of mourning, the rebuilding of a self which has been traumatized, "Shelley must modify the immortal Keats-Adonais," as Peter Sacks asserts, "so as to reflect and accommodate the immortal Shelley."[22] Here, Shelley's depiction of Keats depends on the conventional understanding of the pastoral as a mode of literary adolescence and relative impotence. The dragon, which seems to represent the difficulties of the epic form and the merciless literary critic, overwhelms the shepherd/poet. Those who could have overcome the barbs of jealous critics and the pitfalls of epic text production are those more mature practitioners of poetry or epic heroes themselves, those with the strength and spirit to "[d]are the un*pastured* dragon in his den," namely Byron and Perseus.[23] That Shelley counts himself among such heroes seems clear, especially insofar as his "spirit's bark['s]" departure from the "trodden paths of men" is a movement out of the pastoral mourning community into a quasi-heroic quest-voyage.

Rounding out the concerns of poetic mourning implicit in elegiacal production—rivalry, self-doubt, dependence, admiration, jealousy—is the topic of same-sex desire, most explicitly presented in the tradition's allusions to and representations of same-sex lovers. Familiar with that convention from having translated Bion's "Lament for Adonis" and Moschus's "Lament for Bion" before writing *Adonais*, Shelley had also undertaken a fascinating if finally unconvincing exculpation of classical Athenian culture from charges of a vicious sexual practice. In "A Discourse on the Manners of the Ancients, Relative to the Subject of Love" (1818), he explains Greek pederasty as the logical solution to the cultural problem of women's subordination: excluded from educational opportunity, women in that culture were ineligible to participate in the highest forms of intellectual and spiritual communion. But what is most interesting about this essay, apart from its protofeminist analysis, is that although Shelley can condone passionate object love between men, he cannot accept the manner that such affection might adopt, namely sodomy: "It is impossible that a lover could usually have subjected the object of his attachment to so detestable a violation or have consented to associate his own remembrance in the beloved mind with images of pain and horror."[24] Shelley speculates that the actual Greek practice was roughly equivalent to shared or mutual wet dreams: "the almost involuntary consequences of a state of abandonment in the society of a person of surpassing attractions."[25] Curiously, this tortured explanation resonates with the masturbatory imagery in the self-presentation of Shelley's mourning persona in stanza 33:

> And a light spear topped with a cypress cone,
> Round whose rude shaft dark ivy tresses grew

Yet dripping with the forest's noonday dew,
Vibrated, as the ever-beating heart
Shook the weak hand that grasped it.[26]

I draw attention to this passage and to the literary context out of which Shelley writes, because the pageant of mourners—a central convention of elegiacal practice—so suggestively reconstitutes a community of men whose relationships with one another are modeled on the Greek ideal of pederasty: erotically invested pedagogical and mentoring relationships between men aspiring to transcendental vision or attainment.[27] Indeed, the more elegies I read and the better I understand the various regimes of masculinity and sexuality under which they were produced, the more apparent it becomes that homoeroticism in pastoral elegy is motivated by reasons other than respect for tradition, the sophomoric delight of enshrining prohibited representations within mainstream cultural representations, or the benefits of asserting class membership.[28] Instead, homoeroticism in pastoral elegy, which is almost invariably figured through classical myth, emblematizes the most salient desire of the mode itself: not eternity through an undifferentiating reproduction or natural cycle, but intellectual and spiritual transcendence obtained through a noble, collective, and historically masculine endeavor. Thus, in turning away from the immortalizing power of reproduction—a power still vulnerable to untimely death—Shelley takes up the ideal and transhistorical community of elegy writing, a community to which women as a class in early nineteenth-century England did not belong.

Whatever the mode whereby Greek love is manifest, whether "diabolical and operose" as is the "vulgar imputation" or merely a mutual, almost innocent reverie, Shelley honors the classical paradigm through his use of Apollo's grief over Hyacinthus (a youth of "surpassing attractions," presumably) as the standard of bereavement against which Autumn's and Spring's mourning for Adonais is measured.[29]

Grief made the young Spring wild . . .
For whom should she have waked the sullen year?
To Phoebus was not Hyacinth so dear
Nor to himself Narcissus, as to both [presumably Echo as well]
Thou Adonais. . . .[30]

Nevertheless, despite the Hellenistic sympathies and veneration for classical models apparent in such allusions, Shelley's "Discourse" indicates that certain sexual practices, albeit endemic to its educational institutions, were frowned upon by early nineteenth-century English society, despite the fondness for its idealization among elites. Sociologist and cultural theorist David Greenberg argues that we can best understand British nineteenth-century attitudes toward homosexuality—its diagnosis, its projection, its prohibition—by examining the economic context that produced it. In *The Construction of Homosexuality*, he focuses on the rise of market economies as the most salient historical influence:

> three developments were particularly important in shaping a distinctly modern response to homosexuality: the growth of competitive capitalism, the rise of modern science, and the spread of bureaucratic principles of social organization. The effects of these developments were contradictory, but their net effect was to strengthen anti-homosexual beliefs and attitudes.[31]

Nor can the French Revolution be ignored for its influence on nineteenth-century British politics and culture, especially during the Romantic period. That "catastrophe" was popularly believed to have been provoked by aristocratic decadence and moral turpitude, both euphemisms for homosexuality. Indeed, Greenberg describes the "repressive tone of the moral climate" of the early decades of the nineteenth century as partly the result of British moral reform movements that drew a direct inference from moral (read, sexual) laxity to political rebelliousness.[32] At the same time, economic imperatives and ideological dictates of the new capitalist economy were urging increased competitiveness, self-restraint, female subordination, and exaltation of the family. Within this context, Greenberg concludes, male children of the emergent middle classes would have been raised in ways that "fostered self-assertiveness and competitiveness, while discouraging such traits as emotional expressiveness, dependence, and nurturance—traits that would have been dysfunctional in the competition."[33]

Against this reconstruction of masculinity and corollary vilification of the homosexual, the skills of the successful poet or literary artist, and especially that of a poetic mourner, must have appeared increasingly abnormal and suspect. Henceforth, even their competitions would have seemed of a different order than those of wage earners.[34] In Shelley's case, we know he suffered personally for his public resistance to emergent norms of morality and masculine comportment; his exile suggests as much. Although it is difficult to assess the impact of economic factors on Shelley's labor because of his privileged class and educational background, the homoeroticism in *Adonais* is explicitly chosen and encomiastically intended within this pastoral elegy.[35] Given his writings on the ancient Greeks, Shelley uses homoerotic representation to signify an idealization of same-sex erotic, intellectual, and spiritual intimacy, despite the fact that such relations were variously sublimated, proscribed, and prosecuted in his own culture.

If the sustained attention to such subject matter is one indication of Shelleyan antinominianism, his comparison of Keats to other poets, "all of whom are liberals noted for various forms of resistance to reigning authority," is another.[36] Thus, for Shelley to celebrate Keats's *oeuvre* and radical thought is also to celebrate a similar pursuit in his own work; it suggests a shared political object within their poetics. Hogle names such an objective "the repressed drive for 'unapprehended relations,' " a drive Keats shares with Lucan, Chatterton, and Sidney according to Shelley's reading of their work. Defined as "the pulse of true poetry . . . that has kept generating revolutionary interrelations of figures out of, in defiance of, and in flight from the most established political and symbolic systems," unapprehended relations describe what Shelley seeks to reproduce, represent, and examine in *Adonais*.[37]

At once sublime and abject, unapprehended relations in *Adonais* are fascinating and threatening, abominable like that which juxtaposes and thereby scandalizes category, paradoxical like that which is both sides of an opposition simultaneously.[38] In formal terms, they are the sensible and sensuous overload produced by the tropological, figural, and allusive excess common to pastoral elegy. *Adonais* is literally strewn with such contradictory formulations and descriptions, drunk with its own rhetorical and phonotextual play: the poet/subject represented as both father and prey of his writing, the hunter and the hunted, and later as Cain and/or Christ, murderer and/or savior; the "burning fountain," the "thirst for fire," or Rome as "paradise and grave, city and wilderness." In terms of sound and sense, almost every stanza displays the auditory lushness and the cognitive *frisson* produced by punning or syntactical ambiguity. As poetry, *Adonais* articulates and celebrates what is linguistically indescribable and mentally inapprehensible.

This solicitation in *Adonais* toward that which exceeds or subverts established political and symbolic systems—in the case of Western European culture, typically dualistic and oppositional—corresponds to the expressed political convictions and behavior of Shelley the libertine, atheist, and political radical. Affirming such an intention on the part of the poet is the choice of the pastoral mode for his elegy, a mode whose defining characteristic is the de-construction of binary oppositions and whose signal poetic achieve-ment is the opening out of a space between life and death, speech and silence, where the dead may "live on." The better to anatomize what I have termed *Adonais'* queer work of mourning, I begin with an analysis of Shelley's reimagination of death, seeking thereby to expose such unapprehended relations as are to be traced in his po-etic language but to which only the dead have immediate access.

Instead of recoiling from identification with the dead and denying its power over the deceased, Shelley's poetic persona solicits Keats's benediction and proclaims his envy of the latter's state. Yet according to conventional models of the mourning process, wherein health is equivalent to sublimation and/or renunciation, elegiacal grieving is not supposed to encourage us to seek the primary union represented by death. Nonetheless, that seems to be Shelley's per-verse innovation. Peter Sacks asserts, "It is the very triumph of his mourning imagination, its apparently literal rather than literary thrust, that draws him on to what all mourners most need to avoid—their own drive beyond life and beyond the language whose detours and saving distances keep them alive."[39] For example, consider Shelley's conclusion to *Adonais* in which he offers this astonishing vision:

> The breath whose might I have invoked in song
> Descends on me; my spirit's bark is driven,
> Far from the shore, far from the trembling throng
> Whose sails were never to the tempest given;
> The massy earth and sphered skies are riven!
> I am borne darkly, fearfully, afar:
> Whilst burning through the inmost veil of Heaven,
> The soul of Adonais, like a star,
> Beacons from the abode where the Eternal are.[40]

But is this a suicidal solicitation? Is he acting on the low wind's whispered advice, " 'Tis Adonais calls! Oh, hasten thither"? And, if so, what does such a death-embracing gesture mean?[41] Upon first glance, this conclusion may seem unavoidable; after some study, however, I think we will see that the embarkation is not finally re-ducible to a despairing or self-annihilatory act. Simply put, in writ-ing with fascination and desire about death, Shelley is not actually relinquishing life. Of course the trauma of Keats's death provokes personal anguish and melancholy thoughts, but it also results in po-etic production, a literary clinging to life.

Nominally, Shelley's philosophical solution to the problem of loss and his justification for celebration in the wake of Keats's death exploits neo-Platonic metaphysics and reworks Edmund Spenser's poetic vision in his November *Eclogue* (1579). Shelley names his transcendental and immortalizing force the "One," that "power," even "nature." As the "true reality" concealed by the "dream of life," this power underlying existence is prismatically visible behind or broken up by individual forms that bear the imprint of "the one Spirit's plastic stress."[42] Hence, within *Adonais*, death functions as threshold of reality, a melting of the form and a return to the loving source by the "portion of the loveliness" which had been caught in "th'unwilling dross that checks its flight."[43]

But despite Shelley's transcendental rhetoric, our attention is more forcefully commanded by what separates us from an immediate apprehension of the "One": death and its signifiers. The dead or bleeding body fascinates and propels figuration; and figuration gestures beyond the prison of our "living clay": Urania's feet bleeding flowers as she journeys to Keats's bier, Shelley's pansy-crowned "ensanguined brow," and Keats's flower-strewn corpse. Implicit in such imagery is the mundane but empirically confirmed transformation of death into life according to the natural cycle whereby matter is endlessly reprocessed—that is, wasted bodies supplying the materials for luxuriant vegetable existence.[44] Reflecting on this indifferent kind of immortalization, however, Shelley finds it unthinkable that the body could be endlessly inspirited and reused and thereby partake of eternity while the essence of man— the soul or spirit in our body—remains finite. The poet asks:

> Nought we know, dies. Shall that alone which knows
> Be as a sword consumed before the sheath
> By sightless lightning?[45]

The answer to this rhetorical question is "of course not." For Shelley, the essence of man is to know; that is how the "spirit" expresses itself within the form of "cold clay" that is our body.

But man's knowing (accomplished through representing, ordering, and apprehending) presupposes difference and plurality.[46] This plurality seems a contradictory expression of the "One," a contradiction internal to any attempt to represent it, but one that appears both to frustrate and to energize Shelley. The closing stanzas narrate a wish to leave figuration for illumination, to get beyond the mediation of a dome of many coloured glass, . . . the web of being" to something at once substantially real and transcendental.[47] However, this desire is impossible to achieve in language, because to posit what we need to get beyond, say, figuration or language in its difference, Shelley has no alternative but language and figuration.

This catch-22 in which Shelley appears to be enmired is not, it seems to me, irresolvable. Indeed, I think Hogle is right to read *Adonais* as a radical redefinition of "the One," rather than as a paean to paradox. Instead of a static metaphysical ground, the kind of "One" that Shelley describes is a "'One' of never-ending change." In other words, "the true most beneficial 'One' is really the movement of transference across and through all existence as perceived."[48] Redefining the "One" in this manner transforms what looks like a desperate survey of figures in search of an adequate representation, into a demonstration of the process of becoming that Shelley believes the "One" to be; difference and association are its traces, not its negation.

Perhaps Shelley's most audacious attempt to break through or beyond figuration by means of representation, to imitate the transferential slide of the "One," is made by the reversal of conventional categories and definitions in stanza 39. This assault on experience redefines "death" through an inversion of its ordinary sense and a deconstructive proliferation of its analogues.[49]

> Peace, peace! he is not dead, he doth not sleep—
> He hath awakened from the dream of life—
> 'Tis we, who lost in stormy visions, keep
> With phantoms an unprofitable strife,
> And in mad trance, strike with our spirit's knife
> Invulnerable nothings.—*We* decay
> Like corpses in a charnel; fear and grief
> Convulse us and consume us day by day,
> And cold hopes swarm like worms within our living clay.[50]

Shelley feverishly affirms that Keats is neither dead nor sleeping, but beyond life's decay and awakened into a transcendent reality. Putrefaction and nightmarish dreams are not his; those are not the correlates of his state, which in this stanza is articulated negatively. Rather, dreams, visions, trances, worms, and decay are the conditions of our sleep and our bodily dereliction as readers, mourners, and survivors. This stanza stands as the point of reversal within the movement of the poem, the realization that death means something different than we originally thought.

Indeed, the "dream of life" from which Shelley hopes soon to awaken is described using one figure after another from the poem:

"stormy visions"; "invulnerable nothings" (another name for poetic figures); phantoms in a mourning procession; corpses in a char-
nel; or "cold hopes" (desires producing belief in immortality).
These figures conventionally associated with death, Shelley finds
more appropriate to the description of life and, not coincidentally,
of elegy. Given Shelley's belief that analogy is the "foundation of
all our inferences, from one idea to another," it is only logical that
representations of death will utilize materials available to the living.[51] Thus, in the climax of the elegy, where the denial of death's
victory occurs, Shelley makes clear that what we know about death
is mostly projection, derived from the empirical information we
have concerning dead bodies. What *Adonais* awakens into is inapprehensible, because we do not have images, memories, or sensations pertaining to it.[52]

Attending to the lesson of this stanza and recalling our own appreciation of death's abjection—its status as neither subject nor object is partly what motivates our attempts to situate it through
elegiacal reading and writing—it seems that death is best understood as the transpositional gap between apprehensible states, ideas,
and forms: a nothing that in its interposition makes what is before
and after perceptible. Yet it is a more significant blank space than
those ordinarily intruding between mental states, words, or ideas,
because it seals one mode of "living" from another. Death as a
threshold divides the dream of life from the awakening into a larger,
atemporal reality.

Shelley's redefinition of death as threshold puts what is before
death and what is after it on par; both may be conceptualized as a
series of becomings. In *Adonais*, the movement of spirit links subjective experience across the space of death. Certainly, a problem
with this account is that it still subordinates life as we know it to
the splendor and dazzling immortality of being "made one with Nature," thereby echoing Christian and metaphysical death worship.
Yet insofar as the "One" has been desacralized, reinterpreted as a
continuous becoming modeled on the cyclical alteration of nature,
Shelleyan transcendence is immanently so. And because in writing
we can discern the nature of the "One," we have some foreknowl-
edge of the eternal and multiplicitous "One" within poetic language. Consider, for example,

> Rome's azure sky,
> Flowers, ruins, statues, music, words, are weak
> The glory they transfuse with fitting truth to speak.[53]

Alerted to Shelley's interest in something other than the words themselves by the adjective "weak," our attention shifts to the relations between them. In the passage from sky to flowers to ruins to statues, the "one"—transfused or poured from one to the other—exists or is manifest. The deferral of words and of figures, their crossing, arising, and fading is the spirit's movement and stasis. Indeed, the eternal spirit signifies its presence through the syntactical process whereby these distinctly different nouns become apposite. Shelley's claim about their impotence as words suggests that it is their metonymical relationship that best approximates his vision of a postmetaphyscial "One."[54]

"No more let Life divide what Death can join together," pronounces the poetic persona.[55] As the transpositional threshold to the associative movement of the "One," death describes a time and a space between perception, memory, and event, rather than *a* or *the* thing itself. An abject zone where boundaries are not respected and where meaning constituted according to category and opposition breaks down, death is a cipher that nonetheless determines meaning on either side of itself.

Shelley hints at what is joined together on the other side of death, the becoming everything of the "One," by forging another chain of identifications among non-synonymous words. The series of nouns in stanza 54, "Light," "Beauty," "Benediction," "Love," "Fire," and "Breath," demonstrates this phenomenon of deferral and becoming as each term gives rise to and in turn cedes to the next:

> That light whose smile kindles the Universe,
> That Beauty in which all things work and move,
> That Benediction which the eclipsing Curse
> Of birth can quench not, that sustaining Love
> Which through the web of being blindly wove
> By man and beast and earth and air and sea,
> Burns bright or dim, as each are mirrors of
> The fire for which all thirst; now beams on me,
> Consuming the last clouds of cold mortality.[56]

Their accompanying verbs, "kindles," "work," and "move," "burns bright or dim," "thirst," "descends," literalize the activity, motion, and process that Hogle calls transference and that Shelley understands as the dynamic of writing.

Developing his interest in showing and enacting rather than telling, Shelley reconceptualizes the "One" by the lyrical agrammaticality of the last line, "Where the Eternal are." The startling lack of agreement points directly at Shelley's reimagination of "Spirit." His eternal "One" is only perceptible in its dislocation from one instant of awareness into a different one, in the passage between figures and in the record of becoming that poetry can preserve. Because difference and plurality are requisite for the apprehension of the "One," the eternal as the associative force by which the particular becomes everything is a one that is many. Conceptually the "One" can only be grasped in relation to other matters which it also is or will become. In the movement through everything "the Eternal" ("the One") *are*.

Shelley's *Adonais*—as poem, cultural artifact, and impression of male subjectivity during the Romantic period—should be understood as, in part, a response to the multiple and contradictory claims that pastoral elegy makes on authorship, poetic language, genre, and representation. As biography, it is an uncanny reflection of Shelley's own experience, philosophical demons, and artistic ambition. Approached historically, the poem shows itself as a transition text, disciplined by the residual imperatives of a pre-capitalist and classically oriented aesthetic but reflexively attuned to the reconfigurations of gender, self, community, and art occasioned by the rise of market capitalism and the reorientation of society toward the future. Breaking with the Christian immortalization of the tradition, however, *Adonais* offers consolation of an intellectualized rather than religious spiritualism. But in keeping with convention, *Adonais* also provides figural means and textual methods of "living-on." Yet even as it espouses a radical political philosophy, *Adonais* bristles with classical learning and recondite reference, appearing largely indifferent to questions of accessibility to the newly literate. Lastly, artistic self-assertion reaches new and potentially troubling heights, even within the elegy's competitive tradition: in *Adonais*, the isolated poet claims the mourning mantle from the procession of his fellow poets, ostensibly discounting their contributions in the closing stanzas of the poem.[57]

In fact, greater psychological complexity, individuation, and intimations of a vast interiority within its narrative persona distinguish this elegy from its predecessors and correspond to the emergence in this period of psychological science and modern subjectivity: a *subject for* who is also *subject to* the state, the economy, and mass society. Yet insofar as Shelley's emotional display has been aestheticized, displaced from the public arena into the increasingly private world of literature, this text is not an exception to the limitation and repression of emotional expressiveness that Greenberg describes as consequences of early market capitalism. Indeed, if one lasting and deleterious effect of the new gender dispensation of the early nineteenth century was to dissociate men from capacities of nuturance, empathy, and interdependence that they and the political world they were fashioning needed desperately, it may be that those capacities were entrusted to the elegy and sealed off from everyday life, only to be reanimated when "occasion drear" required that they be experienced vicariously as art.[58]

Nonetheless, Shelley's performance of the initiatory rites of the pastoral elegy suggests how this most artificial of poetic modes elaborates an alternative model of masculine subjectivity—one whose manifestly erotic homosociality and affective displays contrasted with the emerging norms and suppressed eroticism of competitive individualism. Although effectively limited to mutual transports of intellectual reverie and the occasional mourning gesture, same-sex intimacy, and erotic investment are figured within *Adonais* as a *mise-en-abyme* of the function and value of elegiacal tradition itself; they mark a convening of community necessary to transcendental vision and immortality. As in all elegiacal productions, the dependency of the self on the language of others—indeed that self's constitution by words and text—is a distinctive feature of *Adonais*. Furthermore, by positing death as a continuation of being and a mode of existence analogous to the "dream of life," Shelley denies the mutual exclusivity of binary opposition. Androgynous representations and homoerotic allusion in *Adonais* show how proximate ostensibly polar notions can be and how fluid the expressions of masculinity based on them often are.[59]

Shelley's redefinition of the "One"—a term whose theological and metaphysical baggage must give us pause—makes of that word something dynamic, unfamiliar, and queer. This Shelleyan "One" describes an ineffable movement and differentiation, a state of betweenness, that can never be as named, because our very perception of it is at the same time the awareness that it has been displaced. The "One" as becoming instead of being, movement instead of stasis, is already an ironic, oxymoronic coinage. To die, then, is to continue an endless series of transformations concealed behind the becoming of death, the threshold between corporeal and finite life and the endless life for which words and texts offer our best approximation. *Adonais* works to foreground and dissolve this distinction between the living and the dead, between voice and writing, showing how they are separated only by the transpositional field of death, a simple movement, a proximate becoming. In Shelley's poem we see elegy subverting difference, articulating a place and meaning between and alongside.

In the final stanzas of *Adonais*, Shelley narrates his own renunciation of this "dream of life," one that would take place extra-textually all too soon. A year and a half after Keats died, Shelley, "[w]hose sails were [. . .] to the tempest given,"[60] found his watery grave and returned to the embrace of that

> sustaining Love
> Which through the web of being blindly wove
> By man and beast and earth and air and sea,
> Burns bright or dim, as each are mirrors of
> The fire for which all thirst.[61]

This last stanza is commonly read as Shelley's renunciation of life and earth, his exchange of writing for epic and perilous voyage. However, I think we are now in a position to see that what Shelley rejects are inadequate conceptualizations of life, death, subjectivity, and immortality. Shelley implies that the pastoral elegist too may rank with the heroes and writers of epic fiction insofar as all writing—and especially his—is a kind of heroic adventure. Demonstrating this kind of uncanny commerce between presumed opposites, Shelley concludes *Adonais* with a gesture of generic meltdown. In its closing stanza, pastoral elegy becomes epic and, in turn, epic becomes pastoral:

> The breath whose might I have invoked in song,
> Descends on me; my spirit's bark is driven,
> Far from the shore, *far from the trembling throng*
> Whose sails were never to the tempest given;
> The massy earth and sphered skies are riven![62]

In answer to his poetic prayer, Shelley's muse responds with the inspiriting breath that enables the poetic, philosophical, and personal explorations undertaken within *Adonais* and anticipated beyond it. Read in this way, Shelley's poem is not ultimately frustrated by language's "weakness" nor is it a prospectus for suicide; instead, it articulates an investment of self in the risky markets of artistic fame, a vote of confidence for life, for difference, for writing. It exists as the materialist vehicle for immortalizing a unique and particular individual, a supplement to "living on" through reproduction.

NOTES

1. My suspicion is that we can understand the norm, the dominant, or the central from the perspective of the unusual, subordinate, or marginal in ways otherwise inaccessible. I consider this assumption axiomatic of queer theory.

2. This is Shelley's own description of his elegy: *Letters of Percy Bysshe Shelley*, ed. Frederick L. Jones, 2 vols (Oxford: Clarendon Press, 1964), 2 : 294.

3. Jerrold Hogle, *Shelley's Process* (New York: Oxford University Press, 1988). Indeed, Hogle makes explicit the ramifications of his project for other readers of Shelley's work. He writes, "[N]o discussion of Shelleyan thought or identity should avoid how very political both of these are for him, and so no analysis of Shelley's writing should separate transposition from his radical social programme" (15).

4. Ibid., 10–12.

5. Ibid., 15.

6. Ibid., 3.

7. Ibid., 10.

8. Ibid., 13.

9. Ibid., 14.

10. Ibid., 21. Earlier Hogle describes the "transposition constantly displacing the self" to be "inherently iconoclastic and revolutionary, even in the face of its own previous production" (14).

11. What seems remarkable—given Hogle's rhetoric and his reliance on Freudian/Lacanian psychoanalysis, French feminism, and French and American deconstruction to understand and articulate Shelley's philosophy and writing—is the absence of reference to the work of Gilles Deleuze and Felix Guattari. So much of what Hogle says seems to paraphrase their views.

12. Percy Bysshe Shelley, *Adonais*, *Shelley's Poetry and Prose*, ed. Donald Reiman and Sharon B. Powers (New York: Norton, 1977), 390–406, ll. 271–72; all subsequent quotations are from this edition.

13. Ibid., l. 305.

14. Ibid., ll. 406–8.

15. Ibid., ll. 217–61.

16. See specifically the reference to Milton, who wrote and died in ignominy but who lives on in the "light" of his poetic achievement, the allusions to Homer and Dante, the mention of Lucan, Sidney, and Chatterton, as well as the mourning procession composed by contemporary poets Byron, Moore, and Hunt. These suggest the constitution and range of such a community.

17. Stuart Curran, "*Adonais* in Context," *Shelley Revalued*, ed. Kelvin Everest (Bath: Leicester University Press, 1983), 167.

18. Shelley, *Adonais*, ll. 494–95.

19. Ibid., ll. 4–9.

20. See Peter Sacks, *The English Elegy* (Baltimore: Johns Hopkins University Press, 1985) for a comprehensive account of the rivalry, competition, and emotional ambivalence manifest in elegiacal writing.

21. Shelley, *Adonais*, ll. 235–43; my emphasis.

22. Sacks, 160.

23. Shelley, *Adonais*, l. 238; my emphasis.

24. Percy Shelley, "A Discourse on the Manners of the Ancient Greeks Relative to the Subject of Love," *Shelley's Prose on the Trumpet of a Prophecy,* ed. David Lee Clark (Albuquerque: University of New Mexico Press, 1954), 222.

25. Ibid.

26. Shelley, *Adonais*, ll. 291–95.

27. The erastes (older mentor and social superior) guides the eromenos (younger student and social inferior) to the apprehension and contemplation of the ideal forms, for which male beauty is a lesser model. See Michel Foucault, *The

Use of Pleasure, vol. 2 of *The History of Sexuality*, trans. Robert Hurley (New York: Vintage Books, 1990), 187–203, for further discussion and complication.

28. Swinburne's "Anactoria" comes to mind here.

29. Shelley, *Adonais*, ll. 136, 199.

30. Ibid., ll. 136, 139–42.

31. David Greenberg, *The Construction of Homosexuality* (Chicago: University of Chicago Press, 1988), 347.

32. Ibid., 353–54.

33. Ibid., 358.

34. Emily Allen and Dino Felluga, in their unpublished essay, "Minding the Body: Poetry and 'Self-Abuse' at Mid-Century," remind us how the single male poet and his sexuality, pleasures, and nonproductive labor became a source of deep cultural anxiety as Romanticism gave way to Victorianism.

35. With respect to the French Revolution, it seems clear that Shelley interpreted it as the product of liberatory struggle rather than the result of aristocratic decadence.

36. Hogle, 312.

37. Ibid., 312.

38. Another way we might think of unapprehended relations is through Kristevan "poetic language," the irruption of the chaotically material into the regulated and abstract space of the symbolic. For more concerning Kristeva and *jouissance*, see Julia Kristeva, *Desire in Language*, trans. Leon Roudiez (New York: Columbia University Press, 1982).

39. Sacks, 165.

40. Shelley, *Adonais*, ll. 487–95.

41. Shelley, *Adonais,* 1.476. Angela Leighton also believes this elegy should be read otherwise than as a solicitation of death; she finds elegy, whose purported goal is to recapture a lost presence, to be paradigmatic of poetry's (or indeed, language and literature's) signification of a lost presence. When Shelley's poetic persona sets out to sea, his lapse into silence is a recognition of the only fictional presentation of lost presence, the imitation of voice and its "failure" to resurrect the dead. Indeed, Shelley knows the dead to be immortal insofar as they have returned to the immediacy of the natural world; they are once again a part of the eternal becoming of the world, cyclically transformed, always in movement, postlinguistic. "[T]he triumph of the poem," Leighton writes, "is to have discovered the dead to be immortal, and theirs to be the pure voice of creative 'Power' beyond the deceptive fictions of language." Angela Leighton, "Deconstructive Criticism and Shelley's *Adonais*," *Shelley Revalued*, 162.

42. Shelley, *Adonais*, l. 381.

43. Ibid., ll. 379, 384.

44. The burning fountain is a particularly stagey version of this idea.

45. Shelley, *Adonais*, ll. 177–79.

46. See especially stanzas 25–29, in which Urania apostrophizes Adonais' corpse and evinces her inability to restore him. As early as stanza 2, the poetic persona asks, "Where wert thou mighty Mother," thereby accusing her of indifference (l. 10).

47. Shelley, *Adonais*, ll. 462, 482.

48. Hogle, *Shelley's Process* 26.

49. It is a kind of becoming, indebted to what has been known, and anticipating what is not now known but will be.

50. Shelley, *Adonais*, ll. 343–51.

51. This claim by the poet appears in *The Complete Works of Percy Bysshe Shelley*, 7 : 61.

52. Intellectually, however, Shelley expects it to be light and hot.

53. Shelley, *Adonais*, ll. 466–68.

54. Shelley, *Adonais*, 1.460. Hogle writes more about metaphor than metonymy, yet what he says is certainly suggestive of the claim I am making. "Metaphor is but the late *synecdoche* whose operation points back to the movement that underlies all figuration and thence becomes visible only in figures" (Hogle, *Shelley's Process*, 19; my emphasis). Metonymy is the figure through which "living on" is expressed; metaphor is used to image substitutability, the replacement of the lost beloved.

55. Shelley, *Adonais*, l. 477.

56. Ibid., ll. 478–86.

57. Despite Shelley's aloof self-representation, "A phantom among men; companionless" (l. 272) and his claims to immortalizing power, the performance of this poetic act, its conventional solicitation, and his immortalizing vision all subsume the individual poet to a transtemporal community. Even his imaginative hubris cannot displace that mourning community.

58. Interestingly and perhaps ironically, given the privilege accorded homosociality within *Adonais*, the despair over reproductive immortality, and the impotence of Urania's motherhood, Shelley's spiritual rebirth still relies on the imagery and paradigm of parturition. "The massy earth and sphered skies are riven! / I am borne darkly, fearfully, afar" (ll. 491–92). The phonotextual pun on "borne" that allows us to hear "birthed" under the accepted sense of "carried away" also allows us to see how the dark, wet distance of the sea is thematically subordinated and contrasted to the bright, fiery immediacy of heaven. In invoking the abstract and ideal silence of the paternal logos, Shelley relies on the maternal, material, and concretely linguistic.

59. It is difficult to use the words *"masculinity," "subjectivity,"* and *"fluidity"* in one paragraph without thinking of Klaus Theweleit's work on fascism and masculine ego formation and identity. I am contrasting rigidity and a fixed notion of self-conception of identity with a fluid and performative account. The latter is the queerer version and also the one that Shelley privileges in this poem. Klaus Theweleit, *Male Fantasies* (Minneapolis: University of Minnesota Press, 1989).

60. Shelley, *Adonais*, l. 490.

61. Ibid., ll. 481–85.

62. Ibid., ll. 487–90; my emphasis. "Far from the trembling throng" sounds like Gray's "far from the madding crowd," which Hardy uses in a novel by the same title. This phrase signifies the pastoral place, and yet it also suggests the isolation of epic journey. Of course the inspiriting muse is a convention shared by both pastoral and epic.

Part II
Victorian

Benjamin Disraeli, Judaism, and the Legacy of William Beckford

RICHARD DELLAMORA

> You will surely not find it strange that this subject,
> so profound and difficult, should bear various
> interpretations, for it will not impair the face of the
> argument with which we are here concerned. Either
> explanation may be adopted.
>
> —Moses Maimonides

INTRODUCTION

SHORTLY AFTER THE PASSAGE OF THE FIRST REFORM BILL IN 1832, BENjamin Disraeli began to write a romance about a legendary Jewish hero named David Alroy.[1] Why did he do so at a time when he was attempting to launch a political career in England, a country where Jews were not permitted to hold seats in Parliament? Why, moreover, did the book, when published, bring Disraeli to the attention of William Beckford, a wealthy amateur musician and author of an Oriental romance, whose main claim to fame had been his involvement in a notorious sexual scandal? And why did Richard Harris Barham, a noted humorist and Anglican divine, immediately pen a parody of Disraeli's text, in which Barham identifies Jewish literary aspiration with theft and Jewish heroism with an assault on the Established Church? In a poisonous sketch, Barham identifies Alroy and Disraeli with Isaac Solomon, the best known Jewish criminal of the 1830s (and the model of Fagin in *Oliver Twist*, 1838).

In publishing *The Wondrous Tale of Alroy* (1833), Disraeli attempted to constitute himself as a national subject, affirming his identity simultaneously as a *minority* and an *imperial* subject. As a young man, he wrote: "My mind is a continental mind. It is a revolutionary mind."[2] Nor did a single continent suffice. Disraeli's mind and travels included not only Europe but also the Middle East, where he traveled in 1830 and 1831, and extended as far afield as

India. Because his personal and political ambitions were bound up from the outset with an identification with the British empire,[3] he might well be described as an imperial Briton. In Disraeli, this outlook does not merely extend the survey of the nation-state; it changes self-concept as well as the meaning of being a national subject. Commentators today are generally agreed that Disraeli's ability to speak as an "I" on the political stage depended upon his finding a way to affirm the fact that he was of Jewish descent.[4] Regarding himself as an imperial subject enabled him to develop a public persona capacious enough to include Jewish difference, but it was being Jewish that enabled him to make the claim in the first place.

Since both suffrage and membership in Parliament were restricted to men, the work of gender involved in becoming a national subject was necessarily masculine. In this light, the connotations of effeminacy that Barham and reviewers of the book lodge against Disraeli function so as implicitly to deny him the status he sought.[5] By affecting the dandy in his personal and prose style, Disraeli attempted to turn such criticism back upon itself.[6] Even more troubling for some contemporaries, through his investment in the literary heritage summed in the name "Beckford," Disraeli signaled the central place of desire between men in British politics, whether religious or parliamentary. This desire threatens to become as explicitly sexual in *Alroy* as it is in Beckford's *Episodes of Vathek*.

As gay historians and critics such as Alan Bray and Jonathan Goldberg have argued, during the late medieval and Renaissance periods, royal and aristocratic governance depended on the public institution of male friendship—both between equals and between patrons and clients. In these relations, the line between ardent friendship and a sexual relation was indistinct enough to be crossed with relative ease. In particular circumstances, however, it might be recognized—less likely by its participants than by their antagonists—as a sodomitical relationship.[7] Since sodomy was deemed to be a form of both blasphemy and treason, such allegations were as threatening to the political order as they were to the individuals thereby singled out. Friendship was both necessary and potentially dangerous to the existing order.

Recently, Linda Dowling has reminded readers that attacks on sodomy are a standard feature of classic republican discourse from the mid-seventeenth century onward. Tory opponents of Sir Robert Walpole condemned political patronage as a form of "luxury" and "corruption" that was metaphorically and (at times) literally sodomitic.[8] Dowling charts the shift of this rhetoric during the nineteenth century into the realm of aesthetics, where it becomes part of a general Tory onslaught against innovative and, later, vanguard cultural practices. She places in this context the attack on John Keats in *Blackwood's Edinburgh Magazine* for the "emasculated pruriency" of his writing.[9] When *Blackwood's* writer contends that Keats's poetry "looks as if it were the product of some imaginative eunuch's muse,"[10] moreover, he may well be glancing obliquely at Beckford, whose Oriental tales are overrun by eunuchs (as is *Alroy*, for that matter). As the son of a politically radical, former Lord Mayor of London, whose immense wealth was founded on slave labor in Jamaica, the scandal-soiled Beckford was a perfect target for Tory abuse. Not surprisingly, John Wilson Croker, one of Keats's antagonists, also made himself an enemy of Disraeli at the outset of his career.[11] The patterns of patronage and dependence, often between an older and a younger man, in which parliamentary politics in England were played out could be equally construed under the rubric of friendship or sodomy, depending on one's choice of lens. Goldberg argues that these relationships were part of the tradition of aristocratic hegemony.[12] Equally, however, as Dowling reminds us, they were the necessary means whereby eighteenth-century Whigs practiced their "modernizing" politics. It was members of the party of commercial progress and imperial expansion such as Beckford who were most liable to be accused of sodomy.

Some readers will resist extending consideration of "sodomitic" linkages into the nineteenth century on the ground that to do so is anachronistic. But it would be incorrect to conclude on the basis of Dowling's discussion that classical republican rhetoric, shunted into aesthetics, disappears from politics in the nineteenth century. One has to think only of the Liberal Prime Minister Lord Rosebery's liaison with Viscount Drumlanrig, Alfred Douglas's older brother, in the 1890s, to be reminded how the interweave of class, party, and sexual affiliations that I begin to explore in this essay continue during the Victorian period.[13] Indeed, one would be wiser to consider the homosexual connotations of, say, *Punch's* satiric representation of male aesthetes in the 1870s and 1880s and the sexual innuendoes of the Newman-Kingsley controversy in the 1860s as struggles, within aesthetic and religious terms, that intersect at times with explicitly political discourse.[14] Beckford provides a crucial connection both in his reflections on male friendship in the fiction he wrote during the 1780s and in his slyly sexual reading of *Alroy* a half century later.

BECKFORDIAN EROTICS

In *Vathek* (1786; wr. 1782) Beckford affirms the innocence of pederastic desire by dissociating it from property, dynastic power, and family. He focuses on the figure of Gulchenrouz, the thirteen-year-old boy with whom the beautiful young Nouronihar is in love—at least until she falls under the erotic sway of the Caliph Vathek.[15] Vathek's first great crime is to sacrifice fifty of "the most beautiful sons"[16] of his vizirs and great men to the monstrous Giaour who promises to bring him to "the Palace of Subterranean Fire."[17] Beckford arranges to have Gulchenrouz protected from a similar fate by a "good old genius,"[18] who transports him to safety in a Roc's nest above the clouds. There Gulchenrouz finds his fifty youthful companions, whom the genius has likewise saved. The boys live happily ever after in a hypererotic, desexualized paradise:

> Gulchenrouz . . . admitted without fear the congratulations of his little friends, who were all assembled in the nest of the venerable genius, and vied with each other in kissing his serene forehead and beautiful eyelids.—Remote from the inquietudes of the world; the impertinence of harems, the brutality of eunuchs, and the inconstancy of women; there he found a place truly congenial to the delights of his soul. In this peaceable society his days, months, and years glided on; nor was he less happy than the rest of his companions: for the genius, instead of burthening his pupils with perishable riches and vain sciences, conferred upon them the boon of perpetual childhood.[19]

At the end of the tale, Beckford contrasts "the pure happiness of childhood" to Vathek's pursuit of "empty pomp and forbidden power."[20] Beckford, however, purchases this purity at the price of mystifying his own romantic obsession, at the time, with William Courtenay, a young aristocrat the same age as Gulchenrouz. Beckford saves Gulchenrouz, William, himself, and his fictive creations from the tensions of actual friendship and the potential perversity of pederastic desire by relegating these objects of desire to a sensuous but presexual paradise.

Given what I have earlier said about the sexual politics of male friendship in elite English society, Beckford's fantasy was very "Oriental," that is, removed from the actualities of English life, to which he himself would soon fall victim. It was also in the tradition of the genre of the Oriental tale in France and England in the eighteenth century, whereby Oriental alterity provided, through exaggeration or contrast, a moral commentary on the corruption of European existence. In this context, Beckford's tale is harshly critical of domestic norms, especially in male-female relations. Vathek's mother, Carathis, is more depraved than Vathek; and Nouronihar, after rejecting the boy, hastens with Vathek to the depths of hell. In contrast, Beckford affirms the innocence and seductive attraction of a boy. But this polemical affirmation is compromised by the need to withdraw it from temporality.

In the first of the *Episodes of Vathek*, written one year later, in 1783, Beckford turns to the subject of the desire of a beautiful and powerful young man for a boy. Beckford intended to incorporate these short fictions within the longer text in the manner of inserted tales in the *Arabian Nights*. The *Episodes*, however, were so unconventional that they remained unpublished until the twentieth century. In the opening lines of the first of these, "The Story of Prince Alasi and the Princess Firouzkah," Beckford, on the verge of his own scandal, introduces the problematic of friendship between a young man and a boy. Speaking in the voice of Prince Alasi, Beckford writes:

> I reigned in Kharezme, and would not have exchanged my kingdom, however small, for the Calif Vathek's immense empire. No, it is not ambition that has brought me to this fatal place. My heart . . . was armed against every unruly passion; only the calm and equable feelings of friendship could have found entrance there; but Love, which in its own shape would have been repelled, took Friendship's shape, and in that shape effected my ruin.[21]

As in *Vathek*, Beckford instates a binary opposition between "Love," which here means love of a man for a woman particularly in marriage, and "Friendship," which, by sanitary cordon, Alasi defines as excluding "passion." At the very outset, however, Beckford uses the episode to put in question this structural feature of the longer narrative. Alasi acknowledges his sexual aversion to women—by whom he is "repelled." But he is also forced to acknowledge that his desire for his friend—the young stranger, Firouz—is neither "calm" nor "equable."[22]

Beckford pursues this novel situation in two ways. One is by immediately engaging Alasi in the sort of internal examination and confession that Foucault associates with the development of a post-Enlightenment view that identifies the truth of the self with the secrets of one's sexuality.[23] The other is by rehearsing Alasi's discovery within the traditional rhetoric of male friendship as the proper medium of governance. In this respect the date of Beckford's fiction—written in the years immediately preceding the French Revolution—is crucial for, after 1789, it would have been impossible in England, the self-styled land of "liberty," to regard friends active in politics as constituting political representation. Alasi says:

> I felt the need of introspection. This was not at first easy: all my thoughts were in confusion! I could not account to my own self for the agitation of feeling I had experienced. "At last," said I, "heaven has hearkened to my dearest wish. It has sent me the true heart's-friend I should never have found in my court; it has sent him to me adorned with all the charms of innocence—charms that will be followed, at a maturer age, by those good qualities that make of friendship man's highest blessing—and, above all, the highest blessing of a prince, since disinterested friendship is a blessing that a prince can scarcely hope to enjoy."[24]

Alasi's confused efforts at self-analysis indicate Beckford's unease with his growing awareness of sexual implications in the relationship with William. Moreover, Beckford was already growing disillusioned with his beloved, who would grow from angelic boy into an effeminate young man with an excessive interest in fancy dress.[25] Beckford's changing attitude suggests that it is a mistake to identify him exclusively with pederastic interests, as Adam Potkay does, for example.[26] Beckford thinks of intimacy between an adult male and a boy, ardent, embodied, even sexual, as directed toward what will become proper friendship between two grown men active in public life. In other words, as in Foucault's account of Athenian culture, such friendships are envisaged as part of the process whereby the younger male enters into the privileges and responsibilities of citizenship.[27] Alasi's idyll suggests the importance of ideal friendship within aristocratic circles; the irony of the passage suggests how far short of the ideal reality could fall. Beckford's later connection with his agent, George Clarke, and his long, intimate relationship with Gregorio Franchi, a young musician sarcastically dubbed the "Portuguese orange" after he followed Beckford from Portugal to Madrid, provide evidence that he enjoyed close relations with men of various ages who were subjects of same-sex desire.[28] His eventual choice of a condition approaching celibacy indicates as well the near impossibility that attended the complex set of demands that inhabited his ideal of erotic friendship.

Alasi's remarks place in doubt the possibility of a transparent relationship between friendship and the exercise of political responsibility. As he falls under the influence of Firouz, moreover, other men at court grow angry, seeing the prince's favor for the boy as a sign of disorder: Alasi's infatuation disrupts the proper relations of male hierarchy in governance. The resulting tensions closely resemble those between Edward II, the Barons, and Gaveston, the king's "minion," in Christopher Marlowe's play, *Edward II*.[29] Alasi rejects the dynastic need for marriage and embarks with Firouz on a course of ever wilder crime that leads both, literally, to hell.

In *Alroy*, Disraeli attempts to validate erotic friendship in terms of its dedication to achieving a particular religious and national aim. He also validates it insofar as it meets the demands and pleasures of government in a multi-ethnic state. As in Beckford, however, the purity of the male ephebe cannot be preserved. The compromises, revulsions, and contaminations of mentorship capture Alroy in a double bind for they make possible his success only at the price of lost innocence and guarantee his ultimate failure. At the end of *Alroy*, Alroy is betrayed by his Moslem wife, Schirene, and decapitated at the order of a King of Karasmé who is very different from the elegant young Prince Alasi. In the familiar terms of Freudian psychology, David is deprived of his masculinity; he is castrated. In the terms of Jewish nationalism as they were to develop in the course of the nineteenth century, the Jewish seed is dispersed as the seductive possibility of a renewed national center glimmers, then fails.[30]

In view of arguments put forward by Sander Gilman, Daniel Boyarin, and Marc A. Weiner, one could conflate Jewish aspects of Disraeli's text with male homoeroticism through the mediating term of "effeminacy," which, in Gilman and Boyarin's arguments, is understood to render Jews improperly masculine and, in that respect, reducible to the figure of what, by the end of the nineteenth century, is referred to as the sexual invert—the man whose body is inhabited by the "soul" of a woman.[31] To do so, however, would be to telescope a set of stereotypical identifications that become fully elaborated only later on. Moreover, one would emphasize sexological contexts to the neglect of others. Effeminacy in *Alroy* connotes more the danger of the contamination of men by uxoriousness, an excessive desire for women. Anxieties about sexual contamination by another man focus on the institution of male mentorship. Concerning the latter, my claim is that erotic and sexual aspects should be construed at times within religious or political terms; at other times, sexual aspects dominate political ones. Depending on context, moreover, the two terms are reversible.

In 1833, the most salient other context is that of successful passage of the Reform Bill one year earlier. Although the exclusion of working-class men from the vote led to intensified political unrest among workers,[32] the victory of the Whigs in the subsequent na-

tional election ushered in a period of legal reform which seemed to
promise the possibility that at least some excluded others might be
able to improve their position. Men with sexual and emotional ties
to other men hoped that the death penalty for sodomy might be
lifted.[33] Following the achievement of Catholic Emancipation in
1829, Jews hoped that they too might gain full civil rights. And, in
1833, the Jewish Emancipation Bill successfully passed the House
of Commons only to be rejected by the Lords.

The genre of the Oriental tale entailed commentary on contemporary political and moral conditions.[34] In *Alroy*, Disraeli shifts attention from class issues to others: in personal terms, to the proper
function of political friendship in a time of political upheaval; in
social terms, to the need to diversify the bases of citizenship. The
claim to purity that Alroy puts forward at the end of the romance is
made in the name of fidelity to a reclaimed Jewish tradition. He can
do so, however, only in revolt against his uncle, Bostenay, and *both*
his mentors. The first is a Jewish rabbi named Jabaster, who urges
David after the conquest of Bagdad to establish a Jewish state in
Jerusalem; the second is Jabaster's brother, Honain, a medical doctor and "Marrano" or disguised Jew who has abandoned his faith
and concealed his identity in order to achieve wealth, acceptance,
and influence.[35]

"I am pure."[36] With these words, Alroy in contrast rejects the
demand that he become an apostate. His integrity depends upon
being true to his faith—and his "sacred race."[37] But it is also true
that earlier in the novel, at the height of his military success against
the Caliph, Alroy refuses to comply with Jabaster's demand that he
establish Judaic law in his new kingdom. Instead, recognizing the
status of Jews as a minority in the midst of a Mohammedan world,
Alroy declares that "We must conciliate": "Universal empire must
not be founded on sectarian prejudices and exclusive rights."[38]
Alroy/Disraeli points a double moral about the need to reconcile
minority existence with imperial citizenship. The necessity and sanity of this theme, which Daniel Boyarin has argued, in another context, to be a central one in Jewish culture, should not blind us to
some of its implications.[39] For example, as Gauri Viswanathan has
argued, the conciliation of British rule with local practices was a
prime means to maintain British hegemony within the empire.[40]
Later, as prime minister, Disraeli would sponsor initiatives whose
net effect was to increase homogeneity at home while contributing
to the consolidation of imperial power. Secondly, Disraeli the politician was not averse to exploiting the maltreatment of members of
one minority group as an argument to defend the subordination of

other minorities within Great Britain, in particular, Irish Catholics.[41]

Disraeli's emphasis on the need to avoid ethnic and religious fanaticism in constituting governments is very much in the spirit of the Enlightenment. Considered together, the double face of his moral is both rationalistic and universalizing, on the one hand, and, on the other, romantic, emphasizing the necessity of affirming Jewish custom and ritual, the *body*, so to speak, of Jewish existence. Disraeli defends this heritage at the same time that he rejects sectarian exclusivity—as does his father, Isaac, who published his treatment of the Jewish question, *The Genius of Judaism*, in the same year in which *Alroy* appeared.

Disraeli's affirmation of Jewish faith corrects Beckford on this point. In Beckford's tale, Vathek's long descent into hell has the architectonic structure of an opium-induced reverie that one finds in romantic texts by Beckford, Coleridge, and De Quincey. At the end of his progress, Vathek arrives at the tomb of Solomon, an undead creature who is represented, as he is presumably in Moslem tradition, as a fire-worshipping infidel.[42] Solomon tells Vathek:

> In my life-time, I filled a magnificent throne; having, on my right hand, twelve thousand seats of gold, where the patriarchs and the prophets heard my doctrines; on my left, the sages and doctors, upon as many thrones of silver, were present at all my decisions. Whilst I thus administered justice to innumerable multitudes, the birds of the air, hovering over me, served as a canopy against the rays of the sun. My people flourished; and my palace rose to the clouds. I erected a temple to the Most High, which was the wonder of the universe: but, I basely suffered myself to be seduced by the love of women, and a curiosity that could not be restrained by sublunary things. I listened to the counsels of Aherman, and the daughter of Pharaoh; and adored fire, and the hosts of heaven. I forsook the holy city, and commanded the Genii to rear the stupendous palace of Istakhar.[43]

Until he is rescued by the angelic love of his sister, Miriam, Alroy follows a similarly idolatrous path: marrying Schirene, daughter of the Caliph whom he has supplanted, and agreeing to attend Moslem services.

But the dream of Solomon figures very differently in Disraeli's text. There, through a standard quest narrative, Disraeli appears to solve the problem of the potentially degenerative effects of male friendship by presenting Alroy's maturation into a conventional masculine subject. His illumination is conjured not by intoxication but occurs in a dream-vision that climaxes his pilgrimage to Jerusalem. As his Cabalistic mentor, Jabaster, has predicted, Alroy there receives the sceptre of Solomon that confirms him in his role as the long-awaited Jewish Messiah:

> Further on, and far above the rest, upon a throne that stretched across the hall, a most imperial presence straightway flashed upon the startled vision of Alroy. Fifty steps of ivory, and each step guarded by golden lions, led to a throne of jasper. A dazzling light blazed forth from the glittering diadem and radiant countenance of him who sat upon the throne, one beautiful as a woman, but with the majesty of a god. And in one hand he held a seal, and in the other a sceptre.[44]

Alroy approaches and mounts the steps to the throne:

> Pale as a spectre, the pilgrim, whose pilgrimage seemed now on the point of completion, stood cold and trembling before the object of all his desires and all his labours. But he thought of his country, his people, and his God; and, while his noiseless lips breathed the name of Jehovah, solemnly he put forth his arm, and with a gentle firmness grasped the unresisting sceptre of his great ancestor. And as he seized it, the whole scene vanished from his sight![45]

Alroy is empowered as the result of thinking "of his country, his people, and his God." His act offers a rebuke to the secular position taken by Disraeli's father, who, in his book, argues that Jewish heritage is spiritual not material and that Jews can be admitted to full citizenship only when they are prepared to relinquish the detailed observances prescribed by Jewish law.[46] This moment in Alroy's adventures likewise offers a rebuke to the author, who was also a "Marrano." Baptism into the Church of England had been forced upon Disraeli at the age of twelve upon the advice of a friend of his father named Sharon Turner. This influence was determining for, had Turner not intervened, Disraeli would have been ineligible to take part as a candidate, albeit unsuccessfully, for Parliament in 1832. Turner played the role of a latter-day Honain who effectively turned Disraeli into another Honain, a Jew who had to become a Christian in order to enjoy the privileges of being an English gentleman.

The main erotic dramas in *Alroy* occur between men, usually between David and an older man: Bostenay, Jabaster, Honain. Although essential to David's fulfillment of the task of regaining the rod of Solomon, all three relationships are destructive. Bostenay attempts to corrupt David with the "luxury" of Jewish commercial success. Later, when Honain first meets David and declares his affection, he offers him the "luxury" of high office at the court of the Caliph. Jabaster deprives Alroy of the counsel he needs to create a multi-ethnic administration and state. In his role as interpreter of the law, he intends to dominate Alroy's kingdom. David's disillusionment with all three relationships suggests how guarded Disraeli himself found it necessary to be in searching out the path toward an "embodification" that would enable him to link "character" with "career."[47]

CONSTITUTING THE NATIONAL SUBJECT

Shortly after passage of the Reform Bill in 1832, Disraeli became an agent in defining the modern British state by outlining his political philosophy in a series of articles in the *Morning Post*. Earlier, his career had begun in typical nationalist fashion with an effort to establish a national newspaper.[48] Later, in the 1850s, he owned his own journal, *The Press*.[49] In major aspects of his mature career— the extension of the suffrage to 1,000,000 additional males in 1867, the attempt to make the Conservatives the "national party" in the 1870s by espousing a populist imperialism, the declaration of Queen Victoria as Empress of India in 1876—he abetted the process of conventional nation-building that Ernest Gellner defines as "the principle of homogenous [sic] cultural units as the foundations of political life, and of the obligatory cultural unity of rulers and ruled."[50] Yet, as I have said, the very possibility of Disraeli's political career depended on the assertion of Jewish difference. Moreover, in the *Morning Post* essays and elsewhere, he identifies himself against processes that Gellner identifies with nationalism but that Disraeli associates with the perfidy of political opponents: Whigs, Utilitarians, and, later, Liberals. Commentators such as Simon During point out that in the eighteenth century Tories, defining nationalism in terms of "patriotism," had emphasized "love of country" in contrast to the use of politics to pursue "personal ambition." Likewise, they affirmed traditional affiliations in contrast to the exercise of "state power . . . by the Whigs to make room for the free play of the market."[51] In the *Morning Post*, Disraeli writes against Whig reform from within Burkean tradition:

The King of England is the avowed leader of the Conservative party. . . . We have upon our side also the Peers of England; we have upon our side the Gentlemen of England; we have upon our side the yeomanry of England; we have upon our side their armed and gallant brethren; we

have upon our side the universal peasantry of England; we have upon
our side the army and navy, the Church, the learned professions to a
man, the Universities, the Judges, the Magistrates, the merchants, the
corporate bodies of all descriptions, and a large party in every town,
agricultural, commercial, and even manufacturing. What constitutes a
people if these do not afford the elements of a great and glorious nation?[52]

Just as the emphasis on Jewish particularity is at odds with the drive
toward homogeneity, likewise this historically oriented, contingent
view of what constitutes the nation cuts across what Gellner sees to
be the main trend-line identifying processes of industrial development and modernization with the formation of the imperial nation-
state.

The passage also offers a good example of how individual subjectivity, in this case Disraeli's, can be constituted in relation to
identification with a particular political party, a major function, as
Joseph Childers points out, of Disraeli's later novel, *Coningsby*
[1844].[53] Disraeli's Ciceronian period organizes differences into a
"we" that is a multiple corporate body: "we" the Conservative
party and "we" the people, embodied, in atavistic fashion, in "the
King of England." The passage constitutes the continuum of a body
at once real and local (the writer's body, the king's body) and simultaneously social and symbolic (the body of the Conservative
party, the body of the people). Particular bodies (Alroy's in the romance; the king's body here) provide switch points at which these
different embodiments coincide.

Disraeli's best-known reflections on the course that his self-fash-
ioning would take occur in an entry in the so-called "mutilated
diary" that survives in the Hughenden papers at Oxford. Writing at
age twenty-nine, Disraeli weaves together his aspirations, recognizes the prejudice he must overcome, and indexes the narrative of
Jewish self-affirmation in *Alroy*. In the passage, the particular word
that he uses to refer to the process is one of becoming-body, or, to
use his word, "embodification":

> The world calls me "*conceited.*" The world is in error. . . . My mind is
> a continental mind. It is a revolutionary mind. I am only truly great in
> action. If ever I am placed in a truly eminent position I shall prove this.
> I c[ou]ld rule the House of Commons, although there w[ou]ld be a great
> prejudice against me at first. It is the most jealous assembly in the world.
> The fixed character of our English society, the consequence of our aris-
> tocratic institutions, renders a career difficult. Poetry is the safety valve
> of my passions, but I wish to act what I write. My works are the embodi-

fication [sic] of my feelings. In Vivian Grey I pourtrayed [sic] my active and real ambition. In Alroy, my ideal ambition. The P. R.[54] is a development of my poetic character. This Trilogy is the secret history of my feelings. I shall write no more about myself.[55]

Disraeli bases the passage upon a binary distinction between "action" and "writing" that tends to corroborate During's argument that while nineteenth-century nationalism tends to be associated with a militant, masculine ideal, aesthetic production, in particular in the realist novel, focuses increasingly on creating a world parallel to but removed from the "ethical" demands of modern nation-building.[56] During instances Sir Walter Scott's *Waverly* and Jane Austen's novels as examples of this shift in generic development. But he does not mention that what he sees to be an ethical retreat occurs in parallel with the destruction of imperial/republican aspirations at the time of the defeat of Napoleon on the continent. In Disraeli (as in Shelley and Byron), romantic narrative operates so as to keep the ethical demand for political possibilities alive. Disraeli terms the demand a "wish"—but this wish really *is* a demand and not the wish fulfillment in terms of which Freud characterizes aesthetic creation.[57] Moreover, by insisting not upon transcending material existence but on achieving fulfillment in and through it, the wish tends to break down the binary structure upon which the diary entry is based.

The elements of the entry may be diagrammed as follows:

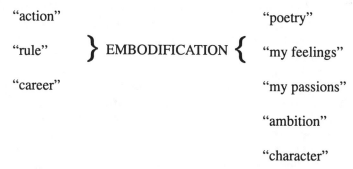

Mediating between these sets is the unusual word "embodification." The term construes the body as a place of active political, personal, and aesthetic formation.[58] Disraeli uses the word as a synonym for his autobiographical fictions. But it also refers to the work that he needs to do to transfer his wishes into the "rule" of others in a political "career."

In *Alroy*, the project is twofold. It occurs in the narrative of a

medieval Jewish warrior, DAvId ALRoY. But, as the partial anagram of Disraeli's name suggests, the text also provides a site
for coming to terms with the problems that concerned its young
politician/novelist/journalist/dandy/author. Alroy's "ideal ambition" is to redeem his people from their subjection to Moslem rule.
In the course of the novel, he comes to believe that this aim can be
achieved only by taking the power of the Caliph of Bagdad to himself in order to establish a new regime based on mutual tolerance
among peoples.

Unlike Iskander, the successful military commander of the short
story of the same title that was published together with *Alroy* in
order to fill out the requisite length of the three-decker book, David
does not look the part of the conquering hero.[59] At the outset, he is
an androgynous youth of eighteen years, who lives comfortably
with his sister, Miriam, and uncle, Bostenay. Despite his ostensible
good fortune, however, he and his fellow Jews exist in abjection
variously marked. For example, in the preface to the novel, Disraeli
remarks that "the natural effects of luxury and indulgence" have
rendered the sultanate of Bagdad vulnerable to invasion at the
hands of the Kings of Karasmé.[60] In turn, the novel begins on the
day of the annual procession when Bostenay, as Prince of the Captivity, must bear tribute to the Caliph.[61] Upon his return, Bostenay
suffers "the audible curses and the threatened missiles of the unbe-
lieving mob" of Moslems outside his door.[62] Even Bostenay's success as a trader signifies inferiority. "Dreams, dreams!" he says.
"We have fallen on evil days, and yet we prosper. I have lived long
enough to feel that a rich caravan, laden with the shawls of India
and the stuffs of Samarcand, if not exactly like dancing before the
ark, is still a goodly sight."[63] The commercial success of the Jewish
community is a sign of its decadence and yet one more aspect of a
general corrupting "luxury." In a statement of his own "Marrano"
mentality, Bostenay says: "The age of power has passed; it is by
prudence now that we must flourish. The gibe and jest, the curse,
perchance the blow, Israel now must bear, and with a calm or even
smiling visage."[64]

Bostenay's nephew, David, who is in line to succeed him as
prince, chafes. As he says, his "pedigree is pure,"[65] by which he
means openly resistant to Moslem dominance. After he leads a successful revolt, however, he refuses to follow his advisor Jabaster's
lead in establishing a "Theocracy": "The Hebrew legislator requires but little musing to shape his order. He has a model which
time cannot destroy, nor thought improve."[66] Jabaster demands that
the Jews leave Bagdad, drive the Crusaders out of Jerusalem, and
reestablish the Temple:

I wish . . . a national existence, which we have not. You ask me what I
wish: my answer is, the Land of Promise. You ask me what I wish: my
answer is, Jerusalem. You ask me what I wish: my answer is, the Temple, all we have forfeited, all we have yearned after, all for which we
have fought, our beauteous country, our holy creed, our simple manners, and our ancient customs. . . . We must exist alone. To preserve that
loneliness is the great end and essence of our law. . . . Sire, you may be
King of Bagdad, but you cannot, at the same time, be a Jew.[67]

Yielding to conspirators, Jabaster lends the authority of his wisdom
and office to a palace revolt. Endorsing it, he uses the rhetoric of
purification that Mary Douglas finds in Leviticus and that Julia
Kristeva argues is directed against a pollution associated with men-
strual blood, female sexuality, and the mother's body[68]: "Who
would have the ark polluted, and Jehovah's altar stained with a
Gentile sacrifice?"[69]

The opposites posed by Jabaster can be construed as a (mascu-
line-identified) logocentrism versus a (feminine-identified) abjection. Jabaster's nationalism, however, requires not the expulsion of
femininity but what he regards as the proper subordination of subject populations, including women, to Jewish Law. The order that
he seeks, including both masculine and feminine efficacy, can be
signified, in psychoanalytic terms, as the maternal phallus.[70] The
association of Jewish existence with an originary "womb" characterized Jewish nationalism during the nineteenth century.[71] David
Kaufmann, the Jewish nationalist who wrote a commentary on
George Eliot's *Daniel Deronda*, refers to the Jewish "species" as
"a wild luxuriance of unceasing growth" with an "inherent prolific
power of propagation," a force of "unceasing fecundity."[72] But
how is this force to be directed?

The work of the Jewish subject is to subordinate this power
within a newly created nation-state. In psychological terms, it
means disciplining feminized aspects of the male subject through
the regulating concept of effeminacy. The ideal formulation of this
order occurs in the relationship between Alroy, his Jewish mentor,
and the Law, whose minister Jabaster claims to be:

the Law

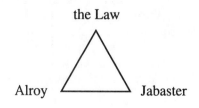

In this formulation, Alroy's subjection to his mentor is mystified in the form of the dedication of both to the Law.[73] In the story, however, Alroy negates both in order to constitute himself as an imperial subject ruling a multi-ethnic state.

Women are implicated in the triangle in three ways. First of all, Esther, the female Jewish prophet, who attempts to stab Alroy to death after he marries Schirene, embodies the view uttered by David in the first chapter that it would be preferable to die rather than to remain the slave of infidels. She represents a gendered, ethnically identified aspect of Alroy's interiority that threatens him with destruction if his subordination to the rabbi should be put in question. She also figures as a danger in the Jewish body politic, its capacity to rise up and destroy an unfaithful leader. The other implicated female presence is that of "the Daughter of the Voice," a legendary oracle that warns Jewish leaders of impending danger. Jabaster introduces Alroy to this oracle.

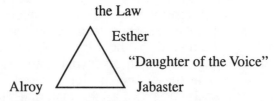

In a note to the text in the manner of Beckford's annotations to *Vathek*, Disraeli quotes a source that reports: "Both the Talmudick and the latter Rabbins . . . make frequent mention of *Bath Kol*, or *Filia Vocis*, or an echoing voice which served under the second temple for their utmost refuge of revelation. For when [the original] oracle was ceased, and prophecy was decayed and gone, they had, as they say, certain strange and extraordinary voices upon certain extraordinary occasions, which were their warnings and advertisements in some special matters." Equivocally, Disraeli cites another source which contends that while the voice "was used for a testimony from heaven, [it] was indeed performed by magic art."[74] Mysteriously, however, after Jabaster's death, the voice is heard one more time at the scene of Alroy's execution.[75] Jabaster's access to the voice offers Alroy access to his own Messianic future. The dubiety of the oracle, however, implies the abuse by the rabbis of secret knowledge in order to secure their objectives. The allegation, a commonplace of modern anti-Semitism, recurs at the end of the novel when, after yet one more turn of the political wheel, Schirene denounces Alroy to the King of Karasmé as a black magician. Predictably, Honain transfers his loyalties to the new conqueror.

While Alroy waits in prison, the forces unleashed by his betrayal of Judaism are brought back into alignment by a re-articulated triangulation. Alroy's devoted, "pure" sister, Miriam, serves as the term that restores Alroy to Jabaster.

Miriam

Alroy   Jabaster

The reconciliation of the pair enables David to be reunited with Jabaster, who returns to him in a vision "full of love."[76] The relation of the trio seems to correspond with Eve Kosofsky Sedgwick's model of male homosocial triangulation, in which the intensities of male-male attraction/repulsion are mediated through a single female figure. But Miriam's function may better be staged in binary terms that emphasize the reliance of this relationship on the Byronic/Shelleyan ideal of twinning affection between a young man and woman, usually brother and sister. In this context, Miriam's unsullied faith in her brother mirrors to him the broken covenant of his relationship with Jabaster as mediated by devotion to Jewish law. The female is the male self's imaginary other. Moreover, this binary relation connotes perversity since brother-sister love, in Byron's biography and in texts such as *Manfred*, has incestuous overtones.[77] Disraeli does not exploit the inversion of this ideal, but it cannot be altogether dismissed from mind in view of the book's emphasis both on infidelity and perversity in closely related contexts.

In the imperial context of the multi-ethnic state, it is, of course, Schirene to whom Honain introduces Alroy and whom he has selected as the vehicle of his continuing influence at court, who provides the familiar Sedgwickian figure of the woman who mediates desire. She mirrors David's androgyny, at first playfully, then with increasing perversity: "If I were only a man!" she exclaims. "What a hero you would be!" Honain rejoins. Schirene continues: "I should like to live in endless confusion." Honain comments: "I have not the least doubt of it."[78] Female gender transgression results in personal and social disorder, ultimately in the execution of Alroy; but Schirene's delight in "confusion" suggests as well Alroy's confusion about his status as a masculine subject.

If the relation to femininity is unruly, Disraeli is even more anxious about the dangers of intimacy in mentor-protégé relations, which seem to put in question the very existence of both the masculine subject and the phallus. This point is suggested at the end of Alroy's dream-vision of Solomon, when the "the unresisting sceptre" that he has seized vanishes "from his sight." Alroy then wakens with a start, to find himself, inexplicably, in the arms of Jabaster.

> He faintly moved his limbs; he would have raised his hand to his bewildered brain, but found that it grasped a sceptre. The memory of the past returned to him. He tried to rise, and found that he was reposing in the arms of a human being. He turned his head; he met the anxious gaze of Jabaster![79]

The sceptre authenticates the experience Alroy has just had. But is it, like the voice of the daughter of the people, just another toy in Jabaster's bag of tricks? Is the dream just ended Alroy's or a hallucination induced by his mentor? And since Alroy is traveling without Jabaster, how does it happen that the latter appears in Jerusalem at this moment? Or is Alroy's entire pilgrimage to Israel yet one more of Jabaster's mirages? There is good reason for Jabaster to be "anxious" about the young man under his "gaze" at this moment. Alroy too has reason to direct an anxious gaze toward the Rabbi, whose very name threatens to disintegrate into a series of words with troubling meanings—jabber, jabster, jokester . . . .

In Beckford's "The Story of Prince Alasi and the Princess Firouzkah," skepticism about the governance of friends quickly degenerates into cynicism; in *Alroy*, cynicism becomes nihilism. Mentorship threatens to dispel as illusory the very knowledge-power that it promises to communicate and instate. The same paradox haunts Alroy's relationship with Jabaster's brother, Honain, the renegade Jew. Honain confesses his love to Alroy shortly before introducing him to Schirene. The "moral" to be derived from the example of Honain, however, is that the one constant of the politician's life is the pursuit and exercise of power—stripped of any group or individual allegiance. Within this context, to become an imperial ruler becomes an act devoid of human significance.

SYMPATHIES AND AVERSIONS

By focusing on Alroy's betrayal by his wife and male mentors or by insisting on Alroy's beheading as the moment of narrative closure, one could find the text to be dominated by sexual panic in the face of any desire directed toward a male. To do so, however, would be to miss the delight in young men that also motivates Disraeli's writing. It's important to recognize the worldliness that welcomed this pleasure and made it possible for Beckford and Disraeli to meet. In addition to the lure of Alroy's androgynous male beauty, the interchange between the two men reinscribes, in an oriental setting, the Neoclassic myth of artistic genius, one of whose cardinal signs is attraction (emotional, aesthetic, and often sexual) to youths. In the scholarly annotation appended to *Vathek*, Beckford links "these supposed intermediate creatures between God and man" in Mohammedan mythology with the Ωντεζ and Εωντες of Platonic tradition.[80]

In the eighteenth century, in contrast to other aestheticians such as Edmund Burke and Immanuel Kant, Johann Winckelmann finds the norm of beauty to exist in the sculpture of a desirable male.[81] Of figures such as the winged ephebe of the Borghese Genius or Eros (Louvre), brought back to Paris by Napoleon after the conquest of Italy,[82] Winckelmann writes:

> What human conception of divinity in sensuous form could be worthier and more enchanting to the imagination than the state of an eternal youth and spring-time of life, whose recollection even in our later years can gladden us? This corresponds to the idea of the immutability of divine being, and a beautiful godly physique awakens tenderness and love, that can transport the soul into a sweet dream of ecstasy, the state of bliss that is sought in all religions, whether they understand it correctly or not.[83]

Winckelmann's transposition of religious idealism into an erotic and aesthetic ideal suffuses both the representation of Alroy and the term, "genius," which was variously ascribed to Disraeli by Beckford, by reviewers, and himself.[84] This particular embodification helps explain both the response of the reviewer for *The Athenaeum*, who recognized "genius . . . stamped on every page" as well as the complaint in the *American Monthly Review* that the style showed the want of gentlemanly "pure taste."[85] In contrast to the pure bliss of Winckelmann's response, the reviewer uses the term in the opposed, Kantian sense of being free from an excessive sensitivity to Apollonian beauty.

Genius is not confined to the realm of taste. As the connection between the Borghese Genius and Napoleon suggests, this figure and others such as the *Apollo Belvedere* that Winckelmann celebrates (and the King Solomon, "beautiful as a woman," whom Disraeli describes) are associated with an aristocratic ideal of heroic action. The conjunction of seductive beauty, aesthetic idealism, and "a true heroic loftiness of soul" throws into relief Alroy's description of himself as a young Alexander.[86] Praising "the heroism of the youthful and still lovely Alroy," Beckford responds to the combination of beauty and adult valor and accomplishment in Disraeli's presentation.[87] This Neoclassic amalgam subtends the erotic tenor of Disraeli's concept of imagination, which refers to a genius both aesthetic and political. The heady combination informs, in turn, his investment in Alroy's relationships with Jabaster and Honain.

In the 1830s, Beckford, now in old age, was about to enjoy renewed literary celebrity as a result of the publication of his travel writing, *Italy: with Sketches of Spain and Portugal* (1834).[88] After having been forced into exile in 1785 as a result of his imaginatively productive but personally disastrous infatuation with Courtenay, later Earl of Devon, Beckford eventually returned to a life of retirement in England.[89] I say "unfortunate" because Lord Loughborough, Courtenay's uncle by marriage, was a bitter rival and political enemy of Beckford's guardian, the Lord Chancellor, Lord Thurlow.[90] Add to this Loughborough's envy and dislike for the witty, effeminate, very wealthy young man; Beckford's irritating show of interest in Courtenay; and the fact that the newspapers were reporting that he was about to be named Lord Beckford of Fonthill, and Loughborough had more than sufficient motive to attempt to entrap Beckford in a sexual indiscretion with his wife's nephew. Even though Loughborough failed in this objective, he used gossip and the press in order to force Beckford to flee the country. The point of these details is not merely anecdotal. The wealth of Beckford and Courtenay, their Parliamentary connections and aristocratic ties, far from shielding their friendship, exposed it to the politics of scandal. Minus these elite entanglements, Beckford is unlikely to have faced disgrace. As for Courtenay, years later he would be forced into exile in order to avoid prosecution for sodomy.[91]

Beckford was implicated in Disraeli's expression of the "secret history of my feelings." Immediately following the passage in the "Mutilated Diary" that I analyzed earlier, he writes:

> Beckford was so enraptured when he read "the Psychological" that he sent Clarke, his confidential agent and publisher with whom alone he corresponds to call upon me on some pretence, or other, and give him a description of the person, converse etc. of the author of what he was

pleased to style "that transcendant work." Clarke called accordingly and wrote back to Beckford that Disraeli was the most conceited person he had ever met in the whole course of his life. B. answered and rated C. roundly for his opinion, telling him that what "appeared conceit in D. was only the irrepressible consciousness of Superior power." Some time after this when Clarke knew me better, he very candidly told me the whole story and gave me a copy of B's letter.[92]

In the trio of Beckford, Clarke, and Disraeli, we find the sort of informal social grouping of privileged men, bound in part by desire for other men, that existed before words like "homosexual" or "subculture" had as yet been invented. For Disraeli, such relations included other persons, often with connections to Lord Byron, such as Edward Bulwer Lytton, Thomas Moore, and John Cam Hobhouse, who were familiar with the poet's sexual divagations. In the early 1830s there was an effort underway in similar groups, for the most part among Disraeli's Whig and Utilitarian antagonists, to relieve the legal sanctions against sodomy. Renewed interest in Beckford as a writer in these years was symptomatic of efforts to alleviate the position of men with sexual and emotional ties to other men. As in the case of Jewish emancipation, in *Alroy* Disraeli intervenes on behalf of legal reform by generating an atmosphere sympathetic to difference.

Beckford met Disraeli on only one occasion, a performance of Rossini's opera, *Semiramide* on 12 June 1834.[93] To his delight, he discovered that, along with a taste for opera, he and Disraeli shared many other interests. After the performance, they conversed for three hours. Enthusiastic about Disraeli's writing, Beckford was eager to learn, with Clarke's assistance, just how sympathetic or, to use Beckford's term, how "partial . . . to French" the young author might be.[94] He considered letting Disraeli read the unpublished manuscript (in French) of the *Episodes of Vathek*.[95] Beckford eventually decided that Disraeli's "french accent" was not good enough to merit sharing the *Episodes*; but Beckford continued to believe that Disraeli's oriental aesthetic closely resembled his own: "He is so strongly imbued with Vathek—the images it presents haunt him continually—the halls of Eblis, the thrones of the Sulimans are for ever present to his mind's eye, tinted with somewhat different hues from those of the original, but partaking of the same awful and dire solemnity."[96] Beckford provides a guide to a sexually dissident reading of *Alroy*, noting not only the attractions of its young protagonist but also the negativity towards women that accompanies Disraeli's investment in relationships between Alroy and older men.

Beckford also recognizes the importance of Honain, which later commentators overlook: "What can be truer to Nature or more admirable than the delineation and development of the character of Honain?"[97]

Beckford also enjoyed Disraeli's sodomitical play with the threat of impalement that impends over Alroy at the end of the novel as punishment for supposedly having engaged in "intercourse with the infernal powers," an allegation traditionally lodged in Christian culture against both Jews and sodomites.[98] Disraeli archly withholds this fate while dangling it before the reader. In a note, he writes: "A friend of mine witnessed this horrible punishment in Upper Egypt. The victim was a man who had secretly murdered nine persons. He held an official post, and invited travelers and pilgrims to his house, whom he regularly disposed of and plundered. I regret that I have mislaid his MS. account of the ceremony."[99] In the 1835 account of his visits to two Portuguese monasteries, Beckford includes a similar sly reference to the mode of execution of Edward II.[100] At the high point of the book, an account of Beckford's introduction to the Portuguese regent in the royal palace at Queluz, Beckford reports: "At this moment, the most terrible, the most agonising shrieks—shrieks such as I hardly conceived possible—shrieks more piercing than those which rung through the Castle of Berkeley, when Edward the Second was put to the most cruel and torturing death—inflicted upon me a sensation of horror such as I never felt before. The [mad] Queen herself, whose apartment was only two rooms off from the chamber in which we were sitting, uttered those dreadful sounds: 'Ai Jesous! Ai Jesous!' did she exclaim again and again in the bitterness of agony."[101]

Because Disraeli associated *Alroy* with his "ideal ambition," commentators assume that he identified with the young protagonist. They ignore his similarly intense engagement with Honain and the sympathies that bind the latter to Alroy. The word "sympathy" is tricky. On the one hand, Alroy's success depends upon "the strong national sympathy" of the Jews.[102] In this light, Honain is chastised for want of sympathy with his brother, Jabaster. Jabaster notes that, when the two men met after having been separated for twenty years, Honain "shrank from my embrace." Someone replies: "Honain is a philosopher, and believes in sympathy. 'Twould appear there was none between you. His system, then, absolves you from all ties."[103] In this context, sympathy based in blood ties is contrasted to a "philosophy" whose concept of sympathy is put in question insofar as it validates ignoring such links. At the same time, Alroy is right in refusing to identify Jewish identity either with blood relationship, subjection to the law, or the re-founding of the kingdom at Jerusalem. His imperial identity is based on coexistence with others and a model of Jewish identity whose emphasis is temporal not spatial, based in shared memory, responsibilities, and aspirations.[104]

Honain is susceptible to another kind of sympathy, which holds open the possibility of developing sociality on a basis of what Edward Said once referred to, in another context, as affiliation in distinction from and contrast to filiation.[105] When Honain meets Alroy, he lays claim to a "prophetic sympathy": "I loved thee from the first."[106] "Our affections are not under our own control; and mine are yours. The sympathy between us is entire."[107] The mutual dedication of the pair leads Alroy, as conqueror of Bagdad, to make Honain his chief vizir.[108] Of course, Honain has developed their sympathy exactly for such a purpose; his relationship to affiliation is altogether "wicked."[109] He plays the role of mentor much as, in the *Episodes*, Firouz plays the role of junior partner. In retrospect, Alasi writes: "Firouz knew me better than I knew myself. He played upon me as he wished. Besides, he had himself well in hand, knew how to act so as to excite my sympathy, and to seem yielding and amenable, as it served his purpose."[110]

As the novel unfolds, the full extent of Honain's cynicism becomes evident. This is the "realism" of the portrayal that Beckford finds so persuasive. From the outset, however, Disraeli has made it clear that Honain is a Jew who is prepared to efface his identity in order to rise to the top. As David remarks when they first meet: "Thou has quitted our antique ark; why; no matter. We'll not discuss it."[111] Honain responds with a sort of Shakespearean soliloquy:

You see me, you see what I am; a Hebrew, though unknown; one of that despised, rejected, persecuted people, of whom you are the chief. I too would be free and honoured. Freedom and honour are mine, but I was my own messiah. I quitted in good time our desperate cause, but I gave it a trial. Ask Jabaster how I fought. Youth could be my only excuse for such indiscretion. I left this country; I studied and resided among the Greeks. I returned from Constantinople, with all their learning, some of their craft. No one knew me. I assumed their turban, and I am, the Lord Honain. Take my experience, child, and save yourself much sorrow. Turn your late adventure to good account. No one can recognize you here. I will introduce you amongst the highest as my child by some fair Greek. The world is before you. You may fight, you may love, you may revel. War, and women, and luxury are all at your command. With your person and talents you may be grand vizir.[112]

Honain's apologia is likewise Disraeli's confession. He too reached
for the highest honors and influence. Becoming a Protestant Englishman, he had relinquished the antique ark. And like Honain, he
knew that the byways to power led not only through women's bou-
doirs but also by way of the ineffable sympathies of male intimacy.
It is important to recognize Disraeli's ambivalent engagement on
Honain's side of the mentor-protégé dyad; it is just as significant as
his cathexis with David Alroy.

Disraeli's partial self-portrait as Honain anticipates the antagonistic, anti-Semitic reaction that he had every reason to expect
proper Englishmen to have against this book. Just as the accident of
the survival of Beckford's letters indicates one important context of
Alroy, the existence of an unpublished manuscript, written immediately after publication of the novel, provides another. The Berg Collection of the New York Public Library holds the manuscript of the
draft outline of a satiric parody of Alroy entitled "The Wondrous
Tale of Ikey Solomons," which, to the best of my knowledge, has
hitherto escaped critical comment. Although corrections indicate
the manuscript to be a working draft not to be read by others, the
text does convey the anti-Semitic attitudes of the English elite
among whom its author, Richard Harris Barham, a well-known
clergyman and comic author, circulated. Barham's parody is based
on the idea of substituting Isaac Solomon for Alroy as hero of the
narrative. Solomon had been in the news in 1831, when at the end
of a long, highly successful career in business and crime on three
continents, he was transported to Hobart Town for receiving stolen
goods. The life of Solomon in *The New Newgate Calendar* (1840)
parodies the typically English story of the poor boy who manages
to parlay a "small capital" into a large fortune.[113] Solomon was
well known for his extraordinary effrontery and success (at the time
of his arrest he was reported to be in possession of £20,000 in stolen
goods).[114]

Barham also includes a parody of Jabaster in the figure of the
High Priest, who looks upon Alroy/Ikey with " 'large luminous
eyes.' " Further details of the description (the "beard" that hangs
"down to his waist-band, red plush breeches with yellow buttons,"
and "greasy hat") indicate that Barham's principal interest is in
conflating Jabaster, the Doctor, and Alroy with popular representations of Jewish immigrants and criminals.[115] Barham's "Wondrous
Tale" conflates anti-Jewish stereotypes with popular attacks on
members of the lower classes, who contaminate the body politic
through crime and grossly excessive consumption of food, drink,
and intoxicants. To these charges are added the further allegations

that Jews, being foreigners, can speak or write in English only on the basis of fraud. To Disraeli's affectations of genius, Barham responds that such "genius" can only be "a Literary Larceny."[116]

Jews likewise threaten the commercial probity of the City. *Newgate Calendar* lives of Jewish criminals emphasize their involvement in counterfeiting paper currency, which they refer to, in thieves' cant, as " 'queer screens.' "[117] Likewise Jews are infidels who subvert the true faith. Although Disraeli is the specific target, the tendency for aspects of the representation to shift between "Asher Levi," the purported author of Barham's "Wondrous Tale"; the "perfidious friend" who steals it; and Ikey alias Isaac Solomon indicates that Levi/Isaac is a generic representation of the tribe of "degenerate brethren."[118] Barham sums these suggestions in the comic raid that Ikey and an associate make upon the pantry of the Archbishop of Canterbury. In another allegation, Barham's worst since it proceeds beyond Solomon to an indictment of Azkenazic Jews generally, Barham reports that "the Hebrew People" of Petticoat Lane have stolen "the Communion Plate from the Sacristy of St. Paul's Cathedral," then had it melted down into " 'white soup,' " a term Barham glosses as thieves' argot for "melted silver."[119] But the phrase also connotes illicit consumption: the milky fluid of opium, a drug that Disraeli smoked during his Eastern tour of 1830–1831.[120] The dissolution of sacred vessels into unidentifiable bars of metal is a metaphor of the destruction of an incorporating national faith.

CONCLUSION

In addition to the writer who is fascinated with both sides of sodomitic political ties, there is yet another Disraeli figured in *Alroy*, namely, the narrator who memorializes the doomed "Prince of the Captivity." Disraeli makes restitution for his apostasy through an act of fidelity to Jewish tradition. Miriam, Alroy's imaginary other—who mirrors Disraeli's sister, Sarah, to whom he dedicated the novel—prophesies this role.[121] Transvaluing the word "usury," traditionally lodged against Jews as the emblem of their perverse relation to the orders of production and reproduction, Miriam tells Alroy in prison: "Great deeds are great legacies, and work with wondrous usury. By what Man has done, we learn what Man can do; and gauge the power and prospects of our race. . . . And so sweet brother, perchance some poet, in some distant age, within whose veins our sacred blood may flow, his fancy fired with the

national theme, may strike his harp to Alroy's wild career, and con-
secrate a name too long forgotten."[122] Since Alroy's fate as a Jew
is not to be able to found a nation-state, it will be left to a later
"poet" to turn the memory of defeat into the portent of a victory
that signifies for both the Jewish and the wider "race."

In the final pages of the novel, Alroy achieves purity at a high
price. If, as Julia Kristeva contends, the human corpse is the most
abjected of objects, mute witness to the inevitable failure of the effort to distance the embodied self from its material constituents,
then Alroy's end (which is the end of Disraeli's narrative) is utterly
abject. At the very moment when Alroy achieves sublime transcendence, his head is cut off by the King of Karasmé. Although the
economy of such a sacrifice is thoroughly conventional, it leaves
Disraeli with a number of as yet unresolved questions.[123] The first
of these is whether it is possible to pursue one's ambitions without
sacrificing the "ideal." This question refers not only to the need to
be true to group loyalties and the faith of one's forebears; it refers
as well to the question of how to avoid a debasing subjection to
political leaders. Disraeli drives this point home by triply subjecting
Alroy to the King of Karasmé; to Princess Schirene; and, most especially, to Honain, who plays the Whiggish role of Sir Robert Walpole at the court of Bagdad. When Honain tempts Alroy to
repudiate his Jewish faith, he invites him to become the sodomitical
accomplice of the dominant political (and religious) order. Unan-
swered is the question whether a like fate awaits Disraeli. Disraeli's
dandyish dress advertised the threat of being unmanned while turning it into a taunt against those like Barham who would convict him
of racial *and* sexual degeneracy.

The second set of questions has to do with the topic of what
Alroy refers to as "strong national sympathy."[124] How can one
transform politics by means of popular patriotism when the members of some religious, ethnic, and economic groups are more equal
than others? In 1833, the Jewish Emancipation Bill, which had successfully passed the House of Commons, was rejected by the Lords.
As I pointed out at the outset, for Alroy the question takes the specific form of how one who belongs to a particular minority can
achieve emancipation within a much larger entity. Although these
questions are not resolved at the end of the novel, their connection
with the abjection of a people is manifest. Equally manifest is the
demand that such abjection be annulled by the practice of an impossible purity. Barham's squib shows that such demands will always
be turned into new allegations of defilement.

Yet Disraeli is not quite through with his Anglo-Saxon antagonists. Disraeli's repudiation of Jabaster's national program comments in displaced fashion on the effort, aggressively pursued in the nineteenth century, to refine differences within British society into a single Christian identity that validated Britain's Anglo-Saxon heritage at the expense of other aspects. Turner, Disraeli's baptismal sponsor, was a leading exponent of a mythically unified definition of English nationality. In his *History of the Anglo-Saxons* (1799–1805), he uses the concept of "conversion" to efface the persecution of Jews in England while praising the process of "improving progress," whereby the Anglo-Saxon developed from the condition of a pirate into that of the modern Englishman.[125] In refusing to heed Jabaster, Alroy/Disraeli revolts against his own godfather's demand for a unitary concept of the body politic. At the same time, in ultimately rejecting Honain, Disraeli repudiates Turner's role in turning the boy Disraeli into a renegade against his heritage.[126]

Disraeli rejected the mystifications and prejudice of nineteenth-century "English" nationalism. However, he would continue to feel its stings. In the mid-1870s, after Jewish emancipation had been achieved, Liberals, Radicals, Nonconformists, and a number of Anglicans led a campaign against Disraeli's foreign policy in which it, he, and Jews generally were attacked on the ground of what William Gladstone referred to as their "Judaic sympathies."[127] After Disraeli returned from the Congress of Berlin in July 1878, having checked Russian influence in the Balkans and gained the island of Cyprus as a British outpost in the Aegean, one commentator wrote: "That day represented the triumph, not of England, not of an English policy, not of an Englishman. It was the triumph of Judea, a Jewish policy, a Jew. The Hebrew, who drove through these crowds to Downing Street, was dragging the whole of Christendom behind the juggernaut car over the rights of Turkish Christians, of which he was the charioteer."[128] In face of the unembarrassed directness of this assault, the radicalism of Disraeli's early oriental romance is yet more evident. Disraeli defended Jewish cultural practices, religious belief, and historical identity at a time when they were under attack even by his own father. Notwithstanding Disraeli's commitment to British imperialism, he endorsed the concept of a futurity for Jewish collectivity while dissociating the state from a singular religious ideology, ethnic or racial identity. This complex outlook is cognate with what Boyarin describes as the double tendency within Jewish cultural tradition to validate both Jewish practices and a vision of universal emancipation. The courage, subtlety, and intellectual toughness of Disraeli's thinking help account for

George Eliot's turn to the rhetoric of Jewish emancipation in expressing her own resistance to a unitary national subject in *Daniel Deronda* (1876), at a time of both belated vindication and continuing vilification for England's Jewish prime minister.

NOTES

1. Jane Ridley, *Young Disraeli: 1804–1846* (New York: Crown, 1995), 125.

2. Benjamin Disraeli, "The Mutilated Diary," *Letters: 1815–1834*, ed. J. A. W. Gunn, John Matthews, Donald M. Schurman, and M. G. Wiebe (Toronto: University of Toronto Press, 1982), 447; hereafter cited in notes as *Letters*.

3. Benjamin Disraeli, *Whigs and Whiggism: Political Writings*, ed. William Hutcheon (London: John Murray, 1913), 85, 96; *Letters* 2: 37.

4. Ridley, *Young Disraeli;* see also Stanley Weintraub, *Disraeli: A Biography* (New York: Truman Talley Books, 1993).

5. Contemporary men of letters frequently reminded Disraeli both of this Jewishness and his effeminacy. For men such as the editor, John Gibson Lockhart—a Lowland Scot with aristocratic and Church connections—Disraeli was never able to overcome being Jewish. Even later, in the 1840s, when he published *Coningsby*, Lockhart remarked to his son: "Ben Disraeli, the Jew scamp, has published a very blackguard novel. . . . Awful vanity of the Hebrew!" (Ridley 124). Commentators enjoyed rewriting his name so as to accentuate its foreignness. In the earliest journalistic literary study of Disraeli, for example, W. Maginn writes: "O Reader dear! do pray look here, and you will spy the curly hair, and forehead fair, and nose so high, and gleaming eye of Benjamin D'Is-ra-el-i, the wondrous boy who wrote *Alroy* in rhyme and prose, only to show how long ago victorious Judah's lion-banner rose" (R. W. Stewart, ed., *Disraeli's Novels Reviewed* [Metuchen, N.J.: Scarecrow Press, 1975], 17). Under the surveillance of a Tory journal, Disraeli is seen to be an exponent of Jewish triumphalism. But he is also effeminate: a girlish "boy," with "curly hair, and forehead fair." He affects aristocratic hauteur, but the very signs of social distinction (the "nose" carried "so high") signify the mortified pride and social abjection of the Jew.

6. Andrew Elfenbein, *Byron and the Victorians* (Cambridge: Cambridge University Press, 1995), ch. 6.

7. Alan Bray, *Homosexuality in Renaissance England* (London: Gay Men's Press, 1982), 67–70.

8. Linda Dowling, *Hellenism and Homosexuality in Victorian Oxford* (Ithaca: Cornell University Press, 1994), 5, 9n.

9. Ibid., 15.

10. Ibid.

11. Ridley, *Young Disraeli*, 38, 41, 275–76.

12. Jonathan Goldberg, *Sodometries: Renaissance Texts, Modern Sexualities* (Stanford: Stanford University Press, 1992), ch. 4.

13. Richard Dellamora, *Masculine Desire: The Sexual Politics of Victorian Aestheticism* (Chapel Hill: University of North Carolina Press, 1990), 211–12.

14. Gary Schmidgall, *The Stranger Wilde: Interpreting Oscar* (New York: Dutton, 1994), 43–63; see also Oliver S. Buckton, *Secret Selves: Confession and Same-Sex Desire in Victorian Autobiography* (Chapel Hill: University of North Carolina Press, 1998), 21–59.

15. William Beckford, *Vathek and Other Stories*, ed. Malcolm Jack (London: Penguin, 1993), 70–71.

16. Ibid., 42.

17. Ibid., 41.

18. Ibid., 84.

19. Ibid., 85.

20. Ibid., 97.

21. William Beckford, *The Episodes of Vathek* (Sawtry, Cambs: Dedalus, 1994), 21.

22. Later, this unnatural attraction is rationalized by the notional fiction that Firouz is, in fact, Firouzkah, a woman in disguise.

23. Michel Foucault, *The History of Sexuality, Volume 1: An Introduction*, trans. Robert Hurley (New York: Pantheon, 1978), 58–61.

24. Beckford, *Episodes*, 24.

25. Brian Fothergill, *Beckford of Fonthill* (London: Faber, 1979), 165–66.

26. Adam Potkay, "Beckford's Heaven of Boys," *Raritan* 13 (Summer 1993): 73–86.

27. Michel Foucault, *The Use of Pleasure*, volume 2 of *The History of Sexuality*, trans. Robert Hurley (New York: Vintage, 1986), 187–246.

28. Fothergill, *Beckford*, 206, 209, 293–96.

29. Christopher Marlowe, *Edward the Second*, ed. W. Moelwyn Merchant (1967; rpt., New York: Norton, 1994), 1.4. 87.

30. I have in mind the terms of Mordecai, in George Eliot's novel, *Daniel Deronda*, including the commentary on the novel by David Kaufmann, *George Eliot and Judaism: An Attempt to Appreciate "Daniel Deronda,"* trans. J. W. Ferrier (1888; rpt. New York: Haskell House Publishers, Ltd., 1970).

31. On sexual inversion, see Christopher Craft, *Another Kind of Love: Male Homosexual Desire in English Discourse, 1850–1920* (Berkeley: University of California Press, 1994), 33–36.

32. Linda Colley, *Britons: Forging the Nation 1707–1837* (New Haven: Yale University Press, 1992), 349; see also E. P. Thompson, *The Making of the English Working Class* (Harmondsworth: Penguin, 1972), 909–10.

33. Louis Crompton, "*Don Leon*, Byron, and Homosexual Law Reform," *Journal of Homosexuality*, 8 (Spring–Summer 1983): 53–71.

34. Beckford, *Vathek*, xvii–xxii.

35. For this and other possible meanings of the word, see Michael Ragussis, *Figures of Conversion: "The Jewish Question" and English National Identity* (Durham: Duke University Press, 1995), 157–59. Like other Jewish commentators, Elaine Marks speaks of Jewish converts to Christianity as "crypto-Jews" (Elaine Marks, *Marrano as Metaphor: The Jewish Presence in French Writing* (New York: Columbia University Press, 1996), 129. In an important study, however, Benzion Netanyahu argues convincingly that Jewish converts did, in fact, adopt Christian belief; see Henry Kamen, "The Secret of the Inquisition," *New York Review of Books*, February 1, 1996, 4–6. Quoting Yirmiyahu Yovel, Marks describes a set of attitudes arising from existence as a Marrano: "A this-worldly disposition; a split religious identity; a metaphysical skepticism; a quest for alternative salvation through methods that oppose the official doctrine; an opposition between the inner and outer life, and a tendency toward dual language and equivocation" (133).

36. Benjamin Disraeli, *Alroy*, Introduction, Philip Guedalla (London: Peter Davies, 1927), 248.

37. Ibid., 261.

38. Ibid., 149, 148.

39. Daniel Boyarin, *A Radical Jew: Paul and the Politics of Identity* (Berkeley: University of California Press, 1994), 3, 8.

40. Gauri Viswanathan, "Raymond Williams and British Colonialism," *Yale Journal of Criticism,* 4 (Spring 1991): 47–66.

41. Already in debate with the Irish nationalist, Daniel O'Connell, Disraeli uses the need to protect heterogeneity as a rationale for continued English domination of Ireland. Despite his defense elsewhere of Jewish difference, Disraeli in a series of political columns in the *Morning Post* is happy to speak—as a *Protestant Englishman*—in mockery of Catholic Irish and the Scots. He dubs O'Connell's supporters "Popish rebels" (85). And Sir John Campbell, the Attorney General, is a "baseborn Scotchman, . . . this booing, fawning, jobbing progeny of haggis and cockaleekie" (89). As so often in English writing in the nineteenth century, ethnic differences close to home become metaphors of the most extreme sort of racial, implicitly sexual degeneracy. Disraeli compares Campbell with "an ourang-outang of unusual magnitude dancing under a banana-tree, and licking its hairy chaps, and winking with exultation its cunning eyes as it beholds the delicious and impending fruit" (Disraeli, *Whigs and Whiggism*, 85, 89, 88–89). Attacks such as this indicate that Disraeli was as capable of xenophobic assaults as were other contemporaries such as Thomas Carlyle and Charles Kingsley. Compare, for example, the latter's infamous comparison of the Irish to "white chimpanzees" (quoted by Anne McClintock, *Imperial Leather: Race, Gender, and Sexuality in the Colonial Contest* [New York: Routledge, 1995], 216).

42. See Beckford's note, *Vathek,* 118.

43. Beckford, *Vathek,* 93–94.

44. Disraeli, *Alroy,* 95–96.

45. Ibid., 96.

46. Isaac Disraeli, *The Genius of Judaism* (London: Edward Moxon, 1833), 256–58.

47. Disraeli, *Letters,* 447.

48. Ridley, *Young Disraeli,* 34–41.

49. Disraeli, *Whigs and Whiggism,* 2.

50. Ernest Gellner, *Nations and Nationalism* (Oxford: Basil Blackwell, 1983), 125. In a classic analysis of Jane Austen's *Mansfield Park*, Edward W. Said sees imperial expansion as an aspect of the modernization of the nation-state (*Culture and Imperialism* [New York: Vintage, 1994], 80–97). For the convergence of Disraeli's foreign policy with cockney jingoism, see David Feldman, *Englishmen and Jews: Social Relations and Political Culture, 1840–1914* (New Haven: Yale University Press, 1994), 94–97, 115–20.

51. Simon During, "Literature—Nationalism's Other? The Case for Revision," in *Nation and Narration,* ed. Homi K. Bhabha (London: Routledge, 1994), 140,141. See Gellner, who suggests that "conservative traditionalists" can find common ground with nationalists on grounds of race and other commonalities (133). One finds both elements in Disraeli's *Morning Post* articles.

52. Disraeli, *Whigs and Whiggism,* 44.

53. Joseph Childers, *Novel Possibilities: Fiction and the Formation of Early Victorian Culture* (Philadelphia: University of Pennsylvania Press, 1995), 53.

54. *Contarini Fleming: A Psychological Romance* (1832).

55. Disraeli, *Letters,* 1: 447.

56. During, 147; but Childers disagrees (*Novel Possibilities,* 52–68). Gary Wihl has argued that generalizations about the relationship between the novel and ideol-

ogy should be treated with caution ("Novels as Theories in a Liberal Society," in *Constructive Criticism: The Human Sciences in the Age of Theory,* eds., Martin Kreiswirth and Thomas Carmichael [Toronto: University of Toronto Press, 1995], (101–113).

57. Sigmund Freud, "Creative Writers and Day-Dreaming" and "Family Romances" in *The Standard Edition of the Complete Psychological Works*, trans. and ed. James Strachey with Anna Freud, 9 (London: Hogarth Press, 1974), 143–53, 237–41.

58. Later in the essay, I connect "embodification" with Teresa de Lauretis's concept of "sexual structuring." See Teresa de Laurentis, "Habit Changes" *Differences,* 6 (Summer-Fall 1994), 296–313.

59. Ridley, *Young Disraeli,* 127.

60. Disraeli, *Alroy,* x.

61. Ibid., 1.

62. Ibid.

63. Ibid., 4.

64. Ibid.

65. Ibid., 6.

66. Ibid., 157.

67. Ibid., 162, 164.

68. Mary Douglas, *Purity and Danger: An Analysis of Concepts of Pollution and Taboo* (Harmondsworth: Penguin, 1966), 54–73. Julia Kristeva, *Powers of Horror: An Essay in Abjection,* trans. Leon S. Roudiez (New York: Columbia University Press, 1982).

69. Disraeli, *Alroy,* 191–92.

70. Jane Gallop, *The Daughter's Seduction: Feminism and Psychoanalysis* (Ithaca: Cornell University Press, 1989), 115, 117.

71. Kaufmann, *George Eliot and Judaism,* 7–8.

72. Ibid., 3, 2, 4.

73. The capital letter refers to Lacan's usage (Jacques Lacan, *Écrits: A Selection,* trans. Alan Sheridan [New York: W. W. Norton, 1977], 311) and, more significantly, to the following passage in the book of Jewish ritual in use in London since 1780: "All *Jewish* Parents are reckoned to be accountable for the Sins of their Sons, till they are thirteen Years old, but no longer; and therefore when Boys arrive to their thirteenth Year, they are for the first Time called up to the Law that is read on the Altar in their Synagogue on the Sabbath-Day, and read a Chapter or more in the Law themselves, . . . entering into Man's State, in Regard of becoming accountable for himself, from that Day" (Weintraub, *Disraeli,* 31).

74. Disraeli, *Alroy,* 271.

75. Ibid., 265.

76. Ibid., 254.

77. Elfenbein discusses the gender anxieties and sexual perversity that accompany the idealization of the brother-sister dyad, in *Byron and The Victorians* (22, 33–35).

78. Disraeli, *Alroy,* 70.

79. Ibid., 97.

80. Beckford,*Vathek,* 99.

81. John Joachim Winckelmann, *History of Ancient Art,* trans. G. Henry Lodge (New York: Ungar, 1968) I, 215; Alex Potts, *Flesh and the Ideal: Winckelmann and the Origins of Art History* (New Haven: Yale University Press, 1994), 118–32; see also Richard Dellamora, "The Androgynous Body in Pater's 'Winckel-

mann,' " *Browning Institute Studies,* 11 (1983), 51–68. For a different articulation of Potts's views, see Alex Potts, "Beautiful Bodies and Dying Heroes: Images of Ideal Manhood in the French Revolution," *History Workshop Journal,* 30 (Fall 1990): 1–21.

82. Alex Potts, "Beautiful Bodies, 20, 27n.

83. Ibid., 2, 12.

84. Beckford describes Disraeli as a "genius" (Oliver 101).

85. Stewart, *Disraeli's Novels Reviewed,* 144, 145.

86. I take Alroy's reference to "the conqueror of the world" (149) as an allusion to Alexander. The quotation is from the *Athenaeum* review (Stewart, *Disraeli's Novels Reviewed,* 144).

87. J. W. Oliver, *The Life of William Beckford* (London: Oxford University Press, 1932), 300.

88. Boyd Alexander, *England's Wealthiest Son: A Study of William Beckford* (London: Centaur Press, 1962), 18.

89. Ibid., chap. 8–9.

90. Ibid., 107–8.

91. Louis Crompton, *Byron and Greek Love: Homophobia in 19th-century England* (Berkeley: Univ. of California Press, 1985), 180–81.

92. Disraeli, *Letters,* 1: 447.

93. Ibid., 1:, 411–12, 419 n. 8.

94. Oliver, The phrase current today is *comme ça.* See D. A. Miller, *Bringing Out Roland Barthes* (Berkeley: Univ. of California Press, 1992), 6.

95. Oliver, 298.

96. Ibid., 299, 300.

97. Ibid.

98. Disraeli, *Alroy,* 244.

99. Ibid., 281.

100. Fothergill, 230.

101. Ibid., 230–31.

102. Disraeli, *Alroy,* 124.

103. Ibid., 182.

104. For a context in contemporary Jewish cultural politics, see Jonathan Boyarin, *Storm from Paradise: The Politics of Jewish Memory* (Minneapolis: Univ. of Minnesota Press, 1992), xvii.

105. Said defines *affiliation* as "a joining together of people in a non-genealogical, non-procreative but *social* unity" (Edward Said, "On Repetition," in *The Literature of Fact,* Selected Papers from the English Institute, ed. Angus Fletcher [New York: Columbia Univ. Press, 1976], 146).

106. Disraeli, *Alroy,* 59.

107. Ibid., 62.

108. Ibid., 181.

109. Ibid., 250.

110. Beckford, *Episodes,* 25.

111. Disraeli, *Alroy,* 61.

112. Ibid., 62.

113. Camden Pelham, *The Chronicles of Crime; or, The New Newgate Calendar* (London: Miles, 1887), 2 : 236.

115. Richard Harris Barham, "The Wondrous Tale of Ikey Solomons" (Berg Collection, New York Public Library), mss. sh. 6.

116. Ibid. sh 1.

117. Pelham 2 : 236.

118. Barham, mss. sh. 2; *The Newgate Calendar or Malefactors' Bloody Register* (London: T. Werner Laurie, 1932), 814.

119. Ibid., sh. 3, 4. Barham glosses "white soup" as thieves' argot for "melted silver."

120. Ridley, *Young Disraeli,* 99; see also Barham, mss. sh. 8.

122. Disraeli, *Alroy,* 255.

123. Elaine Scarry, *The Body in Pain: The Making and Unmaking of the World* (New York: Oxford Univ. Press, 1987), Part One.

124. Disraeli, *Alroy,* 124.

125. Ragussis, *Figures of Conversion,* 93–94.

126. Weintraub, 31–32.

127. Feldman, *Englishmen and Jews,* 103.

128. Feldman, 106, 118.

The Private Pleasures of Silas Marner

DONALD E. HALL

> Bite my lip and close my eyes
> Slipping away to paradise
> Some say quit or I'll go blind
> But it's just a myth.
>
> "Longview," Greenday

THE SOCIALLY DISTANT, APPARENTLY SELF-SUFFICIENT INDIVIDUAL invariably provokes suspicion, but often she or he is confronted with even more intrusive actions. "What are you doing in that room by yourself? Get *outside* and do something!"—how many times did I hear that parental query and command as a bookish (and, yes, rather masturbation-happy) adolescent in the 1970s? Implicitly acknowledged, of course, was that I was already "doing something," but whatever it was that I "was doing" was inappropriately hidden, was disturbing because silent, provoking because unmonitored. More recent, widely expressed worries about the effects of long hours spent by the young playing on computers or with video games similarly point to concerns well beyond those of physical health, even if expressed as "she may hurt her eyes" or "he is rotting his brain." At issue still is a fundamental question concerning proper socialization, the required movement into, acknowledgment of, and continuous proving of allegiance to standards of social propriety, or more specifically, to a social power structure which encompasses demands (meaning, in desired effect, commands) by parents, teachers, religious figures, medical professionals, and other authorities concerning what one may or may not do with one's own body, a body that should (learn to) fit seamlessly into the smooth functionings of the body politic.

Of course "provoke" is not the only verb that one might choose to characterize the (in)action of a relatively motionless and isolated body. Can passivity be said to provoke? Yes, if we recognize that noncompliance of even the most inert sort is a form of agency, that insularity and nonconformity are often perceived as having a viral potential. Ask anyone who has refused to disperse or "move along" at a cop's command. Ask any kid who has silently resisted eating her dinner. Indeed, ask anyone who simply wishes to be left alone. (In the 1995 film *Powder* the happily isolated title character is forced into social contact, is killed by society's desire to "norm" him, by teachers and social workers who scoff at his cry, "I don't *need* a friend.") Imperviousness is impiety, and the symbolic will have its way.

Yet even as I write, computer facility, often achieved in solitude, is acknowledged as a prerequisite for a "good job." At clubs and other music venues, solitary dancing has become relatively common. Today, parents are often simply too busy and overworked to socialize their children aggressively. If we believe William Bennett, George Will, and other conservatives, the last trend, in particular, threatens the very fabric of our society, though, to my mind, that is not an inherently frightening possibility, even if it is far-fetched. Cultural theorists have long recognized that substantially differing subjectivities are practically impossible given the heavy valence of normalizing discourses. Even the adolescent sitting alone in her room reading, with the door decisively locked, is hardly outside of cultural control, just as the heavy-lidded masturbator, relishing a few minutes by himself, clearly indulges in fantasies that come from outside the physical body. Yet relative distance from and skepticism about the rewards for full integration into "society," whether articulated or silently lived, should provoke more than a uniformly sanctioned normalizing imperative, should also provoke us to reflect on who, in fact, manages to distance himself from the most egregious forms of socially uninterrogated abuse of others, who manages, even temporarily, to disengage herself from the mechanistic performance of oppression, and who, therefore, becomes castigated and marked, lamentably, as an object needing formation, social work and reintegration. If the Symbolic is the problem, does anyone achieve even a fleeting moment of dissolution?

Of course the Victorians had their own intense worries about socializing "normality," ones certainly divergent from our own, but also allowing us some insight into the continuing dynamics of cultural reproduction and late twentieth-century uses of "the Victorian" to that very end. In *Making a Social Body*, Mary Poovey traces an aggressive and successful process of social homogenization that occurred in Britain during the early and middle decades of the nineteenth century, one accomplished through the conjoined work of a wide variety of policy-makers, institutions, and texts. Focusing on the development of technologies such as the first census in 1801 and the appearance of "material innovations like affordable transportation, cheap publications, and national museums," Poovey demonstrates how "groups that had rarely mixed [were brought gradually] into physical proximity with each other and [were] represented . . . as belonging to the same, increasingly undifferentiated whole."[1] While I have argued elsewhere that very explicit forms of class differentiation were, in fact, key to the creation of a defensively poised, internationally engaged British "self-hood" during this time period,[2] I do agree with Poovey that "by 1860, the idea that individuals were alike in being responsible (economic and moral) agents was being advanced as a substitute for the tutelary role that the metaphor of the social body had initially assigned to the state."[3] That process of moving from widely articulated threats of punishment to an increasing reliance upon internalized forms of discipline was accomplished through remarkably effective forms of specifically discursive homogenization, through, one might say, colonization of unknown or suspicious, only partially known, internal territories—imprinting a British selfhood upon divergently identifying or opaquely subjectivized, threateningly nonidentifying bodies.

Judith Halberstam has explored recently, and with great insight, the novelistic use of "monstrosity" in furthering this "internal colonization" of Jews during the nineteenth century; she asks, implicitly, of course, who exactly were the real "monsters" here?[4] Indeed, the catalogue of horrors helping comprise many of the most broadly sanctioned forms of Victorian selfhood is well-known and explored at length in the essay collection before you: sexist, racist, classist, increasingly (as language metamorphosed) homophobic, and strikingly xenophobic, the Victorians can be seen as both victims and perpetrators, formed by discourses that depended upon hierarchized binaries and plagued by anxieties that fueled oppressive actions toward others. Indeed, few successfully, multidimensionally resistant figures emerge from the pages of Victorian writing: Jane Eyre is dependent upon colonial exploitation for income no matter how angry she may be concerning her own subjugation; Dickens's and Kingsley's working class heroes usually abet appalling gender ideologies. One would have to be "beyond" language and culture entirely to elude its oppression-producing systems of reference, an impossibility even for the insane or cloistered, who must depend upon and at least sporadically encounter the surrounding world even if they barely participate in it. And in any case, such individuals rarely find their way into the realm of Victorian cultural representation. Even if we wished to congratulate heartily a catatonic Victorian on his success at not oppressing others, his name and life story is hardly to be found in a novel by Thackeray or a poem by Tennyson (though I must confess to having always felt a measure of respect for the Lotos-Eaters).

Yet one character does come to mind, a figure whose relative adiscursivity is marked as "the" problem to be solved in the novel, whose narrative progression allows us to see, in microcosmic form, the process that Poovey focuses on, whose setting (early nineteenth century) and publication (1861) dates even conveniently mirror those of Poovey, and whose use today by agents working to imprint culture highlights the continuing, preventive work required to maintain mass social identity, as new generations are interpellated and as discourses re-form and reproduce. I am referring, of course, to *Silas Marner*, whom I and millions of others were required to study, indeed learn from, in high school, and who today continues to occupy a place on numerous required reading lists. Even though he is relatively silent (and in many ways because he is so silent) Silas Marner tells us much about George Eliot, about the Victorians in general, and about ourselves, as we fill in his blanks in highly revealing ways.

Silas's self-chosen isolation in the first half of the novel bearing his name is insistently presented, and therefore understandably, uniformly perceived, as a problem requiring remediation; it is unhealthy and pathetic. "[W]ithered and yellow," Silas seems to embody at once personal illness and social dis-ease.[5] Indeed, most critics agree that the novel has something of a healing function. For Gillian Beer, it "restores [Silas] to life"[6] as he becomes "again part of the community of humankind"[7]; Bernard Semmel makes almost precisely the same point: "The love of Eppie replaces Marner's preoccupation with accumulation and restores him to the fellowship of *Gemeinschaft*."[8] Indeed, it appears that there is little else to be said about this "poetic novel"[9] of "moral development."[10] But I would like to offer an alternate reading of *Silas Marner*, to resist the nearly irresistible urge to pity (to find a lamentable "lack" in) the early, isolated Silas and, in effect, participate in and continue to enable such trajectories of unquestioned "moral" development. One might disparage such a reading as perverse, and certainly it is, as the novel barely permits it, but perversity has its uses, often allowing us a

starting point for recognizing certain norms going generally unre-
marked upon and therefore substantially uncontested.

So what is wrong with Silas the miserly hermit? Everything?
Anything? Nothing? It does depend upon one's perspective, and,
indeed, one might try placing oneself in Silas's shoes for a moment,
even though the novel makes such a positioning both difficult to
achieve and impossible to maintain. After being erroneously condemned for theft by a judgmental, narrow-minded religious community, Silas flees to the village of Raveloe, where his distrust of
society and skepticism regarding its collective wisdom only deep-
ens. After generously helping an ill woman, Silas is "beset" by in-
quiring villagers who "wanted him to charm away the whooping
cough, or bring back the milk, . . . who wanted stuff against the
rheumatics or the knots in the hands."[11] Knowing nothing about
such quackery, "he drove one after another away with growing irri-
tation," while still "no one believed him when he said he knew no
charms."[12] It is with a sense of "heightened . . . repulsion"[13] that
Silas finally closes his door on the villagers, turning his back on
a community, but, more specifically, on a superstitious, intrusive
discursive community which has summarily overruled all of his assertions and scoffed at his simple claims to fundamental knowledge
about his own abilities. Indeed, Raveloe never stops insisting that it
knows much more than he about what he can, and should, do.

Is it any wonder, then, that Silas turns to inanimate objects for
forms of companionship that do not violate his own beliefs or sense
of fundamental proprietorship over his "self"? Eliot has placed
Silas in two succeeding situations where society misjudges and
mistreats this honest, if nonconforming, individual, where with-
drawal becomes the only form of resistance possible. Thus to protect himself, his "self," Silas chooses solitude, wishing only to be
left alone, to amuse himself, by himself, or rather with his coin collection: "He loved the guineas best, but he would not change the
silver. . . ; he loved them all. He spread them out in heaps and
bathed his hands in them; then he counted them and set them up in
regular piles, and he felt their rounded outline between his thumb
and fingers."[14] Compared to those nosy, noisy villagers, his coins
provide calming, consistent, and nonexploitative forms of fulfillment: "He handled them, he counted them, till their form and col-
our were like the satisfaction of a thirst to him; but it was only in
the night, when his work was done, that he drew them out to enjoy
their companionship."[15] Of course, the second half of that description pushes what could be nascent support for Silas among readers
toward active discomfort, even disgust. Alone in his hovel at night,

caressing his coins, fingering them repeatedly, loving them intensely, Silas is as thoroughly self-absorbed and blissful as he is repulsive to the social observer; after all, repulsion is his express intent, and it is nearly impossible to resist Eliot's castigation of the miser's "narrowing" behavior.[16] His repulsive activity may serve his needs, but how does it serve readers' needs?

And society, the novel insists, must be served. As theorists have long argued, the novel is itself an inherently social form, as it depends upon and replicates key social conventions and, moreover, appeals to our desire for viewing and participating in the resolution of a problem, a "social" activity in itself. For the reader to be "fulfilled," he or she must be allowed "in," which Silas resists. Yet such readerly "nosiness" (in many ways mirroring that of Raveloe—"tell us things," "charm us") does not fully account for the degree of deference to social authority which is finally used in *Silas Marner* as the determiner of all value and success. Diverging memorably from the general pattern in Victorian fiction that Michiel Heyns uncovers in his recent *Expulsion and the Nineteenth-Century Novel*, Silas does not figure as a social scapegoat, because his castigation and exclusion are not presented as a solution to society's problems; instead, they *are* the problem. In unparalleled fashion, *Silas Marner* equates isolation with extinction: "So, year after year, Silas Marner had lived in this solitude, his guineas rising in the iron pot, and his life narrowing and hardening itself more and more into a mere pulsation of desire and satisfaction that had no relation to any other being. His life had reduced itself to the mere functions of weaving and hoarding."[17]

Of course, the imposition above of a "reading" onto Silas's existence is in no way masked, because diverging even from her own previous characterizations, Eliot has little desire to explore Silas's perceptions of his life; instead she gives voice to a social viewpoint that demands visible breadth rather than (nearly) invisible narrowness and social eruptions (one supposes) rather than hidden pulsations. Later, she admits, "it had been an eager life, filled with immediate purpose, which fenced him in from the wide, cheerless unknown. It had been a clinging life; and though the object round which its fibres had clung was a dead, disrupted thing, it satisfied the need for clinging."[18] Of course, the key charge embedded here and elsewhere is that this "satisfaction" of "desire" (however "functional" or sufficient from Silas's perspective) "had no relation to any other being"; it fences us out. That such a fence can help make for a "self"-contented life is even granted: during his miserly existence, Silas's "legs were weary, but his mind was at

ease, free from the presentiment of change."[19] Spinning and hoarding, weaving his cloth and caressing his coins, Silas, "at ease,"
seems to have entered a rather enviable state of something like
meditative transcendence—peaceful, relaxed, and happy within the
small circle of his own existence. But clearly these are not the novel's standards for evaluation, because even though "eager" and purposeful, Silas's existence fails to revolve around other people; his
small "system" of pleasure and happiness is located within his own
hovel, rather than spinning outwards toward a universe that demands his fealty to its physical laws governing attraction, repulsion,
revolution, and entropy.

And those laws insist and depend upon both visibility and perme-
ability, both of which Silas in his "solitary imprisonment" has
managed to resist.[20] Yet Eliot's diction here should at least give us
pause, because if the novel "frees" Silas from his jail, it is only so
that society can better oversee and monitor his existence. Indeed,
Jeff Nunokawa, in *The Afterlife of Property*, has done pertinent
work in isolating the signs that mark Silas as a particularly worri-
some type of solitary "threat" to Victorian society:

> Eliot's account of the revelry of this "pallid, undersized" man, isolated
> among full-bodied strangers, reads like a case study of the solitary prac-
> tice and enervating consequences of self-abuse, imagined by nineteenth-
> century sexology, consequences that range from bodily debilitation to
> homosexuality. Intimations of solitary and more than solitary vices are
> enfolded in the hard cash whose "rounded" and "resistant outlines" the
> miser fondles, outlines and "faces" not only "his own," but also *like*
> his own.[21]

Yet I would not make too much of the hints of quasi-"homosexual"
desire here, because the primary "ill" to be cured in the novel is
that of pleasing oneself *by* oneself; it would hardly matter if the
faces and outlines on the coins were those of Queen Elizabeth or
Susan B. Anthony, because it is the solitariness of Silas's pleasure
that disturbs the social order. As Christopher Looby has argued,

> While it seems true to describe masturbation as in some basic way anti-
> social—it is a turning in upon the self, upon the self's own body, a turn-
> ing away from others . . . it is equally important to notice the ways in
> which even the most intimate phenomenology of masturbation relocates
> selfhood in the socius, as well as the ways in which masturbation and
> the masturbator have been discursively relocated as objects of social
> concern in the modern period. The masturbator may be acting antiso-
> cially, but society will not let the masturbator alone.[22]

Physicians, teachers, clergymen, and parents must intrude aggressively into the masturbator's solitude, says one nineteenth-century commentator, because masturbation is fundamentally "subversive and degrading."[23] Not just the health of the individual, but that of society itself is endangered by the pursuer of private pleasures.

Of course one might usefully relate such medically expressed fears to an industrial-age, reproductive mandate, or to a set of specifically male gender norms insisting upon activity rather than passivity; both would provide credible insights into the novel. But I wish to look for a moment to somewhat broader currents, because to understand the gravity of Silas's social subversion, one need only turn to Thomas Carlyle, whose essay "Characteristics" was published in 1831, midway between *Silas Marner*'s setting and its publication date and very much bound up in the process that Poovey describes above. Carlyle is profoundly distressed by possible assertions of autonomy by any of society's members. He writes,

> In the Body . . . all doctors are agreed, the first condition of complete health is, that each organ perform its function unconsciously, unheeded; let but any organ announce its separate existence, were it even boastfully, and for pleasure, not for pain, then already has one of those unfortunate "false centres of sensibility" established itself, already is derangement there.[24]

All self-awareness, all "feeling" of self, even if pleasurable, is subversive and unhealthy. And what is true for the "animal body" is equally true for the "Body Politic,"[25] as "SOCIETY, the vital articulation of many individuals into a new collective individual" is "the most important of man's attainments on earth."[26]

And Carlyle is uneasy, for around him, in 1831, he finds a still imperfectly constructed "new collective individual," one still too "self-conscious,"[27] too "self-sentien[t]."[28] The "parts" have not yet fully relinquished their separate "selves": "Nothing [yet] acts from within outwards in undivided healthy force; everything lies impotent, lamed, its force turned inwards."[29] And here, social and physical bodies become synecdochically inseparable, as the health of the former is threatened by the weakness of the latter. Carlyle argues that "the solitary man must continue forever folded in, stunted and only half alive,"[30] a representation that Eliot seems to echo—"Marner's face and figure shrank and bent themselves"—as Silas's deformed body figures his own deformation of the social body.[31] But however "impotent" and "folded in" such a part might be, its "in-folding" is perceived as "outwardly-challenging," its

relative inaction highly provocative, its refusal to comply a problem. Vectors of agency here become muddled, as even the language
of agency is confused. While "impotence" is a castigated quality
and passivity is decried, finally, it is nonconformity that is feared,
because the opposite of such "impotence" is not "assertion" or
"action"—those actually seem to be part and parcel of "impotence"—instead, it is submission that is called for. Thus in Carlyle's words, overall social health will be achieved only when "the
weak submit . . . to the strong . . . , giving obedience that he may
receive guidance."[32]

A generation after Carlyle's essay, Eliot reflects upon and dramatizes the process whereby such submission was exacted. Indeed, the
urgency of Silas's social (re)integration highlights the fragility of
national identification during the early years of the nineteenth century. Eliot goes to great length to emphasize the insularity of local
identities at the time of the novel's setting; discursive communities
within Britain could still be highly discrete:

> [I]t was believed that each territory was inhabited and ruled by its own
> divinities, so that a man could cross the bordering heights and be out of
> the reach of his native gods. . . . It seemed to [Silas] that the Power in
> which he had vainly trusted among the streets and in the prayer meet-
> ings was very far away from this land in which he had taken refuge.[33]

Certainly Silas's lack of integration into the discursive community
of Raveloe is clear in the confusion surrounding language that he
and his neighbors experience when trying to communicate. What
he calls a "chapel," they call a "church"; what he terms "baptism," they refer to as "christening." What Carlyle decries as a
"stunning hubbub, a true Babel-like confusion of tongues" is represented microcosmically by Eliot, as even a common national language seems still nascent.[34] As in the biblical story of Babel, such
discursive heterogeneity can only lead to social vulnerability, because if Silas emblematizes the problems of imperfect homogenization, this social breakdown is most clearly demonstrated in his own
catatonic states—ones that remove him wholly from language and
social interaction, ones that leave him defenseless. Indeed, Silas's
life-altering encounter with cruelty, when his best friend betrays
him during their youth, occurs because he is outside of language
and consciousness. Catatonic and passive, unassimilated and unable
to defend himself, Silas is both a rupture in the community and a
figure for that ill-synchronized, unhomogenized community (sick
and vulnerable because not working in harmony), what Carlyle de-

cries as social "dissolution" leading potentially to wholesale "disappearance."[35] Like the ill-prepared youth, the bumpkin, the ingenue, Silas is represented as needing socialization for his own good; equally clear, it is also for readers' good, even as the line between good and evil begins to blur as thoroughly as that separating activity from inactivity.

Socialization inevitably normalizes both proper and laudable "use," as well as egregious forms of "abuse." Even the high-minded propriety invited by a recognition of the former should be met with some suspicion. Certainly the philanthropic among us/ within us would insist that there are much better uses for Silas's money than playing with it. Are there no hungry mouths to feed? Schools to finance? Perhaps, but the silent Silas should continue to challenge us here, should provoke us to question the highly differential qualities of such demands. If he had furnished his hovel nicely—a comfortable sofa, a few paintings—in anticipation of having his neighbors over for tea or bridge, we would hardly feel justified in criticizing his use of his own coins. Or if he lazily fingered a natural history collection while chatting with a friend (as Mr. Farebrother does in *Middlemarch*) we would probably ignore his actions or chalk them up as evidence of time well spent. But he keeps (it) to himself, and that is the problem, as Silas's solitary use (really non-use) of his money has extra-solitary implications that are not unlike the other forms of provocatively passive agency mentioned earlier in this essay. Silas's money does not gather interest in a bank; it does not go back into the local economy. While we are told that he does purchase the supplies of his trade and must provide for his own meagre physical wants, he otherwise takes money out of circulation, absenting it and himself, a singular sin during an age of capital advancement. Of course, in operating as a (very) small drain on the system, Silas, from another perspective, might be considered socially responsible; at the very least, he is not underwriting Britain's colonial projects in the Caribbean and in Asia, helping finance wars in Europe, or abetting the oppression of the Irish. How many other nineteenth-century figures can be commended for even that degree of resistance? His money, stored securely underneath the floorboards or contained in his own caressing fingers is doing no harm, is as passively benign as he is. And that is abnormal and infuriating.

Not that Raveloe's "norms" are themselves anything to praise; beyond the intrusive ignorance mentioned earlier, its townspeople, especially the men, can be abusive and combative: Dunsey and, to a lesser extent, Godfrey Cass wreck drunken havoc on the lives of others; Jem Rodney steals on occasion; the men at the local tavern seem ever-ready to question each other's honesty and manliness. And from such corruption, for a time, Silas has managed to remain aloof. As mentioned above, when he does help his ill neighbor, he does not ask for remuneration and turns away all who arrive at his doorstep seeking miracle cures. Silas does not exploit: "few men could be more harmless than poor Marner. In his truthful, simple soul, not even the growing greed and worship of gold could beget any vice directly injurious to others."[36] Self-centeredness does not equal, necessarily, self-promotion at the expense of others; thus even when his gold is stolen, Silas has no desire for vengeance: "Marner did not want to punish . . . , but only to get back his gold which had gone from him, and left his soul like a forlorn traveller on an unknown desert."[37] Playing by himself, playing with his own coins, Silas has never learned to use or abuse other people; one might say that from the novel's perspective, he only abuses himself and that such abuse must be turned outwards. Thus we find that to redirect socially, properly, his libidinal energy, Silas is "socialized" forcefully by being violently penetrated.

The loss of Silas's money marks the overpowering entrance of the outer world into Silas's life. This penetration is signalled most clearly in Dunstan Cass's larcenous entry of Silas's home:

> [Dunstan] felt the ground before him cautiously with his whip handle, and at last arrived safely at the door. He knocked loudly, rather enjoying the idea that the old fellow would be frightened at the sudden noise. He heard no movement in reply. . . . Dunstan knocked still more loudly, and, without pausing for a reply, pushed his fingers through the latch hole. [38]

But Dunstan's hole-probing fingers aside, it is language that actually "enters" Silas in the most desire-reconfiguring way: "The conversation . . . was at a high pitch of animation when Silas approached the door of the Rainbow"[39]; quite appropriately, that conversation centers on the power of language, itself, as Mr. Macy tells of his concern over a marriage ceremony where the "words" were "contrairy," causing him to wonder, "Is't the meanin' or the words as makes folks fast i' wedlock?"[40] The "glue," he is told, is neither, actually: "it's the re*gest*er does it—that's the glue."[41] Indeed, law, language, and church all combine to form a discursive glue that makes marriage as a social convention, indeed, society itself as a social convention, cohere. Into this conversation, which flows over the various ways of arriving at socially agreed upon definitions of truth, bursts Silas, "uttering no word, but looking round at the company with his strange, unearthly eyes. . . . For a few moments there was a dead silence."[42] But silence is finally broken.

" 'Robber!' said Silas, gaspingly. 'I've been robbed! I want the constable—and the Justice—and Squire Cass—and Mr. Crackenthorp.' "[43] And with that admission of vulnerability and need, Silas becomes a target of intense social work. The town now has not only a reason (which it, in fact, always had) but also a means, for imposing itself upon him:

> "Ay, ay, make him sit down," said several voices at once. . . . The landlord forced Marner to take off his coat, and then to sit down on a chair aloof from everyone else, in the centre of the circle, and in the direct rays of the fire. The weaver, too feeble to have any distinct purpose beyond that of getting help to recover his money, submitted unresistingly.[44]

Silas submits, and following Carlyle, Eliot figures this submission as a moment of moral rebirth. Carlyle writes, "it is in Society . . . that Morality begins; here at least it takes an altogether new form, and on every side, as in living growth, expands itself"[45]; in Eliot's words, "in the warmth of a hearth not his own," the first "circulations of the sap" begin to stir in Silas's heart.[46] But even if Eliot wishes to insist upon this proto-budding as a moment of gain, I would like to see it also as one of loss: the loss of something at least approaching discursive autonomy, the loss of distance from a society that exacts a very high price for inclusion in its disallowance of nonconformity, and the loss of a daily existence that managed to avoid the most active forums for interpersonal abuse— marriage, religion, heterosexual and others demanding interpenetration and a self-hood dependent upon hierarchized, power-deploying interactions.

"[T]he fence was broken down," and in the chapters after the loss of his money, the townspeople, taking turns, discursively penetrate and re-penetrate Silas.[47] Mr. Macey, for one, delivers a harangue on good social behavior: "if you brought . . . knowledge from distant parts, you might ha' been a bit freer of it. And if the knowledge wan't well come by, why you might ha' made up for it by coming to church reg'lar."[48] Though "[d]uring this discursive address Silas had continued motionless," the effects of it and numerous others like it are inevitable and hardly lost on Eliot: "We can send black puddings and potatoes without giving them a flavour of our own egotism; but language is a stream that is almost sure to smack of a mingled soil"[49]—that "mingled soil" also serves as fertilizer of a sort, with an evocation of the scatological (night soil) that reiterates a social productivity in group penetration of Silas. Of course, the metaphors here do become wildly mixed as Eliot strains to find words to characterize Silas's progression from social virgin to man of the world:

> Formerly, his heart had been as a locket casket with its treasure inside; but now the casket was empty, and the lock was broken. Left groping in the darkness, with his prop utterly gone, Silas had inevitably a sense, though a dull and half-despairing one, that if any help came to him it must come from without; and there was a slight stirring of expectation at the sight of his fellow men, a faint consciousness of dependence on their good will. He opened the door wide to admit Dolly.[50]

Emptied of its "treasure" (its "self," actually) his casket must be filled by the town. Unable to amuse himself with his own prop, Silas begins to grope about. Formerly "stirred" only in isolation, he now begins to find himself stirred by other people. And the success of this socialization process is nowhere signaled more clearly than by the fact that as Dolly talks and talks at him, "there was no possibility of misunderstanding the desire to give comfort that made itself heard in her quiet tones."[51] Finally Silas understands; their language becomes his language. Even so, this is hardly the end of the socialization process, because finally Silas must prove his loyalty to the town, must perform in visible fashion if his socialization is to be believed: "The fountains of human love and divine faith had not yet been unlocked, and his soul was still the shrunken rivulet . . . its little groove of sand was blocked up, and it wandered confusedly against dark obstruction."[52] Silas, though certainly never "macho," does learn the joys of phallicism as he, with Eliot's help, pushes through the obstruction.

"Hephzibah"—Hebrew for "my delight is in her." Carlyle, Victorian sexologists, and Eliot all agree that one's delight cannot reside in oneself, one must put it somewhere. Thus no longer will Silas sit alone in his hovel, caressing his own coins; instead, he will find ecstatic pleasure and wide public approval in caressing someone else: his beloved little daughter. And Silas does delight *in* little Eppie, as his proprietorship is made explicit from the beginning: "I can't part with it. I can't let it go. . . . It's come to me—I've a right to keep it."[53] Even as Eppie becomes a "she" rather than an "it," Silas's early claims to ownership of her are often reiterated: "I want to do things for it myself, else it may get fond o' somebody else, and not fond o' me"; "she'll be *my* little un. . . . She'll be nobody else's."[54] "[T]he gold had turned into the child,"[55] but unlike the gold, the child serves as the living vehicle through which Silas proves himself by providing proof of his new social self. Thus his visibly interpersonal delight helps solidify social links: the town meets him "with open smiling faces and cheerful questions, as a person whose satisfactions and difficulties could be understood."[56] There are no threatening secrets, no unnerving differences; society is securely glued.

Carlyle's worries notwithstanding, that glue holds fairly well. Sixteen years later, Silas has been thoroughly normalized:

> Silas had taken to smoking a pipe daily during the last two years, having been strongly urged to it by the sages of Raveloe. . . . Silas did not highly enjoy smoking . . . but a humble sort of acquiescence in what was held to be good had become a strong habit of that new self which had been developed in him since he had found Eppie on his hearth. . . . [H]e had himself come to appropriate the forms of custom and belief which were the mould of Raveloe life.[57]

Of course Silas's new social self includes no critical faculty; even those activities that he finds personally distasteful, such as pipe-smoking, he nevertheless participates in because he is told that he should. Dolly is a guide here, not just transmitting to him many of the local customs, but also modeling blind acceptance of norms: "I can never rightly know the meaning o' what I hear at church, only a bit here and there, but I know it's good words—I do."[58] Her advice to him when she hears of his former trials before coming to Raveloe is "to trusten": "there's trouble i' this world, and there's things as we can niver make out the rights on. And all as we've got to do is to trusten."[59] If he was improperly judged or treated harshly, Silas was simply to accept that and seek no redress, because "if you could ha' gone on trusting, Master Marner, you wouldn't ha' run away from your fellow creaturs and been so lone."[60] Thus in this "poetic novel" of "moral development," social selfhood takes precedence over all; injustice and "morally" sanctioned evil must be endured at even horrific cost, so that loneliness, figured here as the very worst that one can experience, can be staved off. While Dolly's concern is not reflected in Silas's own experience of relative contentment in solitude, he, now fully acculturated, accepts her social "truth" over his own experience: "you're i' the right, Mrs. Winthrop—you're i' the right."[61]

Of course Silas remains a somewhat bumbling social creature, imperfectly performing rituals that he doesn't understand and mimicking, sometimes humorously, his neighbors' actions. Thus he is told by Dolly to "punish" Eppie and therefore locks her in the coal bin, though only to the vacantly smiling little girl's delight. But I, for one, stop smiling altogether when he becomes a mouthpiece for and replicator of wholly predictable gender ideologies (even if the novel does allow Silas a certain maternal, gender-bending quality, as Nancy Paxton and others have discussed). Although Eppie insists that she is strong enough to work on building a wall around their yard, Silas insists, "let us go and sit down on the bank against the stile there, and have no more lifting. . . . You'd need have somebody to work for you."[62] Of course, such working for Eppie is caught up in a highly skewed gender economy whereby she performs a more important form of work for her father: "After a bit . . . I'd got to feel the need o' your looks and your voice and the touch o' your little fingers. You didn't know then, Eppie, when you were such a little un—you didn't know what your old father Silas felt for you."[63] Socially constructed, he no longer "knows" himself, he knows only what he is told, and, now fully cured of his masturbatory tendencies, he no longer even feels himself, he feels (for) her, and she returns the favor, meeting his needs with her "little fingers." Is it any wonder that she has a "slight flush on her cheeks?"[64]

Following the insights of Levi-Strauss and others, it really should come as no surprise that Silas acquiesces when Godfrey Cass shows up to claim Eppie; Silas, the social creature that he is now, knows how to act in response to such demands. "[W]e should like to have Eppie" announces Cass, to which Silas replies "Eppie, my child, speak. I won't stand in your way. Thank Mr. and Mrs. Cass."[65] Eppie, of course, knows with whom she must stay (glued) for the health of Silas and society—after all, he has warned that he might slip back into his old ways without her presence—and after she declines their request, Silas reiterates his proprietorship: "God gave her to me . . . you've no right to her!"[66] "I'll cleave to him as long as he lives," and cleave Eppie does, bringing her new husband Aaron Winthrop to live with them, letting both men feel (for) her, dedicating her body to a patriarchal social body, to serving its needs.[67] It will remain glued in/through her.

Yet even she is not enough to fulfill all of the needs of that national body; continued social solidity demands invariably an outward gesture. The social self must always test itself against new barriers; the "rivulet" will always need another "obstruction" to break through in order to assure itself of its continuing strength. Carlyle tells us that out of social harmony should come international conquest: "before us is the boundless Time, with its as yet uncreated and unconquered Continents and Eldorados, which we . . . have to conquer, to create."[68] Yet equally true is that such conquest works to ensure the very harmony that it celebrates and seeks forcibly to share. In this way, Silas certainly serves both historically and within the Eliot canon as a necessary precursor to Daniel Deronda. Daniel might be Silas's grandchild let loose upon the world, able to move into the international arena because Britain itself is "tamed," indeed needing to move into that arena because Britain is not only tamed, it is in need of revitalization. Daniel Born makes this point well in *The Birth of Liberal Guilt in the English Novel*, when he argues that "the great concentrations of power and wealth, embodied in the character of Grandcourt, are rotting England from the inside out. . . . Eliot attempts to posit over against England's decadence a salutary form of nationalism —Zionism."[69] At the end of his novel, Daniel Deronda moves outward on a quest to re-make, re-invigorate himself through an attachment to an international cause. *Daniel Deronda* exemplifies the process described by Poovey near the beginning of this essay, a process whereby the national identity is inscribed upon British "subjects" through a host of cultural "mechanisms" and then policed both through surveillance and through engagements "outside," for "[t]he consolidation of a national identity or national character is necessarily a protracted and uneven process, just as its maintenance is always precarious and imperfect."[70] Thus the two dates of *Silas Marner*, ca. 1800 and 1861, its setting and publication dates, mark a date of internal conquest and one of pointed reminder of (always) threatening fragmentation.

Indeed, society must be ever watchful; thus it is entirely fitting that Silas's home with Eppie and her husband invites inspection: "[t]he garden was fenced with stones on two sides, but in front there was an open fence, through which the flowers shone with answering gladness."[71] This image closes the novel, and works well as one signaling its construction of social identity, not separated, but open, bounded on the sides certainly, but still always responsive to the community, answering back with reassuring "gladness" the greetings and inquiries posed to it. Always enterable by "us," always defendable from "them," indeed, always providing visible proof that "we" have not turned into "them."

And this leads us back to *Silas Marner* among high school students, ones whose loyalty to adult society must be assured because it is still so questionable, ones whose unviewed "activities" always unnerve because they potentially diverge from social norms. And for this reason *Silas Marner* is taught to complaining students to this day. Its messages so baldly serve the interests of parents, teachers, and of a society that reproduces itself through the educational system: stop playing with yourself, engage yourself heterosexually in the world, conform to its norms, "trusten" the powers that be, do not rebel or you may end up lonely.

Because the fear remains that social identity, so compromised and, at times, so corrupt, may crumble, that dissolution may be actively embraced by the young or social malcontents. And, to my mind, it is to that end that *Silas Marner* might be used profitably as a teaching tool.

> The wall that fortifies the Subject is its collective share; its psychic habitat, the stronghold of its membership in the social body. The expression "social body" defines the shackles that must be destroyed: an enormous flesh made up of constraints and customs, of conventional gestures and paths taken, an invisible and everyday network—the socius, citizenship, relations, are suddenly unbearable.[72]

Catherine Clement, in *Syncope: The Philosophy of Rapture*, finds in a very few moments "outside" of social identity—moments of orgasm, ecstatic dance, madness, music, solitary excess—cause for celebration. What Clement describes, appropriately, as rapturous "catatonia"[73] can in fact gloss life, can supplement it by superseding it:

> this glaring weakness contains a raging force. This prostration is creative; from its disorders unknown energies are often born. . . . I am speaking of politics in the long term. . . . The world in which I have lived until now idolizes power and force, muscle and health, vigor and lucidity. Syncope opens onto a universe of weakness and tricks; it leads to new rebellions.[74]

As we have seen, passivity can be a form of activity. It can unnerve and challenge; it can undermine and incite. And conversely, social activity is often static, as it normalizes and stupefies, as it makes one forget. Yet if we *can* remember, if we can dislodge our comfort in being *told* that truth lies in "common knowledge," then yet again out of inaction can come impulse, out of distance can come engaged critique.

For neither I nor (to my understanding) Clement is arguing that catatonia is our best hope for challenging narrow discursive norms.

And certainly I am not suggesting that opting out of the system represents the most effective way to alter it. But at the very least (and, maybe, at best), as literary critics, teachers, and parents, *let us not be so quick to applaud socialization*. If, as many of us seem to know, Victorian society, in general, and Victorian masculinity, in particular, normalized grotesque injustices (much as our own society and manifestations of masculinity continue to do) then we should question our unthinking complicity in applauding and reproducing *the same*. The social body must be continuously remade, as young bodies are socialized and as their barriers are broken down, and indeed, as old bodies are socially served through that interaction. Is it any wonder that Jocelyn Elders lost her job as Surgeon General for telling the young that in playing with "oneself" there are relatively few opportunities for doing harm? Society has for years found a few moments of lapsed sociality far more threatening than any disease or form of distress caused by interpersonal contact.

Thus Silas Marner should provoke us to reflect on the concomitant losses involved in all developmental gains, to acknowledge how resilient our belief is, to this day, that one must act forcefully *upon* the world in order to have fully lived, and to recognize how lives lived differently continue to challenge us, testing our respect for difference, certainly, but, more often, simply proving our loyalty to convention.

NOTES

1. Mary Poovey, *Making a Social Body: British Cultural Formation 1830–1864* (Chicago: University of Chicago Press, 1995), 4.

2. See Donald E. Hall, "On the Making and Unmaking of Monsters: Christian Socialism, Muscular Christianity, and the Metaphorization of Class Conflict," in *Muscular Christianity: Embodying the Victorian Age*, ed. Donald E. Hall (Cambridge: Cambridge University Press, 1994), 45–65.

3. Poovey, 22.

4. Judith Halberstam, *Skin Shows: Gothic Horror and the Technology of Monsters* (Durham: Duke University Press, 1995), 14.

5. George Eliot, *Silas Marner* (1861; reprint, New York: Signet Books, 1960), 22.

6. Gillian Beer, *George Eliot* (Bloomington: Indiana University Press, 1986), 131.

7. Ibid., 132.

8. Bernard Semmel, *George Eliot and the Politics of National Inheritance* (New York: Oxford University Press, 1994), 26.

9. Jennifer Uglow, *George Eliot* (New York: Pantheon Books, 1987), 158.

10. Nancy Paxton, *George Eliot and Herbert Spencer* (Princeton: Princeton University Press, 1991), 96.

11. Eliot, 20.
12. Ibid., 20.
13. Ibid., 20.
14. Ibid., 23.
15. Ibid., 21.
16. Ibid., 22.
17. Michiel Heyns, *Expulsion and the Nineteenth-Century Novel: The Scapegoat in English Realist Fiction* (Oxford: Oxford University Press, 1994), 21–22.
18. Eliot, 78.
19. Ibid., 42.
20. Ibid., 20.
21. Jeff Nunokawa, *The Afterlife of Property: Domestic Security and the Victorian Novel* (Princeton: Princeton University Press, 1994), 103.
22. Christopher Looby, " 'The Roots of the Orchis, the Iuli of Chestnuts': The Odor of Male Solitude," in *Solitary Pleasures: The Historical, Literary, and Artistic Discourses of Autoeroticism*, ed. Paula Bennett and Vernon A. Rosario II (New York: Routledge, 1995), 178.
23. Joseph W. Howe, *Excessive Venery, Masturbation and Continence* (1887; reprint, New York: Arno Press, 1974), 76.
24. Thomas Carlyle, "Characteristics," 1831, in *A Carlyle Reader*, ed. G. B. Tennyson (Cambridge: Cambridge University Press, 1984), 67.
25. Ibid., 77.
26. Ibid., 76.
27. Ibid., 83.
28. Ibid., 82.
29. Ibid., 85.
30. Ibid., 75.
31. Eliot, 22.
32. Carlyle, 76.
33. Eliot, 17.
34. Carlyle, 94.
35. Ibid., 80.
36. Eliot, 44.
37. Ibid., 46.
38. Ibid., 40.
39. Ibid., 47.
40. Ibid., 52–53.
41. Ibid., 53.
42. Ibid., 57.
43. Ibid.
44. Ibid., 58.
45. Carlyle, 75.
46. Eliot, 59.
47. Ibid., 78.
48. Ibid., 80.
49. Ibid.
50. Ibid., 83–84.
51. Ibid., 85.
52. Ibid., 89.
53. Ibid., 119.
54. Ibid., 126, 128.

55. Ibid., 127.
56. Ibid., 135.
57. Ibid., 145.
58. Ibid., 146.
59. Ibid., 148.
60. Ibid.
61. Ibid.
62. Ibid., 151.
63. Ibid., 168.
64. Ibid., 169.
65. Ibid., 171.
66. Ibid., 169, 173.
67. Ibid., 175.
68. Carlyle, 70.
69. Daniel Born, *The Birth of Liberal Guilt in the English Novel: Charles Dickens to H. G. Wells* (Chapel Hill: University of North Carolina Press, 1995), 52.
70. Poovey, 55.
71. Eliot, 185.
72. Catherine Clement, *Synecope: The Philosophy of Rapture*, trans. Sally O'Driscoll and Deirdre M. Mahoney (Minneapolis: University of Minnesota Press, 1994), 251.
73. Clement, 117.
74. Ibid., 20.

Homosexuality at the Closet Threshold in Joseph Sheridan Le Fanu's "Green Tea"

ANDRÉ L. DeCUIR

ONE MIGHT FIND IT ODD TO BEGIN A STUDY OF A POSSIBLE ACKNOWL-edgment of male homosexual identity in a piece of Victorian fiction with a reference to Joseph Sheridan Le Fanu's most famous work, the vampire tale, "Carmilla." Critical attention has almost always centered on the homoerotic relationship between Laura, the narrator of the story, and the vampire, Carmilla. Nina Auerbach asserts in *Our Vampires, Ourselves*, perhaps the most recent work to analyze "Carmilla," that "Carmilla is one of the few self-accepting homosexuals in Victorian or any literature."[1]

The perceived relationship between the two women in the story has led inevitably to speculation about Le Fanu's own sexuality, but the sparse critical studies of Le Fanu's life and works provide no conclusive evidence that Le Fanu was either a practicing or latent homosexual. W. J. McCormack in *Sheridan Le Fanu and Victorian Ireland*, perhaps the definitive study of Le Fanu, points out that "Le Fanu's last five years [he died in 1873] were passed largely in isolation"[2] and that "for the year 1870 virtually nothing is known, apart from his non-payment of bills and non-attendance at church."[3] McCormack alludes to the writer's sexual identity in one line: "That Le Fanu may have been a latent homosexual has a certain clinical interest."[4]

This essay certainly does not attempt to set forth irrefutable evidence of Le Fanu's homosexual identity. Rather, through a close reading of the short story, "Green Tea," with the lens provided by recent gay literary criticism, I wish to show that Le Fanu was certainly aware of same-sex desire which undoubtedly manifested itself within enclaves of accepted examples of masculinity: circles of professional men such as those in the Victorian medical profession.

While McCormack does not make any claims about Le Fanu as

a possible homosexual, he does provide evidence and speculates more comfortably, though not clearly, about Le Fanu's attitudes toward the medical profession which perhaps formed because of his and his wife's ill health: "Ill-health dogged both Joseph and Susanna—scarletina, rheumatism, gout in his case, and a recurring ailment probably of psychosomatic origins in Susanna's."[5] Susanna died on 28 April 1858, and in letters written by Le Fanu after her death, McCormack finds that husband and wife may have "held diverging views on medicine."[6] Le Fanu himself may have favored homeopathy as opposed to conventional medical practice of his day as suggested by a 22 May 1858 letter to his mother in which he advises her on her health: "You, my dear little mother, must consult somebody upon the symptoms which you mention. If you will not, at least apply a wet towel to your head . . . but you ought to see a homeopathist."[7]

The intersection of Le Fanu's questionable sexuality and his possible doubting of conventional medicine transform "Green Tea" from the status of a standard Gothic horror tale into a medium through which a male homosexual identity is acknowledged and one which simultaneously criticizes a medical establishment for seeking to "cure," deny, or suppress it. "Green Tea" is introduced as a case-study of the late Dr. Martin Hesselius, a physician with a Freud-like interest in the analysis of the human mind and who attempts to use his abilities in feats of Sherlock Holmes-like detection. An unnamed editor who claims to have acted as Dr. Hesselius's medical secretary, "[f]or nearly twenty years,"[8] is in the process of "arrang[ing], index[ing], and bind[ing] the papers of Hesselius, supposedly to share the deceased physician's greatness with the public:

> In Dr. Martin Hesselius, I found my master. His knowledge was immense, his grasp of a case was an intuition. He was the very man to inspire a young enthusiast, like me, with awe and delight. My admiration has stood the test of time and survived the separation of death. I am sure it was well-founded.[9]

At the conclusion of "Green Tea," however, critics find that Hesselius falls short of the above praises. Barbara T. Gates, for example, writes that "He [Hesselius] is a careless empiricist, a derelict in duty, and a very materialistic spiritualist."[10] However, no one has explored the relationship between the editor and Dr. Hesselius in order to account for what the editor writes in his prologue and then reveals throughout "Green Tea." The piecing together of this rela-

tionship based upon what the editor reveals about himself ultimately shows Le Fanu's acknowledgment of alternative male
sexual identities and his own personal criticism of the medical profession expanded into an indictment of its attempts to keep such
identities concealed.

In the "Prologue" to the story, the editor describes himself as
"carefully educated in medicine and surgery," and just about to
embark on this "honourable calling" which would then allow him
to carve a niche for himself in an exclusive realm of men sharing a
common body of knowledge and a system of language with which
to access this storehouse and participate within it. On the threshold
of this exclusive realm, however, the editor suffers an accident
which drastically changes the direction of his life:

> Neither idleness nor caprice caused my secession from the honourable
> calling which I had just entered. The cause was a very trifling scratch
> inflicted by a dissecting knife. The trifle cost me the loss of two fingers,
> amputated promptly and the more painful loss of my health, for I have
> never been quite well since, and have seldom been twelve months to-
> gether in the same place.[11]

The editor is "demoted" to the position of "medical secretary," an
inferior position, as the editor is not an active participant in the
medical field, but merely a recorder of the cases of one of its members. The editor's vague description of his "loss of . . . health" and
his admission that "I have never been quite well since" assign him
the marginal status of patient/subject/object, the role which Sandra
Gilbert and Susan Gubar suggest that women are socialized by the
patriarchy to assume.[12] This "feminization" of the editor imbues
the narrative with a subversive element, because, as in "Carmilla,"
Le Fanu clearly recognizes a potential for the disruption of a culture
which seeks to prevent a deviation from the norm through regulatory and often repressive measures.[13] Since women were excluded
from the public/economic sphere and relegated to the home, emotions and desires could flourish uninhibited, behind closed doors,
all potentially erosive to the value system of a society which se-
questered women behind the walls of the Victorian mansion, "a society which was patriarchal, hierarchical, and ultimately, justified
by God the Father, [and] depended on every level on the supremacy
and potency of the male."[14]

For example, in an isolated castle in Styria, desire between
women can flourish as Laura, the lonely narrator of "Carmilla," becomes the recipient of Carmilla's amorous affections which she describes in her narrative:

She used to place her pretty arms about my neck, draw me to her, and laying her cheek to mine, murmur with her lips near my ear, . . . And when she had spoken such a rhapsody, she would press me more closely in her trembling embrace, and her lips in soft kisses gently glow upon my cheek.[15]

Like the female narrator that, according to McCormack, "allows the novelist to speak through a role of apparent passivity and weakness which is also subversively a source of strength and integrity,"[16] the editor, in a seemingly powerless role, can manipulate discourse in order to fracture the reputation of the authority figure, Hesselius ("my master"), and display the "ruins" to "a lay reader"[17] or one who may feel excluded from a system of knowledge and language made privy to a certain few in a "patriarchal, hierarchical" society. Nevertheless, the editor can be seen as doubly marginalized, especially when certain homoerotic elements of the text are gleaned and examined.

Helen Stoddardt identifies "a homosexual potential" in "Green Tea,"[18] specifically in the relationship between Dr. Hesselius and the Rev. Mr. Jennings, the patient within the story, without acknowledging, however, that this relationship is being structured by the editor who changes names and makes "slight modifications, chiefly of language."[19] To complicate further matters of credibility, the editor reveals that the narrative, "Green Tea," is pieced together from letters shuttled between Hesselius and "his friend Professor Van Loo of Lyden," letters "in English, some in French, but the greater part in German."[20] The editor then admits that he is by "no means a graceful translator" and that "here and there" he has *omitted* some passages, *shortened* others and disguised names. This admission is not to say that the homosexual theme Stoddardt recognizes is absent in the narrative, but because of the narrator's admitted relationship, the "homosexual potential" might be better investigated within the relationship between the editor and Hesselius.

The editor elaborates on the similarities between Hesselius and himself, likenesses which would inscribe them into what Eve Kosofsky Sedgwick calls the " 'Male homosocial desire' " continuum: "In my wanderings I became acquainted with Dr. Martin Hesselius, a wanderer like myself, like me a physician, and like me an enthusiast in his profession."[21] According to Sedgwick, this spectrum includes "men-promoting-the-interests-of-men"[22] but also male homosexual desire as she hypothesizes that the "homosocial," which "describes social bonds between persons of the same sex,"[23] cannot be entirely separated from the "homosexual." The realization and fear of "the potential unbrokenness of a continuum between homosocial and homosexual"[24] results in the constraining of desire by "intense homophobia, fear and hatred of homosexuality"[25] and ultimately the regulation of "a nascent or already-constituted minority of homosexual people or desires."[26]

The editor appears to cross the sketchy line dividing the homosocial and the homosexual as suggested by the language he uses in describing his personal feelings toward Hesselius. He inspires the younger man "with awe and delight," and perhaps more telling is the editor's assertion, "In Dr. Martin Hesselius, I found my *master*."[27] The ambiguous meanings of the word beautifully illustrate and underscore the tenuousness of that boundary dividing the homosexual from the homosocial within Sedgwick's continuum. Within the context of male homosocial bonds through which men-promote-the-interests-of-men, "master" could explain that Hesselius is simply an expert in the male-dominated field of medicine. Such a reading is questionable, however, as the narrator's initial praise does not correspond to the image of Hesselius he presents at the end of the tale.

The Victorian cultural milieu undoubtedly contained excursions into alternative sexualities. Victorian readers, particularly physicians such as the editor and Hesselius, could have attributed a distinctly *sexual* and perhaps homosexual meaning to the word "master," especially within the context of the study of sadomasochistic behavior during the Victorian period. The German physician, Krafft-Ebing, for example, in *Psychopathia Sexualis* (1882), "coined the term 'sadism' as an allusion to the notorious Marquis de Sade," and added the sexual component to the violent behavior inherent in sado-masochism, a behavior possibly already familiar to Victorians who read the novels of the Marquis de Sade, "coveted underground commodities"[28]:

> The master-serf relationship still existed in eastern Europe and Russia as late as 1860. The master-servant relationship thrived throughout the Victorian period in Europe and America. Similarly, man-woman and adult-child relationships often indicate mastery and submission, which were considered good and natural. Krafft-Ebing's original formulation of these terms ["sadism," "masochism"] did not encompass the more subtle forms of mental domination and submission that we might refer to as sadistic or masochistic today. He meant a mingling of frankly lustful and openly violent, even murderous feelings.[29]

Victorians may have understood sadomasochistic behavior defined by Krafft-Ebing as a distinct feature of homosexual relationships, because, as Drinka argues, Krafft-Ebing's *Psychopathia* intermingled "the lust murderer and the homosexual" as cases of "lust murders, rapes, fetishism, sadomasochism and necrophilia . . . appeared alongside cases of homosexuals, many of whom [were] doctors, judges, and government officials."[30]

Steven Marcus in *The Other Victorians* points out those works concerning sexualities that may have been available to mid-Victorian readers. William Acton's *A Practical Treatise on Diseases of the Urinary and Generative Organs in Both Sexes* was published in 1841 "and was successful enough to have gone through four editions by the time of Acton's death in 1875."[31] Acton's *The Functions and Disorders of the Reproductive Organs* which focused on "men and male sexuality"[32] was published in 1857: "within a year a second edition was called for: a translation into French was made in 1863, from the third edition; it went through a number of editions in America and was still being printed twenty years after Acton's death, an eighth edition [published] in Philadelphia in 1894."[33] Marcus suggests that such works were responsible for the burgeoning "pornographic publishing trade" in the nineteenth century.[34]

When read within such a context, the editor's revelations about himself in the prologue take on a sexual tinge and indicate that he perceives social position or lack of it based upon sexuality. His amputated fingers, members which would have allowed him full participation in the medical profession, a male-centered sphere of knowledge, experience, and language, and his "more painful loss of . . . health" resulting from the dismemberment, certainly suggest castration and impotency and underscore the editor's frustration at his removal to the margins of the male homosocial continuum. As a result, he no longer has the opportunity to step discreetly over the homosocial and into the homosexual where he can possibly reveal and act upon his desire for Hesselius. In a professional and social sense, his removal to the margins of the male homosocial continuum render him unable to participate actively in the field. In a culture in which work or occupation was so closely associated with masculine identity, the editor is "emasculated" by being removed to a position where he assumes the inferior, submissive, feminine position of medical secretary.

In the editor, then, Le Fanu has created a figure, who, when studied within the context of Sedgwick's male homosocial continuum, is a suddenly demasculinized male who cannot fully participate in either the professional or (homo)sexual component of this continuum. Le Fanu has created a marginalized character who becomes empowered, however, through picking up the pen, and who becomes an element most subversive for those who are removed from the center to the margins of the continuum. In short, he can release information about certain "privileged" groups to the general reading public. Thus Le Fanu, through the editor's transformation of Hesselius's papers into the piece of written discourse, "Green Tea," exposes the perceived incompetency of his era's medical practices and ultimately his recognition of this profession's attempt to censure alternative sexualities.

After his interview with Jennings, Hesselius decides to "devote some hours" to the case, not at his usual lodgings, but at "an inn two miles out of town." As Jennings's condition deteriorates, his servant frantically tries to locate Hesselius who does not leave an address. Jennings commits suicide, and all Hesselius can do is blame the dead man:

> Poor Mr. Jennings made away with himself. But that catastrophe was the result of a totally different malady, which, as it were, projected itself upon the disease which was established. His case was in the distinctive manner a complication, another complaint under which he really succumbed, was hereditary suicidal mania. Poor Mr. Jennings I cannot call a patient of mine, for I had not even begun to treat his case, and he had not yet given me, I am convinced, his full and unreserved confidence. If the patient do not array himself on the side of the disease, his cure is certain.[35]

Significantly, the only time the editor interrupts the narrative itself is after Hesselius resolves to retire to an inn for the study of the case, because he apparently wants to stress that Hesselius *deliberately* makes himself unavailable:

> (There occurs here a careful note of Dr. Hesselius' opinion upon the case, and of the habits, dietary, and medicines which he prescribed. It is curious—some persons would say mystical. But, on the whole, I doubt whether it would sufficiently interest a reader of the kind I am likely to meet with, to warrant its being here reprinted. The whole letter was plainly written at the inn where *he had hid himself for the occasion.* The next letter is dated from his own lodgings.)[36]

An argument that the editor's criticisms of Hesselius and the Victorian medical profession stem from frustration over his own vocational shortcomings can perhaps be answered by juxtaposing "Green Tea" to a work such as Charlotte Perkins Gilman's "The Yellow Wallpaper," which has as its sources medical practices deemed as threatening because of sexual difference.[37]

According to Drinka, Silas Weir Mitchell, the prominent Phila-delphia physician and originator of the Rest Cure, which he pre-scribed to Gilman, "exhibited an almost ruthless male chauvinism and Victorian roguishness":

> One woman who pleaded paralysis was essentially inert, perhaps de-pressed. Mitchell took her for a ride in his carriage. Some distance from her home he drew his team to a halt and sternly bade the woman alight and walk home. This she did. Though cured, she never particularly cared for Mitchell again. With another woman who refused to get out of bed, pleading an indisposition, Mitchell used a similar method. First he tried to persuade her to walk by telling her that he intended to crawl into bed with her. She did not believe him. Even after he had undone his coat and vest she remained motionless. It was only when he started to unbutton his trousers that she leaped up angrily.[38]

There is of course Freud's famous case of Dora, who does not re-turn to him for treatment after he misdiagnoses her condition. Freud's self-justification remarkably echoes Hesselius's blaming of Jennings for the collapse of the case which would have added a fifty-eighth to "Fifty-seven cases" he has solved without failure: "I knew Dora would not come back again. Her breaking off so unex-pectedly, just when my hopes of a successful termination of the treatment were at their height, and her thus bringing those hopes to nothing—this was an unmistakable act of vengeance on her part."[39] Drinka believes that Freud's sexual (mis)interpretation of her dreams frightened her away: "Freud's sexual monomania fright-ened the girl, and it is not surprising that she let him know on 31 December 1900 that she would stop [seeing] him."[40] The incident in which the physician unbuttons his trousers and Freud's sexual interpretation of Dora's dreams show clearly the dynamics of the power structure the editor gradually sketches out in "Green Tea." The title "physician" is equated with authority, which is fortified further by male heterosexuality and ultimately can be used to threaten into submission those who might challenge social and sex-ual authority.

A look at the Gothic qualities which permeate and layer the nar-rative's excursion into medical exposé can point out yet another purpose in the editor's manipulation of Hesselius's papers into "Green Tea"—the release of his suppressed homosexual desire for Hesselius and the revelation of his true sexual identity despite his encounter with professional and social barriers.

Sedgwick writes that "the Gothic was the first novelistic form in England to have close, relatively visible links to male homosexuality"[41] as usually in "Romantic novels . . . a male hero is in a close, usually murderous relation to another male figure, in some respects his 'double.' "[42] This antagonistic/desirous relationship between men is indicated in the Gothic through a doubling, as Sedgwick notes, and the editor of "Green Tea" draws similarities, not between *Jennings and Hesselius*, but between *himself and Hesselius*: "In my wandering I became acquainted with Dr. Martin Hesselius, a wanderer *like myself, like me* a physician, and *like me* an enthusiast in his profession."[43] The editor then attempts to make himself more akin to Mr. Jennings. He reveals that he has never been in perfect health and also that "Mr. Jennings' health does break down in, generally, a sudden and mysterious way."[44] Just as the editor has given up the practice of medicine, he also reveals that Mr. Jennings has given up writing through a conversation between Hesselius and Lady Mary Heyduke:

> "He has been writing, that is he *was*, but for two or three years perhaps, he has not gone on with his work, and the book was upon some rather abstract subject—perhaps theology."
> "Well, he was writing a book, as you say; I'm not quite sure what it was about, but only that it was nothing that I care for; very likely you are right, and he certainly did stop—yes."[45]

More suggestion of "doubling" is apparent in the editor's descriptions of Mr. Jennings's study in his lodgings at Blank Street as the room seems to contain pairs of furnishings:

> This was really a study—almost a library. The room was lofty, with *two* tall slender windows, and rich dark curtains. . . . The upper carpet—for to my tread it felt that there were *two* or three—was a Turkey carpet. . . . I stepped into this perfectly silent house, with a peculiar foreboding; and its darkness, and solemn clothing of books, for except where *two narrow looking-glasses* were set in the wall, they were everywhere, helped this somber feeling.[46]

Perhaps the clearest indication of Gothic doubling occurs when Hesselius looks into one of the two mirrors and sees Jennings reflected behind him: "Directly before me was one of the mirrors I have mentioned, in which I saw reflected the tall shape of my friend, Mr. Jennings, leaning over my shoulders, and reading the page at which I was busy, and with a face so dark and wild that I should hardly have known him."[47]

If we are to accept a relationship between two men characterized by both infatuation and loathing as part of the economy of the traditional Gothic narratives, then the relationship between the narrator and Hesselius is more exemplary of this ambivalence because of the editor's contradictory accounts of Hesselius's reputation rather than that of Hesselius and Jennings. Since the editor is not present as a character in the narrative, however, he provides a vehicle through which to project or duplicate himself and interact more closely with his object of desire: Hesselius. This vehicle is the character Mr. Jennings. This need may account for the description of Jennings's and Hesselius's reflections as framed together in the mirror. The unrecognizable, "dark and wild" face recalls the standard description of the Gothic double, but also serves as a description of the external manifestation of the seething but suppressed emotions of the editor, unrecognized by Hesselius during his lifetime, which are about to be released as he "leans over Hesselius's shoulders" reading and manipulating his text.

The editor's repressed homosexual desire for Hesselius surfaces through his depiction of Mr. Jennings's "visions" of a "small black monkey."[48] Peter Penzoldt writes that the monkey "is the symbol of suppressed sex desire"[49] and Julia Briggs relates the monkey to the libido,[50] but when examined within the context I have been presenting, the monkey can be seen, more specifically, as representing the editor's repressed homosexual libido. The physical movements of the monkey within the "phallic" chimney described by Jennings during one of his first encounters with the creature and then recounted by the editor seem to simulate male masturbation and climax: "and it draws nearer and nearer to the chimney, quivering, it seems, with rage, and when its fury rises to the highest pitch, it springs into the grate, and up the chimney, and I see it no more."[51] The squatting position which the monkey assumes upon Mr. Jennings's book as he reads to his congregation suggests anal eroticism, but it is in a note sent by Jennings to Hesselius while he is studying the case at an inn that Hesselius becomes more clearly the object of this embodied homosexual desire:

Dear Dr. Hesselius.—it is here. You had not been an hour gone when it returned. It is speaking. It knows all that has happened. It knows everything—it knows you, and is frantic and atrocious. It reviles. I send you this. It knows every word I have written—I write. This I promise; and I therefore write, but I fear very confused, very incoherently. I am so interrupted, disturbed.

Ever yours, sincerely yours,
Robert Lynder Jennings.[52]

The monkey appears or the libido surfaces only an hour after Hesselius's lengthy interview with Jennings and is now focused on an object of desire—Hesselius: "it knows you." If we are to consider that the narrator is manipulating the text as an editor and author for the purpose of venting his resentment at a profession which marginalizes him, then this frustration becomes apparent in the description of the monkey/libido as "frantic," "atrocious," and reviling. These adjectives add a resentful tinge to a libido which has the potential to explode into violent forms of expression upon being released from a long suppression, evoking the Victorian association of "frankly lustful and openly violent, even murderous feelings" with sadomasochism and homosexuality.

While Krafft-Ebing came to intermingle "the lust murderer and the homosexual,"[53] the narrator's revelations and editorship, in his "coming out," revise this notion as his resentment is not manifested in a sexual violation of Hesselius. Rather, as the narrative builds toward a climax, the editor becomes, more discernibly, a "master" in a profession, that of letters, as this once repressed character, now empowered through written discourse, is about to reveal overtly the incompetence of one of the medical profession's most respected members. He simultaneously becomes "master" in a sexual sense as he reveals that the entire written discourse is informed by desire through a line from Jennings's letter: "It [the monkey] knows every word I have written—I write."[54]

Jennings's use of the present perfect, "I have written," and the sudden use of the present, "I write," may seem confusing as the only present information anyone could gain from the letter *by itself* is simply Jennings's description of his own writing as "very confused" and "incoherent." If we are to read Jennings as a representation of the editor and Jennings's case as editorially manipulated, then the use of the present-tense verb becomes more revealing when read as alluding to the *entire narrative*, "Green Tea." All that the editor has presented until now and all he will present afterward has been and will continue to be inspired by his frustrated desire for Hesselius.

The death of Jennings signals the exposure of Hesselius as a bruised egoist and allows him, as part of his own conscience-clearing, to ruminate upon Jennings's possible malady. He recalls a paper he has written called " 'The Cardinal Function of the Brain' " in which he speculates that the human brain produces a fluid, "spiritual, though not immaterial."[55] If this fluid is altered through the abuse of a substance such as green tea, "an inner eye" could be opened through which one may communicate with the spirit world. This "interior vision" can easily be blocked "by the simple application of iced eau-de-cologne."[56] The editor's inclusion of such a fantastic theory not only serves to call into question Hesselius's reputation, but it also acts as a metaphor for the editor's sexual desire, which must be kept suppressed by society and, more specifically, the medical profession.

After being removed from the threshold opening into the "interior" of the medical profession, the editor empowers himself through the position of frame narrator of the traditional Gothic narrative. Through the manipulation of written discourse, he suggests the existence of a sexuality which for many must remain "internal" and illustrates the dangers of repression. Jennings's suicide, for example, can be read as a result of a Victorian clergyman's guilt after experiencing sexual desire, heterosexual or homosexual, which can no longer be locked away in the interior of the psyche.

If readers are to construe Jennings as a representation of the editor in the interior narrative, then his death occurs as the narrator's "killing off" of a previous closeted lifestyle and, simultaneously, as an act of defiance. Jennings never has that "inner eye" sealed with "iced eau-de-cologne," a treatment which could have caused "that permanent insensibility which we call numbness, and a little longer, muscular as well as sensational paralysis."[57] Similarly, the editor, through a narrative which suggests his sexuality and criticizes a rising institution, asserts his refusal to have his sexuality "numbed" and "paralyzed" in the dark interior of the closet by a "patriarchal, hierarchical" society's prejudices and suppressive measures.

Evidence of the editor's newly expressed sexual identity becomes most clear in his note preceding "Carmilla," the last tale in *In a Glass Darkly*, as this account of erotic affection between women seems to validate his own feelings. Briefly, Carmilla becomes the houseguest, after an accident, of the narrator Laura and her father, who is retired from the Austrian service, in a remote castle in Styria. The account the editor reads is written in Laura's own hand and addressed to an unnamed "town lady," and has inexplicably fallen among Dr. Hesselius's papers.[58] As the friendship between Laura and Carmilla develops, Laura experiences "a strange tumultuous excitement that was pleasurable, ever and anon, mingled with a vague sense of fear and disgust," especially when Carmilla caresses her with the "ardour of a lover": "she drew me to her, and her hot lips travelled along my cheek in kisses; and she would whisper, almost in sobs, 'You are mine, you *shall* be mine [italicized in text], and you and I are one forever.' "[59] Eventually,

Carmilla's identity as vampire is deduced, and she is executed in the traditional fashion in the presence of Laura's father, General Spielsdorf, whose daughter died as a result of a previous encounter with Carmilla, and "two medical men." Carmilla is staked through the heart, decapitated, and then cremated.[60] Laura then goes on a year-long "tour through Italy" with her father.[61]

Critics point out, however, that Carmilla, cannot be readily dismissed as yet another representation of "homosexual as monster." Michael Begnal, for example, believes that Le Fanu's purpose in "Carmilla" is "not to attack the practice of homosexuality but rather to comment on the self-destruction of a total submission to sexuality."[62] Nina Auerbach in *Our Vampires, Ourselves* points out that Carmilla is more "human," both physically and emotionally, than other male literary vampires as "[t]here are no fangs, no slavering, no red eyes, no mesmerism, and no dematerialization, . . . she is all body."[63] In the previously reproduced lines from the story, Carmilla's flesh is "hot" against Laura's, and her passionate commands uttered with a breaking voice ("almost in sobs"), perhaps an indication of Carmilla's sadness at having to express her love for Laura by taking her human life:

> "Dearest, your little heart is wounded; . . . if your dear heart is wounded, my wild heart bleeds with yours. In the rapture of my enormous humiliation, I live in your warm life, and you shall die—die, sweetly die—into mine. I cannot help it; as I draw near to you, you, in your turn, will draw near to others, and learn the rapture of that cruelty, which yet is love; so, for a while, seek to know no more of me and mine, but trust me with all your loving spirit."[64]

Camilla offers Laura a sexual relationship based upon mutual sharing and exchanging, a characterization which would again attempt to revise Krafft-Ebing's and other Victorian physicians' deduction that homosexual relationships are based upon lustful or murderous feelings.

Laura's initial "disgust" over Carmilla's expression of affection eventually diminishes as shown by her actions after hearing the narrative of General Spielsdorf which attempts to characterize Carmilla as "monster." In a carriage heading to "the deserted village and ruined castle of Karnstein," ancestral home of Carmilla, the general relates the complete story concerning his daughter's mysterious death to Laura and her father.[65] He tells how a young woman, Millarca, was left in his care by her mother and how he was "too happy to have secured so charming a companion for [his] dear girl."[66] As his daughter's health deteriorates, she is haunted "by appalling dreams; then as he fancied by a spectre, something resembling Millarca, sometimes in the shape of a beast, indistinctly seen walking around the foot of the bed, from side to side."[67] After a pause in the general's story, Laura admits to herself that she recognizes her own situation in his story:

> You may guess how strangely I felt as I heard my own symptoms so exactly described in those which had been experienced by the poor girl who, but for the catastrophe which followed, would have been at that moment a visitor at my father's chateau. You may suppose also, how I felt as I heard him detail habits and mysterious peculiarities which were, in fact, those of our beautiful guest, Carmilla![68]

Even after recognizing Millarca's "mysterious peculiarities" as Carmilla's, however, Laura is never suspicious as demonstrated by her congenial thoughts when she sees Carmilla in the churchyard of the castle Karnstein, after hearing the general's story: "I saw very gladly the beautiful face and figure of Carmilla enter the shadowy chapel. I was just about to rise and speak, and nodded smiling, in answer to her peculiarly engaging smile."[69]

The last line of "Carmilla" is often cited as proof that Carmilla survives in Laura's affections long after she has been destroyed by male authority figures (father, general, physician): "and after from a long reverie I have started, fancying I heard the light steps of Carmilla at the drawing-room door."[70] According to Waller, not only does Carmilla survive, but also "a world of sentiments and sensations apart from the father, yet as close as the drawing-room door."[71]

McCormack characterizes Le Fanu's fiction as turning upon "suggestion and negative statement" and "obliquity and concealment as well as revelation and exposure."[72] True to this assessment, in "Green Tea," male homosexual desire lands upon the closet threshold under the guise of criticism of the medical profession. This criticism is formed by suggestion and "obliquity" as it is built by what the editor chooses to reveal about himself and Hesselius and what the reader can deduce from these bits of information. "Carmilla," however, which concludes the volume, *In A Glass Darkly*, can be seen as an attempt on the part of the editor to focus, clarify, and affirm the themes introduced in the collection's first story, "Green Tea."

The editor decides to *remove* the "rather elaborate note, which he [Dr. Hesselius] accompanies with a reference to his Essay on the strange subject which the Manuscript illuminates" that is attached to Laura's narrative. The editor elects "to abstain from presenting any precis of the learned Doctor's reasoning" and to "publish the case, in this volume, simply to interest the 'laity.' "[73] After reading the tale, the editor apparently recognizes the repression of sexual desire and identity which, I believe, he has experienced. When the editor decides not to include Hesselius's note attached to Laura's narrative (one, we must remember, which was originally intended for the eyes of another woman only, a "town lady," and not those of a heterosexual male) in an attempt to rationalize her (homosexual) experience, he acknowledges Carmilla and the alternative desires she represents and attests to their flourishing despite any barriers built by society's authorities. More than a year after Carmilla's execution, Laura writes that "the image of Carmilla returns to memory," undoubtedly accompanied by the memories of the eroticism once shared with her, despite the authorities' (which includes "two medical men") witnessing of Carmilla's death and their signing of the Imperial Commission's report of the death.[74] Similarly, at the end of "Green Tea," Dr. Hesselius fails to "cure" Mr. Jennings, the character through which the editor attempts to express his homosexual identity, an identity which is clarified by the relationship between the two women foregrounded in "Carmilla."

Why Le Fanu becomes more "bold" in his acknowledgment of same-sex desire in "Carmilla" is certainly arguable. Perhaps he believed that casting the homosexual as a fictional monster and the recipient of her affections as a young female with absolutely no opportunity to attain a position of power would be less innocuous to his readership. Nevertheless, when elements of "Green Tea" are examined closely and then placed in relief by a reading of "Carmilla," along with its more frank portrayal of homosexual desire, the acknowledgment of a male homosexual identity in Victorian fiction edges closer to the threshold.

NOTES

1. Nina Auerbach, *Our Vampires, Ourselves* (Chicago: University of Chicago Press, 1995), 41.

2. W. J. McCormack, *Sheridan Le Fanu and Victorian Ireland* (Oxford: Clarendon Press, 1980), 268.

3. Ibid., 207–8.

4. Ibid., 247.

5. Ibid., 122.

6. Ibid., 130.

7. Ibid., 130.

8. Joseph Sheridan Le Fanu, "Green Tea," in *Best Ghost Stories of J. S. Le Fanu* (New York: Dover, 1964), 178.

9. Le Fanu, "Green Tea," 178.

10. Barbara T. Gates, "Blue Devils and Green Tea: Sheridan Le Fanu's Haunted Suicides," *Studies in Short Fiction* 24 (1987): 22.

11. Le Fanu, "Green Tea," 178.

12. Sandra Gilbert and Susan Gubar, *The Madwoman in the Attic: The Woman Writer and the Nineteenth-Century Literary Imagination* (New Haven: Yale University Press, 1979), 53–54.

13. Gilbert and Gubar argue that disorders such as anorexia and agoraphobia can be attributed to "patriarchal socialization in several ways" (53–54). For example, anorexia results from the carrying of the "patriarchal definition of 'femininity' to absurd extremes" as a woman goes to devastating lengths to fulfill her role as "beautiful object" (54). Agoraphobia, a fear of public places, stems from women being "reared for, and conditioned to, lives of privacy, reticence, domesticity" (54).

14. McCormack, *Sheridan Le Fanu*, 244.

15. Joseph Sheridan Le Fanu, "Carmilla," in *Best Ghost Stories of J. S. Le Fanu* (New York: Dover, 1964), 291–92.

16. McCormack, *Sheridan Le Fanu*, 249.

17. Le Fanu, "Green Tea," 179.

18. Helen Stoddardt, " 'The Precautions of Nervous People Are Infectious': Sheridan Le Fanu's Symptomatic Gothic," *Modern Language Review* 86 (1991): 19.

19. Le Fanu, "Green Tea," 179.

20. Ibid.

21. Ibid., 178.

22. Eve Kosofsky Sedgwick, *Between Men: English Literature and Male Homosocial Desire* (New York: Columbia University Press, 1985), 3.

23. Ibid., 2.

24. Ibid.

25. Ibid.

26. Ibid., 86.

27. Le Fanu, "Green Tea," 178; my emphasis.

28. George Frederick Drinka, M. D. , *The Birth of Neurosis: Myth, Malady and the Victorians* (New York: Simon & Schuster, 1984), 172.

29. Ibid., 171.

30. Ibid., 174.

31. Steven Marcus, *The Other Victorians* (New York: Humanities Press, 1965), 3.

32. Ibid., 13.

33. Ibid., 12.

34. Ibid., 65.

35. Le Fanu, "Green Tea," 207.

36. Ibid., 202; my emphasis.

37. Charlotte Perkins Gilman, *The Living of Charlotte Perkins Gilman: An Autobiography* (New York: Arno, 1972), 119–21. In her autobiography, Charlotte Perkins Gilman writes that "the real purpose of the story ['The Yellow Wallpaper'] was to reach Dr. S. Weir Mitchell, and convince him of the error of his ways" (121). Gilman describes the "inevitable result" of her own treatment by Mitchell

for a nervous breakdown as "progressive insanity" (119). A patient undergoing Mitchell's rest cure first had to be isolated for at least six weeks "from family worries, and the overstimulation of city life." She was not allowed to feed or dress herself and had to stay in bed "with no exercise for the first two weeks." Gradually, the patient was allowed to sit up, walk around the room, and take solid food (Drinka 200–201).

38. Drinka, 339.

39. Sigmund Freud, *Dora: An Analysis of a Case Hysteria* (New York: Macmillan, 1963), 131.

40. Drinka, 339.

41. Sedgwick, *Between Men*, 91.

42. Eve Kosofsky Sedgwick, *Epistemology of the Closet* (Berkeley: University of California Press, 1990), 186, n. 10.

43. Le Fanu, "Green Tea," 178; my emphasis.

44. Ibid., 180.

45. Ibid., 183.

46. Ibid., 185; my emphasis.

47. Ibid., 187.

48. Ibid., 194.

49. Peter Penzoldt, *The Supernatural in Fiction* (New York: Humanities Press, 1965), 77.

50. Julia Briggs, *Night Visitors: The Rise and Fall of the English Ghost Story* (London: Faber, 1977), 40.

51. Ibid., 197.

52. Ibid., 203.

53. Drinka, *The Birth of Neurosis*, 174.

54. Le Fanu, "Green Tea," 203.

55. Ibid., 207.

56. Ibid.

57. Ibid.

58. Ibid., 293.

59. Ibid., 292.

60. Ibid., 336.

61. Ibid., 339.

62. Michael H. Begnal, *Joseph Sheridan LeFanu* (Lewisburg: Bucknell University Press, 1971), 44.

63. Auerbach, 45.

64. Le Fanu, "Carmilla," 291.

65. Ibid., 316.

66. Ibid., 326.

67. Ibid.

68. Ibid., 327.

69. Ibid., 332.

70. Ibid., 339.

71. Gregory A. Waller, *The Living and the Undead: From Stoker's "Dracula" to Romero's "Dawn of the Dead"* (Urbana: University of Illinois Press, 1986), 54.

72. McCormack, *Sheridan Le Fanu*, 207, 208.

73. Le Fanu, "Carmilla," 274.

74. Ibid., 336.

The Seduction of Celibacy:
Threats to Male Sexual Identity in
Charles Kingsley's Writings

LAURA FASICK

AMONG THE MANY CHARGED TERMS THAT HAVE BEEN USED IN THE debates over homosexuality as activity and as identity, few have been as emotion-laden as the words "manliness" and "effeminacy." For some time, "effeminacy" has served many people virtually as a synonym for male homosexuality[1]—a usage that would horrify many past and present practitioners of homosexual behavior.[2] "Manliness," or its more common modern equivalent, "masculinity," conversely suggests heterosexual desire and activity. Yet the many ironies accompanying attempts to define homosexuality itself must surely include the way in which the holders of all positions along the spectrum of possibilities repudiate "effeminacy" and attempt to associate "manliness" with their own stand and its practitioners. As a result, masculinity has assumed a baffling array of guises—a salutary reminder that masculinity itself is best understood as a social construction, but an obstacle to being sure how to understand the word in particular contexts in which it appears.[3] In fact, as numerous commentators have pointed out, the idea of homosexuality *as an identity* dates, like the word "homosexuality" itself, from the late nineteenth century,[4] so much so that some earlier practitioners of sodomy could perceive their homosexual acts as distinct from themselves and their own sexual identity.[5] In a somewhat different fashion, one might argue that "masculinity" or "manliness" has constituted a separate identity from biological membership in the male sex.[6] Why else would such comments as "He's a real man!" be used (by some people) as praise that differentiates one male not from women but from other, less worthy men?

This still leaves open the question, however, of the extent to

215

which sexual desire and activity are components in this admirable "manliness." In *Hellenism and Homosexuality in Victorian Oxford*, Linda Dowling argues eloquently and persuasively that eighteenth- and early nineteenth-century denunciations of effeminacy need to be understood as polemics not against homosexuality, but against the abandonment of former military and civic ideals in favor of luxurious and selfish self-indulgence. According to Dowling, "effeminate" men's sexual behavior was the least of their attackers' concerns. Although certainly perceived as sexually ambiguous, their ambiguity resided in their failure to resemble the heroic warriors and self-denying statesmen of an idealized classical antiquity. True masculinity required patriotic self-sacrifice, nobility of character, and a chaste asceticism that rose above the allure of purely personal pleasures, whatever those pleasures might be.[7] The true man was more committed to the public good than to his own private life. Effeminacy, by contrast, was evil because it prized individual self-indulgence above the welfare of the state.[8]

Dowling's argument thus provides one example of the need to move beyond the binary opposition of homosexuality and heterosexuality, just as Randolph Trumbach points out the inadequacy of "[t]he paradigm that there are two genders founded on two biological sexes."[9] "Effeminacy," rather than designating a particular sexual orientation among members of one sex, can apply to heterosexuals as well as homosexuals and even to women as well as to men. One of its most important meanings historically has been to categorize (and stigmatize) a selfish sensuality associated with heterosexual passion. That same association with selfish sensuality remained during the nineteenth century, even though for some the effeminacy in question was seen to manifest itself through voluntary celibacy rather than heterosexual indulgence.

Charles Kingsley's 1864 skirmish with John Henry Newman over the vices or virtues of the Roman Catholic clergy is most famous today for having inspired Newman's *Apologia Pro Vita Sua*. Recently, Oliver Buckton has examined this skirmish as an example of nineteenth-century veiled allusions to homosexuality and appeals to homophobic feeling under the guise of a religious debate.[10] Certainly Kingsley's language is riddled with references to gender identity, normalcy, and abnormalcy—particularly effeminacy. In *all* of Kingsley's attacks on Roman Catholicism—and they are legion—clerical celibacy and the ideal of perpetual virginity are among his foremost objects of detestation. Yet one might question whether Kingsley's attacks on celibacy are really euphemistically worded references to homosexuality. Rather, an examination of his writings leads to the conclusion that, for Kingsley, the lifelong celibate male who *prefers* celibacy to marriage (for Kingsley, the only acceptable arena for sexual activity), is as abnormal and as corrupt a figure as nineteenth-century popular prejudice perceived the homosexual to be.

Today, of course, we are used to the idea of heterosexual feeling helping to define gender identity, so that "masculinity" stereotypically includes sexual attraction to women and sexual involvement with them. Yet by looking at Kingsley's writings against the backdrop of a key literary motif repeated across centuries—that of the male warrior weakened and effeminized by heterosexual desire—one gains a sense of how radically Kingsley and his fellow-thinkers in the nineteenth century are revising earlier conceptions of manhood. This essay therefore divides into two parts. The first section examines the long-standing tradition that sexual interest in women is destructive of male identity. The second part explores Charles Kingsley's anti-Catholic writings, including his famous dispute with John Henry Newman, as representative of a new and growing tendency to perceive sexual abstinence, not sexual indulgence, as one important source of male effeminacy.

I

In Virgil's *Aeneid* (19 B.C.), model and inspiration for so many later literary works, the reader encounters a paradigmatic moment of male identity crisis, the significance of which expands far beyond its immediate context. Aeneas, the hero of Virgil's epic, has deviated from his mission to found Rome by sinking into a love affair with the Carthaginian Queen Dido. Mercury, directed by Jupiter to rebuke Aeneas for his lapse from duty, encounters him thus.

> [Mercury] noted well the swordhilt the man wore,
> Adorned with yellow jasper; and the cloak
> Aglow with Tyrian dye upon his shoulders—
> Gifts of the wealthy queen, who had inwoven
> Gold thread in the fabric. Mercury
> Took him to task at once:
> "Is it for you
> To lay the stones for Carthage's high walls,
> Tame husband that you are, and build their city?
> Oblivious of your own world, your own kingdom!
> From bright Olympus he that rules the gods
> And turns the earth and heaven by his power—

He and no other sent me to you, told me
To bring this message on the running winds:
What have you in mind? What hope, wasting your days
In Lybia? If future history's glories
Do not affect you, if you will not strive
For your own honor, think of Ascanius,
Think of the expectations of your heir,
Iulus, to whom the Italian realm, the land
Of Rome, are due."[11]

Aeneas, already identified as "Sir Paris" with "[h]is chin and perfumed hair tied up in a Maeonian bonnet," the leader of "half-men"[12] has clearly been emasculated by his "sweet life"[13] of sexual gratification. His pleasure in amorous dalliance with the besotted Dido has alienated him from what should be his primary loyalties and concerns: his place in a masculine line of patriarchal descent and his authority as the military leader of a male fighting force. Earlier moments in Greek literature have presaged this treatment of feminine sensuality as a threat to masculinity: Heracles, for example, is reduced to women's garb and women's work by the beautiful Queen Omphale.[14] Homer's Odysseus, by contrast, retains his manhood because, although he lives for a time as lover of the seductive Circe, he does so on his own terms and is able to leave her when he wishes. Unlike his followers, he is not betrayed by sensual greed into bestial subjugation. It is Virgil's handling of this theme, however, that echoes most clearly throughout centuries of literature as successive generations of poets replayed different versions of Mercury's encounter with Aeneas using their own heroes to replace the Roman forefather.

In Ariosto's *Orlando Furioso* (1516) Alcina lures Ruggiero into luxurious idleness,[15] just as Tasso's Armida does to Rinaldo in *Gerusalemme Liberata* (1580), while in *The Faerie Queene* (1590) Spenser's Duessa literalizes the idea of the Roman Catholic Church as the "Whore of Babylon" through her seduction of the Red Cross Knight.[16] Spenser's is the loosest adaptation of Virgil's scene, but in Ariosto's and Tasso's closer imitations only the shock of recognizing that heterosexual desire has effeminized them, weakening their masculine identity, restores the erstwhile heroes to their former status as fighters: military rather than sexual conquest obviously being the measure of manhood.[17] Different though *Orlando Furioso* and *Gerusalemme Liberata* are, each contains some of the same essential elements in the treatment of this moment: the hero who has slipped into becoming a lover invariably is dressed foppishly in clothes suitable for court rather than for camp life, has lost strength and vigor through the luxury with which he is now surrounded, and focuses his energies upon his emotional and sexual relations with his inamorata rather than on winning immortal glory through the defeat of male foes. In short, he is remarkably like a woman: his flourishing heterosexuality has destroyed his masculinity.

The following lines from the Edward Fairfax translation of Tasso's poem, the English title of which is *Jerusalem Regained*, show the remarkable continuity of Virgil's theme through their description of the knight-warrior Rinaldo's recognition of his own fall through his love affair with the beautiful Armida. Two of Rinaldo's fellow knights have just forced him to look at his own reflection in a shield and Tasso/Fairfax present the scene thus:

> Upon the targe his [Rinaldo's] looks amazed he bent,
>   And therein all his wanton habit spied,
> His civet, balm, and perfumes redolent,
>   How from his locks they smok'd and mantle wide;
> His sword, that many a Pagan stout had shent,
>   Bewrapt with flow'rs hung idly by his side,
> So nicely decked that it seem'd the knight
> Wore it for fashion sake, but not for fight.[18]

Armida's evil triumph here has been to turn Rinaldo from his religious, national, and masculine duty to fight and to fight specifically for the glory of his nation and his God. She has thereby destroyed his masculine identity; although far more erotically alive and active than previously, he is effeminate, not virile, as a result.

Rinaldo's horror at the sight of what sexuality has done to him underscores one of the paradoxes of male sexual identity: although men traditionally have been freer to explore and to assert their sexuality than women, they nonetheless have been less restrictively identified through sexuality alone. Whereas female virtue has usually meant chastity, men have been perceived as requiring a variety of virtues in order to pursue their many duties in their nation, their occupation, and the other spheres they occupy. Thus, although the sexually "conquering" male has often had some glamour, extreme sexual susceptibility or even interest paradoxically has been associated with a man's seduction into effeminacy. Indeed, as Peter N. Stearns points out, "pre-nineteenth-century Western culture assumed that women, not men, were the insatiable sexual aggressors, with men as vulnerable creatures in need of protection."[19] Specifically, the danger of the sexually tempting woman, then, is that she leads males away from the larger world of men—whether that world be military or economic—into a fantasy world of sensual self-indulgence. By separating men from their proper roles in a wider sphere than sexual, she robs them of their masculinity even as—paradoxically—she encourages their phallic prowess through sexual play.[20] Heterosexual desire itself, rather than an essential component of manliness, actually is a detraction from it, as illustrated by Romeo's cry, after his pacific passivity has led to the death of his comrade Mercutio, "O sweet Juliet, / Thy beauty hath made me effeminate / And in my temper soft'ned valor's steel!"[21]

Romeo's love for Juliet is an exemplar of romantic devotion, of course, far removed from the sottishness of Circe's prey. Yet so dangerous is heterosexual love that even its "pure" varieties can be psychologically and physically self-destructive. Participation in a same-sex world shows respect for men and for masculinity, including one's own. Men in groups, it appears, reinforce each other's gender identity by modeling, mirroring, and thus strengthening commitment to a univocal male ideal. Fascination with a woman, on the other hand, depreciates manliness by reversing the "normal" hierarchy of genders in which maleness is superior to femaleness.[22] Even Milton's Adam, who has no other human males with whom to join, suffers a severe rebuke from the archangel Raphael for doting excessively on Eve.[23] Effeminacy in this context is largely an undue susceptibility to female attractions and a consequent relinquishment of masculine prerogatives.[24]

This unease over the slipperiness of a specifically male identity continues across cultural shifts. In times when the warrior-ideal was paramount, the lover of women became *like* a woman by turning away from a same-sex male world of military combat, physical rigor, and ascetic living to an interiorized, emotion-centered existence in a feminine realm of sensual and sexual indulgence. Even a more sedentary model of masculinity, such as the merchant life extolled in George Lillo's *The London Merchant* (1731), assumes that same-sex bonding between master and apprentice and between fellow apprentices is normal and normative in a way that young George Burnwell's involvement with the courtesan Millwood is not. Thus when financial probity and industry are primary masculine virtues, Protestant morality tales recast the weakened warrior as an upright businessman led astray by an expensive woman who encourages sharp dealing or disrupts the secure passage of family estates. In Lillo's play, had Barnwell remained loyal and devoted to his master Thorowgood, to his uncle, and to his fellow apprentice

Trueman (a telling name!), he himself would have been a "true man" as opposed to Millwood's slave of passion.[25]

If the sameness of an all-male group reinforces masculinity, women's difference from men makes women's company an inferior and therefore deteriorating influence. This neatly illustrates Thomas Laqueur's observation that pre-Enlightenment thought typically perceived women as inferior versions of men while consequent centuries of medical and gender theory have viewed the sexes as incommensurate and complementary. This more recent development has made it possible to assume that sexual segregation might actually threaten rather than maintain gender identity. Defining themselves in opposition to each other, men and women need each other in order to realize fully their own masculine and feminine qualities. Thus Charles Kingsley writes of "[t]his binary law of man's being [as] the want of a complementum, a 'help meet,' without whom it is not good for him to be, and joined to whom they two became one being of a higher organization than either had alone."[26] For Kingsley, a passionate advocate of marriage, a man who does *not* link himself with a woman is thereby less of a man.

Kingsley's almost hysterical detestation of celibacy and his zealotry for marriage undoubtedly have some roots in his own psychological conflicts, amply documented not only by biographer Susan Chitty but by historian Peter Gay.[27] Yet his arguments also represent one increasingly dominant voice in the polyphony of Victorian discourses about marriage. Linda Dowling points out the continuity of thought from earlier centuries in Victorian idealizations of civic virtue as crucial to manhood. In arenas as different as Oxford tutorial rooms and Crimean battlefields, Victorian men were subject to a rhetoric of public responsibility that was deemed incompatible with an immersion in private life.[28] The domesticity that was idealized on one hand, on the other could be viewed with suspicion as dangerously weakening. As James Eli Adams shrewdly remarks, if manliness is essentially a form of physical and psychological toughness, then perhaps "manhood cannot be *sustained* within domesticity, since the ideal is incompatible with ease."[29] At its most extreme, the exaltation of public-spirited manhood could "lead some to the conclusion that society was carried upon the shoulders of unwed males."[30] The members of the Oxford Movement seized upon this idea with particular fervor: a "common antagonism to domesticity" links "Tractarian discipline to Carlylean heroism."[31] As former Tractarian R. W. Church eloquently put it, "To shrink from [celibacy] was a mark of want of strength or intelligence, of an unmanly preference for English home life, of insensibility to the generous devotion and purity of the saints."[32] Note that in this equation, the respectable *husband* is insufficiently masculine, guilty of a contemptible weakness.[33] Not only wanton profligacy but even domestic stability could tempt men away from the "ideal of martial and civic 'virtue.' "[34] Once domesticity has become a symbol of comfort, even of luxury, then it fits neatly into the definition of effeminacy offered by William Hazlitt in the decade before Victoria's ascension to the throne. According to Hazlitt, effeminate people (Hazlitt never confines effeminacy to males) are distinguished by their addiction to "ease and indolence" and their "appetite of enjoyment."[35] In Hazlitt's definition, effeminacy indicates neither a sexual orientation nor a gender identity. It indicates only a preference for an easy life—and that raises the question of what kind of life is easiest.[36]

John Henry Newman, Kingsley's most famous antagonist on the subject of clerical celibacy, is foremost among those who stress the heroic manliness of the sexually abstinent and the despicable self-indulgence of the domestically united. In his history of the Oxford Movement, R. W. Church notes that "the idea of celibacy, in those whom it affected at Oxford, was in the highest degree a religious and romantic one." [37] The embrace of that idea was an implicit choice of "the loftier and bolder . . . standard of Roman piety" over the Anglican Church's allegiance with "home life."[38] That romantic idealism emerges in *Loss and Gain* (1848) through the terms in which Newman's hero defends his decision to remain single. Charles Reding argues that "surely the idea of an Apostle, unmarried, pure, in fast and nakedness, and at length a martyr, is a higher idea than that of one of the old Israelites sitting under his vine and fig-tree, full of temporal goods, and surrounded by sons and grandsons?"[39] Here Newman stresses the strength of the celibate male and the spirit-sapping sensuality of family life itself. His association of domesticity with the appetites tempted and sated by the products of "vine and fig-tree," and with the materialism glutted by "temporal goods" undercuts standard Victorian pieties about the sacredness of home.

Yet Kingsley's strictures lay a counterpoint stress upon the duty to marry and the avoidance of that duty by the abnormally self-focused.[40] He therefore detests above all the exaltation of celibacy as an ideal. He will allow and even admire the celibacy that is endured as a sacrifice to God and a necessary hardship. So long as "a man . . . says to himself, 'I know marriage is the highest, because the most symbolic of all human states; but it is not for me, I have a great work to do . . . and must bear that cross,' " he "would deserve all names of honor which men could heap on him, just because the sacrifice is so great—just because he gives up a present and manifold honor and blessing."[41] But Kingsley's numerous writings on the subject attest to his suspicion that the choice of celibacy too often is an act of self-indulgence rather than self-denial: the "present and manifold honor and blessing" seems all too easy to give up in favor of selfish—and therefore effeminate—singleness.

II

Kingsley retains the rhetorical opposition of effeminacy and duty that literary predecessors had bequeathed him, but he gives the material some new twists. In his "intense preoccupation with the matter of celibacy,"[42] Charles Kingsley radically revises the trope of the seduced man: the promising youth led astray from proper masculine development by an enticing but corrupting "other." In Kingsley's hands, the seducer is not a woman and the threat is not that of unbridled and therefore enervating sexual indulgence. Instead, men seduce other men: specifically, Roman Catholic priests and their sympathizers subtly emasculate their male followers by persuading them to adopt celibacy. Sexual repression, not sexual excess, is the danger to masculine identity. To him, "that terrible question of 'Celibacy versus Marriage' . . . is the cardinal point. It is to religion, what the Malthusian doctrine is to political economy the crux in limina, your views of which must logically influence your views of everything afterwards."[43] The theory that "celibacy [is man's] highest state" is the "cause," according to Kingsley of "the lie of lies—the formulized and organized skepticism of Jesuitry," which Kingsley characterizes as "utter skepticism."[44] Such a theory is the source of all that is "unmanly" and "everything which we abhor" even in so admirable a pre-Protestant figure as St. Francis of Assisi.[45] The proselytizers of such a theory destroy the "independence, self-respect, self-restraint" of their converts and reduce them from "men and brothers" to "infants" or even "to the level of the Irish or Neapolitan savage."[46]

Thus it arises that Kingsley accuses Newman of effecting a sinister metamorphosis among his young male followers. As Oliver Buckton has shown, Kingsley couched his accusation by deploying "terms of quasi-sexual seduction and penetration" to describe Newman's preaching.[47] According to Kingsley, Newman's sermons were crafted to contain "one little barbed arrow which . . . he delivered . . . as with his finger-tip, to the very heart of an initiated

hearer, never to be withdrawn again."[48] The phallic arrow of Newman's teaching "[i]n proportion as young men absorbed it into
themselves, . . . injured their straightforwardness and truthfulness"
and thereby "spread misery and shame into many an English
home."[49]

Newman, in Kingsley's terms, is literally a "homewrecker," and
a far more potent one than the wayward female usually thus characterized. In Kingsley's account, Newman's male followers begin as
"hot-headed" and "fanatic": not milksops, but ardent young men
burning with misdirected zeal.[50] Once exposed to Newman's seductive preaching, however, and even more to his intimate counsels,
they lose their putatively masculine qualities of straightforwardness, vigor, and (in the positive sense of the word), worldliness.
They are all too likely to slip into that "element of foppery . . . a
fastidious, maundering die-away-effeminacy" that Kingsley identified in a private letter with the Oxford Movement.[51] No longer full
of "all manful energy, self-respect, all self-restraint, all that the true
Englishman has, and the Greek and Spaniard have not," they "mis-
tak[e]" effeminacy "for purity and refinement."[52] Yet just as this
"effeminacy" is certainly not "purity," so Newman's Catholic belief in miracles reveals his spirituality to be "stuff and nonsense,
more materialist than the dreams of any bone-worshipping Bud-
dhist."[53]

Ostensibly, Kingsley's persistent use of the word "materialism"
to describe Newman's beliefs comes from his revulsion at a hagiog-
raphy (endorsed by Newman) that describes Saint Walburga's di-
vinely inspired compassion as resulting in a literal "flow of oil or
dew."[54] Yet Kingsley's accusations of materialism function just as
do his accusations of "luxury" and "foppery." In both cases, he is
performing a dizzying turnaround. In Kingsley's hands, the miracu-
lous—through which invisible and divine powers defy physical
laws—becomes materialist; religious asceticism, which renounces
bodily self-indulgence, becomes "foppery," the "most carnal"
choice of a "luxurious aristocracy."[55] The result is to suggest that
Newman and his followers operate out of sensuality rather than
spirituality. The mortification of the flesh becomes, in Kingsley's
interpretation, self-indulgent luxuriousness.

Yet these implications of sensuality and even Kingsley's consistent accusations of prurient sensuality among the Roman Catholic
priesthood do not mean Kingsley identified this corrupt Catholic
sexuality as homosexual in nature. Buckton indicates the stereotypes of masculinity and the resulting potential homophobia that
underlie the reactions of Kingsley (and many of his contemporar-

ies) to Newman, but those same stereotypes of masculinity militate against celibacy as well as homosexuality. Certainly Kingsley, whose brother Henry apparently was homosexual,[56] would not have been ignorant about different sexual orientations, and there can be no doubt what his attitude toward them was.[57] But Kingsley seems to have feared and hated vowed sexual abstinence itself, not simply as a mask for homosexuality, but as what Kingsley would have considered a distinct and separate "perversion." Kingsley's many ferocious attacks on religious celibacy focus on its supposed propensity for inducing hysteria: a desire that Kingsley, even more strongly than other Victorians, linked to sexual repression rather than to sexual indulgence. Kingsley, indeed, anticipates Freud in the vigor with which he insists upon the return of the repressed, the process whereby Kingsley accounts for the mystical ecstasies, visions, and even many of the "miracles" of Catholic saints. By "[p]rurience," Kingsley writes, "I mean lust, which unable to satisfy itself in act, satisfies itself by contemplation, usually of a negative and seemingly virtuous and Pharisaic character, vilifying, like St. Jerome in his cell at Bethlehem, that which he dare not do, and which is, after all, only another form of hysteria."[58] The cult of the Virgin Mary, likewise, emerges in Kingsley's handling as an example of misdirected—but certainly heterosexual—erotic feeling among sex-starved monks and priests. Deprived of the blessing of actual female presence, these yearning males sink into "prudish and prurient foul-mindedness."[59] They thereby demonstrate two things: both the apparent universality of heterosexual feeling (the celibate clergy are obsessed with the absence of women from their lives, not with the presence of men), and the deleterious effects of suppressing that heterosexual feeling.

Thus, one of the most striking aspects of Kingsley's anti-Catholicism is that it does *not* draw upon long-standing traditions, richly revived in Victorian England, of scurrilous and obscene imputations about the supposed sexual habits of theoretically celibate Catholic clergy.[60] Indeed, Kingsley writes that

> it is a sin to disbelieve that God's grace will be vouchsafed in answer to prayer and earnest struggles to preserve that state [celibacy], as I think the biographies of pious monks and nuns fully show . . . they . . . prayed for grace to avoid that which in them would have been sin, and they obtained it.[61]

As is usual for Kingsley, he is far more willing to praise the celibate clergy of pre-Reformation times than of his own period; after all, he could hardly blame the former for their failure to be Protestants. His tone is markedly less respectful toward contemporary Catholic priests, yet during a period when there were both public and anonymous claims that supposedly celibate clergy were often sexually active (and often heterosexually so), Kingsley's writings focus almost exclusively on the effect of sexual inactivity upon these men. He attributes neither hidden heterosexual nor homosexual activity to them. Kingsley suggests that "the [Catholic] priest [is] unsexed by celibacy,"[62] but it is largely modern commentators who have assumed that "unsexing" equals homosexuality. Kingsley, rather, assumes both the priest's heterosexual feeling and his success in denying that feeling any physical expression. He believes further, however, that such "success" warps and corrupts the entire soul.

Thus, in the novel *Westward Ho!* (1855), Kingsley draws parallel pictures of two priestly paths. Both Jack Brimblecombe, the Protestant, and Eustace Leigh, the Catholic convert, are romantically drawn to the beautiful Rose Salterne, although both realize that they have no chance of winning her. Jack, who begins the novel as a comic caricature of plump sloth and cowardice—vices that Kingsley clearly feared the public too easily associated with clergymen— joins a quasi-military expedition on Rose's behalf and there receives lessons in manliness from his stalwart companions. He proves himself a fierce swordsman and *therefore* a more effective priest and ends his life as a husband, the patriarch of a large family, and a model clergyman. His earlier gluttony, laziness, and timidity—all sins of self-indulgence—disappear, and his apotheosis as a family man at the novel's end is the culmination of his training in self-discipline and endurance. Eustace, on the other hand, having chosen Catholicism though not yet Catholic priesthood, has only a celibate in whom to confide his love-anguish, and his confessor, naturally, can only lead him further astray. Rapidly degenerating, Eustace becomes not merely a convert but a priest, and not merely a priest but a Jesuit, and thereby he also becomes an "it." In Kingsley's scathing words, Eustace is "a man no longer; he is become a thing, a tool, a Jesuit which goes only where it is sent, and does good or evil indifferently as it is bid; which . . . has lost its soul . . . ; without a will, a conscience, a responsibility (as it fancies), to God or man."[63] The Jesuit, then, neither male nor female but rather neuter, has renounced every form of self-control because "it" has renounced human selfhood. "It" has attained the perverse ease that comes with giving up a volition, choice, moral struggle.

A neuter might not seem like a compelling romantic rival to pit against a fully sexed individual, but Kingsley even presents clerical advocacy of a sexually abstinent life as resulting in a new version of the romantic triangle. He thus participates in what James Eli Adams terms "the . . . bizarre paradox that contemporary attacks on celibate priests . . . tend to figure them as at once emasculate and sexually predatory."[64] The rival most likely to threaten a Kingsley hero's amorous happiness is a religious zealot bent on persuading the hero's beloved to embrace celibacy. This twist undoubtedly reflects Kingsley's own experience, since his future wife was tempted by the prospect of religious celibacy before marrying him. In Kingsley's literary renditions of this threat, the unsexed "seducer" plays as much upon feminine weakness, vanity, and love of flattery as would a more traditional "lady's man." Thus Lancelot Smith in *Yeast* (1849) must struggle to save his beloved Argemone from the corrupting temptation to enter an Anglican sisterhood, a spiritual trap into which the village vicar is trying to lure her.

Kingsley's most extended treatment of the man/woman/celibate triangle is in *The Saint's Tragedy* (1847), in which he retells the story of St. Elizabeth of Hungary as the story of an unscrupulous monk's alienation of a wife from her husband. The sexually abstinent man, then, becomes exactly the type of exploitative manipulator and destroyer more customarily envisioned in Victorian writings as the sexual seducer. For example, Kingsley responds to Newman's admiring description of a convent with his own description, in which convent life produces the physical and psychological deterioration that we are more used to associating with Victorian accounts of "fallen women." But, perhaps, for Kingsley, the nun is "fallen." He describes her as "[a] poor girl, cajoled, flattered, imprisoned, starved, maddened, by such as Dr. Newman and his peers, into that degrading and demoralizing disease, hysteria."[65] Distrust of Newman, he goes on to claim, is necessary "for the sake of the ladies of this land."[66] Newman must be an object of suspicion "as long as Englishmen know how to guard the women who God has committed to their charge."[67] These words sound like a ringing cry to arms against a lecherous tempter, but Englishmen here are being counseled to guard their women, not from sexual corruption in the usual sense of the term, but from a life of sexual repression that will lead to hysteria and such perverse acts of self-inflicted stigmata.

Yet at the same time that Kingsley imagines nuns as starving, deranged captives, he simultaneously pictures their original entry into celibacy as enabled by their own dreams of luscious self-gratification. Mourning his own failure to "rescue a woman out of ———'s hands," Kingsley explains that "I could not pamper her fancies as he could; for I could not bid her be more than a woman, but only to be a woman. I could not promise a safe and easy royal road to lily crowns, and palms of virginity, and the especial coronet of saints."[68] In *Yeast*, Argemone's "lust for singularity and self-glorification," "laziness," and "luxury" are the motivations for her abortive movement toward convent life.[69] Kingsley's terms here are remarkably similar to those used by William Hazlitt in his study of "effeminacy" and by Kingsley himself in his account of why the Oxford Movement is proving so attractive to an effeminate aristocracy. Once again religious asceticism, in Kingsley's hands, becomes its polar opposite: materialist self-pampering.

Kingsley objects even to the celibate's aspiration to "do the more good, . . . [to] be the more good."[70] The real attraction of celibacy, Kingsley suggests, is the lure of "mere selfish safety and easy saving of one's own soul," and the appeal of "selfishness" disguised as "devoutness."[71] Thus even the seemingly uncontroversial duty of a Christian to strive for salvation becomes a form of culpable self-centeredness here. By contrast, Kingsley repeatedly depicts the joys and comforts of conjugal union in forbiddingly austere language. By marrying, a man must give himself up to "self-humiliation" and endure "fear and trembling."[72] "[T]rue love" brings with it "wholesome fear," "awe," and "dread."[73] No wonder that Kingsley's widow remarks that for her husband "married love [was] the noblest education a man's character could have."[74] Marriage emerges here as a continual trial: "blissful," according to Kingsley,[75] but a stern and purifying bliss that purges and mortifies those who experience it. In one affectionate but disconcerting letter to his wife, Kingsley writes, "What would life be without you? What is it with you but a brief pain to make us long for everlasting bliss?"[76] Kingsley's youthful attraction toward bodily austerities, self-mortification, and even the idea of turning "papist and monk" has been well-documented.[77] Obviously, Kingsley ended by rejecting "papism" vehemently and embracing life as a husband and father. Yet he seems to have retained the sense that through this choice he overcame the temptation toward ease in order to enter the more difficult path. Part of his case against celibates is his charge that they choose the easier way, and hence arises his hostility toward their "luxurious" effeminacy.

The association of celibacy with selfish ease explains the apparent incongruity of Kingsley's rewriting the seduction motif from earlier literature with a priest, rather than a beautiful and sexually available woman, as the tempter. In this version, the priest fulfills the same function as a *femme fatale* because, like her, he entices the young (especially but not exclusively young men) away from duty and into self-indulgence: a vice whose most extreme form is effeminacy. Spenser's lewd Duessa and the celibate Newman might seem an unlikely pair at first glance, but Kingsley links them by making Newman his real-life model (as Duessa had been Spenser's allegorical one) of Roman Catholic seductiveness. Yet where Spenser had used sexual excess to represent Catholic immorality, Kingsley insists on the spiritual dangers latent in sexual abstinence. In both cases, the form that corruption takes is a despicable effeminacy.

NOTES

1. David Hilliard, "UnEnglish and Unmanly: Anglo-Catholicism and Homosexuality," *Victorian Studies* 25 (1982): 188.

2. Ibid., 183–84; see also Oliver Buckton, "Closet Dramas: Strategies of Secrecy and Disclosure in Four Victorian Autobiographies," (Ph.D. diss., Cornell, 1992), 21–23, 327–28.

3. David D. Gilmore's *Manhood in the Making: Cultural Concepts of Masculinity* provides a useful anthropologically based overview of different constructions of masculinity. Peter N. Stearns's *Be a Man! Males in Modern Society*, although assuming male "physical powers and freedom from the hearth" along with "female receptivity and nurturing functions," offers a discussion of the subject that concentrates on Western cultures (4).

4. Jeffrey Weeks, *Sex, Politics and Society: The Regulation of Sexuality Since 1800*, 2d ed. (London: Longman, 1981), 102.

5. Richard Dellamora, *Masculine Desire: The Sexual Politics of Victorian Aestheticism* (Chapel Hill: University of North Carolina Press, 1990), 3.

6. In *The Wilde Century*, Alan Sinfield points out that even definitions of homosexual behavior can vary dramatically. In Turkey, he asserts, "mutual male masturbation is regarded as heterosexual behaviour, and hence . . . is free from stigma" (181–82). In an additional twist, men who take the "insertive" role with other men may claim a "manliness" that they deny to their "receptive" partners (192).

7. Ultimately, of course, this conception of masculine virtue reaches back to the Platonic allegories that show "[m]oral progress" as "a struggle to transcend the feminine. The virtuous life, in which Reason gains its rightful supremacy over the lower aspects of human nature, comes through a process of, as it were, becoming male—shedding the influence and intrusion of femaleness" (Genevieve Lloyd, *The Man of Reason: "Male" and "Female" in Western Philosophy*, 26).

8. George L. Mosse demonstrates the continuance of this idea in modern society, most notably under German's Nazi regime, in *Nationalism and Sexuality: Respectability and Abnormal Sexuality in Modern Europe*.

9. Randolph Trumbach, "London's Sapphists: From Three Sexes to Four Genders in the Making of a Modern Culture," *Body Guards: The Cultural Politics of Gender Ambiguity*, ed. Julia Epstein and Kristina Straub (New York: Routledge, 1991), 112.

10. See Buckton's article, " 'An Unnatural State': Gender, "Perversion," and Newman's *Apologia Pro Vita Sua*."

11. Virgil, *The Aeneid*, trans. Robert Fitzgerald (New York: Random House, 1981), 104–5.

12. Ibid., 103.

13. Ibid., 105.

14. This enforced "feminization" has its own history as a literary trope of male degradation at the hands of a virago. In *The Faerie Queene*, Spenser dooms Artegall to such humiliation from Radigund (Book 5, Cantos 5–7).

15. Lodovico Ariosto, *Orlando Furioso*, 7.26–32, 53–65.

16. Edmund Spenser, *The Fairie Queen*, ed. Thomas P. Roche, Jr. and C. Patrick O'Donnell, Jr. (Harmondsworth: Penguin, 1978), 1.2.26–30, 1.7.1–7.

17. Ariosto's version does contain one surprising deviation from the Virgilian model: the monitor who rebukes Ruggiero is herself female, the sorceress Melissa. However, since her purpose in confronting him is to send him back to his masculine military duties, she affirms the importance of same-sex bonding despite her own sexual difference from the hero.

18. Torquato Tasso, *Jerusalem Regained*, trans. Edward Fairfax, intro. Roberto Weiss (Carbondale: Southern Illinois University Press, 1962), book 16, st. 30.

19. Peter N. Stearns, *Be A Man! Males in Modern Society* 5.

20. Alan Sinfield uses this same passage to illustrate his point that effeminacy in Shakespeare's time and "[u]p to the time of the Wilde trials . . . often . . . involved excessive cross-sexual attachment" (*The Wilde Century*, 27).

21. William Shakespeare, *Romeo and Juliet*, ed. J. A. Bryant, Jr. (New York: Signet, 1964), 3.1.115–17.

22. Milton's similar warning against the dangers of uxuriousness in *Samson Agonistes* indicates how significant—and potentially destructive—he considers this temptation.

23. John Milton, *Paradise Lost. Complete Poems and Major Prose*, ed. Merritt Y. Hughes (New York: Odyssey Press, 1957), 8:521–94.

24. There is an interesting parallel between the disapproval of a man who gives up masculine privilege through infatuation with a woman and of one who assumes the "inferior" sexual role vis-à-vis another man. George L. Mosse is one of numerous commentators to point out that historically male homosexuals who took the "female positions [in sexual activity] were often punished with greater severity than those who had taken the male position" (25). Even in the context of generally prohibited behavior, then, there appears to be a further stigma attached to, and animus against, men who are perceived as "lowering" themselves to the position of women.

25. The chaste and unrequited love that Maria, Thorowgood's daughter, bears for Barnwell is also held out as preferable to Millwood's seduction, of course. Maria, however, is a virtual cipher in the play compared to the male characters and the charismatic Millwood. The most she does is to mirror palely her father's idealized mercantile values and Trueman's passionate attachment to Barnwell.

26. Charles Kinglsey, *Charles Kingsley: His Letters and Memories of His Life*, ed. F. E. Kingsley, 2 vols. (New York: Fred De Fau, 1899), 1 : 162.

27. Peter Gay, *The Tender Passion*, vol. 2 of *The Bourgeois Experience: Victoria to Freud* (New York: Oxford University Press, 1986), 297–309.

28. Linda Dowling, *Hellenism and Homosexuality in Victorian Oxford* (Ithaca: Cornell University Press, 1994), 39–40, 46–47.

29. James Eli Adams, *Dandies and Desert Saints: Styles of Victorian Manhood* (Ithaca: Cornell University Press, 1995), 10.

30. George L. Mosse, *Nationalism and Sexuality: Respectability and Abnormal Sexuality in Modern Europe* (New York: Howard Fertig, 1985), 20.

31. Adams, 82.

32. R. W. Church, *The Oxford Movement: Twelve Years 1833–1945* (London: Macmillan, 1932), 370.

33. Dowling, 42.

34. Ibid., 55.

35. William Hazlitt, "On Effiminacy of Character," *Table Talk: Essays on Men and Manners* (1822; reprint, London: Oxford University Press, 1933), 332, 334.

36. As evidence of the semantic confusion that Victorians (like all of us!) experienced with key cultural terms, scholars from Claudia Nelson (*Boys Will Be Girls*, 38) to Peter Gay (*Cultivation of Hatred*, 3:101) have noted that nineteenth-century writers applauded females as well as males for being "manly." Indeed, Nelson points out that not only is manliness "possible for women as well as men," but it "may come more easily to the woman than to the man" since it involves some virtues, such as patience and chastity, that in other contexts have been seen as stereotypically feminine (37–38). Thus the self-effacement of the ideal Victorian woman and the self-control of the masculine man can blur into one.

37. Church, 370.

38. Ibid.

39. John Henry Newman, *Loss and Gain: The Story of a Convert*, ed. Alan G. Hill (1848; reprint, Oxford: Oxford University Press, 1986), 139.

40. Gay, *Tender Passion*, 2 : 300.

41. Kingsley, *Letters*, 1 : 165.

42. Brenda Colloms, *Charles Kingsley: The Lion of Eversley* (London: Constable, 1975), 18.

43. Kingsley, *Letters*, 1 : 222.

44. Ibid., 1 : 225.

45. Ibid.

46. Ibid., 1 : 221.

47. Oliver Buckton, " 'An Unnatural State,' " 375.

48. Charles Kingsley, "What, Then, Does Dr. Newman Mean?" *Newman's Apologia Pro Vita Sua: The Two Versions of 1864 & 1865 Preceded by Newman's and Kingsley's Pamphlets*, intro. Wilfred Ward (1864; reprint, London: Oxford University Press, 1931), 33.

49. Ibid., 34–35.

50. Ibid., 34.

51. Kingsley, *Letters*, 1 : 217–18.

52. Newman, 220, 218.

53. Kingsley, "What, Then," 41.

54. Ibid.

55. Kingsley, *Letters*, 1 : 218.

56. Susan Chitty, *The Beast and the Monk: A Life of Charles Kingsley* (London: Hodder & Stoughton, 1975), 53.

57. Norman Vance, *The Sinews of the Spirit: The Ideal of Christian Manliness in Victorian Literature and Religious Thought* (Cambridge: Cambridge University Press, 1985), 112–13.

58. Kingsley, *Letters*, 2 : 281–82.

59. Charles Kingsley, "The Poetry of Sacred and Legendary Art," *Fraser's* 39 (1849): 287.

60. Louis Crompton, *Byron and Greek Love: Homophobia in 19th-Century En-*

gland (Berkeley: University of California Press, 1985), 53–54; see also Hilliard, 191–92.

61. Kingsley, *Letters*, 1 : 163–64.
62. Ibid., 1 : 228.
63. Charles Kingsley, *Westward Ho!* (1855; reprint, London: Dent, 1925), 428.
64. Adams, 105.
65. Kingsley, "What, Then," 52.
66. Ibid., 52–53.
67. Ibid., 52.
68. Kingsley, *Letters*, 1 : 218.
69. Charles Kingsley, *Yeast* (1849; reprint, New York: Fred De Fau, 1899), 166–67.
70. Kingsley, *Letters*, 1 : 165.
71. Ibid., 1 : 165.
72. Ibid., 1 : 164.
73. Ibid., 1 : 166–67.
74. Ibid., 1 : 166.
75. Ibid.
76. Ibid., 1 : 168.
77. Ibid., 1 : 225.

The Comic Promiscuity of
W. S. Gilbert's Dandy-Aesthete

DENNIS DENISOFF

MANY THEORISTS SEE THE NINETEENTH CENTURY AS ONE OF THE
most influential periods in Western history for the formation of
identities defined by unconventional sexualities. The view is based
in large part on Michel Foucault's well-known claim—articulated
in *Discipline and Punish* and the first volume of *The History of Sexuality*—that identities are constructed through macro-political systems that also influence the ways in which people perceive and
communicate with each other in private or domestic spaces. Although various institutions did begin attempting to categorize and
contain sexual deviancy at this time, simplified adaptations of Foucault's argument risk attributing excessive control to medical, juridical, religious, and other institutional discourses, thereby leaving no
room for addressing the positive and affirming articulations of
those identities that the institutions debase.[1] Sexual identities form
neither entirely through established institutions nor solely through
the construction of counter-discourses by individuals attempting to
communicate their oppressed desires and actions to select others.
Rather, the formation and ongoing re-formation of sexual identities
are the unpredictable result of strategic and random acts that are not
always predefined by institutional taxonomies.

The nineteenth-century Aesthetic Movement makes apparent
some of the subtleties, ambiguities, and misreadings that were an
important part of the formation of identities based on unconventional sexualities.[2] While Walter Pater's aestheticist description of
sympathy and his homoerotic idealization of sensuous pleasure advocated a supportive notion of sexual diversity, literary reviewers'
almost entirely negative affirmation of this diversity helped to establish the discourse in mainstream society, thereby informing a
broader range of people who experienced unconventional desires
that they were not alone.[3] Parodists and satirists were especially important in making aestheticism one of the most popular movements

in nineteenth-century England; their depictions of the doctrine and the dandy-aesthete, however, turned the ambiguities surrounding gender, sexuality, and identity to comic advantage, and therefore were often vague in their moral position.

W. S. Gilbert's *Engaged* and *Patience*, two works from his *oeuvre* of extremely popular and often mimicked plays and comic operas (for which Arthur Sullivan wrote the music), demonstrate the role of parody and satire in the articulation of a homosexual identity that was not wholly contingent on negative institutional taxonomies. Gilbert positioned his work between, on the one hand, comic condemnation of unconventional male sexuality and, on the other, an appreciation of erotic titillation that can be, and was, read as a sympathetic deflation of the image of such diversification as threatening. As the Victorian affiliations of his work with same-sex desire make apparent, the creative use that Gilbert found for the sexually unconventional dandy-aesthete persona helped sustain the space in which various individuals, including Oscar Wilde, constructed sympathetic identities defined by marginalized sexual desires.

During the 1870s, the permeation of bourgeois culture by aestheticist characters and an appreciation for refined taste further enmeshed the already interwoven communities of sincere admirers of aestheticism's tenets, people who felt the doctrine supported their developing identities to a degree and gave a usefully elusive discourse for communicating them, those who adopted aestheticist codes in order to articulate their individuality in public, and those who simply viewed the movement as an entertaining novelty. Aestheticism's rise in popularity also fostered a familiarization of the unconventional phenomena associated with it. As Esmé Amarinth, an aesthete character in Robert Hichens's 1894 novella *The Green Carnation*, puts it, "when æstheticism became popular in Bayswater—a part of London built for the delectation of the needy rich—I felt that it was absurd no longer."[4] Ironically, it was through popular parody and satire seemingly intended to discredit aestheticism that some of the most provocative intersections between sexuality and the doctrine were established.

Gilbert, Hichens, W. H. Mallock, Vernon Lee, and other writers based much of their humor on images of apparent deviancy such as male effeminacy and erotically inflected rhetoric that were intended to evoke the hidden depths of unconventional attractions. By so doing, these writers encouraged people to read texts (including nonhumorous and nonverbal ones) against the grain, in search of those moments when the subtexts so entertainingly derail the normative narrative movement. Even if they were not necessarily sympathetic to the sexual desires that they insinuated, the writers, in an effort to amuse an audience that not only enjoyed aspects of aestheticism but also found pleasure in mocking traditional notions of love and the family, popularized dandy-aesthete characters that could be, and were, read as supportive portrayals of people who identified themselves by less familiar sexual traits and proclivities.

Dandy-aesthetes were the unique result of aesthetic, class-based, and sexual concerns. Aesthetes are basically people who view, or claim to view, life as art, a common nineteenth-century synopsis of aestheticism's central tenets. The image of the aesthetes echoes considerably that of the Victorian dandies, who were people (primarily men) interested in fashioning *themselves* as art, with the process of artistic commodification leading to a major overlap between presenting oneself as art and presenting oneself as valuable. To fashion oneself as a dandy, in other words, was to claim membership in an elite class of men with refined tastes and values—a class beyond the dictates of everyday society. Class was also a crucial factor that helped to determine whether individuals were likely to identify themselves by their unconventional sexual interests. As Jeffrey Weeks points out, the relatively immobile, poor laboring classes were less suited to the formation of marginal identities; a lack of the social power that arises from financial security appears to have greatly inhibited the acceptance of identities defined by, for example, same-sex desires.[5]

During the Victorian period, culturally privileged males' sexual transgressions were institutionally defined in such a way as to direct punishment for these transgressions at women and lower-class men.[6] The secretive womanizing dandies and the dandies who found pleasure in same-sex intimacy (not to mention those with other proclivities) were united through the greater social freedoms bestowed upon them as a result of their actual or assumed wealth, class, lack of a traditional partner, and higher proportion of discretionary income than men who supported wives and children.[7] Moreover, the womanizer was tolerated and even admired by many within Victorian culture, a situation that offered individuals having same-sex encounters an excellent guise for their actual clandestine identities; in the eyes of most of the public, they could "pass" as "ladies' men." Of course, not all dandies were wealthy or upper class, but this did not hinder the dandy-aesthete image from becoming a signifier of cultural elitism that included the right to a relatively high level of secrecy about one's affairs. As such, the persona and its aestheticist context became an attractive site of self-definition for people otherwise forced to deny and despise their own feelings.

In light of the negative stigma attached to marginalized sexual desires and activities, it is not surprising that few records exist that represent ways in which less famous Victorians who experienced these desires and activities reacted to aestheticism. Charles Edward Hutchinson's anonymous pamphlet *Boy Worship* (1880) thus offers a rare insight into the influence of W. H. Mallock's *The New Republic* (1877) on individuals who experienced same-sex erotic attraction. In his novel, Mallock mocks Pater's theories by personifying aestheticism as an elitist, effeminate, and ineffectual aesthete named Mr. Rose. The homoeroticism of Pater's work comes through in the character's admiration of Lady Grace's page, "a pretty boy with light curling hair,"[8] and his description of "life as a chamber, which we decorate as we would decorate the chamber of the woman or the youth that we love." At various points in the novel, Mr. Rose, making use of the coded discourse popularized by Pater, discusses "passionate friendship," "the lust of Rome," Narcissus's beauty, and the "keener and profounder passions" of "Achilles and Patroclus, David and Jonathan, our English Edward and the fair Piers Gaveston."[9] Mallock's aim was to deflate Pater's views by presenting them as impractical and ineffectual, and presenting the Paterian aesthete as a sexual deviant.

Hutchinson, who wrote his text as a supportive discussion of the "boy worship" that took place at Oxford University, uses the opening lines of a poem read aloud by Mr. Rose as a headnote to his pamphlet's title page and first page. Despite the fact that Hutchinson discusses such attraction among Oxford men in general, the quotations most directly implicate Pater and aestheticism. Hutchinson undermines Mallock's intentions by appropriating the comic attack to support his argument that same-sex erotic relations did exist in British society. Regardless of the fact that many Victorians may not have even recognized the dandy-aesthete as an important social character, a number of men who possessed same-sex desires (as well as other unconventional attractions and interests) would have seen him as one of the few familiar signifiers of their own generally concealed sexual traits. Oppressed individuals such as Hutchinson might very well have made a habit of searching the dandy-aesthetes, whether defined by their public persona or their writings, for implicit approval of their own unconventional desires.

Unlike Mallock's *New Republic*, texts by Gilbert such as *Engaged*, first produced in 1877, and *Patience*, first produced in 1881, do not aggressively mock or criticize aestheticism, dandy-aesthetes, or the sexual ambiguity they supported. Even if the positive reading of same-sex loyalty, devotion, and attraction that can be brought to bear on Gilbert's work does not accord with the author's intentions (I have found nothing strongly suggesting that Gilbert approved of same-sex desire), his successful exploitation of aestheticism and the dandy-aesthete's titillating qualities suggest that he courted suspicions of unconventional sexual inclinations among dandy-aesthetes.

Gilbert recognized that the attraction of the dandy-aesthete persona, in all its sexual ambiguity, was related to the thrill that many members of the middle class got from mildly mocking conventional family-based models of identity. The amount of pleasure that members of late-Victorian society derived from poking fun at bourgeois norms associated with finances, family position, and courtship paradigms suggests just how entrenched these values were. The jokes, cartoons, and comedies that proliferated around the "family" signified both its centrality to the dominant social structure and the confidence many had in its stability. At the same time, however, the humor suggests potential points of tension that were ripe for re-evaluation.

It is easy to see that Gilbert intended his spoof of courtship and marriage rituals to be only mildly deprecating, but it is less obvious that his representations of aestheticism and the dandy-aesthete were sympathetic; the two categories, however, are never entirely separate in Gilbert's work, operating as foils for each other. Thus, Jay Newman felt it necessary to warn against dismissing Gilbert's representation of aestheticism as wholly antagonistic:

There is bountiful evidence that Gilbert, Sullivan, and Carte sincerely appreciated and respected the serious aspects of the Aesthetic Movement and indeed maintained cordial relations with some of the leading figures associated with the movement, such as Whistler.[10]

Discussing the central aesthete character in the comic opera *Patience*, Newman concludes that "Gilbert could well have empathized with Bunthorne up to a point"—that is, regarding his need for attention, his admiration for the image of "the artistic rebel, the charming rogue, or the literary man," and his appreciation for the house design popularized during the Aesthetic Movement.[11] Other than arguing that Gilbert disapproved of "unmanly oddities[,] . . . weird manners and outrageous behaviour,"[12] Newman attempts to forestall suspicion of Gilbert and Bunthorne's connections to sexual or gender-based interests.

Sexual suggestion, however, figures centrally in Gilbert's humor. His erotically inflected *Bab Ballads* were first published as a collection in 1869 by John Camden Hotten, best known for having risked publishing Algernon Swinburne's *Poems and Ballads* three years earlier. Gilbert based his 1874 play *Topsyturvydom* on the notion of a gender-inverted society where women are men and men are women. In an 1873 letter to J. B. Buckstone, the manager of the Haymarket Theatre, Gilbert also mentions the idea of writing a serious play centered on female same-sex affection:

> I should like to write her [the actress Mrs. Kendal] a part either of the "Leah" or "Lucrezia Borgia" style—a powerful part with strong dramatic capabilities—a passionate vindictive devil with some *one* accessible weak point—such as love for a child or for some other *woman*—which weak point is to be the means of reclaiming her.[13]

Gilbert's play *The Wicked World*, first produced in 1873, depicts a land of fairies who are pure and superior to "wicked" mortals in every way, save for one flaw, "an overweening sense of righteousness."[14] Rather than enjoying "mortal" love, the males experience only "tranquil brotherhood" and the women wade in the "placid lake of sister-love."[15] After some of the fairies, whom Gilbert consistently portrays sympathetically, get a taste of what earth's inhabitants call "love," they unanimously reject it. A critic for the *Pall Mall Gazette* described the play as vulgar, coarse, offensive, and indecent, and Gilbert took him to court, where the critic's attorney pointed to a passage bearing an ambiguous sexual reference and another in which the Fairy Queen retains a knight in "the dark recesses of her bower" for six hours. The jury concluded that the play was not offensive, but found for the defendant anyway.[16]

Gilbert's interest in, and sympathy for, aestheticism reverberates in his attention to non-normative sexual desires and activities. It is only to be expected, then, that *Patience*, Gilbert's playful jab at aestheticism, makes heavy use of sexual innuendo. Produced at the Opéra Comique in spring 1881, the opera is one of Gilbert and Sullivan's most successful pieces, having had a lengthy run and having been generally well-received by the critics.[17] Gilbert's libretto for the opera is a light piece clearly designed to benefit from the Aesthetic Movement's popularity. The insinuations of what most of the audience would have seen as sexual deviancy seem intended to add titillation to a relatively uncommitted narrative chock full of witticisms and catchy rhymes that mock conventional courtship as much as they do Bunthorne's more unique desires. The characters in the opera bring to mind aspects of D. G. Rossetti, Swinburne, Wilde, and other people associated with aestheticism. When Grosvenor, for example, asks the milkmaid Patience if she loves Bunthorne, she offers the Swinburnean reply: "With a heart-whole ecstasy that withers, and scorches, and burns, and stings!"[18] Meanwhile, Bunthorne, from his long hair to his penchant for lilies and china, is an exaggerated version of Wilde's dandiacal image at that time. In comic retaliation against Gilbert's caricature, Wilde would later have the two young dandies in *The Importance of Being Earnest* "whistle some dreadful popular air from a British opera."[19]

Patience does not offer a strong eroticized narrative, but neither does it attempt to forestall any connection of aestheticism to unconventional sexuality when it presents Bunthorne's rejection of most women, and claims that the aesthete must settle for a "vegetable love," "an attachment *à la* Plato for a bashful young potato, or a not-too-French French bean!"[20] Notably, *Punch* interpreted these implications of sexual difference as contributing specifically to a rhetoric of same-sex desire. Less than a year after the 1889–90 Cleveland Street Scandal, in which the police discovered that male telegraph workers were making additional money as prostitutes for men, the magazine published the following bit of verse, "[w]ith acknowledgments to the Author of 'Patience,' " from which it takes both meter and some of its language:

If you aim to be a Shocker, carnal theories to cocker is *the* best way to begin. / And every one will say, / As you worm your wicked way, / "If that's allowable for *him* which were criminal in *me*, / What a very emancipated kind of youth this kind of youth must be."[21]

The parody also associates the youth—who, we are told, has a penchant for books that "display the 'deeper mysteries' of strange and subtle Sin"—specifically with aestheticism.[22] It includes an acknowledged quotation of Wilde and describes the youth as "anxious to develop to a true hedonic 'swell,' " as "prattl[ing] about Art," as believing that "emotion for the sake of emotion *is* the aim of Art," and so on. Wilde is clearly implicated as the "flabby fellow" being described, the image echoing a *Punch* cartoon published a few months earlier of Wilde as the fat "Fad Boy" who wants to make Mrs. Grundy's "flesh creep."[23] Not only individuals who were developing elusive codes for the communication of burgeoning identities based on suspicious sexual desires and actions, therefore, but even a popular, unsympathetic journal of the period

associated Gilbert's enterprise with a depiction of the aestheticist
community and same-sex male desire.

Patience itself is not wholly derogatory with regard to the aesthete, implying as it does that the persona is as essential to some
people's identities as more common ones are to others'. Bunthorne
does tell the audience that his self-presentation is insincere: "Am I
alone, / And unobserved? I am! / Then let me own / I'm an æsthetic
sham! / This air severe / Is but a mere Veneer!"[24] Despite this claim,
however, he remains patiently devoted to the aesthete image, even
while all the other characters change their personae in drastic ways.
The comedy ends with everybody paired up—everybody, that is,
except for Bunthorne, who has never dropped aestheticism and
"will have to be contented / With a tulip or li*ly*!"[25] In this sort of
comedy, Bunthorne's acknowledgment of his persona's artificiality
is not surprising, but his devotion to something that he admits is
false, even when everybody has left him because of it, does seem
queer. Gilbert and Sullivan's aesthete appears not to believe in his
own image, yet he nevertheless retains it. Bunthorne's unrequited
attachment to the naive dairy maid Patience signifies an indefinite
deferral of sexual fulfillment, and, when Patience takes Grosvenor
as her partner, the opera ends with Bunthorne seemingly married to
eternal "patience" or, more precisely, the aestheticist community
symbolized by the flowers.

The sexual connotations of *Patience* gain greater potency in light
of Gilbert's play *Engaged*, which was first produced at the Haymarket Theatre four years before *Patience* and in the same year that
Mallock's *New Republic* was published. Without making any
strong references to aestheticism, the play elucidates the mutual
support of the Aesthetic Movement and the popular trend for mocking family traditions. This relation is further buttressed by the ambiguities surrounding the dandy-aesthete's private relations.
Engaged also offers more complex representations than *Patience*
does of the sexually ambiguous dandy-aesthete's social role by
questioning not only *his* desires but also those of less eccentric individuals, particularly those considered central to the family unit. Indeed, the negative reviews that Gilbert garnered indicate that it was
his mockery of family bonds that was probably most instrumental
in the play's short run. With no levelheaded character like Patience
as a foil for the money-hungry individuals who dominate the stage,
most critics found *Engaged* too cynical.

Max Sutton's attempt to justify the lack of a moral foundation to
the play by turning to the ethics of Gilbert's earlier works is not
convincing. Sutton argues that the positive foils for the immoral at-

titudes in *Engaged* are to be found in the author's previous writing: "Echoes of Gilbert's serious plays could remind the audience of the need for charity, in contrast to the over-prizing of money and one's own image"; an awareness of the author's pre-*Engaged oeuvre* "allows human foils—persons with conscience, self-knowledge, and feeling—to stand just off-stage from the compulsive role-players in this farcical comedy."[26] Sutton's claim seems over-extended; Gilbert could not have assumed that audience members would be familiar with his previous works or, even if they were, that they would juxtapose the values in these plays with those of the characters in *Engaged*. The lack of even one character with standard morals or manners means that, whether Gilbert intended it or not, the dandiacal sexual ambiguity appears not as a unique and unforgivable transgression, but as simply one humorous peculiarity among many. If one looked to *Patience* and *Engaged* for representations of transgressive sexuality, stronger support would be found in the earlier *Engaged* because it uses the sexually mysterious dandy (the "aesthete" quality being less apparent in this text) to weave questions of same-sex friendship and devotion into the dominant narrative of affection and coupling.

The first act begins unassumingly with the presentation of heterosexual trysts in a country garden. A Glasgow-bound train has derailed somewhere off stage, but Cheviot Hill (who shares his surname with an infamous Fanny), Belinda Treherne, and the other passengers continue their romantic antics, at least until Major McGillicuddy, the intended from whom it turns out Belinda is escaping, catches up to them on the next train. "I am betrothed to this lady," he explains, "we were to have been married this morning. I waited for her at the church from ten till four, then I began to get impatient."[27] "I really think you must be labouring under some delusion," replies the dandiacal young Cheviot. "Delusion? Ha! ha! Here's the cake!" exclaims the major triumphantly, as his two friends bring forward the delectable marriage symbol that they have dragged with them across England.

Whether it be cake or bannock, porridge or celery, tarts or what have you, food seems to appear in *Engaged* whenever the topics of marriage, family, or home are being defended. But, as McGillicuddy's cake suggests, the comedy mocks the notion of social stability that is often associated with food. Appropriately, the program from the play's first run shows two dapper young men struggling to cross a rickety bridge as they balance an unwieldy white wedding cake over their heads. The pastry stands for the excessive emphasis placed on the symbolic puffs of affection, as opposed to "true love" itself. Along similar lines, it turns out that the seemingly honest country folk who feed their bannock to Cheviot, Belinda, and the rest actually earn their living by derailing trains and charging the distraught passengers for sustenance. Later in the play, Belinda stuffs herself with tarts while lamenting the possible death of her possible husband, whose name she does not recall. And, when Cheviot orders a cake for his own marriage, he selects one that is three-fourths wooden: "I thought at first of ordering a seven-eighths article; but one isn't married every day—it's only once a year—I mean it's only now and then. So I said, 'Hang the expense; let's do the thing well.' And so it's a three-quarters."[28] Food becomes, in Gilbert's comic criticism of Victorian values, a sign of familial insincerity.

The farce attains a sharper critical edge when finances are added to the mix. In *Engaged*, money supersedes affection as the catalyst for marriage. People are willing to sell themselves into wedlock for as little as—in the case of the "Lowland lassie" Maggie Macfarlane—three shillings. Mr. Symperson, who will gain an annuity upon Cheviot's marriage, does not care who the young man marries, eagerly offering up his own daughter as, to use his terminology, the sacrificial lamb.[29] Cheviot's friend, Belvawney, works against any such union because he will lose his own annuity should Cheviot marry or die. In both of these examples, and indeed throughout the text, marriage and death are constantly coupled. The cash nexus is even apparent when Belvawney, after pronouncing his love to Belinda, attempts to prevent his friend's suicide:

> *Bel. (desperately).* You shall have Belinda; she is much—very much to me, but she is not everything. Your life is very dear to me; and when I think of our old friendship—Cheviot, you shall have anything you like, if you'll only consent to live!
> *Ch.* If I thought you were in earnest; but no—no. *(Putting pistol to head.)*
> *Bel.* In earnest? of course I'm in earnest! Why what's the use of Belinda to me if I'm ruined?[30]

Belinda will not marry Belvawney without his money, but he loses his income upon Cheviot's death or marriage. Cheviot intends to kill himself because he has apparently lost his fortune, which means he has lost Belinda. In Gilbert's play, the importance of being earnest is always financial, with friendship and love being budgeted in relation to it. Belvawney's gigolo economics lead him to weigh his affections for Cheviot and Belinda on the same scale.

Even if Gilbert presented this monetary model of affection only to mock Victorian bourgeois values, the rhetoric inevitably equalizes opposite-sex and same-sex attachments by predicating both on financial reward.

Despite the multifold complications of three women and one man wanting Cheviot each to themselves, and everybody wanting more money, Gilbert succeeds in tying up the plot, albeit very loosely, on the last page. A letter arrives that proves that Cheviot and Belinda's unintentional marriage in a country garden is valid, and the play ends: "Cheviot embracing Miss Treherne. Belvawney is being comforted by Minnie. Angus is solacing Maggie, and Mrs. MacFarlane is reposing on Mr. Symperson's bosom."[31] Belvawney and Maggie are being comforted because they have each lost Cheviot, while Mrs. MacFarlane and Mr. Symperson's affections had not even been insinuated until this moment. By using stock dramatic convention, Gilbert mocks the idea of happy heteronormativity one last time. Notably, Belvawney—the Bunthorne-like dandy left single at the end—is not excluded from the closing group hug.

Besides money, Belvawney and Cheviot's friendship is the clearest threat to the traditional family narrative. The oral overlap of Belinda and Belvawney's names suggests the similar relations that the fiancée and best friend have to Cheviot. The wealthy Cheviot, Belvawney explains, is "cursed with a strangely amatory disposition" having "contracted a habit of proposing marriage, as a matter of course, to every woman he meets."[32] Cheviot's father, fearing that his son will contract an "undesirable" marriage, and knowing that the financially desperate Belvawney, whom Gilbert depicts at one point as "Satanic,"[33] has "all but supernatural influence over his son,"[34] pays the young man £1000 annually if he keeps Cheviot unmarried. In his dependent role, Belvawney might have reminded some audience members of the lower-class "trade" who maintained relations with wealthy dandies for financial reasons.[35]

Belvawney has the peculiar ability to hypnotize Cheviot with his eyes, thereby deterring the dandy from following the conventional amorous route. The two bachelors maintain this forced but fixed friendship until Belvawney unwittingly dons tinted glasses (due to illness) and Cheviot escapes his seductive powers; "Belvawney," Cheviot declares,

> it may not be denied that there was a time when, owing to the remarkable influence exercised over me by your extraordinary eyes, you could do with me as you would. . . . They were strange and lurid eyes, and I bowed to them. That time has gone—for ever![36]

Cheviot's uncontrollable attraction to Belvawney is the closest thing to a romantic conception of intense love in the play, possibly parodying the whole Petrarchan discourse of lovers' eyes. When no longer subject to Belvawney's seduction, however, Cheviot is let loose on the sanctified world of marriage, and he proposes to three women in rapid succession.

Gilbert's thematic pairing of same-sex attraction and critique of Victorian family traditions seems to have made a strong impression on at least one, highly influential Victorian homosexual—Oscar Wilde. In a letter written to George Grossmith (who played Bunthorne) after the production of *Engaged* but before Wilde saw *Patience*, the author offers the following praise: "With Gilbert and Sullivan I am sure we will have something better than the small farce of the Colonel [an aestheticist spoof written by *Punch* editor F. C. Burnand]. I am looking forward to being greatly amused."[37] Not only did Wilde find Gilbert amusing, but he also found him useful for his own later complex suggestions of same-sex desire in *The Importance of Being Earnest*.

Wilde's play shadows many elements of its precursor. Both texts split scenes between the city and the country; Parker is the name of a maid in *Engaged* and of a solicitor in *Earnest*.[38] Belinda's ravenous appetite foreshadows Jack's consumption of cucumber sandwiches and muffins, and Wilde repeats her plea "Who am I?" in Jack's desperate request that Miss Prism tell him who he is.[39] The rhythm of lines like Mr. Chasuble's "I spoke metaphorically. My metaphor was drawn from bees"[40] follows that of Mr. Symperson's "[T]hese clothes are symbolic; they represent my state of mind."[41] Miss Prism's grievance that Bunbury's revived health is a sign of bad manners strongly echoes Mr. Symperson's complaint regarding Cheviot's decision not to kill himself:

> [Y]ou threaten to commit suicide; your friends are dreadfully shocked at first, . . . and when they have brought themselves to this Christian state of mind, you coolly inform them that you have changed your mind and meant to live. It's not business, sir—it's not business.[42]

All in all, Wilde appears to be indebted to Gilbert for effects of syntax, humor, and plot line.

If *Earnest* offered only these minor echoes of Gilbert's play, one might not be able to do more than acknowledge yet another source for some of Wilde's ideas and expressions. The parallels, however, are not simply formal and stylistic. *Engaged* and *Earnest* both critique the middle-class concern with financial stability and the sanctity of love and marriage. Almost all the characters treat marriage proposals as frothy entertainment, and both plays discuss marriages that result from misunderstandings. In both, the young female characters, displaying affected ignorance and false manners, argue politely over being engaged to the same man. Each play has a confusion over a husband's name and a potential marriage delay of a number of years. Both also repeat hyperbolic catch phrases to suggest a wooer's insincerity; in *Earnest*, Algernon refers to loving "wildly, passionately, devotedly, hopelessly," while, in *Engaged*, Cheviot claims to love women "madly, passionately, irresistibly" and tells each woman to whom he proposes that she is "my Past, my Present, my Future—my own To Come." Furthermore, both Gilbert and Wilde mock the conventional theatrical ending of heterosexual coupling. In addition to the spoof of opposite-sex devotion, both plays also offer alternative narratives in men's relations—the friendship of two dandies toying with each other's marital plans. Wilde's writing never overtly presents a scenario of same-sex erotic attraction; rather than deterring critics from offering queer readings of the author's work, however, this obfuscation has fostered more complex studies that take into account the need for subterfuge and strategic maneuvering within the coded discourse of the texts themselves.[43] The resulting critical tools allow analyses of not only Wilde's work but also that of other authors such as Gilbert, Mallock, and Lee.

Alan Sinfield has argued that a reading of Algernon and Jack's relationship in Wilde's play as homoerotic caves in under the weight of a plot in which the two dandies spend most of their time talking about property and women, and in which the one "Bunburying" scene centers on a man's visit to a woman and involves extensive opposite-sex wooing. The homoeroticism or queerness of Wilde and his "effete, camp, leisured or aspiring to be, aesthetic, amoral, witty, insouciant, charming, spiteful, dandified" characters, Sinfield argues, is a quality that readers, at the end of the twentieth century, have anachronistically transposed back onto Jack and Algernon.[44] However, a recognition that, in Victorian culture, the dandy-aesthete's womanizing image and financial security offered a cover for men with less accepted erotic interests encourages a modification of this thesis. While Sinfield is correct to suggest that the two dandies should not be simply defined as homosexual or queer, the fact that dandies discuss property and women does not guarantee an identity defined wholly by opposite-sex attractions either; as noted, the dandy-aesthete's womanizing image and financial security offered a cover for men whose predominant erotic interests were directed toward their own sex. In addition, even though Wilde's play makes us an audience to an opposite-sex Bunburying, the somewhat heavy-handed wordplay also suggests sodomitical possibilities (which were predominantly associated with same-sex male desire). Wilde's "Bunbury" seems to be a not-too-distant acquaintance of Gilbert's own sexually ambiguous "Bunthorne."

Christopher Craft points to various passages in which Wilde's text associates Bunburying with vague, unarticulated but repeated practices. He also notes other allusions within the play either to Wilde's own same-sex experiences or to social events with which some audience members would have been familiar, such as the conflicts between Alfred Douglas and his father, the Marquess of Queensberry, and the popular 1871 case of *Regina v. Boulton and Others* that involved the arrest and prosecution of the two transvestites Stella and Fanny, aka Edward Boulton and Frederick William Park. As Wilde was well aware, he was communicating with more than one audience, and, by leaving the term "Bunburying" ambiguous, he made it available to more than one reading.

Craft acknowledges that, despite *Earnest*'s same-sex innuendos, Wilde never clarifies what exactly Bunburying entails.[45] Although the text's only representation of Bunburying involves opposite-sex subterfuge, the term appears to refer more generally to the act of covering up any social transgression. The term is not only ambiguous with regard to sexuality, but it does not even specifically signify *sexual* adventure. However, in contrast to Wilde's discussion of Bunburying, which does not (at least in the surface narrative) mean making love to Bunbury, Gilbert's earlier coinage "Belvawneying," in *Engaged*, explicitly refers to having some sort of relations with Belvawney—a character who, unlike Bunbury, does exist within the reality of the play. The risqué connotations of the neologism arise primarily from the sexual humor of the rest of the text; Cheviot uses the term when chastising two of his fiancées for allowing themselves to be entertained by the hypnotic dandy's parlor tricks (What the man can do with a live hen, two hair brushes, and a pound and a half of fresh butter![46]) A previous "slave" to the man's magnetism, Cheviot knows better than anyone else the risks of Belvawneying. Even as Cheviot uses the term in a conventional opposite-sex context, he offers support for the potentiality of other options by intoning it with a plurality of possibilities: "I will permit no Belvawneying of any kind whatever, or anything approaching thereto."[47] "Belvawneying" thus connotes a broader range of interactions than simply conventional flirtation, enhancing the sexual innuendo and offering a precursor for Algernon's, and Wilde's, later practices.

Both of the dandies in *Engaged* have convenient alibis for their mutual devotion. By basing Cheviot's attraction to Belvawney on hypnotism, Gilbert takes the responsibility for the attachment out of Cheviot's passive hands. Belvawney, conversely, revolves on the monetary fulcrum that, as noted earlier, also defines the heterosexual attractions. At the end of *Engaged*, Cheviot and Belvawney are no longer together and the latter has lost his income. Belvawney, however, is not the only loser, and he is not cast out of the community. The wrap-up, furthermore, is far from secure. Belinda, in her final speech, tells Belvawney that she loves him "with an intensity of devotion that I firmly believe will last while I live" and then, turning to her fiancée, offers virtually the same proposal: "if the devotion of a lifetime can atone for the misery of the last few days, it is yours."[48] It appears that marriage will not change Cheviot's ways either, as he responds to Belinda with the now tired cliché, "My Past, my Present, my To Come!" Couched within the Victorian context of a dandy's sexual ambiguity, Cheviot's weakness under Belvawney's magnetism, combined with his role as seductive swell and his flippancy regarding his relations with women, offers an alternate reading for people such as Wilde. As with everybody else, hope springs eternal for those individuals who, experiencing unconventional sexual desires, are in search of identity reinforcement. By presenting the sexually ambiguous dandy in a same-sex relation that has a social value and relevance similar to that of opposite-sex relations, *Engaged* offers support for such hope.

While *Patience* acknowledges the relation between unorthodox desires and pleasures, on the one hand, and aestheticism and the Aesthetic Movement on the other, the operatta does not celebrate Bunthorne's particular sexuality, just as Gilbert's representation of same-sex attraction in *Engaged* does not clearly enforce the sexual connotations of such a relationship. However, these texts—along with *Topsyturvydom*, *The Wicked World*, and others—show that Gilbert acknowledged unconventional sexuality and attraction, at least as a major source of plot, and that his depictions of nontraditional attractions and pleasures, even if intended to be humorous, were not entirely insulting or dismissive. In addition, they did not suggest that such attractions were less essential to an individual's identity than those that were more commonly valorized. Introducing ambiguous sexual attractions into mainstream culture, Gilbert not only enhanced people's familiarity with diverse sexual preferences, but also offered potential support for those individuals on the lookout for moments when their otherwise proscribed sexual identities seemed to merge with mainstream discourses of affection and desire. As the responses of Victorians from *Punch* cartoonists to Wilde make apparent, Gilbert's writing was a vehicle for British society's growing awareness of the diverse identities within its own makeup, a function that, while not a serious threat to heteronormativity, nevertheless bolstered awareness and legitimation of sexual diversification.

NOTES

1. For analyses of Foucault's notion of a "reverse" discourse, and for alternative models of identity formation by subcultures and otherwise marginalized groups, see Ross Chambers's *Room for Maneuver* and "Poaching and Pastiche," James Creech's *Closet Writing/Gay Reading*, and Jonathan Dollimore's *Sexual Dissidence*.

2. While the aestheticist view of same-sex male attraction as ideal offered positive reinforcement for some unconventional identities, it was also often misogynistic. The virtual absence of women in Walter Pater's *Renaissance*, except as represented in art, reflects this tendency. The phenomenon is discussed by Regenia Gagnier (*Idylls of the Marketplace*, 160), Eve Kosofsky Sedgwick (*Between Men*, 207–13), and Elaine Showalter (*Sexual Anarchy*, 172–77).

3. Isobel Armstrong (*Victorian Poetry*), Laurel Brake (*Subjugated Knowledge*), and Thaïs Morgan ("Reimagining . . . Pater") all analyze the sexualized discourse of nineteenth-century literary criticism. Pater's politics of same-sex male desire is discussed in, to name only some of the texts, James Eli Adams's *Dandies and Desert Saints*, Richard Dellamora's *Masculine Desire*, and Linda Dowling's *Hellenism and Homosexuality in Victorian Oxford*.

4. Robert Hichens, *The Green Carnation* (1894; reprint, New York: Dover, 1970), 103.

5. Jeffrey Weeks, *Against Nature: Essays on History, Sexuality and Identity* (London: Rivers Oram, 1991), 66.

6. Ibid., 21.

7. For a discussion of class and nineteenth-century male same-sex activity, see Weeks's *Against Nature* and Randolph Trumbach's "London's Sodomites: Homosexual Behaviour and Western Culture in the 18th Century."

8. W. H. Mallock, *The New Republic: Culture, Faith and Philosophy in an English Country House*. 1877 (Gainesville: University of Florida Press, 1950), 232.

9. Mallock, 188, 189, 270, 189.

10. Jay Newman, "The Gilbertianism of Patience," *Dalhousie Review* 65, no. 2 (Summer 1985), 266. Richard D'Oyly Carte was the theatrical agent and manager responsible for bringing Gilbert and Sullivan together.

11. Ibid., 269.

12. Ibid., 266.

13. W. S. Gilbert, *Letter to J. B. Buckstone* (1873), quoted in Hesketh Pearson, *Gilbert: His Life and Strife* (London: Methuen, 1957), 42–43.

14. W. S. Gilbert, *The Wicked World*, in *Gilbert's Original Plays*, vol. 1 (1873; reprint, London: Chatto & Windus, 1875), 4.

15. Ibid., 11, 62.
16. Pearson, 43. According to Norman St. John Stevas, Gilbert also wrote, in collaboration with Arthur Sullivan, a homoerotic farce entitled *The Sod's Opera*, with the characters Count Tostoff, the Brothers Bollox ("a pair of hangers on"), and "the wrinkled old retainer" Scrotum (*Obscenity and the Law,* 189).
17. Newman, 264.
18. W. S. Gilbert and Arthur Sullivan, *Patience, or Bunthorne's Bride* in *The Complete Plays of Gilbert and Sullivan* (1881; reprint, New York: Modern Library, 1936), 219.
19. Oscar Wilde, *The Complete Works of Oscar Wilde* (New York: Harper & Row, 1989), 370.
20. Gilbert, *Patience,* 200.
21. "Development," *Punch* 20 September 1890: 135.
22. "Development," *Punch,* 135.
23. [E. R.,] "Parallel," *Punch* 19 July 1890: 25.
24. Gilbert, *Patience,* 198.
25. Ibid., 233.
26. Max Keith Sutton, *W. S. Gilbert* (Boston: Twayne, 1975), 81.
27. W. S. Gilbert, *Engaged* in *Gilbert's Original Plays,* vol. 2 (1877; reprint, London: Chatto & Windus, 1875), 56.
28. Ibid., 34.
29. Ibid., 57.
30. Ibid., 80.
31. Ibid., 85.
32. Ibid., 45.
33. Ibid., 68.
34. Ibid., 45.
35. See Weeks's *Against Nature.*
36. Op. cit., 48–49.
37. Quoted in Richard Ellmann, *Oscar Wilde* (1987; reprint, London: Penguin, 1988), 129.
38. Parker is also the name of a butler in *Lady Windemere's Fan* and of a valet who testified against Wilde during the 1895 trials.
39. Gilbert, *Engaged,* 6; and Wilde, *Complete Works,* 380.
40. Wilde, *Complete Works,* 341.
41. Gilbert, *Engaged,* 81.
42. Ibid., 81–82.
43. For theoretical approaches that address the queer ambiguities of Wilde's writing, see Ed Cohen (*Talk on the Wilde Side*), Christopher Craft (*Another Kind of Love*), Jonathan Dollimore (*Sexual Dissidence*), and Alan Sinfield (*The Wilde Century*).
44. Alan Sinfield, *The Wilde Century: Effeminacy, Oscar Wilde and the Queer Moment* (New York: Columbia University Press, 1994), vi.
45. Christopher Craft, *Another Kind of Love: Male Homosexual Desire in English Discourse, 1850–1920* (Berkeley: University of California Press, 1994), 116.
46. Gilbert, *Engaged,* 75.
47. Ibid., 76.
48. Ibid., 85.

Disguising the Self in Pater and Wilde

JAY LOSEY

W HEN WILDE PROCLAIMED "[T]HERE IS NO PATER BUT PATER, AND Oscar Wilde is his prophet," he created an impression that the naturally reserved Pater must have found unsettling.[1] In his biography of Pater, Thomas Wright asserts that even though the two men were intimate, "Pater, in his heart of hearts, regarded Wilde with continuous dislike."[2] Writing in the aftermath of Wilde's fall and death, Wright may have wanted to preserve the image of Pater as Pater—despite the pronouncements of his fallen disciple.[3] Wright portrays Pater as moving toward conservatism, as refashioning his early subversive, radical self into a pious, proper Victorian: "He had passed from Cyrenaicism to Platonism, and from Platonism to Christianity. Already the Bible, the Prayer-Book, and the Breviary were, as he told a friend, his chief reading."[4] Why would Wright intentionally stress Pater's "Christianity"?[5] He contends that, after professional setbacks early in his academic career, Pater waged a lifelong campaign to appear less daring than he actually was. Wilde also states his disappointment in aestheticism's apostle: "poor dear Pater has lived to disprove everything that he has written."[6] Similarly, Wright is fuzzy in his rendering of the Pater-Wilde relationship.[7] Pater's letters to Wilde appear to attest to their friendship.[8] Further, Pater read the manuscript version of *Dorian Gray* in 1890 and so knew that Wilde had appropriated many passages from *The Renaissance* (1873) and *Marius the Epicurean* (1885); he made Wilde's quip about living up to his blue china "the epigraph to the unpublished part of his last book, *Gaston de Latour*"[9]; he, by all accounts, maintained cordial relations with Wilde at least until 1891, the fateful year in which Wilde met "Bosie," Lord Alfred Douglas;[10] and both writers shared a lifelong concern to promote a new Hellenism to lighten Victorian England.

Wright may have found objectionable the same-sex relationships that Pater and Wilde subversively present in their work.[11] In any case, he unconvincingly divides Pater and Wilde by portraying Pater as one who follows the madding crowd. But from beginning to end, Pater calls into question the prevailing sentiment on sexuality, arguing for the naturality of homo- and heterosexual love. As Pater intimates in an early essay, "Diaphaneitè" (1864), which he read to the Old Mortality Club at Oxford,[12] the rare but ideal crystalline type focuses on "the fine edge of light, where the elements of [his] moral nature refine themselves to the burning point."[13] He deploys the same metaphor, slightly modified, in his celebrated "hard, gem-like flame" statement in the "Conclusion" to *The Renaissance*.[14] He and Wilde knew the risk they were taking, as revealed by their brushes with institutional power at Oxford[15] and by the "homosexual oppression" pervading Victorian society.[16] Alan Sinfield persuasively asserts: "we need to bear in mind that Pater could not have published what he did if a same-sex construction was likely."[17] But had the cultural taboo about same-sex passion waned by the 1870s? It had from a late twentieth-century perspective, but Pater and Wilde were caught in the middle. So they disguised the self by creating a counter-discourse on sexuality, one that originates in Greek literature.[18] In this essay, I focus on the love that dared to speak its name in the only complete novels by Pater and Wilde.[19] I explain how their autobiographical disclosures concerning their sexual orientation are an attempt to engage in a kind of polemical debate with institutional power, to argue for the naturality of same-sex passion, and to develop an emergent discourse on the inseparability of sexuality and identity.

REGULATING

For the Greeks, according to Michel Foucault, "reflection on sexual behavior as a moral domain was not a means of internalizing, justifying or formalizing general interdictions imposed on everyone; rather, it was a means of developing . . . an aesthetics of existence, the purposeful art of a freedom perceived as a power game."[20] The Greeks inscribed sexual behavior in law or social codes, because they viewed sexual behavior as an ethical concern.[21] "They had never been taught," according to John Addington Symonds, "to regard the body with a sense of shame, but rather to admire it as the temple of the spirit, and to accept its needs and instincts with natural acquiescence. Male beauty disengaged for them the passion it inspired from service of domestic, social, civic duties."[22] Such a view reflects Socrates' assertion in the *Phaedrus* (after 386 B.C.) regarding the passionate reciprocity of same-sex love; a " 'flood of passion' " passes between lovers, giving them "fresh vigor" and intensifying their love, which, for Socrates, is spiritual rather than physical because while looking at one another each lover "holds himself" as though looking in a mirror.[23] In short, same-sex love should enable one to master the self, to become temperate. Paul Cartledge indicates that Wilde's classical learning, especially under the tutelage of Edward Mahaffy, enabled him to study original Greek sources that would "have taken [him] to ancient Athens, of course, the setting of Plato's *Symposium* and also through Plato's work to Elis and Thebes, where—as Mahaffy observed with barely stifled astonishment—the law actually sanctioned physical homosexuality and not only idealized spiritual intimacy."[24] In the *Symposium* (after 386 B.C.), Pausanias asserts that the man who falls in love with a youth must be prepared to educate him and refuse "to take advantage of the lad's youth and credulity by seducing him."[25] After reading Plato, especially the *Phaedrus* and *Symposium*, Symonds memorably asserts, "Socrates described his philosophy as the science of erotics."[26] This eroticism has for the Greeks a carefully prescribed context: individuals must learn to regulate their sexual appetite through austerity and self-discipline.[27] This regulation is crucial in Pater's blending of asceticism and aestheticism, the chaste manly figure imbued with sensuality.

For the Victorians, however, political and juridical measures curbing sexual freedom transformed an "aesthetics of existence" into a different kind of power game. "The conventions of Greek life— *paiderastia, symposia, dialektike*"—were not the conventions of Victorian life.[28] For instance, the Labouchère amendment to the Criminal Law Amendment Act of August 1885 stated that "[a]ny male person who, in public or private, commits . . . any act of gross indecency with another male person, shall be guilty of a misdemeanour," punishable by a "term not exceeding two years, with or without hard labour."[29] When authorities discovered in July 1889 that telegraph boys were making extra money by "going to bed with gentlemen" at 19 Cleveland Street, near the West End, an investigation revealed that, among other aristocrats, Lord Arthur Somerset, an equerry of the Prince of Wales, frequented the male brothel.[30] After the telegraph boys were prosecuted in what became known as the Cleveland Street affair, Labouchère and others in Parliament discovered an attempted government cover-up. When it became clear that Lord Somerset would be arrested and charged under the Labouchère amendment, he, unlike Wilde five years later, fled the country.[31] I dwell on this one political scandal to indicate how it is possible to trace, in Foucault's words, "the theoretical effort to reinscribe the thematic of sexuality in the system of law, the symbolic order, and sovereignty."[32] Foucault, among others, shows how juridical and medical debates appear in fiction. But fiction also influences these debates about same-sex relationships. A "thematic of sexuality" permeates the fictive discourses of Pater and Wilde, notably *Marius the Epicurean* and *The Picture of Dorian Gray* (1890; rev. 1891), two novels that set the tone for the fin-de-siècle cultural debate on art, politics, religion, society, and self.

While Pater and Wilde understood the potential juridical response to same-sex relationships, only Pater took measures to protect himself. Although Pater's conflict with Benjamin Jowett would not have had public ramifications, Jowett's decisive action to quash the Pater–William Money Hardinge love affair of 1874 resembles an institutional response to punish wrongdoing.[33] That Pater grasped the meaning of Jowett's response is revealed in two late imaginary portraits: "Apollo in Picardy" and "Hippolytus Veiled."[34] To counteract juridical measures that would make them victims or scapegoats, Victorian writers like Pater and Wilde sought freedom through their work.[35]

Pater and Wilde knew that there were regulatory measures to silence them. To counteract this possible punishment, they blurred the distinction between art and life, fiction and reality.[36] Foucault argues that institutional discourses provide the language for counter-discourses.[37] Pater and Wilde attempt, with varying success, to employ such discourses, striving, among other concerns, to naturalize same-sex love; and although Pater became warier as he got older, he nonetheless continued to wage his discursive fight to legitimize same-sex relationships. Denis Donoghue asserts that Pater's anxiety over receiving good reviews of his books, especially after the fiasco over *The Renaissance*, revealed his determination to fit in a traditional or mainstream Victorian mode.[38] On the contrary, I argue that Pater's careful management of who reviewed his books, how he returned favors for generous reviews, and why he never replied to negative reviews all indicate a need to manage the reception of his books. The books themselves are still antinomian, even though Pater deliberately obscured his message through a hesitant, circumspect prose style. And as Christopher Craft, among others, has shown, Wilde always mastered the double entendre. After Algy explains to Jack the necessity of knowing "Bunbury" in *The Importance of Being Earnest* (1895), Craft concludes, "Bunbury thus operates within the heterosexual order as its hidden but irreducible supplement"—literally, that is, as a site of burying in the bun.[39]

CONFESSING

For both Pater and Wilde, identity reveals a number of essential characteristics: a reliance on sensations, impressions, and experiences; a nondiscursive and receptive response to influences; a love of art for its own sake; and an affinity for male beauty. These characteristics all mark Pater's Marius and Wilde's Lord Henry Wotton, Dorian Gray, and, most notably, Basil Hallward.[40] Although Wilde refers to Pater's *Renaissance* and *Marius the Epicurean* in his novel, he more significantly employs Pater's narrative strategy: to legitimize same-sex relationships through confession. As arbiters of cultural taste, Pater and Wilde strive to use this confession to establish a counter-discourse. Although Wilde plumbs the depth of despair in his confessional *De Profundis* (1897), he, like Pater, produces a confessional mode in which erotic fictive selves are fashioned. Such a narrative strategy would enable Pater, Wilde, or anyone else, as Foucault notes, to confront "the infinite task of extracting from the depths of oneself, in between the words, a truth which the very form of confession holds out like a shimmering mirage."[41] In other words, Pater and Wilde establish their own sexuality by stressing the totality of identity; every sensation, every impression, every thought, every experience reveals the veracity, however hesitantly conveyed, of their sexual confession. Although juridical systems rely on confessions to exact the truth, to cause the individual, in some instances, to inform against himself, Pater and Wilde adopt a similar stance toward confession to shape a new cultural attitude toward same-sex relations.

But there are some significant, fundamental differences in Pater's and Wilde's tone. These tonal differences indicate, above all, that while Pater offers a tentative, defensive, ambiguous confession, Wilde provides one that is decisive, paradoxical, and undisguised, a confession that riveted readers of the 1890 *Lippincott's* first edition of *Dorian Gray*.[42] Both writers acknowledge these tonal differences in reviews of one another's work. Reviewing *Imaginary Portraits* (1887), Wilde asserts that "[a]sceticism is the keynote of Mr. Pater's prose; at times it is almost too severe in its *self-control*, and makes us long for a little more freedom."[43] As in the longer imaginary portrait, *Marius the Epicurean*, Pater strives to complicate his confession on same-sex passion by deliberately employing an austere and disciplined prose.

And in a review of *Dorian Gray*, a review based on the revised 1891 edition of the novel, Pater seems to recoil at Wilde's paradoxical rendering of Epicureanism:

> Clever always, this book, however, seems to set forth anything but a
> homely philosophy of life for the middle-class—a kind of dainty Epicu-
> rean theory, rather—yet fails, to some degree, in this; and one can see
> why. A true Epicureanism aims at a complete though harmonious devel-
> opment of man's entire organism. To lose the moral sense therefore, for
> instance, the sense of sin and righteousness, as Mr. Wilde's heroes are
> bent on doing as speedily, as completely as they can, is to lose, or lower,
> organisation, to become less complex, to pass from a higher to a lower
> degree of development.[44]

Pater appears conflicted, extremely troubled in this passage. The
strained syntax, the frequent punctuation, and the tentative language all reveal Pater's attempt to identify with Wilde while appearing to chastise him. In *Plato and Platonism*, Pater presents a
radically different notion of "development": "The entire modern
theory of 'development,' in all its various phases, proved or unprovable,—what is it but old Heracliteanism awake once more in a
new world, and grown to full proportions?"[45] Pater's criticism, in
my reading, is less like an attack on Wilde than a defense of his
confessional strategy in *Marius the Epicurean*. Pater anxiously ad-
dresses middle-class Victorians, signifying that his brand of Epicureanism which includes morality as Wilde's does not is "true,"
"complete," "harmonious," "entire." Although clearly intrigued
by Wilde's narrative, Pater argues that Wilde fails in his narrative
strategy because he neglects to make his philosophy ageeable to
middle-class beliefs—or at least to diguise his confession on sexuality so that middle-class Victorians would fail to discern its hedonism.

Although this review appeared in November 1891, over six years
after the publication of *Marius*, Pater appears to explain his brand
of Epicureanism and repudiate charges that, as he puts it in the celebrated note added to the "Conclusion" of *The Renaissance* (third
edition), he "might possibly mislead some of those young men into
whose hands it might fall."[46] Because Pater intended *Marius* to be
his fictive explanation of the "Conclusion," he appears to defend
his philosophical position on relativism, Heraclitean flux, and Epicureanism. Wilde perceptively rejected Pater's confessional strategy in *Marius* perhaps because Pater overdetermines the moral and
physical purity of Marius, painting a triptych of him during various
phases of *ascêsis*, *salus*, and chastity. From childhood on, Marius
loves religious activities and leans toward "the sacerdotal function"
because of "the sort of mystic enjoyment he had in the abstinence,
the strenuous *self-control* and *ascêsis*, which such preparation in-

volved."[47] The self-control of Pater's prose, as Wilde notes in his review, also applies to the self-control associated with *ascêsis*.[48]

Like the concept of *ascêsis*, Paterian *salus* and chastity involve self-control. *Salus* is the pagan equivalent of Christian chastity.[49] Pater stresses celibacy, whether in pagan or postpagan traditions, as a way to complicate his discourse on sexuality: "Chastity— [Marius] seemed to understand—the chastity of men and women, with all the conditions and results proper to that chastity, is the most beautiful thing in the world, and the truest conservation of the creative energy which men and women were first brought into it."[50] Why does Pater assert that chastity is "the truest conservation" of creative energy? The word "truest," in this context, denotes a strategy on Pater's part to appear to uphold this conservation/creativity myth.

Pater also reminds Wilde in his 1891 review that Epicureanism must contribute to the complexity and higher development of human beings—an unmistakable sign of Darwin's strongly felt presence. In this regard, Pater espouses an aesthetic idealism antithetical to Wilde's confessional strategy. Unlike Pater, Wilde does not mind including the blemishes, warts and all, on his canvas. Whereas Pater, for example, suppresses the erotic features of his aestheticism, Wilde celebrates them:

> Soul and body, body and soul—how mysterious they were! There was animalism in the soul and the body had its moments of spirituality. The senses could refine, and the intellect could degrade. Who could say where the fleshly impulse ceased, or the psychical impulse began? . . . Was the soul a shadow seated in the house of sin? Or was the body really in the soul, as Giordano Bruno thought?[51]

Although Wilde is here referring to Wotton's seduction of Dorian Gray, he stresses the eroticisim of his fictive discourse, a discourse that fuses body and soul by way of the senses. He may have developed this notion of Platonic eros while at Oxford; in a commonplace book entry, he asserts that eros "is the beginning of the mysticism of neo-platonism: it is like the fruitio Dei of the mediaeval saint, or Dante's love for Beatrice, or the hunger and thirst after righteousness."[52] But because Wilde overdetermines his fictional eroticism, some critics have confidently identified a sexual difference between Pater and Wilde; for example, Ellmann asserts that "Pater's homosexuality was covert, Wilde's was patent."[53] On the contrary, their counter-discourse enables them to appear overt and covert, latent and patent simultaneously. Richard Jenkyns expresses this paradox cogently: "[Pater] more than anyone gave the aesthetic movement its homoerotic tone, and within the limits imposed by the mores of his age and his own sense of decorum, he was open enough—at moments, remarkably explicit."[54]

As Brian Reade and Gary Schmidgall have suggested, Wilde and his entourage may have felt that they could flaunt their sexuality because they mistakenly believed the Hellenic ideal was being accepted in late-Victorian culture. In what may appear, for instance, as a Wildean response to Pater's aesthetic idealism, Dorian believes that

> Experience was of no ethical value. It was merely the name we gave to our mistakes. Men had, as a rule, regarded it as a mode of warning, had claimed for it a certain moral efficacy in the formation of character, had praised it as something that taught us what to follow and showed us what to avoid. But there was no motive power in experience.[55]

Wilde takes as axiomatic the Paterian notion, presented in the "Conclusion" to *The Renaissance*, that human beings must remain receptive to all forms of experience: "What we have to do is to be for ever curiously testing new opinions and courting new impressions, never acquiescing in a facile orthodoxy, of Comte, or of Hegel, or of our own."[56] In *De Profundis*, Wilde admits to falling short of this aesthetic ideal: "That is why, in the subtle epilogue to the first edition of his essays, Pater says that 'Failure is to form habits.' When he said it the dull Oxford people thought the phrase a mere wilful inversion of the somewhat wearisome text of Aristotelian *Ethics*, but there is a wonderful, a terrible truth hidden in it."[57] Wilde confesses that he had allowed himself to become too predictable. Moreover, he failed to acknowledge the fact that Pater continued to refine his position on Heraclitus, stressing his spiritualism in *Marius the Epicurean* and *Plato and Platonism* (1893).[58]

Still, Wilde raises a crucial theoretical concern regarding Pater's expanded same-sex discourse in *Marius*. In appealing to Victorians for acceptance, had he reconfigured the process that enables an individual to form identity by sifting through sensations, impressions, and experiences? Again, Wilde misread, perhaps wilfully, Pater's fictive strategy. Marius is like the sensitive, perceptive, idealized individual Pater presents in the "Conclusion" to *The Renaissance*. After witnessing Flavian's death, for example, Marius discerns that "the individual is to himself the measure of all things, and [that he must] rely on the exclusive certainty to himself of his own impressions."[59] Possibly Wilde objected to Pater's humanist appeal to counter, according to Dollimore, an "idealist culture generally."[60] Or possibly he objected to Pater's idealistic rendering of Marius: "And while he learned that the object, or the experience, as it will be in memory, is really the chief thing to care for from first to last, in the conduct of our lives; all these things were feeding also the idealism constitutional with him—his innate and habitual longing for a world altogether fairer than that he saw."[61] Like Florian Deleal, the protagonist of "The Child in the House," Marius relies on memory not only to create a storehouse of impressions but also to transform experience.

This confessional mode reveals a familiar Paterian narrative strategy: cloak Marius's hedonism in religious and mystic language and make the language of romance obscure the homoeroticism that marks Marius's identity. As Lesley Higgins asserts, "*Marius the Epicurean* depends upon a literally and figuratively embodied discourse to inscribe, and legitimate, same-sex desire within 2nd century A.D. Roman culture."[62] That Pater strives to spin or control his counter-discourse clearly appears in those narrative breaks when he refers to Victorian England and when he invites readers to accept his interpretation of Marius's sexual identity. He may have done so, according to Wright, because "[t]he newspapers had . . . attributed to Pater as many aesthetic extravagances as were reported of Oscar Wilde, and they called him a 'Hedonist'—a term to which he objected 'because it made a wrong—an unpleasant—impression on those who did not understand Greek.' "[63] In the chapter "New Cyrenaicism," for instance, Pater defends himself against the charge that he had promoted a kind of hedonism in the "Conclusion" to *The Renaissance*:

> Really, to the phase of reflection through which Marius was then passing, the charge of "hedonism," whatever its real weight might be, was not properly applicable at all. Not pleasure, but fulness of life, and "insight" as conducting to that fulness—energy, choice, and variety of experience—including noble pain and sorrow even,—loves such as those in the exquisite old story of Apuleius.[64]

Despite the strategy to create an austere, disciplined prose and a protagonist who adheres to principles of *ascêsis* and *salus*, Pater nonetheless affirms Marius's sexual identity by reminding readers of the idyllic afternoon Marius and Flavian spent "half-buried in a heap of dry corn, in an old granary," reading Apuleius's tale of Cupid and Psyche, a tale that both blurs and glosses the intense friendship between Marius and Flavian.[65] Such a reference to Apuleius reveals the eroticism related to Pater's notion of identity;[66] by overdetermining *ascêsis* and *salus*, Pater simply complicates his discourse, embedding same-sex passion in another fictional text by Apuleius.[67]

What Wilde found objectionable was Pater's conflation of hedonism and religion. In *De Profundis*, Wilde comments on this Paterian strategy:

> In *Marius the Epicurean* Pater seeks to reconcile the artistic life with the life of religion in the deep, sweet and austere sense of the word. But Marius is little more than a spectator: an ideal spectator indeed, and one to whom it is given "to contemplate the spectacle of life with appropriate motions," which Wordsworth defines as the poet's true aim: yet a spectator merely, and perhaps a little too much occupied with the comeliness of the vessels of the Sanctuary to notice that it is the Sanctuary of Sorrow that he is gazing at.[68]

Wilde before, during, and after his jail term rejected the self-discipline of Pater's approach to life.[69] Unlike Pater, Wilde proclaims in *Dorian Gray* a "new hedonism," one that will lessen, according to the narrator, our "terror about passions and sensations that seem stronger than ourselves, and that we are conscious of sharing with the less highly organized forms of existence."[70] No wonder that in his review of Wilde's novel Pater expresses alarm. Wilde appropriates Pater's hedonistic discourse in the "Conclusion" to *The Renaissance*, aligning Pater's pleasure principle with "less highly organized forms of existence":

> Yes, there was to be, as Lord Henry had prophesied, a new hedonism that was to re-create life, and to save it from that harsh, *uncomely puritanism* that is having, in our day, its curious revival. It was to have its service of the intellect, certainly; yet it was never to accept any theory or system that would involve the sacrifice of any mode of *passionate experience*. Its aim, indeed, was to be experience itself, and not the fruits of experience, sweet or bitter as they might be. Of the asceticism that deadens the senses, as the vulgar profligacy that dulls them, it was to know nothing. But it was to teach man to concentrate himself upon the moments of a life that is itself but a moment.[71]

Wilde may be mocking in a phrase like "uncomely puritanism" Pater's finicky, repressive language. Wilde wants to create a same-sex discourse using the very language of hedonism. Such a narrative strategy reveals an undisguised attack on religious and cultural customs; the emphasis on "passionate experience" indicates

Wilde's blending of sexuality and identity. This "passionate experience," a coded term for same-sex passion, pervades *Dorian Gray*, making it, as Eve Sedgwick asserts, "a perfect rhetorical distillation of the open secret, the glass closet, shaped by the conjunction of an extravagance of deniability and an extravagance of flamboyant display. It perfectly represents the glass closet, too, because it is in so many ways *out* of purposeful control of its author."[72] It may be true that Wilde displayed political and juridical naiveté, but he did realize the danger of blurring the distinction between art and life in his attacks on religious and cultural institutions.[73] Discussing the radically different ways in which Pater and Wilde sought to present themselves to the public, Laurel Brake reveals a personality trait that pertains not only to their public *personae* but also to their counter-discourses on sexuality: "Pater's careful behind-the-scenes regulation of what should be published on diverse occasions in different discourses, and Moore's and Wilde's explicit interventions to alter public opinion and behavior provide two models of responses to censorship."[74] For example, Wilde supported the anarchists accused in the Chicago Haymarket Riots of 1886, having signed a petition circulated by Shaw.[75] Further, "Wilde's transgressive aesthetic includes an acute political awareness and often an uncompromising political commitment."[76] Whereas Pater appeared to compromise, Wilde paid a heavy price for "playing with that tiger life."[77]

DEFYING

Despite the tonal and strategic differences between Pater's and Wilde's aesthetics, their discourses on same-sex relations share two common tropes: a stress on male beauty and a depiction of intense male friendships. For both Pater and Wilde, seeing or, as Pater puts it, "a diligent promotion of the capacity of the eye" enables them to establish a homoerotic component in their aesthetics of existence.[78] Pater makes vision a vital function of his rendering of aestheticism: "In this way, the true 'aesthetic culture' would be realisable as a new form of the 'contemplative life,' founding its claim on the essential 'blessedness' of 'vision.' "[79] He restates the same idea in a late, unfinished essay, "The Aesthetic Life": "The life of sensation suggests its own moral code, has its own conscience, dear and near, and with no problematic assumptions. If he must live by 'sight,' by sense, then the sense of hands as realised by eye and ear . . . will become for him a law or ideal, a new 'ethick.' "[80] In "A Child in the House" (1878), he is suggestive in his discourse: Florian Deleal discovers early "the activity in him of a more than customary sensuousness, 'the lust of the eye,' as the Preacher says, which might lead him, one day, how far!"[81] For Pater as for Augustine, the "lust of the eye" enables the individual to record impressions; but whereas Pater celebrates sensuousness for its own sake, Augustine recoils against it: "This futile curiosity [seeing] masquerades under the name of science and learning, and since it derives from our thirst for knowledge and sight is the principal sense by which knowledge is acquired, in the Scriptures it is called *gratification of the eye*."[82] Although Pater strives to idealize his confession, he nonetheless appears to find ogling beautiful boys irresistible.[83] His depiction of ogling may have had its origin at Oxford, where, according to a number of cultural critics, a cult of boy worship developed in the 1860s.[84] In their recent biographies, for example, Norman White and Robert Bernard Martin both indicate that Hopkins habitually ogled choirboys; as he discloses in a 1865 diary entry: "Looking at a chorister at Magdalen, and evil thoughts."[85]

In this way, Pater's rendering of Marius's gaze may be a kind of autobiographical confession.[86] When Marius and Cornelius part one evening, "Marius gazed after his companion of the day, as he mounted the steps to his lodging, singing to himself, as it seemed."[87] Marius's homoerotic sensibility marks his relationships, first with Flavian and then with Cornelius. Pater reveals this homoerotic appeal by stressing the physical beauty of the two friends. Flavian stands out from the "gifted youth" at school: "Prince of the school, he had gained an easy dominion over the old Greek master by the fascination of his parts and over his fellow-scholars by the figure he bore."[88] And Cornelius, Flavian's replacement, seems more pagan than Christian in Pater's rendering: "the discretion of Cornelius, his energetic clearness and purity, were a charm, *rather physical than moral*; or at least his exquisite correctness of spirit accorded so perfectly with the regular beauty of his person, as to seem to depend upon it."[89] In his reminiscence, William Sharp comments on this same homoerotic desire in Pater: "he would now and again go out of his way to hail and speak cordially to some young fellow in whom he had a genuine interest."[90]

Like Pater, Wilde makes seeing a necessary trope in his same-sex discourse, most notably in *Dorian Gray*. As Lawler's textual notes indicate, Wilde and his editor at *Lippincott's*, John Stoddart, suppressed explicit statements pertaining to same-sex passion in the original manuscript. Wilde made many changes and additions when he revised the novel for publication in book form; Stoddart emended or deleted explicit pronouncements based on the typescript Wilde submitted.[91] Prudish readers of the *Lippincott's* version no doubt found Wilde's rendering of Dorian Gray sensational, even scandalous. Like Pater, who successfully disguises Marius's and Flavian's same-sex passion in the tale of Cupid and Psyche, Wilde also uses a tale from Greek myth: Narcissus. According to many commentators, Wilde himself was called "Narcissus" by the press.[92] Like the green carnation worn by Wilde and his entourage, the Narcissus flower is an emblem of same-sex desire; and Wilde makes the association between Dorian Gray, Narcissus, and flowerlike beauty so suggestively that the narcissus flower has a coded meaning in Wilde's counter-discourse.[93] At their first meeting, Lord Henry says to Hallward, "Why, my dear Basil, he is a Narcissus and you—well, of course you have an intellectual expression, and all that."[94] After his fall and imprisonment, Wilde did not disguise his discourse; in a letter indicating his intention to go to Italy, he says to Robbie Ross, "Wire, or write at once to me, chez Mellor, Gland, Vaud, and tell me a good hotel. Also bed out some Narcissi. It is their season."[95]

The Narcissus myth is the favored trope of another Oxonian, Charles Edward Hutchinson, whose pamphlet *Boy Worship* (1880) is a how-to on seducing young men. He uses as a headnote "the first two and a half lines from the sonnet which Mr. Rose reads in the *New Republic*, the one written, he says, by an eighteen-year-old boy.[96] 'Three visions in the watches of one night / Made sweet my sleep—almost too sweet to tell / One was Narcissus."[97] In the pamphlet, Hutchinson indicates that youth worshipping was a manifestation of all-male university life at Oxford.[98] He presents, for example, a reverie in which an Oxford undergraduate encounters two youths in a bookstore. Additionally, he refers to specific places where youths might be seen: "The Upper River, as well as a certain College Chapel [Magdalen], has its little band of *habitués*."[99] Like Pater and Wilde, Hutchinson associates the "loves of men and boys" with Greek mythological figures,[100] citing the love of Heracles and Hylas.[101] Pater refers to Heracles and Hylas in "Aesthetic Poetry"[102] and Wilde in "Charmides" and here in "The Garden of Eros": "The Hidden secret of eternal bliss / Known to the Grecian here a man might find, / Ah! you and I may find it now if Love and / Sleep be kind. / There are the flowers which mourning Herakles / Strewed on the tomb of Hylas."[103] But the paradigm myth is that of Narcissus, revealed in Greek statuary as "youth on the verge of manhood."[104] Wilde ingeniously deploys the Narcissus myth by having Dorian Gray fall in love with his own reflection in Hall-ward's painting[105]: "The sense of his own beauty came on him like a revelation . . . as he stood gazing at the shadow of his own loveli-ness."[106] Like Pater, Wilde makes gazing an essential detail of his discourse, even when, as in this instance, he causes Dorian Gray to fall in love with himself.[107]

Wilde also includes a type of gazing that involves homoerotic de-sire. Basil Hallward's desire for Dorian Gray is so great that he in-stinctively realizes he has succumbed to same-sex passion; recounting to Lord Henry his first meeting with Dorian, he says, "I suddenly became conscious that some one was looking at me. I turned half-way round, and saw Dorian Gray. . . . When our eyes met, I felt that I was growing pale. A curious instinct of terror came over me."[108] More like Medusa than Narcissus, Dorian turns Hall-ward into stone, thereby making him subservient. In the *Lippin-cott's* version, there is a statement affirming Hallward's femininity, a statement Wilde deleted in the revised version: "Rugged and straightforward as he was, there was something in his nature that was purely *feminine in its tenderness.*"[109] Wilde may have sup-pressed the statement because of its misogynistic tenor. James Eli Adams argues that Pater, Arnold, and others were labeled dandies, in part because they conflated gender distinctions: "As both dandy and priest resist participation in economic life, and—perhaps more important—as they seem to display a theatrical self-consciousness, they intrude on a position that in Victorian life is reserved for the feminine."[110] Or perhaps he recalled Pater's critical rendering of the sensual Lucius Verus, Aurelius's co-consul: "Lucius Verus, in-deed, had had a more than womanly fondness of fond things, which had made the atmosphere of the old city of Antioch, heavy with centuries of voluptuousness, a poison to him: he had come to love his delicacies best out of season, and would have gilded the very flowers."[111] Verus lacks discipline, austerity, and, more important, a love of beauty for its own sake; this last attribute Wilde would certainly not have wanted to attach to Hallward. Pater and Wilde prefer their flowers green, not gilded.

The emphasis on male gazing enables Pater and Wilde to make the love that dare not speak its name "speak in its own behalf," as Foucault asserts, "to demand that its legitimacy or 'naturality' be acknowledged."[112] In Pater's confession, same-sex love reveals the most refined type of love.[113] Invoking the Platonic tradition, Pater stresses the necessity of same-sex love to make Marius complete. Whether with Flavian or Cornelius, Marius attains a wholeness or completeness he does not have by himself. In the episode in which

Marius sleeps with the dying Flavian, Pater stresses the selflessness of Marius's gesture, thereby spinning his discourse to make it less sensational:

> The thunder which had sounded all day among the hills, with a heat not unwelcome to Flavian, had given way at nightfall to steady rain; and in the darkness Marius lay down beside him, faintly shivering now in the sudden cold, to lend him his own warmth, undeterred by the fear of contagion which had kept other people from passing near the house.[114]

Pater contaminates the same-sex passion between Marius and Flavian by stressing the disease, destruction, and death being visited on the Roman Empire, thereby not only confessing to his own sense of guilt but also identifying the debilitating, plaguelike effects of Victorian homophobia.

Like Pater, Wilde strives in his counter-discourse to force juridical and medical institutions to acknowledge the naturality of same-sex love. Wilde does so when Hallward confesses his erotic desire for Dorian, a confession condemned by many reviewers of the first version of *Dorian Gray*. Hallward's confession is a *locus classicus* of coming out, of shattering the glass closet:

> "Don't speak. Wait till you hear what I have to say. It is quite true that I have worshipped you with far more romance of feeling than a man usually gives to a friend. . . . I wanted to have you all to myself. I was only happy when I was with you. When I was away from you, you were still present in my art. It was all wrong and foolish. It is all wrong and foolish still. Of course I never let you know anything about this. It would have been impossible. You would not have understood it; I did not understand it myself. One day I determined to paint a wonderful portrait of you. It was to have been my masterpiece. But, as I worked at it, every flake and film of color seemed to me to reveal my secret. I grew afraid that the world would know of my idolatry. I felt, Dorian, that I had told too much."[115]

Stoddart must have felt the same way because after the sentence ending "reveal my secret" he canceled the following statement from the typescript: "There was love in every line, and in every touch there was passion."[116] I find the statement noteworthy because it conveys the meaning of Wilde's coded term "passionate experience."

In the revised version of the novel, Wilde also made many changes to this passage, mainly, I suspect, because he received so many hostile reviews.[117] For example, in a July 1890 review written by Charles Whibley for the *Scots Observer*, Wilde read the following: "Mr. Wilde has brains, and art, and style; but if he can write for none but outlawed noblemen and perverted telegraph boys, the sooner he takes to tailoring (or some other decent trade) the better for his own reputation and the public morals."[118] The reference to Lord Arthur Somerset and the Cleveland Street scandal is significant because it was under the Labouchère amendment that Wilde was found guilty of acts of "gross indecency." In fact, Edward Carson read Hallward's confession to Dorian at Wilde's first trial in March 1895. When Carson asked Wilde if he had "ever adored a young man madly," he replied, "No, not madly; I prefer love—that is a higher form. . . . I have never given adoration to anybody except myself," a reply that evoked loud laughter in the courtroom.[119]

The cultural climate of Victorian England, as I have argued, fostered the same-sex discourses on sexuality put forward by Pater and Wilde. Following Arnold, both advocate for a more genial response to Hellenism in England.[120] Like Winckelmann and his adherent Goethe, Pater and Wilde strive in their discourses to move culture forward, to bring Victorian England into the next age: "Hellenism," Pater asserts in the "Winckelmann" essay, "is not merely an absorbed element in our intellectual life; it is a conscious tradition in it."[121] Both writers lament that the Hellenic ideal has been devalued in Victorian culture.[122] Just like Winckelmann, who brought the Renaissance to eighteenth-century Germany, Pater would like to bring a new renascence to Victorian England: "For the thoughts of the Greeks about themselves, and their relation to the world generally, were ever in the happiest readiness to be transformed into objects for the senses."[123] Pater steadfastly adheres to this Greek precept throughout his writing, most notably in *Plato and Platonism*, the last work he published before his death in 1894.

For Pater and Wilde, developing the senses and the intellect makes an individual complete, thereby making artistic creation possible. As Pater asserts in the "Winckelmann" essay,

On a sudden the imagination feels itself free. How facile and direct, it seems to say, is this life of the senses and the understanding, when once we have apprehended it! Here, surely, is that more liberal mode of life we have been seeking so long, so near to us all the while. How mistaken and round-about have been our efforts to reach it by mystic passion, and monastic reverie; how they have deflowered the flesh; how little have they really emancipated us![124]

One can imagine the effect of these words on Wilde. Playing Goethe to Pater's Winckelmann, Wilde revolted against nineteenth-century culture, striving to make it feel the "pulsation of sensuous life."[125] Moreover, he would have truly become a crystalline type so revered by Pater: "It is a thread of pure white light," Pater asserts in "Diaphaneitè," "that one might disentwine from the tumultuary richness of Goethe's nature."[126] Had Wilde followed Pater's circumspect, cautious lead, both in art and life, he, like Goethe, might have carried on Pater's agenda; he might have affected a change toward a more liberal cultural attitude. Predictably, Wilde's energetic discourse on same-sex passion only entrenched more deeply homophobic attitudes in late-Victorian England.[127] As David Hilliard asserts, "the late nineteenth century saw homosexuality acquire new labelling, in the context of a social climate that was more hostile than before."[128] Indeed, the Vagrancy Act of 1898 made homosexual solicitation a punishable offense.[129] A century later, as we engage in our own fin-de-siècle debate on art, politics, religion, society, and self, how much progress have we made toward accepting the light sparked by Pater's and Wilde's "aesthetics of existence"?

NOTES

1. Thomas Wright, *The Life of Walter Pater*, 2 vols. (London: Everett, 1907), 2 : 126.

2. Ibid.

3. Curiously, Denis Donoghue makes the same claim with some of Wright's cadence: "The friendship flourished, but Pater never really liked Wilde" (81).

4. Wright, 2 : 125.

5. F. W. Bussell also refers to this anecdote in his eulogy of Pater; see Seiler, *Walter Pater: A Life Remembered*, 179.

6. Quoted in Frances Winwar, *Oscar Wilde and the Yellow Nineties* (New York: Harper, 1941), 144.

7. At least Wright deals with the Pater-Wilde friendship. Arthur Benson does not refer to Wilde at all in his critical biography of Pater, published the year before Wright's. He may have remained silent because, according to Brian Reade, he "owed a great deal directly to Pater" (*Sexual Heretics*, 36). He may have modeled his professional life—much more successfully—after Pater's: "One of three homosexually inclined sons of an Archbishop of Canterbury, he settled down to being a Fellow" (36). Robert Ross gets beneath Benson's mask in his playful review. He identifies Benson's habit of dissociating Pater from his flamboyant friends (like Rossetti, Swinburne, and Wilde) as a failed attempt to erase Pater's homosexuality:

Anticipating something of the kind [negative criticism], Mr. Benson is careful to insist on the divergence between Rossetti and Pater. . . . If self-revelation can be traced in *Gaston*, it can be found elsewhere. There are sentences in *Hippolytus Veiled*, the *Age of the Athletic Prizemen*, and *Apollo in Picardy* which not only explode Mr. Benson's suggestions, but [also] illustrate the objections he urges against *Denys l'Auxerrois*. They are passages where Pater thinks aloud. If Rossetti wore his heart on his sleeve, Pater's was just above the cuff, like a bangle; though it slips down occasionally in spite of the alb which drapes the hieratic writer not always discreetly. (*Masques and Phases*, 133–34)

I would like to thank Laurel Brake for bringing the Ross article to my attention.

8. Walter Pater, *Letters of Walter Pater*, ed. Lawrence Evans (Oxford: Clarendon Press, 1970), 39, 40, 43, 46, 132, 181.

9. Richard Ellmann, *Oscar Wilde* (New York: Vintage Books, 1987), 45.

10. Unlike Ellmann, Gerald Monsman discerns anxiety in Pater's decision not to include the quip in the novel:

Pater saw an important distinction between Wilde's flippant dictum to "Live up to your blue china" and his own strenuous desire "to burn with a hard, gem-like flame." He selected Wilde's witticism as a chapter epigraph for "An Empty House" to inaugurate his 1890 continuation of *Gaston*—at least until he canceled it as a too direct attack upon his admirer. (xli)

Monsman rightly notes the anxiety Pater felt when *Dorian Gray* appeared in *Lippincott's* (July 1890). But, as I argue, Pater suppressed the witticism to preserve his closeted identity, and not because it would have antagonized Wilde.

11. Alan Sinfield uses the term "same-sex passion" "to avoid anachronism" (vii). Sinfield's terminology does mitigate the sexism implied by Richard Dellamora's term "male-male desire," as presented in *Masculine Desire*. In fact, Sinfield appears to designate Dellamora when he asserts elsewhere, " 'same-sex passion' is the best term I have been able to find for the period up to 1900 ('passion' is intended to include both an emotional and a physical charge, while avoiding the fraught term 'desire')" (11). I prefer "relationships" because the word evokes a gender rather than a sexual orientation.

12. Denis Donoghue argues that the "fine edge of light" is, for Pater, associated with Hellenism. Further, the light or flame is associated with "male homosexual love," revealing Pater's "homosexual code" (112). Pater's flame is Plato's flame all over again. In the *Symposium*, Phaedrus argues that same-sex love ennobles a lover, even causing him to die in battle rather than be seen as unmanly, cowardly by his mate: "Nor is there any lover so faint of heart that he could desert his beloved or fail to help him in the hour of peril, for the very presence of Love kindles the same flame of valor in the faintest heart that burns in those whose courage is innate" (*Collected Dialogues*, 533). In "Humanitad," Wilde has Pater in mind when he refers to "flame": "To burn with one clear flame, to stand erect / In natural honor, not to bend the knee / In profitless prostrations whose effect / Is by itself condemned, what alchemy / Can teach me this? what herb Medea brewed / Will bring the unexultant peace of essence not subdued?" (*Works of Oscar Wilde: Poems*, 1:225). For a counter-argument to such a reading, see Dowling's "Ruskin's Pied Beauty and the Constitution of a 'Homosexual' Code."

13. Walter Pater, "Diaphaneitè," *Miscellaneous Studies*, vol. 8, *The Library Edition of the Works* (London: Macmillan, 1910), 248.

14. Walter Pater, *The Renaissance: Studies in Art and Poetry*, the 1893 text, ed. Donald L. Hill (Berkeley: University of California Press, 1980), 189.1.

15. Linda Dowling, *Hellenism and Homosexuality in Victorian Oxford* (Ithaca: Cornell University Press, 1994), 99–103; see also Ellmann, *Oscar Wilde*, 59–61.

16. Jeffrey Weeks, *Coming Out: Homosexual Politics in Britain from the Nineteenth Century to the Present*, 2d ed. (London: Quartet Books, 1990), 7.

17. Alan Sinfield, *The Wilde Century: Effeminacy, Oscar Wilde, and the Queer Moment* (New York: Columbia University Press, 1994), 89.

18. Although Richard Terdiman focuses on nineteenth-century French literature, his counter-discourse concept applies to my argument. I prefer Terdiman's
phrase to Thäis Morgan's "minoritizing discourse," mainly because the latter implies a minority/majority binarism, a binarism that does not convey the reciprocity
of discourse/counter-discourse: "Briefly defined, a minoritizing discourse is one in
which the solidarity—and essential alikeness—of a group that perceives itself to
be in a minority position is supposed and invoked at the same time as it is being
constructed in the discourse itself" (Morgan, "Reimagining Masculinity in Victorian Criticism," 316).

19. By 1895, according to Linda Dowling, "The 'love that dare not speak its
name' could be spoken of, to those who knew their ancient history, as *paiderastia*,
Greek love" (*Hellenism and Homosexuality in Victorian England*, 28). Symonds
makes a similar point in *A Problem in Greek Ethics*, 6–7, 13–14.

20. Michel Foucault, *The History of Sexuality: The Use of Pleasure*, vol. 2,
trans. Robert Hurley (New York: Pantheon Books, 1985), 252–53.

21. I realize that there is a backlash against Foucault and his nonempirical,
sometimes ideologically slanted assertions about Victorian sexual practices. But I
agree with Richard Dellamora who, in a recent review essay, asserts that "the
crossing of sexual with other discourses holds promise of continuing discoveries
in cultural history. In this work, Foucault's foundational insights continue to be of
the utmost value" ("Victorian Homosexuality in the Prism of Foucault," *Victorian
Studies* 38, no. 2 [Winter 1995], 272).

22. Symonds, *A Problem in Greek Ethics*, 54.

23. Plato, *Phaedrus*, trans. Hackforth in *The Collected Dialogues of Plato*, ed.
Edith Hamilton and Huntington Cairns (Princeton: Princeton University Press,
1961), 501.

24. Paul Cartledge, "The Importance of Being Dorian: An Onomastic Gloss on
the Hellenism of Oscar Wilde," *Hermathena* 147 (1989): 11.

25. Plato, *Symposium*, in *The Collected Dialogues of Plato*, ed. Edith Hamilton
and Huntington Cairns (Princeton: Princeton University Press, 1961), 535.

26. Symonds, *A Problem in Greek Ethics*, 30.

27. I disagree with Herbert Sussman who links Pater's subversive discourse to
that of "the ideal contemporary artist as modern-day monk" (*Victorian Masculinities*, 175). Pater's discourse involves a careful regulation of passion, but not, as I
argue, "the withholding of desire to create a highly eroticized interior life and thus
an erotically charged poetry [that] praises in coded form a homoerotic masculine
poetic and homoerotic masculine criticism" (175). Sussman forces his monastic
model, which does fit nicely with Carlyle, Browning, and the Pre-Raphaelites, onto
Pater and his early work. His monastic model would work more plausibly in the
later writing, not the earlier; he constrains himself too narrowly by his focus on
early Victorian literature.

28. Dowling, *Hellenism and Homosexuality in Victorian England*, 124.

29. F. B. Smith, "Labouchere's Amendment to the Criminal Law Amendment
Bill," *Historical Studies* 17 (October 1976): 165.

30. Montgomery H. Hyde, *The Cleveland Street Scandal* (New York: Coward,
1976), 21.

31. Ibid., 13–30; see also Richard Dellamora, *Masculine Desire: The Sexual
Politics of Victorian Aestheticism* (Chapel Hill: University of North Carolina Press,
1990), 10–11, 204–5; see also Wolf Von Eckardt, Sander L. Gilman, and J. Edward
Chamberlin, *Oscar Wilde's London: A Scrapbook of Vices and Virtues, 1880–
1900* (New York: Anchor Press, 1987), 259–61.

32. Foucault, *History of Sexuality*, 1:150.

33. Billie Andrew Inman, "Estrangement and Connection: Walter Pater, Benjamin Jowett, and William M. Hardinge," *Pater in the 1990s* (Greensboro: ELT Press, 1991), 15–20.

34. Laurel Brake convincingly argues that Benson concealed Pater's same-sex passion even though he knew from reliable sources about its role in Pater's professional setbacks at Oxford. In a diary entry dated 12 November 1904, Benson records some information he received from Edmund Gosse: "Jowett was said to have some mysterious letters, which he vowed he would produce if P. ever thought of standing for any University office" ("Judas and the Widow," 45).

35. For an explanation of how Victorian writers veiled their discourses while still appealing to the converted, see Peter Gay's "Problematic Attachments," *The Tender Passion*, 198–254. And for a discussion of a male homosexual subculture in Victorian England, see Jeffrey Weeks's "Movements of Affirmation," 164–67. Like Foucault, Weeks views "[t]he medicalisation of homosexuality—a transition from notions of sin to concepts of sickness or mental illness—a significant move" (167). In *Discipline and Punish*, Foucault focuses on the emerging attitudes toward punishment in the nineteenth century. The idea of the panopticon, derived from the work of Bentham, is for Foucault a central image of institutional power (see "Panopticism" 195–228).

36. Clyde De L. Ryals, "The Concept of Becoming in *Marius the Epicurean*," *Nineteenth-Century Literature* 43, no. 2 (September 1988): 172–73; Gerald Monsman, *Walter Pater's Art of Autobiography* (New Haven: Yale University Press, 1983), 10–13; Lawrence Danson, "Oscar Wilde, W. H., and the Unspoken Name of Love," *ELH* 58 (1991): 93–95; Eve Kosofsky Sedgwick, *Epistemology of the Closet* (Berkeley: University of California Press, 1990), 160–62.

37. Foucault, *History of Sexuality*, 1:101.

38. Denis Donoghue, *Walter Pater: Lover of Strange Souls* (New York: Knopf, 1995), 66–77.

39. Christopher Craft, "Alias Bunbury: Desire and Termination in *The Importance of Being Earnest*,"*Representations* 31 (Summer 1990): 27.

40. According to Gary Schmidgall, "Oscar thought he was—and *was* indeed—like Hallward. He, too, was an artist hopelessly and ruinously infatuated with beautiful young men" (*The Stranger Wilde*, 23).

41. Foucault, *History of Sexuality*, 1:59.

42. I have decided to use the July 1890 *Lippincott's* version for two primary reasons: Wilde removed many professions of same-sex passion from the revised edition published by Ward, Lock, and Co. in April 1891; and Edward Carson, Queensberrry's defense attorney, read passages from this version of the novel during his cross-examination of Wilde. According to Wilde, Carson read his works badly. See Hyde, *Trials*, 124–33.

43. R. M. Seiler, ed. *Walter Pater: The Critical Heritage* (Boston: Routledge, 1980), 165; my emphasis.

44. Walter Pater, "A Novel by Mr. Oscar Wilde," *Selected Writings of Walter Pater*, ed. Harold Bloom (New York: Columbia University Press, 1974), 264.

45. Walter Pater, *Plato and Platonism*, vol. 6, *The Library Edition of the Works* (London: Macmillan, 1910), 19.

46. See Pater, *Renaissance,* 186.

47. Walter Pater, *Marius the Epicurean*, 2d ed. (London: Macmillan, 1885), 1:31; my emphasis.

48. Because Wilde would have read the first or second edition of *Marius*, I use

throughout the second edition published in November 1885. Like Wilde, Pater presents a more complete confession in the earliest versions of his fictive discourse.

49. Pater, *Marius the Epicurean*, 1 : 33–34.

50. Ibid., 2 : 113.

51. Oscar Wilde, *The Picture of Dorian Gray*, ed. Donald L. Lawler, A Norton Critical Edition (New York: W. W. Norton, 1988), 204–5.

52. Oscar Wilde, *Oscar Wilde's Oxford Notebooks*, ed. Philip E. Smith and Michael S. Helfand (New York: Oxford University Press, 1989), 149.

53. Richard Ellmann, "Henry James Among the Aesthetes," *Proceedings of the British Academy* 69 (1983): 218.

54. Richard Jenkyns, "Recline and Fall," Review of *The Stanger Wilde: Interpreting Oscar* by Gary Schmigdall, *The New Republic* 211 (16 May 1994): 40.

55. Wilde, *Dorian Gray*, 205.

56. Pater, *Renaissance*, 189.20–24.

57. Oscar Wilde, *Letters of Oscar Wilde*, ed. Rupert Hart-Davis (New York: Oxford University Press, 1962), 430.

58. William F. Shuter, "Pater's Reshuffled Text," *Nineteenth-Century Literature* 43 no. 4 (March 1989): 519–21; and Ryals, 73–74.

59. Pater, *Marius the Epicurean*, 1 : 134.

60. Jonathan Dollimore, *Sexual Dissidence: Augustine to Wilde, Freud to Foucault* (Oxford: Clarendon Press, 1991), 7–8.

61. Pater, *Marius the Epicurean*, 1 : 49–50.

62. Lesley Higgins, "Jowett and Pater: Trafficking in Platonic Wares," *Victorian Studies* 37 no. 1 (August 1993): 53.

63. Wright, 2 : 127.

64. After quoting a passage from the "Conclusion" of *The Renaissance*, John Morley, in his sympathetic review of the work which appeared in the *Fortnightly Review* (April 1873), is the first to use the term: "The Hedonist, and this is what Mr. Pater must be called by those who like to affix labels" (Seiler, *Walter Pater: The Critical Heritage*, 68.

65. Pater, *Marius the Epicurean*, 1 : 152.

66. In *Plato and Platonism*, Pater indicates that, for him, there is a connection between austerity and sensuousness, as revealed in his portrait of Plato: "Austere as he seems, and on well-considered principle really is, his temperance or austerity, aesthetically so winning, is attained only by the chastisement, the control, of a variously interested, a richly sensuous nature" (6 : 126).

67. See Richard Dellamora, "Critical Impressionism as Anti-Phallogocentric Strategy," *Pater in the 1990s*, ed. Laurel Brake and Ian Small (Greensboro: ELT Press, 1991), 128.

68. Wilde, *Letters*, 476.

69. According to Timothy d'Arch Smith, Wilde along with Aubrey Beardsley and others seized the "aesthetics of Pater and the Greek ideal" and refashioned it: "The resulting rather heady hermaphroditism, so clear in Beardsley's drawings and in the pages of *The Picture of Dorian Gray*, set off a flood of paederastic material in the form of verse, prose and paintings as well as initiating a new trend in the art of photography" (*Love in Earnest*, 2).

70. Wilde, *Dorian Gray*, 244.

71. Ibid., my emphasis.

72. Sedgwick, *Epistemology of the Closet*, 165.

73. Peter Allan Dale convincingly argues that Wilde obsessively blends crimi-

nality and artistry to complicate his discourse on sexuality: "He may write about treason, adultery, embezzlement, forgery, murder, and so on, but all these transgressions are arguably encodings of the sexual 'crime' at the center of his own life" ("Oscar Wilde: Crime and the 'Glorious Shapes of Art,' " 2).

74. Laurel Brake, "The Discourses of Journalism: 'Arnold and Pater' Again— and Wilde," *Pater in the 1990s*, ed. Laurel Brake and Ian Small (Greensboro: ELT Press, 1991), 57.

75. Schmidgall, 24.

76. Dollimore, 73.

77. Wilde, *Letters*, 779.

78. Pater, *Marius the Epicurean*, 1 : 37.

79. Ibid., 1 : 149.

80. Walter Pater, "The Aesthetic Life," Harvard University Library (bMS Eng 1150), 9.

81. Walter Pater, *Imaginary Portraits*, ed. Eugene J. Brzenk (New York: Harper, 1964), 23.

82. Augustine, *Confessions*, trans. R. S. Pine-Coffin (New York: Penguin, 1988), 241.

83. I wish to thank Jim Adams for pointing out to me this passage in the *Confessions*. The biblical verse Pater and Augustine have in mind is 1 John 2 : 16.

84. Inman, "Estrangement," 14.

85. Quoted in Robert Bernard Martin, *Gerard Manley Hopkins: A Very Private Life* (New York: Putnam's, 1991), 63; and Norman White, *Hopkins: A Literary Biography* (Oxford: Clarendon Press, 1992), 110–16.

86. For an account of the relations between Pater and Hopkins and how Pater influenced his student, see Jude Nixon's "The Handsome Heart: Hopkins, Pater, and Victorian Aesthetics," *Gerard Manley Hopkins and His Contemporaries*, 165–234.

87. Pater, *Marius the Epicurean*, 1 : 185.

88. Ibid., 1 : 54.

89. Ibid., 1 : 231; my emphasis.

90. R. M. Seiler, ed. *Walter Pater: A Life Remembered* (Calgary, Alberta: University of Calgary Press, 1987), 87.

91. Donald L. Lawler, "A Note on the Texts," *The Picture of Dorian Gray*, A Norton Critical Edition (New York: Norton, 1988), xi–xii.

92. Wright, 2 : 121.

93. Elaine Showalter, *Sexual Anarchy: Gender and Culture at the Fin de Siècle* (London: Penguin, 1990), 176.

94. Wilde, *Dorian Gray*, 174.

95. Wilde, *Letters*, 819; see Showalter, 154.

96. I would like to thank Billie Inman for kindly sharing her copy of this remarkable document with me.

97. Inman, "Estrangement," 14.

98. Alan Sinfield, *The Wilde Century: Effeminacy, Oscar Wilde, and the Queer Moment* (New York: Columbia University Press, 1994), 65–6.

99. Charles Edward Hutchinson, *Boy-Worship* (Oxford, 1880), 13.

100. Wilde also refers to this chapel at Magdalen in "The Critic as Artist": "the dulness of tutors and professors matters very little when one can loiter in the grey cloisters at Magdalen, and listen to some flute-like voice singing in Waynfleete's chapel" (*The Critic as Artist* 396). For an explanation of boy-worship at Oxford, see Dowling, *Hellenism and Homosexuality at Victorian Oxford*, 114; and for an

explanation of British educational practices that sought to mold boys into men, see Ed Cohen, *Talk on the Wilde Side*, 38–44.

101. Hutchinson, 8.

102. Walter Pater, "Aesthetic Poetry," *Selected Writings of Walter Pater*, ed. Harold Bloom (New York: Columbia University Press, 1974), 197.

103. Oscar Wilde, *Works of Oscar Wilde: Poems*, Sunflower Edition, ed. Richard Le Gallienne (New York: Lamb Publishing, 1909), 1 : 65.

104. Hutchinson, 8.

105. Mark Pattison, Rector of Lincoln College, records in a 5 May 1878 diary entry an episode that suggests Pater's own attraction to young men:

> To Pater's to tea, where Oscar Browning, who was more like Socrates than ever. He conversed in one corner with four feminine-looking youths "paw dandling" there in one foursome, while the Misses Pater and I sat looking on in another corner. Presently Walter Pater, who, I had been told, was "upstairs" appeared, attended by two more youths of similar appearance (Seiler, *Walter Pater: A Life Remembered*, 57).

106. Wilde, *Dorian Gray*, 190–91.

107. Ibid., 226–27.

108. Ibid., 177.

109. Ibid., 230; my emphasis.

110. James Eli Adams, *Dandies and Desert Saints: Styles of Victorian Manhood* (Cornell: Cornell University Press, 1995), 210.

111. Pater, *Marius the Epicurean*, 1 : 193–4.

112. Foucault, *History of Sexuality*, 101.

113. In his essay on "Winckelmann," Pater includes a passage from one of Winckelmann's letters to a close male friend, adhering to the notion put forth by Winckelmann: "As it is confessedly the beauty of man which is to be conceived under one general idea, so I have noticed that those who are observant of beauty only in women, and are moved little or not at all by the beauty of men, seldom have an impartial, vital, inborn instinct for beauty in art. To such persons the beauty of Greek art will ever seem wanting, because its supreme beauty is rather male than female" (*Renaissance*, 153.17–23).

114. Pater, *Marius the Epicurean*, 1 : 119.

115. Wilde, *Dorian Gray*, 232–33.

116. Ibid., 233; n. 6.

117. During Wilde's first trial, Carson asked Wilde if had made "a good deal" of modifications to *Dorian Gray* because of the hostile criticisms. Somewhat misleadingly, Wilde replied, "No. Additions were made. In one case it was pointed out to me—not in a newspaper or anything of that sort, but by the only critic of the century whose opinion I set high, Mr. Walter Pater—that a certain passage was liable to misconstruction, and I made an addition" (Hyde, *The Trials of Oscar Wilde*, 124). In fact, as Lawler shows, Wilde made many deletions and additions.

118. Wilde, *Dorian Gray*, 346.

119. Montgomery H. Hyde, ed., *The Trials of Oscar Wilde* (London: William Hodge, 1948), 129.

120. It is in Platonic aesthetics that we can "find ourselves under the more exclusive influence of those qualities in the Hellenic genius [Plato] has thus emphasised" (*Plato and Platonism*, 6 : 280). Here, Pater agrees with Arnold concerning the need for Hellenism, but still seems to dissent from Arnold's advocacy of disinterested, objective criticism: "What [Plato] would promise, then, is the art, the literature, of which among other things it may be said that it solicits *a certain effort*

from the reader or spectator, who is promised a great expressiveness on the part of the writer, the artist, if he for his part will bring with him a great attentiveness" (6 : 280; my emphasis).

121. Pater, *Renaissance*, 158.26–27.

122. According to Billie Inman, Ernest Renan and Karl Müller initiated the distinction "between paganism, as a primitive, practised religion, and Hellenism, which emerged relatively late and whose growth is the growth of the human mind, the intellect" (*Walter Pater's Readings: A Bibliography of His Library Borrowings*, 98). Both Pater in the "Winckelmann" essay and Wilde in *Dorian Gray* seize upon this distinction, presenting Hellenism, with its expansiveness, as a major influence on Victorian culture.

123. Pater, *Renaissance*, 163.4–7.

124. Ibid., 146.26–147.1.

125. Ibid., 146.18–9.

126. Pater, "Diaphaneitè," 8 : 254.

127. For a commentary on Wilde as a cultural prophet, see Philip Rieff's "The Impossible Culture." Rieff perceptively indicates why Wilde became a scapegoat: "Wilde can never win. For he imagined an impossible culture, one inhabited by consummate individuals, freed from the inherited inhibitions necessary, at least until our own time, to culture itself" (411).

128. David Hilliard, "UnEnglish and Unmanly: Anglo-Catholicism and Homosexuality," *Victorian Studies* 25 no. 2 (Winter 1982): 183; also Jeffrey Weeks, *Coming Out: Homosexual Politics in Britain from the Nineteenth Century to the Present*, 2d ed. (London: Quartet Books, 1990), 2; and Montgomery H. Hyde, *The Other Love; An Historical and Contemporary Survey of Homosexuality in Britain* (London: Heinemann, 1970), 152–53.

129. Weeks, *Coming Out*, 15.

Part III
Late Victorian

"The bricklayer shall lay me": Edward Carpenter, Walt Whitman, and Working-Class "Comradeship"

WILLIAM A. PANNAPACKER

Edward Carpenter (1844–1929) has always stood in the shadow of the American poet Walt Whitman (1819–1892); Havelock Ellis even referred to Carpenter's major literary production, a collection of poetry called *Towards Democracy* (1883–1905), as nothing more than "Whitman and water."[1] Carpenter's generally conceded status as a second-rate author brings the example of his *life* to the fore among those who cherish his reputation as pioneer of socialism and gay liberation. E. M. Forster's praise of his "constancy" and Henry Bishop's claim that "Carpenter's life was of a uniform texture" have become critical commonplaces.[2] Carpenter's abandonment of a respectable clerical position at Cambridge University, his move to Sheffield as a University Extension lecturer, his quest for a productive life of farming, and his long-term homosexual relationships with working-class men are often presented as examples of heroic opposition to the snobbery and repression of Victorian England. Chushichi Tsuzuki's recent biography, *Edward Carpenter 1844–1929, Prophet of Human Fellowship* (1980), for example, asserts that Carpenter's "whole life presented an open revolt against this society."[3] The referent of "this," however, never seems completely clear, for it assumes the stability of culturally and historically specific social categories such as middle-class and working-class, heterosexual and homosexual. Carpenter's writings *and* the record of his life suggest that his allegedly subversive masculinity, based as it was on the transgression of the boundaries of class and gender, was inherently unstable and often supported the social categories he is said to have resisted. Carpenter's *masculinities* were an ongoing negotiation of competing and overlapping discourses: elitism and populism, conservatism and radicalism, effeminacy and manliness, submissiveness and dominance, refinement and primi-

277

tivism, noblesse oblige and working-class "comradeship" to name a few. Like the poet who inspired his break with middle-class, heterosexual conformity, Edward Carpenter "contained multitudes."

I

On 2 May 1877, a handsome Englishman of thirty-two arrived at 431 Stevens Street in Camden, New Jersey. It was the residence of Walt Whitman, notorious in the United States as the immoral author of *Leaves of Grass* (1855–1892). The three-story row house occupied by Whitman suggested the genteel aspirations of the poet's brother and sister-in-law with whom he lived, but to Edward Carpenter industrial Camden must have seemed like the North of England, ideal for a political poet who shunned the collegiality of bourgeois literati like Lowell and Longfellow for the "comradeship" of uneducated working men like Peter Doyle and Harry Stafford. A socialist who hated hypocrisy and sexually desired other men, Carpenter felt "cut off from the understanding of others," but Whitman's writings had given him "a ground for the love of men" that was not only sexual, but also political and religious.[4] For Carpenter, an ex-minister, this long-delayed journey was tantamount to a spiritual pilgrimage.

Carpenter seems to have had fairly clear expectations about Whitman's appearance and surroundings. The frontispiece to the 1855 edition of *Leaves* presented Whitman as a surly and sensuous workman, "one of the roughs," and Carpenter expected the poet to be "eccentric, unbalanced, violent."[5] By 1877, however, the actual Whitman appeared to have little in common with this vigorous image, and the house in which he lived seemed incongruous with proletarian simplicity. "Walt" was upstairs when Carpenter arrived; he lived on the third floor, and it took him some time to descend, as his left foot was paralyzed by a recent stroke. Carpenter waited in the sitting room, noting the accoutrements of middle-class respectability with some disdain: "one or two ornamental tables," "photograph books," and "things under glass shades, & c."[6] The young man was surprised at Whitman's appearance; he was "an old man with long grey, almost white, beard, and shaggy head and neck."[7] As they exchanged pleasantries, Carpenter found, contrary to his expectations, that Whitman was "considerate" and "courteous," with a "large benign effluence and inclusiveness" combined with a "sense of remoteness and inaccessibility."[8] Although Carpenter still detected "a certain untamed 'wild hawk' look" in Whitman,

Walt Whitman. The frontispiece to *Leaves of Grass*, 1855.

the sexually assertive, politically radical poet of *Leaves* was now, as John Burroughs describes him, "not an athlete, or a rough, but a great tender mother-man."[9]

Whitman could not live up to his robust physical image, but Carpenter was soon pleased to learn that the poet's habitat was not this bourgeois interior but the open-air life of the street and country. Whitman suggested that they go out, walk to the Delaware River, and take the ferry across to Philadelphia. Along the way Whitman hailed his unreserved working-class comrades: "The men on the ferry steamer were evidently old friends," as were "the tramway conductor" and "the loafers on the pavement."[10] To Whitman, Carpenter observes, "The life of the streets and of the people was so near, so dear."[11] In Philadelphia the once reserved Englishman even claims to have witnessed something like a re-enactment of Whitman's relationship with Peter Doyle: Whitman met "an old Broadway 'stager,' " who " 'had not seen Walt for three or four years'; and tears were in his eyes as he held his hand."[12] In Camden and Philadelphia, all working men, it seems, were the comrades of Walt Whitman.

In contrast to these urban scenes, Carpenter's account also presents Whitman in a tableau of pastoral comradeship at a small farm in New Jersey that belonged to the parents of Harry Stafford, a young printer's assistant who was a "favourite of Walt's."[13] Carpenter describes the other Stafford children as flocking to Whitman: "the little boy would lie coiled, on his knees, half-asleep, half-awake, Walt's hand covering and compressing his entire face."[14] When he was not communing with nature, Whitman would hold forth on his poetry in the midst of Stafford's large, picturesque family: "my original idea was that if I could bring men together by putting before them the heart of man," Whitman says, "it would be a great thing." He continues, apparently for Carpenter's benefit, "I have had America chiefly in view, but this appreciation of me in England makes me think I might perhaps do the same for the old world also."[15] Despite his initial impressions, Carpenter finally claims that "Whitman seemed to fill out 'Leaves of Grass,' " adding that "all he had written there was a matter of absolute personal experience."[16]

Undoubtedly, Whitman both affirmed *and* denied Carpenter's preconceptions about him, and the allegory of Carpenter's first visit to Camden highlights the visual and textual complexities of Whitman's significance in the emerging discourses of same-sex desire. Carpenter describes Whitman's face as being formally structured, "like a Greek temple."[17] He also drew a sketch of Whitman, noting that "the likeness to Christ is quite marked." But as Gay Wilson Allen observes, "the drawing looks nothing like Whitman . . . except possibly the frontispiece of the 1855 edition of *Leaves of Grass*."[18] Just as Carpenter's visual images of Whitman are caught in a tension between the Hellenic and the Christian models of same-sex relations in circulation at that time, Carpenter's narrative presents a series of images which transform the basis of their relationship from the erotic to the paternal. The child in Whitman's lap, whose face is conveniently covered, seems an infantilized substitute for Carpenter himself, whose initial expectations of a sexual relationship with the rough, manly lover of 1855 were now transformed into a filial one with the kindly father of 1877, the "good, gray poet."[19]

As Scott McCracken observes, Carpenter uses the textual Whitman "to write a masculine identity for himself," and Carpenter's account of Whitman attempts to demonstrate a continuity between text and reality that accommodates the transformation of masculine roles over time. He returned to England apparently more convinced than ever that Whitman's masculinities, as transitory as they may have seemed, were models on which to base his own development. Though once a refined member of the clergy, Carpenter continued to seek a more "manly," economically independent existence as a poet, lecturer, writer, farmer, and craftsman in the countryside near industrial Sheffield, where, like Whitman, he could be close to both nature and the life of urban streets. And like Whitman, Carpenter began a series of semi-public domestic and sexual relationships with working-class men. Carpenter continued to be subject to the emerging negative discourses of the "homosexual," but this visit to the United States enabled him to construct a new identity for himself, paradoxically, as the "English Whitman."

II

According to Michel Foucault, the "homosexual" was constructed as "a type of life, a life form, and a morphology" in the elite discourses of medical journals after 1870. As a result, sodomy was transformed from an isolated sin into a means of characterizing a "species" suffering from "hermaphrodism of the soul."[20] The "homosexual" male, either as a result of congenital "inversion" or moral "perversion," demonstrated behaviors culturally designated as female, possibly including sexual desire for "normal" males. By the beginning of the twentieth century, effeminate behavior, rather than sexual acts, became the predominant sign of the homosexual in both countries, and effeminacy was the chief basis for attacks on men assumed to be homosexuals, who were now regarded as essentially different from other men. In 1911 Chicago vice investigators, for example, describe inverts as those who "affect the carriage, mannerisms, and speech of women," and "are fond of many articles dear to the feminine heart."[21] A 1913 study of Whitman by W. C. Rivers, published in London and "restricted to Members of the Legal and Medical Professions," identifies the poet as a homosexual for the following reasons: "he cared nothing for sport," he delighted "in cooking," "he can talk about clothes with a woman's knowledge," and he had "feminine devotion and aptitude" for nursing during the American Civil War.[22] "No true man could feel like that," Rivers writes, "however full of compassion and patriotism."[23] As Joseph Bristow observes, the notorious trials of Oscar Wilde for sodomy in 1895 finally established this link between effeminacy and male same-sex desire in both England and the United States.[24] Ironically, it was not same-sex acts between men that presented the greatest social risk. Men who engaged in sexual activity with other men but did not assume the passive or feminized role were regarded as normal; conversely, effeminate men were often regarded as homosexual even if they were exclusively heterosexual.

Carpenter is recognized as one who responded to these emerging discourses but also helped to create them. He was particularly influenced by the Continental sexologists Albert Moll, Richard von Krafft-Ebing and, most importantly, Karl Heinrich Ulrichs (1825–1895), an early campaigner for homosexual rights who proposed the "Uranian" or "Urning" as a sexual type. Carpenter's construction of himself as a Uranian is an example of the "reverse" discourse that Foucault also describes: one that demands "its legitimacy or 'naturality' be acknowledged, often in the same vocabulary, using the same categories by which it was medically disqualified."[25] Carpenter uses Ulrichs's model to reverse the negative discourses of perversion and inversion, making the Uranian's transgendering a source of physical, moral, intellectual, and social virtue. In his poem "O Child of Uranus," for example, Carpenter describes the Uranian as a "Woman-soul within a Man's form dwelling . . . With man's strength to perform, and pride to suffer without sign, / And feminine sensitiveness to the last fibre of being."[26] Although the male Uranian derives a heightened sensitivity from his "woman's soul," he is not "effeminate" or "degenerate" in any way; on the contrary, Carpenter describes Uranians as "fine, healthy specimens of their sex, muscular and well-developed in body, of powerful brain, high standard of conduct, and with nothing abnormal or morbid of any kind."[27]

Carpenter's conception of the Uranian seems contradictory; at times polemically masculine and homosexual, at times androgynous and bisexual, the Uranian is generally portrayed as an *Übermensch*, belonging to a "third" or "intermediate" sex. The Uranian model transforms what appears to be same-sex relations into something superior to opposite-sex relations: "Urning-love was of a higher order than the ordinary attachment."[28] Although same-sex love was not procreative, the children of Uranus could lead the way to a new society. In Carpenter's view, the sexual activity practiced by Uranians should not only be legal but privileged, for "the Uranian class of men are destined in their turn to lead to another wide-reaching social organization and forward movement in the direction of Art and Human Compassion."[29] Uranians, though "Misjudged and crucified" through history, are ultimately destined to foster something like the Christian millennium in which the Uranian "form in glory clad shall reappear."[30]

Carpenter's writings such as *Towards Democracy* (1883–1905), *Love's Coming of Age* (1896), *An Unknown People* (1897), *The Intermediate Sex* (1908), and *Intermediate Types Among Primitive Folk* (1914) may be rightly viewed as a dialogue with other upper-middle-class English intellectuals like John Addington Symonds, Olive Schreiner, and Havelock Ellis. As a whole, these writings constitute an intellectually ambitious and morally courageous attempt to defend those who were increasingly persecuted for their same-sex desires—a circumstance for which Carpenter suffered significant personal abuse. However, his lifelong defense of Uranianism actually reinforced the link between biological sex and socially constructed gender. Moreover, it undermined Carpenter's commitments to socialist egalitarianism, because the Uranian, whom Carpenter generally constructs as an act of self-definition, simply constitutes an alternative elite. Although he did much to promote other progressive social issues, Carpenter's theoretical writings, as Sheila Rowbotham laments, fail to "free sexuality from the tyranny of gender" and engage in bourgeois antihomosexual discourses on their own terms.[31] As a result, Carpenter's practices would never precisely correspond with his theories about sex or socialism.

III

Carpenter's significance is not limited, however, to his articulation of the reverse discourse of Uranianism among English intellectuals—Carpenter is most interesting for his contradictions. The instability of Uranian masculinity was partly the result of Carpenter's emphasis on the transgression of class boundaries. "It is noticeable how often Uranians of good position and breeding," he writes, "are drawn to rougher types, as of manual workers."[32] After his adoption of socialism, Carpenter's sexual desires and relationships generally included only working-class men, and he became increasingly susceptible to their attitudes about masculinity. As George Chauncey has shown in *Gay New York* (1994), there were well-established cultures of same-sex desire among the working classes before the "homosexual" was institutionalized in medicine and law. Medical discourse, Chauncey observes, "represented simply one of several powerful (and competing) sexual ideologies."[33]

Indeed, the circulation of masculine identities predicated on same-sex desire circulated endlessly through every level of social class, both downward and upward. The most visible homosexuals—the ones most readily identified in elite discourses—were primarily working-class men who signified their same-sex desires by becoming "fairies," who externalize the so-called woman within by emphasizing their feminine qualities. Carpenter observes with some frustration that fairies "excite a good deal of attention" and that most people believe all homosexual men fall into this category.[34] It is unclear whether fairies were a source of the elite characterization of the homosexual as an invert or whether they were responding to this characterization; it is most likely that both processes occurred at the same time, but the visibility of fairies did increase in the late nineteenth century as sexuality became increasingly bifurcated. In either case, like Carpenter's model of the Uranian, fairies supported the dominant gender conventions by preserving the model of opposite-sex attraction. As Chauncey observes, "fairies reaffirmed the conventions of gender even as they violated them."[35]

Although fairies constituted a minority of homosexual men, even among the working classes, their effeminacy contributed to the oppression of homosexuals in general. Consequently, they were resented by many masculine men who experienced same-sex desire, particularly those in the middle class. Although the Uranian male possesses feminine qualities, Carpenter always distances himself from the effeminacy of fairies, whom he calls "extreme and exaggerated types of the race." In contrast with the vigorous image of the Uranian, Carpenter describes the fairy as "sentimental, lacka-daisical, mincing in gait and manners, something of a chatterbox, skillful at the needle and in woman's work, sometimes taking plea-sure in women's clothes." Moreover, the body of the fairy was also different from that of the muscular Uranian: "his figure not infre-quently betraying a tendency toward the feminine, large at the hips, supple, not muscular, the face wanting in hair, the voice inclined to be high-pitched."[36] "Straight-acting" homosexuals like Carpenter, it seems, participated with vice investigators in the broader cultural pattern of defining effeminate males as a separate species.

The stronger and more pervasive the construction of the homo-sexual as a fairy—a transgressor of gender roles—became in the general culture, the more men who were unwilling to risk identifi-cation as homosexuals had to differentiate themselves from any-thing effeminate. This need to defend oneself from the accusation of effeminacy became endemic to middle-class men, particularly those in the professions, who had the most to lose in terms of social status. The need to avoid the risks of effeminacy as a signifier of same-sex desire accelerated the circulation of other homosexual subjectivities between classes. Some homosexuals, as Chauncey observes, "created a place in middle-class culture by constructing a persona of highly mannered—and ambiguous—sophistication," which was based on the emulation of the English aristocratic style of connoisseurship and extreme refinement.[37] Oscar Wilde is, per-haps, the most prominent example of this style, which could ob-scure and dismiss antihomosexual attacks with the charge of philistinism.

Carpenter's alienation from the middle class and the ministry was not a direct result of his homosexuality. Carpenter, it seems, was aware of his homosexuality from an early age; he writes, "from the first, my feeling, physically, towards the female sex was one of in-difference, and later on . . . positive repulsion."[38] Meanwhile, from the "age of eight or nine," Carpenter claims, he "felt a friendly attraction" toward his own sex, which later developed into a "pas-sionate sense of love."[39] Homosexuality was not perceived by Car-penter at first as an impediment to middle-class status. He was, perhaps, justified in this perception, because his near contemporary John Addington Symonds (1840–1893) managed to integrate nu-merous homosexual relationships into a conventionally procreative marriage. Moreover, Symonds's extramarital relationships were al-most exclusively with younger working-class men, but these acts of sexual class transgression do not seem to have alienated Symonds from his class at all; in fact, they seem to have cultivated in him a sense of aristocratic patronage. Symonds referred to long-term lover Angelo Fusato as "My magnificent Venetian gondolier & manservant."[40] As Eve Sedgwick observes, Symonds's homosexual relationships were based on "noblesse oblige" and "condescension"; they were "not structurally threatening to the class system as he experienced it."[41] In his youth, Carpenter seems to have adopted this aristocratic pose; he claims to have chosen Trinity Hall at Cambridge in 1864, for example, because it was "a *gentlemanly* college."[42] Photographs of Carpenter as a somewhat dandified young man reinforce this impression.

After Carpenter's conversion to socialism in the 1870s, he became as repelled by those who seem "glib or refined" as he was by fairies. "Anything effeminate in a man," Carpenter writes, "or anything of the cheap intellectual style, repels me very decisively."[43] Nevertheless, it is problematic to take Carpenter's statements about his sexual identity and preferences as absolute, for the qualities of Carpenter's personae and the objects of his desire were continually renegotiated over time and in different contexts. Broadly defined, the evolution of Carpenter's masculinities reflects a process in which the more feminized models of homosexual masculinity coincided with the emergence of their own opposite, which, for socialists like Carpenter, intersected with an increasing sentimentalization of the working classes as somehow more "authentic," closer to human nature, and more masculine than the overly civilized middle-classes.

According to Peter Stearns, working-class men seemed to have "a clearer, more elementary notion of what manhood was."[44] A belief emerged among many intellectuals in the late-nineteenth century that the middle class and its desire for "respectability" had confined sexual acts to the bedrooms of the procreative, married, heterosexual couple, and had abandoned the ancient sexual freedom of the ordinary folk. Sex became a hushed matter, and physical needs were suppressed with dire psychological consequences. The working classes had somehow escaped the excesses of sexual repression endemic to the bourgeoisie; they represented a more primitive state of sexual openness. Sexual expression was not codified into normal and deviant; men, women, and children could wink and laugh knowingly about sex, which was not obsessively concealed. Even "homosexuality," though unnamed, was expressed in the rough play and labor of the men, whose often exposed bodies, muscular from the habit of honest toil, were free to sing, dance, and carouse with each other. Their very being seemed a rebuke to the

MAYALL PHOTO.   BRIGHTON

**Edward Carpenter in his late twenties. Carpenter Collection photographs 8/6,
courtesy of Sheffield City Council.**

pale, starched-collar effeminacy of their domesticated middle-class brethren.

This somewhat impressionistic image of class difference is reflective of a broadly based sense of social alienation rather than substantial differences in values between classes.[45] As Michael Mason observes, even in the first half of the nineteenth century there was a persistent "drive to working-class sexual respectability."[46] Nevertheless, Carpenter's rejection of middle-class culture seems to have resulted from a desire to seek a "cure" for the hypocrisies of civilized life, "the insuperable *feeling* of falsity and dislocation," rather than simply from his homosexuality.[47] Carpenter's break with the ministry in 1874 was, in part, precipitated by being told that " 'religious doctrinal is all such tomfoolery . . . it doesn't matter whether you say you believe in it, or whether you say you don't.' "[48] Carpenter wished "To feel downwards and downwards through this wretched maze of shams for the solid ground—to come close to the Earth itself and those that live in direct contact with it."[49] Whitman may have given Carpenter a "ground for the love of men," but it was the poet's apparent frankness that attracted him most; Whitman, Carpenter writes, "made men to be not ashamed of the noblest instinct of their nature."[50] Carpenter was unable to integrate his changing beliefs with his profession; consequently, he abandoned his ministerial position at Cambridge and began a correspondence with Whitman, sending him a manifesto that clearly equates the middle class with effeminate artificiality and the working class with masculine authenticity:

> There is no hope, almost none, from English respectability. The Church is effete . . . I was in orders; but I have given that up—utterly. It was no good. Nor does the University do: there is nothing vital in it. Now I am going away to lecture to working men and women in the North. They at least desire to lay hold of something with a real grasp. [51]

Posing as a missionary among "the mass of the people and the manual workers," Carpenter declared to Whitman, "my work is to carry on what you have begun. You have opened the way: my only desire is to go onward with it."[52]

Carpenter's evolving construction of a masculine homosexual identity suggests that a driving impulse of social progressivism among middle-class men in the late-Victorian era was sexual desire for other men. By avoiding the stereotype of homosexual gender transgression the middle-class male who sought masculine sexual partners among the working classes could engage in homosexual

activity without as great a risk to his class status. Many homosexuals, including Carpenter, came to believe that their desires for men
need not make them effeminate; rather, as Chauncey observes, "it
was more *masculine* than love for women." "Walt Whitman,"
Chauncey continues, "was heralded as a prophetic spokesman by
many such men." [53]

IV

Nearly a decade before Carpenter's visit to Camden in 1877, he
was a student at Cambridge University struggling to reconcile his
own forbidden same-sex desires with the emerging medical and
legal categorization of the "homosexual" as an invert or a pervert.
In the summer of 1868 or 1869 one of the Fellows of Trinity Hall
gave him a blue-colored book and asked him, "Carpenter, what do
you think of this?"[54] It was the first English edition of Whitman's
Leaves (1868), edited by William Michael Rossetti, and it soon attracted a growing body of young English men who found in Whitman's poetry a language that enabled them to construct a
transnational, imaginary community as "comrades," or members of
a "fellowship." In contrast with the effeminate constructions of
male same-sex desire, Whitman's *Leaves* seemed to offer a masculinity that included same-sex affections that did not seem effeminate or immoral:

> A glimpse through an interstice caught,
> Of a crowd of workmen and drivers in a bar-room around
>   the stove late of a winter night, and I unremark'd
>   seated in a corner,
> Of a youth who loves me and whom I love, silently
>   approaching and seating himself near, that he may
>   hold me by the hand,
> A long while amid the noises of coming and going, of
>   drinking and oath and smutty jest,
> There we two, content, happy in being together,
>   speaking little, perhaps not a word. [55]

Poems like "A Glimpse," in the "Calamus" section of *Leaves*, presented working-class social relations in the United States as less
structured and more sexually permissive than the hierarchial, reserved relations of middle-class men in England. Readable as neither heterosexual nor homosexual, to Carpenter Whitman seemed a
harbinger of "Love's Coming-of-Age"; he possessed a fluid mas-

culinity that seemed to dissolve the socially constructed boundaries of class and gender, placing him outside the disciplinary power of categorization. The poet of *Leaves* declares that he will "accept nothing which all cannot have their counterpart of on the same terms" and asks provocatively, "What is a man anyhow?"[56] Whitman's declarations and questions were always ambiguous, but he suggested a new integration of mind and body, an authenticity of experience that resonated on so many levels that they affected Carpenter with the force of a religious conversion. After his first reading of Whitman Carpenter claims, "a profound change set in within me."[57] Whitman had "spoken the word which is on the lips of God," permitting Carpenter, the former minister, to "see the new, open, life which is to come."[58]

Whitman's writings, particularly his "Calamus" poems, first published in 1860–61, may be considered an example of a means by which working-class discourses of same-sex desire opened up new social spaces in which men like Carpenter could enact alternative subjectivities that avoided the elitism of the aristocratic style and eluded the classificatory discipline suffered by the fairy. Carpenter's exposure to Whitman's conception of American working-class "comradeship" facilitated his shift from the artificiality of sexual relationships with men of his own social standing to the perceived authenticity of relationships with English working-class men. "You hardly know, I think, in America," Carpenter says in his first letter to Whitman in 1874, "what the relief is here to turn from the languid inanity of the well-fed to the clean hard lines of the workman's face."[59] Although Whitman's vision of working-class comradeship was not the only alternative discourse in circulation, it offered a masculinity that could include same-sex contact but nonetheless avoided the effeminacy of the working-class fairy and the decadent immorality of the aristocratic homosexual.

Carpenter did not turn to Whitman only for his apparent celebration of same-sex relationships. According to Whitman, "the special meaning of the *Calamus* cluster of LEAVES OF GRASS . . . mainly resides in its Political significance."[60] But what political role could be played by those whose activities placed them outside the primary structural element of a capitalist society, heterosexual marriage? Could men who took pleasure in nonprocreative homosexual activities—who understood the fluidity of social identity constructions—restore the authenticity of pre-capitalist social relations? For Carpenter, among others, Whitman seemed to provide an overwhelmingly affirmative answer:

I will make the most splendid race the sun ever shone
        upon,
I will make divine magnetic lands,
    With the love of comrades,
    With the life-long love of comrades.[61]

Whitman uses "comradeship" as a term to describe the complex interplay of physical and emotional relations between men ranging from the homosocial to the homosexual, "the beautiful and sane affection of man for man."[62] "Comradeship," he writes, provides "the counterbalance and offset of our materialistic and vulgar American democracy."[63] Whitman implies that the revolutionary potential of comradeship is characteristic of the free, sexually ambiguous relations of working-class men, who, in contrast to middle-class men, are nearer to material reality and, by implication, unashamedly expressive of their physical desires:

I am enamour'd of growing out-doors,
Of men that live among cattle or taste of the ocean or
    woods,
Of the builders and steerers of ships and the wielders
    of axes and mauls, and the drivers of horses,
I can eat and sleep with them week in and week out.[64]

As portrayed by Whitman, the American ambiguity of class boundaries coincided with the ambiguity of sexual relations. Carpenter describes Whitman's "love" as "piercing through the layers and folds of caste, through differences of race, climate, character, occupation, despising distances of space and time."[65]

Whitman's depiction of the freedom of masculine relations among the American working classes had divergent implications for his English readers. On the one hand, Whitman seems to justify middle-class sexual "slumming," which implies the inferiority of the working-class partner and is based on a model of aristocratic patronage. As Eve Sedgwick observes, Whitman's poetry and his intimate relationships with young, working-class men seem to "sacralize something like the English homosexual system whereby bourgeois men had sexual contacts only with virile working-class youths."[66] On the other hand, Whitman's blurring of the boundaries of gender and class seems to use sexual contact to facilitate social revolution. It was Whitman's "fervid adhesiveness," according to Carpenter, that would draw "members of the different classes together."[67] Such relationships would not necessarily be based on the subordination of the working-class partner. Carpenter describes his ideal lover as sexually dominant, "a powerful, strongly built man, of my own age or rather younger—preferably of the working class."[68] Correspondingly, in his long, Whitmanesque poem, "Towards Democracy," Carpenter subordinates himself to a series of working-class male partners whose labor is indistinguishable from the sexual domination of the poet:

> The ploughman shall turn me up with his ploughshare
>   among the roots of the twitch in the sweet-
>   smelling furrow;
> The potter shall mould me, running his finger along my
>   whirling edge (we will be faithful to one another, he and I);
> The bricklayer shall lay me; he shall tap me into place with the handle
>   of his trowel. [69]

Ideally, Whitman inspired cross-class contacts that were not predicated on exploitation but on equal partnership, and possibly the physical subordination of the middle-class partner to the more masculine working-class youth, thus inverting the social order of capitalism.[70]

Whitman's influence was not limited to Carpenter's writings; the semiotics of Whitman's bodily self-presentation also affected Carpenter, whose personal style seemingly became an expression of political and sexual radicalism. "[S]omewhere in the early 'eighties," Carpenter writes, "*I gave my dress clothes away*, I did so without misgiving and without fear that I should need them again."[71] Carpenter seems to have adapted Whitman's style; his clothing became more casual, he wore broad-brimmed hats, and his moustache was replaced by a full beard. Although educated and affluent, Carpenter became, at least in appearance, "one of the roughs," full of Whitmanian "nonchalance," basing his appearance on the defiant workman-poet of the frontispiece of the 1855 *Leaves*.[72]

V

"One of the pathetic things of the Socialist movement," Carpenter complains, "is the way in which it has caused not a few people of upper class birth and training to try and leave their own ranks and join those of the workers." Most such men, Carpenter writes, are "more or less pitied or ridiculed by both classes."[73] Perhaps there is a redeeming hint of self-reflexive irony in Carpenter's ob-

Edward Carpenter at age 43 in 1887. Carpenter Collection photographs 8/24, courtesy of Sheffield City Council.

servation, because he never fully succeeded in extricating himself from the discourses of his upbringing. Although Whitman seemed to give political legitimacy to the activity, Carpenter's turn to working-class men for sexual partners was not predicated simply on socialist politics. In addition to their reputation for masculinity and physical prowess, there were social and economic reasons why working-class men were sexually attractive to middle-class men like Carpenter.

Chauncey presents evidence to suggest that "straight-acting" working-class men were more likely to accept homosexual propositions than middle-class men.[74] On the one hand, this suggests a greater tolerance for sexual variation; the prohibition of all same-sex acts that had become pervasive among the middle-class had not yet permeated working-class attitudes. Working-class men could engage in sexual acts with men without losing status provided they assumed the dominant or masculine role. The availability of working-class men also suggests a greater need among them for patronage and protection. There seems to be a direct correlation between poverty and the receptiveness to homosexual advances; the most common group to accept them, Chauncey observes, was "Common day laborers."[75]

This does not imply that it is simply a matter of sexual exploitation of the poor by the more affluent. A lack of secure income and propertylessness made heterosexual relationships unavailable for many working-class men. "A propertyless man," according to Stearns, was "prevented usually from marriage, from normal sexuality."[76] For sailors, day-laborers, prisoners, and other men at the bottom of the labor system, a sexual relationship was often most feasible with another man, preferably a wealthier one who, because he possessed an income of his own, need not be concerned with the social status of his sex partners. The relationship of Carpenter and George Merrill, his partner of many years, suggests that homosexual bonds across class lines had the potential to be mutually beneficial and democratic; however, the economic inequality of the relationship seems to have provoked in Carpenter the emergence of supposedly rejected discourses of paternalism, patronage, and slumming.

Although theoretically classless, life at Millthorpe, Carpenter's farm, was highly stratified. Merrill was twenty years younger than Carpenter and his social inferior; Carpenter describes him as "Bred in the slums quite below civilization."[77] "I knew of course that George had an instinctive genius for housework," Carpenter writes, "and that in all probability he would keep house better than most

John Johnston on left, Carpenter on right, and George Merrill standing. Carpenter Collection photographs 8/53, courtesy of Sheffield City Council.

women would."[78] Described by Edith Ellis as Carpenter's "facto-tum and friend in one," Merrill assumed the housekeeping func-tions at Millthorpe and permitted Carpenter the leisure to pursue his writing and lecturing, much as Whitman's later comrades had done for him.[79] Carpenter's patronage of young, uneducated, working-class men like Merrill while beneficial in many respects to both partners, frequently echoed the discourses of bourgeois marriage and the aristocratic homosexual system that Carpenter claimed to oppose. Merrill was always encouraged to regard Carpenter as both husband and father, and surviving images of Merrill and Carpenter reinforce this impression of inequality. As such, Carpenter's *masculinities*—even after committing himself to socialism and homosexuality—both resisted and complied with the dominant models.

NOTES

1. Havelock Ellis, *My Life* (London: Heinemann, 1940), 163.
2. Gilbert Beith, *Edward Carpenter: In Appreciation* (1931; reprint, New York: Haskell House, 1973), 81, 15.
3. Chushichi Tsuzuki, *Edward Carpenter 1844–1829, Prophet of Human Fellowship* (Cambridge: Cambridge University Press, 1980), 2.
4. Edward Carpenter, *Selected Writings*, vol. 1, *Sex*, ed. Noel Grieg (London: Gay Men's Press, 1984), 289; and Horace Traubel, ed., *With Walt Whitman in Camden*, vol. 1 (Boston: Small, Maynard, 1906), 160.
5. Walt Whitman, *Leaves of Grass, Comprehensive Reader's Edition*, ed. Harold W. Blodgett and Sculley Bradley (New York: New York University Press, 1965), 52; see also Edward Carpenter, *Days With Walt Whitman* (London: George Allen, 1906), 5.
6. Carpenter, *Days*, 3–4.
7. Ibid., 4.
8. Ibid., 5–6.
9. Ibid., 7; Clara Barrus, *Whitman and Burroughs: Comrades* (Boston: Houghton Mifflin, 1931), 339.
10. Carpenter, *Days*, 8.
11. Ibid.
12. Ibid., 8–9.
13. Ibid., 11.
14. Ibid., 15–16.
15. Ibid., 14.
16. Ibid., 31.
17. Ibid., 7.
18. Randall Waldron, "Whitman as the Nazarene: An Unpublished Drawing," *Walt Whitman Quarterly Review* 7, no. 4 (1990): 192.
19. The relationship between Carpenter and Whitman was certainly physical on some level; whether it was sexual or not is unclear. According to Charley Shively, Whitman and Carpenter had sex during this visit, but there is little evidence to prove this assertion. Shively, ed., *Calamus Lovers: Walt Whitman's Working-Class*

Camerados (San Francisco: Gay Sunshine Press, 1987), 146. Carpenter says he left Whitman with "real reluctance" after falling under "the added force of bodily presence" and admired that "wonderful genius of his for human affection and love" (*Days with Walt Whitman*, 32). Whitman later said that Carpenter "is ardently my friend—ardently" (Traubel 1 : 104).

20. Michel Foucault, *The History Of Sexuality. Volume 1: An Introduction*, trans. Robert Hurley (New York: Pantheon, 1978), 43.

21. E. Anthony Rotundo, *American Manhood; Transformations in Masculinity from the Revolution to the Modern Era* (New York: Basic Books, 1993), 276.

22. W. C. Rivers, *Walt Whitman's Anomaly* (London: George Allen, 1913), 20–22.

23. Ibid., 22–23.

24. Joseph Bristow, *Effeminate England: Homoerotic Writing After 1885* (New York: Columbia University Press, 1995), 2.

25. Foucault, *History of Sexuality*, 1 : 101.

26. Edward Carpenter, *Towards Democracy* (London: Swan Sonnenschein, 1905), 410.

27. Edward Carpenter, *An Unknown People* (London: n. p., 1897), 13.

28. Ibid., 9.

29. Edward Carpenter, *My Days and Dreams: Being Autobiographical Notes* (London: Allen & Unwin, 1916), 98.

30. Carpenter, *Towards Democracy*, 411. Carpenter implies that Jesus (as well as Whitman who resembled him to Carpenter) was a Uranian.

31. Sheila Rowbotham and Jeffrey Weeks, *Socialism and the New Life: The Personal and Sexual Politics of Edward Carpenter and Havelock Ellis* (London: Pluto Press, 1977), 111.

32. Carpenter, *Selected Writings*, 1 : 237.

33. George Chauncey, *Gay New York: Gender, Urban Culture, and the Making of the Gay Male World, 1890–1940* (New York: Harper, 1994), 27.

34. Carpenter, *An Unknown People*, 23.

35. Chauncey, 57.

36. Carpenter, *An Unknown People*, 21.

37. Chauncey, 106.

38. Carpenter, *Selected Writings*, 1 : 290.

39. Ibid., 1 : 289.

40. John Addington Symonds, *The Letters of John Addington Symonds*, 3 vols., ed. Herbert Shueller and Robert Peters (Detroit: Wayne State University Press, 1969), 3 : 815.

41. Eve Kosofsky Sedgwick, *Between Men: English Literature and Male Homosocial Desire* (New York: Columbia University Press, 1985), 210.

42. Carpenter, *My Days*, 46.

43. Carpenter, *Selected Writings*, 1 : 290.

44. Peter N. Stearns, *Be A Man!: Males in Modern Society*, 2d ed. (New York and London: Holmes & Meier, 1990), 81.

45. See T. J. Jackson Lears, *No Place of Grace: Antimodernism and the Transformation of American Culture, 1880–1920* (New York: Pantheon Books, 1981).

46. Michael Mason, *The Making of Victorian Sexuality* (New York: Oxford University Press, 1994), 139.

47. Carpenter, *My Days*, 58.

48. Ibid., 74.

49. Carpenter, *Towards Democracy*, 28.

50. Traubel, 1 : 160.
51. Ibid.
52. Carpenter, *My Days*, 77; and Traubel 3 : 416.
53. Chauncey, 105.
54. Carpenter, *My Days*, 64.
55. Whitman, *Leaves*, 131–32.
56. Ibid., 52, 47.
57. Carpenter, *My Days*, 64.
58. Traubel, 1 : 159.
59. Ibid., 1 : 160.
60. Whitman, *Leaves*, 751.
61. Ibid., 117.
62. Ibid., 751.
63. Walt Whitman, *Prose Works 1892*, 2 vols., ed. Floyd Stovall (New York University Press, 1963–64), 2 : 414.
64. Whitman, *Leaves*, 41.
65. Carpenter, *My Days*, 58.
66. Sedgwick, 204.
67. Edward Carpenter, *Homogenic Love* (London: Redundancy Press, n. d.), 24.
68. Carpenter, *Selected Writings*, 1 : 290.
69. Carpenter, *Towards Democracy*, 73.
70. "The thick-thighed hot coarse-fleshed young bricklayer with the strap round his waist" emerges more than once in *Towards Democracy* (69).
71. Carpenter, *My Days*, 149.
72. Whitman, *Leaves*, 709.
73. Carpenter, *My Days*, 170.
74. Chauncey, 108.
75. Ibid., 118.
76. Stearns, 81.
77. Carpenter, *My Days*, 159.
78. Ibid., 161.
79. Edith Ellis, *Personal Impressions of Edward Carpenter* (Berkeley Heights, NJ: Free Spirit Press, 1922), 11.

The Impossibility of Seduction in James's *Roderick Hudson* and *The Tragic Muse*

> If on a rare occasion one of these couples might be divided, so,
> by as uncommon a chance, the other might be joined; the only
> difference being in the gravity of the violated law. For which
> pair was the betrayal greatest?
>
> —Henry James, *The Sacred Fount*

How COULD HENRY JAMES REPRESENT INDIVIDUALITY IN NOVELS that stress his characters' shared traits? Applying this question to James's rather "stolid" novel *The Tragic Muse* (1889; 1890) highlights two related problems. According to its narrator, the novel's characters fail to resolve "the opposition of [their] interest and desire"; in "a torment of unrest" they confront "the impossibility of being consistent."[1] When James tried to explain these problems in his "Preface to *The Tragic Muse*," he confirmed that the novel inadvertently raises profound questions about the nature and stability of character. The initial object of James's complaint is Miriam Rooth; allegedly, her "theatrical" personality is inauthentic. However, James raises an important, if less severe, charge against masculinity that is only partly veiled by his preoccupation with femininity's ability to ensnare its masculine admirers.

This essay interprets the tension between individuality and desire in *The Tragic Muse*. It asks why James conflates Miriam's "theatrical" personality with femininity, and why the novel's aesthetic failure exceeds James's difficulties with his characters' credibility and sexuality.[2] I contend that James's conventional association of femininity with instability is only the most symptomatic "problem" of this novel; the narrative confronts another challenge in trying to unify its central "object," for its attention shifts from the vagaries of a female character (Miriam Rooth) to the thoughts and desires of her closest male friend (Gabriel Nash). I address the consequence of this shift by assessing the widespread gap between desire and

299

meaning in fin-de-siècle British literature. Arguing that James finally was unable to distinguish among artistry, masquerade, and interpersonal deceit, I'll approach the meaning of sexual dissimulation in his fiction in terms of the significance his narratives attach to physical desire and same-gender intimacy.

By keeping these textual and contextual questions in play and avoiding the assumption that homosexual desire is simply the "truth" of *The Tragic Muse*—or that its protagonists, Nick Dormer and Gabriel Nash, would have been lovers had James had the courage to write otherwise—I examine the pressure shaping this novel's ending and the reason Nash's disappearance at the end of the novel can't rescind its conflicting economies of desire or "correct" its oscillation between female and male desires. Contrary to James's claim that the novel's difficulties stem from its theatricality, I approach *The Tragic Muse* with the premise that failure is its strongest weakness; failure indicates both the novel's inconsistency about sexual difference and its turbulent symbolization of masculinity.

Before addressing the novel's convoluted plot and James's rueful misgivings about its structure, let me make clear my proposition about failure, which recurs throughout James's fiction as a pressing concern. It is now commonplace to argue that James focuses on individual and social duplicity and superficiality; that his heroines (such as Miriam Rooth) often betray a scandalous absence of "deep substance." These heroines invest so much energy in constructing their appearance and sustaining illusions that many relationships collapse when their lovers realize that these women's characters are merely the result of their artful manipulation of roles. But despite the urgency informing this realization—and in novels such as *The Bostonians* (1885–86) and *The Awkward Age* (1899), puncturing feminine "masquerade" seems close to a masculine imperative— the character of each woman endures. What is redefined in interesting ways is the idealizing consciousness that formerly passed between subjects as an elaborate projection of intrigue and fascination.[3] As Sharon Cameron brilliantly suggests, James struggled to reorient this consciousness, rendering it less "false" by circumscribing his characters' intentions.[4] This reorientation produces startling results that, as James sometimes concedes, form an unwanted union of interests and a traumatic merging of identities. The drive informing James's urgent bid for his characters' ontological integrity is thus important; it highlights a crisis of proximity among his male characters.

Although James and his male protagonists usually indict femininity for "betraying" the limits of personality, the drama of differentiation and stability that James explores isn't unique to his fiction; the same charge against women can be found in many turn-of-the-century texts. Consider the undoing of Undine Spragg in Edith Wharton's *The Custom of the Country* (1913), Lena's alleged manipulation of Axel Heyst and Schomberg in Joseph Conrad's *Victory* (1915), and Mildred Rogers's egregious mistreatment of Philip Carey in W. Somerset Maugham's *Of Human Bondage* (1915). Yet although James does examine the "character" of women in *The Tragic Muse* (1889; 1890) and *Roderick Hudson* (1874; 1875), his indictment is not of women alone. He similarly accuses his male protagonists in these novels.

To advance this proposition, let me turn briefly to a contemporaneous text—Oscar Wilde's *The Picture of Dorian Gray* (1890, revised 1891). In Wilde's novel, the "character" and consistency of femininity and masculinity are discussed and finally elided. Connecting James's and Wilde's texts is also worthwhile because Wilde's debt to *The Tragic Muse* is often unrecognized, and because the actress in Wilde's book, Sibyl Vane, proves a disappointment to Dorian Gray when her role points too obviously to her impoverished identity; this occurs, significantly, when she falls in love with Dorian. His complaint about Sibyl's identity assumes in part that Dorian and the reader notice when Sibyl ceases to act—the moment, that is, when her character appears most "true." Attention to such issues downplays the emphasis Wilde placed on the art of successfully exchanging roles. The point is that Sibyl's deficient acting, in her move from offstage to onstage performances, renders the transition apparent; the broken illusion is what galls Dorian. As the narrator of *Dorian Gray* remarks, "[T]he staginess of her acting was unbearable, and grew worse as she went on. Her gestures became absurdly artificial. She over-emphasized everything that she had to say. . . . It was simply bad art. She was a complete failure."[5] Although Dorian's proficient offstage acting goes by another name and generates different crises about credibility and passing, the end of Wilde's novel indicates that masculinity possesses an equal, or greater, capacity for dissimulation. We can attribute this capacity, in part, to masculinity's ability to draw on a greater number of social roles (if not desires), and to the other characters' ignorance of Dorian's disguise; they assume that his gender signifies ontological integrity and that his appearance denotes sincerity and youth.

In James's "baggy" and less elegant novel, *The Tragic Muse*— which the *Atlantic Monthly* serialized throughout 1889, one year before *Dorian Gray* first appeared in *Lippincott's Monthly Magazine*—a similar drama about integrity arises when the narrative's bid to establish the true character of Miriam Rooth merges with a related question about the intentions of her male entourage: Peter Sherringham, Basil Dashwood, Nick Dormer, and Gabriel Nash. Adopting the perspective of Peter Sherringham, Miriam's suitor, the first half of the novel tries in vain to determine what Miriam's character would be if she left the theater and stopped acting; that is, if she endorsed Sherringham's career as a diplomat by becoming his wife (a role, apparently, in which women can be guileless). *The Tragic Muse* illustrates Sherringham's dilemma about his future by juxtaposing his interest in Miriam Rooth with Nick Dormer's comparable interest in Gabriel Nash—a man who acts in many ways, and whose character ultimately proves more elusive.[6] The narrative's oscillation between Sherringham and Dormer, its two "centres of consciousness," initially seems deliberate. However, as James later acknowledged, the novel's focus shifts disproportionately onto the ties binding the two men, which generates a discussion about intimacy that James seemed unwilling—but later compelled—to pursue in the book. Following the logic of this novel, I'll begin with Sherringham's investigation of Miriam to accentuate the subsidiary relationship between Dormer and Nash. This second relationship, as James ruefully acknowledged, almost succeeds in displacing the novel's precarious interest in heterosexuality.

Exhibiting the anxious pursuit of self-knowledge and the narcissism characterizing many love relations in James's short stories (for instance, "The Beast in the Jungle" [1903] and "The Jolly Corner" [1908]), Peter Sherringham tries in vain to discover the "true" personality of Miriam Rooth in order to explain *his* fascination. Sherringham's realization that Miriam never ceases to "act"—that her beauty is "elastic," her character "plastic," and her entire personality an elaborate "embroidery"—is a joyous epiphany to him because it resolves her enigma: She is nothing *more* than an enigma.[7] This limits her appeal and his transference because Sherringham has invested financially and emotionally in her career: he thought he had wanted her acting to improve. When Miriam later displaces this support (she no longer needs to hide her "act"), Sherringham's courtship of her wavers between annoyance at her role-playing and admiration of her performance. But he is appalled by the ease with which she shifts from one role to another: "she was already in a few weeks an actress who could act even at not acting."[8] As Miriam becomes more adept at managing her career, her ambition becomes voracious while her fame partly hides her lack of "character" and "integrity."[9] Sherringham later decides that Miriam has neither quality; her subjectivity consists of parts and roles whose center is fundamentally hollow.

Considering James's overall remarks about this situation, to which I'll soon turn, Sherringham's bid to expose Miriam's "fraudulence" partly displaces his own identity crisis and those of other male characters.[10] Sherringham reacts cynically to Miriam's "exposure" by rationalizing his interest as a test. Despite his repeated disavowals, however, Sherringham confronts similar, if less intense, questions about his own psychic instability and professional impermanence. The narrator answers some of these questions by claiming that men's doubts about their careers shouldn't trouble their identities: Sherringham is merely torn between assisting Miriam and promoting his own career by taking another, more "amenable" woman—Biddy—to the colonies. His problem is thus existential and momentary; it isn't the kind of crisis that threatens many of James's women, whose pleasure hinges on finding vicarious fulfillment in their spouses and whose professional and "private" identities are entirely overdetermined. In this respect, Miriam chooses between the relative stability of marriage and the likely (and, for James, moral) annihilation of her "character" in a series of transient acts. *The Tragic Muse* implies that men are too stable to experience such conflict; nevertheless, Sherringham's claims of autonomy are implausible and disingenuous. As the narrator declares, "Poor Sherringham . . . was much troubled these last days; he was ravaged by contending passions; he paid, every hour, in a torment of unrest, for what was false in his position, the impossibility of being consistent, the opposition of interest and desire."[11]

The Tragic Muse repeatedly makes and withdraws the suggestion that its male and female characters face comparable ontological crises. Without overlooking the difference in magnitude between Sherringham's and Miriam's dilemmas, I claim that the narrative represents Miriam as the most extreme example of a crisis that hinges, for women and men, on exactly this "impossibility of being consistent, the opposition of interest and desire." In this way, the novel's account of men's impossible consistency generates questions about the conflicts determining "interest and desire" among Sherringham, Dashwood, Dormer, and Nash; indeed, the structure of *The Tragic Muse* renders inevitable this comparison among the men.

The novel implies that Sherringham identifies in Miriam's subjectivity the indeterminacy he finds deplorable in himself. Thus the narrator observes that "Sherringham's reserve might by the ill-natured have been termed dissimulation,"[12] though this remark is ap-

parently redeemed several pages later by Sherringham's joke:
" 'Well, after all I'm not an actor myself.' "[13] Miriam responds
adroitly, " 'You might be one if you were serious.' "[14] It seems that
Sherringham's laughter negates an embarrassing contiguity between his and Miriam's "dissimulation[s]." The joke masks his
own unstated problems: If he is flippant about his professional rigidity, she is paradoxically rigid about her ontological "elastic[ity]."[15]

The "opposition between interest and desire" in Sherringham
proves easy to "resolve": the women he pursues (Miriam and
Biddy) "correspond" exactly to specific vocations (Miriam to the
theater, Biddy to his career as a diplomat); his choice of one or the
other will thwart his professional goal or satisfy it. However, the
same conflict is hopelessly confused for the novel's other "centre of
consciousness," Nick Dormer. The relations among Sherringham,
Dormer, and their mediating "object" (initially Miriam, later Gabriel Nash) indicate *The Tragic Muse*'s intent to unify its characters' interests and desires, despite their opposition. As I argued
earlier, the narrative's shift from Sherringham's to Nick Dormer's
point of view allows it to substitute the latter's insoluble existential
dilemma (Nick can't decide whom he wants or what he wishes to
be) for the former's problem of courtship: by rejecting Miriam and
choosing Biddy, Sherringham "resolves" one half of the novel.

The narrative repeatedly highlights the similarity between Sherringham's and Dormer's dilemmas before substituting the latter for
the former. This comparison requires a mediator to offset the novel's preoccupation with masculine similarity. We might consider
this preoccupation an effect of James's concern to maintain individual consistency, for consistency raises questions about resemblance
and difference. How then can identities in this novel remain discrete
and reliable? Invariably, Miriam Rooth is a symptom of this problem. At one point the narrator describes her as "a beautiful, actual,
fictive, impossible young woman, of a past age and undiscoverable
country, who spoke in blank verse and overflowed with metaphor."[16] Poorly executed, the role Miriam assumes "bleeds" into
other identificatory possibilities. By displaying excessive artistry,
her performance ruins the fragile link that James and his characters
try hopelessly to sustain between a role and the illusion it creates.[17]

If we extend this notion of roles "overflow[ing] with metaphor"
to all forms of illusion and characterization in *The Tragic Muse*,
"character" seems unable to prevent the condensed weight of metaphor from dissipating into erratic metonymy: "something mon-
strously definite kept surging out."[18] Indeed, the problem of

relation is so extensive in this novel that any attempt to control it is liable to produce volatile effects. We've already seen this propensity in Miriam Rooth, and we'll encounter it again in the figure of Gabriel Nash. Let us temporarily suspend this account of *The Tragic Muse*'s overproduction of meaning, however, and compare this novel with an earlier one by James that presents similar identificatory and sexual dilemmas: *Roderick Hudson*.

In his preface to *Roderick Hudson*, James acknowledges that his characters' identities threaten to merge: "[R]elations stop nowhere, and the exquisite problem of the artist is eternally but to draw, by a geometry of his own, the circle within which they shall happily *appear* to do so."[19] James later conceded that he couldn't resolve this "perpetual predicament"[20]; it persisted as an aesthetic problem, complicating

the plain moral that a young embroiderer of the canvas of life . . . began to work in terror, fairly, of the vast expanse of that surface, of the boundless number of its distinct perforations for the needle, and of the tendency inherent in his many-coloured flowers and figures to cover and consume as many as possible of the little holes. The development of the flower, of the figure, involved thus an immense counting of holes and a careful selection among them. That would have been, it seemed to him, a brave enough process, were it not the very nature of the holes so to invite, to solicit, to persuade, to practise positively a thousand lures and deceits. The prime effect of so sustained a system, so prepared a surface, is to lead on and on; while the fascination of following resides, by the same token, in the presumability *somewhere* of a convenient, or a visibly-appointed stopping-place.[21]

In the ensuing alignments among characters in *Roderick Hudson*, and in the complex erotic configuration that governs (or seems to govern) relations among men and women, James's "problem" emerges from the lack of an agent capable of securing these relations and of thus preventing a "marriage" between its male protagonists—Roderick Hudson and his mentor and confidant, Rowland Mallet. Only Roderick's violent suicide seems able to foster a reciprocal desire between Rowland and Mary Garland, who mourn the same lost object. Without their shared grief over Roderick's death, the metonymy governing *Roderick Hudson* would impede reciprocity; as the narrator reveals, Rowland "desires" Mary, who desires Roderick, who "desires" Christina Light, who desires, perhaps, to be desired.

I put both men's desire for women in quotation marks because—in addition to these structural displacements, which Freud once called the "aim" of desire, as distinct from the "object" representing it—the novel renders masculine desire inseparable from artistic and ontological deceit.[22] Nothing short of death can prevent the formation of an erotic relation between men in *Roderick Hudson*. The narrative overemphasis on Rowland's improbable attachment to Mary and his jealousy of Roderick for achieving but never clearly returning Mary's interest creates an obsessive, anxious intimacy between Rowland and Roderick. This is a problem for James that exceeds the basic "erotics" of masculine tutelage: Rowland was seduced by Roderick's art when he examined his sculpture. In return, Roderick admitted that the "young Water-drinker," his sculpture, is "thirsty [for] . . . knowledge, pleasure, experience. Anything of that kind!" Roderick's sculpture seems to displace Rowland's palpable interest in Roderick's body and voice—"a soft and not altogether masculine organ."[23] The heterosexual imperative governing Rowland and Mary's marriage, which marks and even scars the end of this novel, seems to obscure Rowland's rivalry with Mary for Roderick; Rowland's conventional (that is, "homosocial") rivalry with Roderick for Mary only partly subsumes his "homosexual" interest in the younger man.

In this narrative of precarious sexual and subjective mastery, James struggles to present the "appearance" of delimiting every relation—a control that the text and its preface subsequently belie.[24] As in other Jamesian narratives—including "The Pupil" (1891), "The Great Good Place" (1900), and *The Ambassadors* (1903)—the "high felicity" of masculine friendship draws here on the discipline of a patron or mentor who oversees the talent and "salvation" of a younger artist.[25] However, in ways that repeat the problem of Miriam's acting in *The Tragic Muse*, these relations of tutelage "overflow" their assigned meanings, creating a metonymic surplus that is either ambiguously erotic in content or diffused by an aesthetic ideal that cancels the opportunity for physical intimacy. As Roderick insists, "The artist performs great feats in a dream. We must not wake him up lest he should lose his balance."[26] The "dream" in this instance conceals a tradition of mentorship already suffused by homo- and ephebephilia: "Rowland took a great fancy to him, to his personal charm and his probable genius. He had an indefinable attraction—the something tender and divine of unspotted, exuberant, confident youth."[27] This "attraction" generates a profound intimacy: "They talked on these occasions of everything conceivable, and had the air of having no secrets from each other. . . . [Roderick's] unfailing impulse to share every emotion and impression with his friend . . . made comradeship a high felicity, and interfused with a deeper amenity the wanderings and contemplations that beguiled their pilgrimage to Rome."[28]

The peripeteia with which *Roderick Hudson* closes is considerably more violent than is Rudyard Kipling's analogous turn in *Kim* (1901), in which Kim's mentor, the Lama, announces his emotional attachment to the young boy, his "beloved," before dying in his arms. James's novel is arguably more violent because Roderick's suicide is the only act that can bring this novel's persistent homo/sexual metonymy to an abrupt halt (even marriage seems to be an inadequate defense against this desire). *The Tragic Muse* may be more daring than either of these texts, however, because its sexual excess creates a bungled ending with an awkward prominence of homosexual desire. Since the narrative has exposed—and all but excised—Miriam's theatricality as a "monstrous" aberration, the figure *necessarily* most contiguous to Miriam is the puzzling Gabriel Nash.

Miriam and Nash share a symbolic function. Yet as several critics have noted, Nash's ability to connect characters renders him more convincing than is Miriam as a narrative "object."[29] Indeed, as James remarked in his preface to *The Tragic Muse*, the novel's conflicting aims derive from the stubborn indeterminacy of its principal object:

> The influence of *The Tragic Muse* was . . . exactly other than what I had all earnestly (if of course privately enough) invoked for it, and I remember well the particular chill, at last, of the sense of my having launched it in a great grey void from which no echo or message whatever would come back. . . . [P]erversely, incurably, the centre of my structure would insist on placing itself *not,* so to speak, in the middle. . . . [T]he terminational terror was none the less certain to break in and my work threaten to masquerade for me as an active figure condemned to the disgrace of legs too short, ever so much too short, for its body. I urge myself to the candid confession that in very few of my productions, to my eye, *has* the organic centre succeeded in getting into proper position.[30]

James's difficulty in stabilizing the center of *The Tragic Muse* suggests that the novel eventually loses its focus; it has at least two protagonists and pursues several themes, including art, politics, drama, and representation. To James, the novel's division between two protagonists signified an "incurab[le]" collapse of order because it allowed another term to masquerade in the position he had designated for "good art"; there's no limit to dissimulation or acting in this novel. James considered *The Tragic Muse* disappointing also because its unruly center defied the position he'd assigned it:

"In several of my compositions this displacement has so succeeded, at the crisis, in defying and resisting me, has appeared so fraught with probable dishonour, that I still turn upon them, in spite of the greater or less [sic] success of final dissimulation, a rueful and wondering eye."[31] James acknowledged that one of his disappointments was Nick Dormer[32]; the other, whose "defiance" relates to his "usurpation" of the novel's implied object (Miriam), appears to have been Gabriel Nash.[33]

Despite Nash's important symbolic function in *The Tragic Muse*, he is curiously not named in the preface to the novel. Nash is "unmanned" by the novel's split between Sherringham and Nick because the novel offers no other path to masculinity. When James refers to his intention to make Miriam the "object" of this novel[34]—and his failure to achieve this end—he signals the vigilance necessary *not* to structure the novel around Nash, apparently admitting the failure and even the effort required to conceal it without alighting on its possible solution. Although he deplores Miriam's duplicity, James himself confronts "the question of artfully, of consummately masking the fault and conferring on the false quantity the brave appearance of the true."[35] The irony of his being compelled to adopt artifice while condemning it in his characters is itself "artfully . . . mask[ed]"; James considers artifice the unhappy consequence of *this* novel, not a problem endemic to all representation.

James's conviction that the aesthetic failure of *The Tragic Muse* derives from the poverty of its supports—"legs . . . ever so much too short, for its body"—suggests that his novel's difficulty lies where its "legs," or protagonists, meet. The site of anxiety and contraction is arguably the novel's distended midriff, for it is here that the text's sublime "body" contains a genital region that James tried alternately to hide and "elevate." Thus the "perverse . . . centre" of his novel has an important function: it demonstrates the weight of sexual meaning that must fall outside the narrative's purview. Nash embodies all the difficulties informing this novel's sexual and marital relations; the narrator observes with uncharacteristic precision that Nash's body is overweight and physically incongruous: "this young man was fair and fat and of the middle stature; he had a round face and a short beard, and on his crown a mere reminiscence of hair. . . . Bridget Dormer, who was quick, estimated him immediately as a gentleman, but a gentleman unlike any other gentleman she had ever seen."[36]

Like Maria Gostrey in *The Ambassadors*, Nash is a *ficelle*, or narrative "thread": he encourages intimacy among others, making clear their intentions without seeming to possess any of his own.[37] In this respect, he is a vanishing mediator for the novel's heterosexual couples. The narrator poorly explains Nash's motives, but he is an important influence on Nick Dormer because he represents a man who lives entirely for art and pleasure—that is, the pleasurable art of appearing artless.

How does this embodiment of masculine pleasure influence the novel's conclusion and engender its author's bitter disappointment? Several critics have noted that the novel's simplicity lies in its allegorical rigidity: Julia Dallow is its "political" representative, while Sherringham stands for diplomacy and Miriam embodies drama.[38] Considering this economy, Nick Dormer is significant because he doesn't choose between the two options before him—politics or painting. As I argued earlier, a character's vocational aim in *The Tragic Muse* determines his choice of object: Sherringham chooses between Miriam/the theater and Biddy/colonial diplomacy. Since Nick faces a comparable choice between politics and painting, James can't give Nash a specific vocation because Nick would then be deciding between a female and male partner (that is, between Julia/politics and Nash/"art"). Although Nick's family pressures him to commit to Julia, his heterosexual complacency grants Nash an influence that verges on seduction. James seems to obviate this problem by assigning Nash an intangible—if no less constitutive— role as Nick's "imagination"; the narrator's suggestion that Nash has an internal influence alleviates some of James's misgivings about Nick's physical intimacy with Nash. Nick is, as it were, already penetrated by this absent presence.

From the start of the novel, when the narrator and Biddy Dormer observe a reunion between Nick and Gabriel that is by Jamesian standards palpably erotic,[39] Nash shapes Nick's interest in aesthetics. Mrs. Dormer later characterizes British aesthetics as effeminate and irresolute—"a horrible insidious foreign disease . . . is eating the healthy core out of English life (dear old English life!)."[40] Indeed, aestheticism represents a counterforce that diminishes the influence of Julia's political and marital ambition for Nick. Mrs. Dormer has reason for concern: Nash's influence on Nick and the legacy of their former friendship at Oxford are so extensive that the "opposition of interest and desire" within Nick seriously jeopardizes his future. Given the burden of these competing demands and his family's panic, it isn't surprising that Nick suffers from indecision. What is surprising is the narrator's inability to name his difficulty: "The explanation . . . consist[ed] . . . of the simple formula that he had at last come to a crisis. Why a crisis—what was it, and why had he not come to it before? The reader shall learn these things in time, if he cares enough for them."[41]

The factors causing this "crisis" remain vague, and the promised explanation never comes. Of course, Nick's "crisis" has certain obvious, identifiable causes: the overbearing demands of his benefactor, Mr. Carteret; the relentless expectations of his mother and those she attributes to his dead father; and Nick's own disinclination to conform. He poignantly summarizes these factors as "my family, my blood, my heredity, my traditions, my promises, my circumstances, my prejudices, my little past, such as it is; my great future, such as it has been supposed it may be."[42] All these factors resurface with Nick's intended marriage to Julia, though he repeatedly confuses affection for Julia with gratitude for her continued professional support. Nash asks bluntly,

> "Are you in love with her?"
> "Not in the least."
> "Well, she is with you—so I perceived."
> "Don't say that," said Nick Dormer, with sudden sternness.[43]

Nash poses this question in a chapter that takes up how the two men might negotiate Nick's marital and professional future: "the more they said the more the unsaid came up."[44] The "unsaid" is ambiguous here, referring either to Nick's marriage as an unspeakable obstacle to their friendship, or to their friendship as an "unsaid" means of averting all other claims to intimacy. Nash implies the second possibility by adopting an antagonistic stance toward Julia, offering to rescue Nick from her: " 'It's her place; she'll put me in,' Nick said. 'Baleful woman! But I'll pull you out!' "[45]

Whatever meaning the narrative attributes to Nick's "salvation" (both men consider Julia's appetite for Nick's success—as Sherringham considered Miriam's—voracious and unappeasable), Nick's uninterest in Julia suggests to his family and friends that he cannot love. As in *The Picture of Dorian Gray*, in which desire and convention are split between incompatible demands, Nick's dilemma produces an acute crisis: " 'I don't know what I am—heaven help me!' [he] broke out . . . 'I'm a freak of nature and a sport of the mocking gods! . . . I'm a wanton variation, an unaccountable monster.' "[46] This assertion of monstrosity draws on the same Gothic trope that Wilde successfully reinvoked in *The Picture of Dorian Gray*. More generally, Gothic fiction often conflates monstrosity and homosexual desire to exaggerate the uncanny shock—and apparent "horror"—of sameness.[47] But though the question of monstrosity surfaced much earlier in *The Tragic Muse*, with Miriam's "elastic" disposition, Nick's claim is particularly significant because it is "unaccountable" and unaccounted for. Despite the narrator's promise to explain it, Nick's problem remains an enigma.[48] The reader can connect Nick's crisis with this novel's conflict between marriage and masculine friendship only by assuming a generic conflict between men's vocations and their unacceptable desires.

Although this novel is concerned with Nick Dormer's relation to marriage, Nick's problem doesn't resurface with much force. When the subject of marriage arises for Gabriel Nash, however—and it does so repeatedly—the narrator is much less cautious: The novel's association of decadence with "irresponsible" pleasure is sufficient to mark Nash as one of James's most persistent bachelors. The narrator also describes Nash as "the mysterious personage," "an anomaly," "a strange man," "Nick's queer comrade," "cheerfully helpless and socially indifferent," "unregenerate . . . the merman wandering free," "a little affected," "this whimsical personage . . . a slippery subject," "the recreant comrade," "romantically allusive," and generally "different."[49] The idea that Nash would ever marry seems not only unlikely, but a source of mirth: "This was a law [of courtship and desire] from which Gabriel Nash was condemned to suffer, if suffering could on any occasion be predicated of Gabriel Nash. His pretension was, in truth, that he had purged his life of such incongruities, though probably he would have admitted that if a sore spot remained the hand of a woman would be sure to touch it."[50] Nash later volunteers, "Oh, I'm never another man . . . I'm more the wrong one than the man himself."[51] The narrator describes Nick and Nash's friendship so soon after this remark that the following statement seems intimately connected to his observation: "one of them [was] as dissimulative in passion as the other was paradoxical in the absence of it."[52]

The narrator consistently declares Nash to be "outside" the novel's circuit of suitors and possible partners; Nash is the overseer of others' relationships. However, since James's fiction never entirely detaches his observers from their surrounding dramas, they become implicated in the scenes they evaluate.[53] The central problem of *The Ambassadors* therefore hinges less on the rescue of Chad Newsome (the principal "object" that Strether must redeem from Europe's vices) than on Strether's vicarious participation in the younger man's passions and follies. While Nash also confirms that James's observers perform a crucial task of detection, Nash's role as narrative *ficelle* and his replacement of Miriam Rooth as the novel's mediating "object" destroy his capacity for detachment. After this substitution, most of the remaining characters represent Nash as a perverse muse with growing influence on Nick. When the two men reminisce about their undergraduate days at Oxford, for example—a university that spawned both aestheticism and the homoerotic underpinnings of Victorian neo-Hellenism in Britain[54]—Nick invokes Nash as " 'very bad company for me, my evil genius; you opened my eyes, you communicated the poison. Since then, little by little, it has been working within me; vaguely, covertly, insensibly at first, but during the last year or two with violence, pertinacity, cruelty. I have taken every antidote in life; but it's no use—I'm stricken. It tears me to pieces, as I may say.' "[55] In other words, by detailing the prehistory of the two men's friendship, the novel slyly invokes homoerotic aspects of the Oxford Movement.

Although much of the novel's melodrama and humor derive from Nick's mock-heroic attempt to rid himself of Nash, we can't discount these remarks as banter. A serious, redemptive expectation underlines this melodrama, which raises pressing questions about Nick's ontology and his unsettled relation to male and female objects. At this juncture the reader may discover—in the "cruelty" of Nash's influence, the impatience of Nick's family, and the agony arising from his indecision—partial reasons for Nick's crisis. One might ask, too, whether "stricken" implies seduced.

I argued earlier that Miriam personifies a split in Sherringham's character that he resolves by breaking off their intimacy. Nick can't resolve his dilemma by comparable action. He circumvents the dilemma by seeing the demand for resolution as a reason for his dual identity: "He was conscious of a double nature; there were two men in him, quite separate, whose leading features had little in common and each of whom insisted on having an independent turn at life."[56] The text later aligns this "double nature" with the public and private division of his character. When Nick decides to run for a seat in Britain's Parliament, he becomes fascinated with employing political rhetoric, which convinces others of an integrity he doesn't possess. He finds he must decide whether to stand for his constituency as their political representative or remain "true" to his own volition and maintain his "private" and creative desire without the symbolic legitimacy of public office: "The difficulty is that I'm two men; it's the strangest thing that ever was. . . . One man wins the seat—but it's the other fellow who sits in it."[57]

The question of Nick's nomination and election to Parliament doesn't resolve his earlier struggle to align every impulse with an acceptable object; it repeats this struggle in an urgent, public form. Although the problem of sexuality seems to fall outside this conflict, the success of Nick's political career still hinges on his dissimulating a "private" self ("He had . . . above all to pretend").[58] This masquerade creates such distress that Nick declines the nomination; were he to take up public office, he would begin a career as a hypocrite. By exposing politics as another form of acting, however, Nick not only indicts the hypocrisy of British (and perhaps all) political representatives, but covertly declares his preference for "the other fellow" whose career lies in painting, and whose constitutive desire is now remarkably *legible*.[59] "The other fellow" refers to aspects of Nick's character he hasn't explored (that is, painting), as well as to Nash, the signifier of his "imagination," who inspires and later displaces this pursuit by making it tangible. Within this field of ambition and partly realized desire, Nash regains some of his former influence by representing Nick's aesthetic fantasies: "There were two voices which told him that all this [marriage and political career] was not really action at all, but only a pusillanimous imitation of it: one of them made itself fitfully audible in the depths of his own spirit and the other spoke, in the equivocal accents of a very crabbed hand, from a letter of four pages by Gabriel Nash."[60] When Nash is later meant to "interpose" for Nick by preventing his fall into marital "perdition" (according to the narrator, Nash "was to have dragged [Nick] in the opposite sense from Mrs. Dallow"), Nash materializes in the place of both of Nick's dissenting "voices," as if to embody Nick's redemption from politics and heterosexuality: "[Nick] had stayed in town to be alone with his imagination, and suddenly, paradoxically, the sense of that result had arrived with Gabriel Nash."[61]

We should note the consequence of substituting Nash for the conventionally feminine muse. The narrator earlier described Nash as an ontological—perhaps sexual—"paradox"; his sudden appearance at this point interrupts conventional behavior, expectations, and marriage. Besides the obvious fact that Nick is inspired—and partly seduced—by this aesthetic embodiment, Nash is provocative because he compels Nick to question all his assumptions and demands. Nash, however, never embodies *more* than a fantasy; as James suggests in the preface to this novel, the removal of Nash's body represents the novel's frantic erasure of homosexual meaning. Nash disturbs the marital arrangements of this novel by intruding, facilitating, and then vanishing. When other characters reflect on Nash's aesthetic and hedonistic pursuits, however, they indicate his enigmatic relation to Nick: "[T]his contemplative genius seemed to take the words out of [Nick's] mouth, to utter for him, better and more completely, *the very things he was on the point of saying.*"⁶²

Given Nash's "paradoxical" status, and the enduringly "tragic" dimension of Nick's muse, Nash seems to embody James's title more completely than Miriam can. At the beginning of the novel, and with considerable irony, Nash describes Miriam as a muse because her performance lacks immanence. However, the narrative can't detach Nash's power to inspire from his ability to perplex. Thus Nash and Miriam are initially related because her "haunting" of Nick resembles Nash's. Sherringham describes Miriam as "an angel" whose properties invoke the ethereal qualities and eventual vanishing of *Gabriel* Nash.⁶³ Later, however, the tragic aspects of James's muse occur more consistently in Nash. Although early in the novel Nick calls Nash "my evil genius" and "the merman wandering free," he later calls him "Mephistopheles," the spirit of seductive evil to whom Faust sold his soul.⁶⁴

The most significant impediments to representing Nash surface when Nick tries to paint him. Although Nick's portrait of Miriam confirms her strength as a muse, Nash proves an unwilling and finally impossible subject. As in such related James texts as "The Madonna of the Future" (1873) and "The Liar" (1888), portraiture seems to frame its subjects' psychic history.⁶⁵ Nick's attempt to paint Nash consequently reveals how little he knows of him. The place where he lives, the people with whom he associates, and the terms of his privacy constitute an enigma that consistently evades representation:

> Nick . . . never caught, from the impenetrable background of [Nash's] life, the least reverberation of flitting or flirting, the smallest aesthetic ululation. . . . [I]t qualified with thinness the mystery he could never wholly dissociate from him, the sense of the transient and occasional, the likeness to vapour or murmuring wind or shifting light. It was for instance *a symbol of this unclassified condition, the lack of all position as a name in well-kept books,* that Nick in point of fact had no idea where he lived.⁶⁶

The narrative adopts metaphors evoking the ethereal (vapor, wind, light) here because a signifier seems incapable of representing Nash; his name designates an "unclassified condition" for which there is no corresponding signified. Here, we could compare James's novel with Wilde's *The Picture of Dorian Gray*, since Dorian's secret indicates a gap between his "actual" identity (the picture of unsullied youth) and his "painted" identity (the grotesque image of an unrepentant "sinner"). While Dorian widens an already palpable split between his utterance and the place from which he has symbolically spoken, Nash seems to repress his private life and identity; his relations to others consistently flounder when they request more information. Nick knows only that Nash belongs to a club without a name—a club whose obvious importance to this text can't sustain specification: "Nash had a club, the Anonymous, in some improbable square, of which Nick suspected him of being the only member."[67] What escapes definition in lexical terms guarantees speculation among other characters; Nash's meaning as a composite of others' fantasies and projections eclipses his probable banality and the vague, conjectural images accompanying his hedonism. As Nick remarks to Julia about his family's judgments, "Excuse my possibly priggish tone, but they really attribute to Nash a part he's quite incapable of playing."[68] With poignant relevance for both contemporary homophobia and the narrative's obsession with "parts" (roles, arbitrary divisions, and discrete elements of anatomy), Nash himself observes that others represent him according to their own projections: "Ah, for what do they take one, with *their* presumptions?"[69]

Questions about the painter's "desire" surface at this point, anticipating Wilde's novel by forcing us to ask, What does Nick Dormer *want*? While Dorian Gray's portrait generates concern about the desire the painter "put . . . into it,"[70] horror at its exhibition,[71] and the drama surrounding its eventual recovery,[72] Nash's unsuccessful portrait in *The Tragic Muse* comes close to erasing not only the meaning of painting in this novel but the "truth" of the portrait's avatar. The image of Nash is not simply "killed" (as in James's "The Liar") or brutally returned to its source (as in Wilde's novel); the narrative deprives it of authority by compelling it to fade. Nash vanishes "without a trace"[73] when he can't "interpose" between the novel's heterosexual partners: "Nick had the . . . diversion . . . of imagining that the picture he had begun had a singular air of gradually fading from the canvas. He couldn't catch it in the act, but he could have a suspicion, when he glanced at it, that the hand of time was rubbing it away little by little . . . making the surface indistinct and bare—bare of all resemblance to the model."[74]

William Hall usefully notes that this sense of fading or *aphanisis* is somewhat delusive, because Nick's "diversion" allows him to forget his sudden loss of Nash and to relive Nash's departure in a more bearable form: "He's only dead to me. He has gone away."[75] In this respect, Nick's projection of loss onto the painting relin-

quishes the object he formerly incorporated as his "Imagination."
While the "fading" of Nash's portrait overdetermines his mysterious departure, Nash's portrait still betrays the novel's inability to
close upon his absence.[76]

This conflict between representation and sexual fantasy suggests
that Nash's disappearance is the precondition for marriage in this
text; his disappearance binds characters who no longer depend on
their *ficelle*. Nash's departure also releases meanings that are un-
writable in this text because they constitute the enigma that betrays
all previous identifications (especially Nick's). Miriam makes this
explicit when she proposes Nash as a substitute for herself. According to Miriam, Nick's decision to externalize Nash would allow
Nick—and presumably the text—to abreact an obsessional fantasy:

> "You'll find other models; paint Gabriel Nash."
> "Gabriel Nash—as a substitute for you?"
> "It will be a good way to get rid of him. Paint Mrs. Dallow too . . . if
> you wish to eradicate the last possibility of a throb."[77]

The advice proves correct insofar as the painting of Nash hastens
his literal and figurative departure. However, the consequences for
Julia, Nick's fiancée, are anticipated but never shown. This advice
is intimately connected with the anxiety surrounding the novel's
heterosexual conclusion. Thus the novel ends with a mild resur-
gence of interest between Nick and Julia; he promises to begin a
full-length portrait of her. From this indication alone, we see that
The Tragic Muse connects painting with seduction. Nick's wavering
consent implies both his promise to seduce Julia (and, by implication, Nash) and the unstable meanings that circulate from the impossibility of either event. Although these developments confirm
relations among painting, acting, and seduction, painting exacer-
bates the novel's problem of courtship by producing a visible
"scar"; by contrast, Miriam's acting seems indistinguishable from
most behavior in this text.

Nash's incomplete painting seems to haunt Nick as a visible reminder of their unfinished business; the painting clearly fails to
"eradicate . . . the last possibility of a throb." Unlike the picture of
Dorian Gray, Nash's painting denotes neither "homosexual" duplicity nor the "sin" of an illicit desire (none is ever avowed); it
represents a powerful "resentment" and irrational shame: "[Nick]
seized it and turned it about; he jammed it back into its corner, with
its face against the wall. . . . The embarrassment however was all
his own."[78]

As in Wilde's novel, the "homosexual" meaning of Nash's painting remains enigmatic; the subject's haunting look is defaced similarly to Dorian's portrait. The drama of masculine desire in *The Tragic Muse* is paradoxically revealed when Nash "disappears" from his canvas. Whereas Miriam was an "embroidery" without genuine form, the significance of Nash *supersedes* the narrative's "overflow" of "metaphor." By generating more meanings than does Miriam's acting, Nash's painting reproduces—then disfigures—the drama of identification in James's novel. Every protagonist in *The Tragic Muse* is propelled by a volatile set of drives and fantasies that painting seems to "realize" with remarkable accuracy.[79]

What makes the fading of Nash's portrait so poignant, finally, is that the character most supportive of others' identifications ultimately is shorn of his own. Having established a tenuous intimacy between Sherringham and Biddy, and between Nick and Julia, Nash is expelled from the novel as a trope of psychic instability. In his preface James explains that in his perversity as this novel's muse, Nash's "fading" cancels its awkward expression of desire by reshaping others' fantasies into acceptable form.

By leaving the text, Nash relieves the group of its surplus member: the confirmed bachelor whom the novel couldn't pair off. His departure conveniently arrests the novel's sexual metonymy by allowing the tentative formation of a partnership between Nick and Julia. The narrator alludes to their marriage, but it is unclear whether Nash's residual influence will finally make Nick's career in politics—and thus in heterosexuality—intolerable. More obviously, *The Tragic Muse*'s conclusion demonstrates that painting's meanings surpass the delineations of its subjects. If the painting of Nash expresses Nick's "spiritual" seduction, it also exhibits a putative identification that its artist and subject find impossible to express. Put another way, Nash's painting illustrates a relation that exceeds masculinity's existing boundaries and that is unrepresentable for Nick or Nash *because of* this excess.

Given the obvious danger here of men painting and seducing other men, *The Tragic Muse* and *Dorian Gray* engage the limits and possibilities of "pleasure." Considering the legal constraints that Britain imposed on pleasure at the turn of the last century, it is perhaps unsurprising that the erotic project of painting fails in James's and Wilde's texts, and that *The Tragic Muse* and *Dorian Gray* find no answer to this failure, reaching instead for violence and death to destroy their homoerotic "interest and desire." Without a referent more specific than "pleasure" to signify seduction and the aesthetic practice of Gabriel Nash and Dorian Gray, these men's "interest" can't signify more than a generic "opposition" to their cultural and symbolic structures. Unable to represent "pleasure" in detail or at length, these novels have no alternative but to excise it in the interests of narrative consistency and resolution. One recalls this startling observation, made by the narrator of *The Tragic Muse*, about portraiture: "unlike most other forms, it was a revelation of two realities, the man whom it was the artist's conscious effort to reveal and the man (the interpreter) expressed in the very quality and temper of that effort. It offered a double vision, the strongest dose of life that art could give, *the strongest dose of art that life could give.*"[80] Since its "vision [is] double," painting indicates why desire is constantly at odds with itself. To put this another way, *The Tragic Muse* and *The Picture of Dorian Gray* offer the "strongest dose of art that life"—at least in 1890s Britain—seemed able to tolerate.

NOTES

1. Henry James, *The Tragic Muse* (1889; 1890; reprint, Harmondsworth: Penguin, 1978), 382.
2. For an account of the novel's aesthetic failure that ignores the conceptual value of the text's deficiencies, see Lyall H. Powers, "James' *The Tragic Muse*—*Ave Atque Vale*" *PMLA* 73 (1958): 270–74.
3. See Leo Bersani, "The Jamesian Lie," in *A Future for Astyanax: Character and Desire in Literature* (Boston: Little, Brown, 1976), 129–30.
4. Sharon Cameron, *Thinking in Henry James* (Chicago: University of Chicago Press, 1989), 47–53.
5. Oscar Wilde, *The Picture of Dorian Gray* (1890, revised 1891; reprint, Harmondsworth: Penguin, 1982), 95–96.
6. See Susan Elizabeth Gunter, "The Russian Connection: Sources for Miriam Rooth of James's *The Tragic Muse*," *South Atlantic Review* 53, no. 2 (1988), 85.
7. *The Tragic Muse*, 230, 131, 146, 145.
8. Ibid., 279.
9. "Integrity": L. *integer*—"intact, making up a whole," in T. F. Hoad, ed., *The Concise Oxford Dictionary of English Etymology* (Oxford: Clarendon Press, 1986), 238.
10. For related discussion of the woman's "masquerade" and the man's "parade," see Joan Rivière, "Womanliness as a Masquerade," in *Formations of Fantasy*, ed. Victor Burgin, James Donald, and Cora Kaplan (London: Methuen, 1986), 35–44; Stephen Heath, "Joan Rivière and the Masquerade," in *Formations of Fantasy*, 45–61; and Jacques Lacan, *The Seminar of Jacques Lacan, Book II: The Ego in Freud's Theory and in the Technique of Psychoanalysis, 1954–1955*, ed. Jacques-Alain Miller, trans. Sylvana Tomaselli (New York: Cambridge University Press, 1988), 37, 227.
11. *The Tragic Muse*, 382.

12. Ibid., 147.

13. Ibid., 153.

14. Ibid., 153.

15. Ibid., 153, 131.

16. Ibid., 457.

17. See Joseph Litvak, *Caught in the Act: Theatricality in the Nineteenth-Century English Novel* (Berkeley: University of California Press, 1992), 243, 264, and Jonathan Freedman, *Professions of Taste: Henry James, British Aestheticism, and Commodity Culture* (Stanford: Stanford University Press, 1990), 182–92. The principles of artistry recur in modern camp—an aesthetic that lays bare, and ruins, the *semiotics* of performance by reproducing it to excess. Nash arguably performs a similar excess by representing all life in aesthetic terms: "[T]o live is such an art; to feel is such a career!" (27).

18. *The Tragic Muse*, 457.

19. James, "Preface" to *Roderick Hudson* (1874; 1875; reprint, Harmondsworth: Penguin, 1986), 37; original emphasis.

20. Ibid., 37.

21. Ibid., 37; original emphasis.

22. Sigmund Freud, "Instincts and Their Vicissitudes" (1915), *The Standard Edition of the Complete Psychological Works of Sigmund Freud* XIV, ed. and trans. James Strachey (London: Hogarth, 1957–74), 122.

23. *Roderick Hudson*, 66, 63. Consider the novel's frequent allusions to physical and artistic tumescence—for instance, Rowland's remark: " 'Of course when a body begins to expand, there comes in the possibility of bursting; but I nevertheless approve of a certain tension of one's being. It's what a man is meant for' " (81).

24. Cameron, *Thinking in Henry James*, 48–49.

25. For elaboration on this relation between mentor and artist or pupil, see Michael Moon, "A Small Boy and Others: Sexual Disorientation in Henry James, Kenneth Anger, and David Lynch," in *Comparative American Identities: Race, Sex, and Nationality in the Modern Text*, ed. Hortense Spillers (New York: Routledge, 1991), 141–56; Michael A. Cooper, "Discipl(in)ing the Master, Mastering the Discipl(in)e: Erotonomies in James' Tales of Literary Life," in *Engendering Men: The Question of Male Feminist Criticism*, ed. Joseph A. Boone and Michael Cadden (New York: Routledge, 1990), 66–83; Eve Kosofsky Sedgwick, "The Beast in the Closet: James and the Writing of Homosexual Panic," *Epistemology of the Closet* (Berkeley: University of California Press, 1990), 182–212; Robert K. Martin, "The 'High Felicity' of Comradeship: A New Reading of *Roderick Hudson*," *American Literary Realism* 11 (1978): 101–2; Richard Hall, "Henry James: Interpreting an Obsessive Memory," *Journal of Homosexuality* 8, no. 3–4 (1983): 86–87; Freedman, *Professions of Taste*, 183; and Mildred E. Hartsock, "Henry James and the Cities of the Plain," *Modern Language Quarterly* 29 (1968): 305–11.

26. *Roderick Hudson*, 66.

27. Ibid., 68.

28. Ibid., 101, 107.

29. Judith E. Funston, " 'All Art Is One': Narrative Techniques in Henry James's *Tragic Muse*," *Studies in the Novel* 15 (1983): 353–55; William R. Goetz, "The Allegory of Representation in *The Tragic Muse*," *Journal of Narrative Technique* 8 (1978): 160–62; William F. Hall, "Gabriel Nash: 'Famous Centre' of *The Tragic Muse*," *Nineteenth-Century Fiction* 21 (1966): 167–70; and W. R. Mac-

naughton, "In Defense of James's *The Tragic Muse, The Henry James Review* 7, no. 1 (1985): 7.

30. James, "Preface to *The Tragic Muse*," *The Art of the Novel: Critical Prefaces* (New York: Scribner's, 1934), 80, 85; original emphases.

31. *The Tragic Muse*, 86.

32. Ibid., 96.

33. See James, ibid., 90: "[T]he multiplication of *aspects*" culminates in "a *usurping* consciousness" (original emphases). James's explanation for Nick's failure is also significant. Having acknowledged that he "strove in vain . . . to embroil and adorn this young man on whom a hundred ingenious touches are thus lavished" (97), James first concludes that the idea of an artist "in triumph" would be uninteresting; his triumph should exist as a matter of what he *produces*. In relation to the novel's ending and the profound ambivalence that Nash's portrait generates, however, this conclusion seemed curious and unworkable even to James, whose explanation for Nick's failure became elliptical thereafter: "The better part of him is locked too much away from us, and the part we see has to pass for—well, what it passes for, so lamentably, among his friends and relatives" (97).

One answer to the failure, which may also account for James's admission that Nick's "better part . . . is locked . . . away," surfaces in an earlier statement: "What he produces . . . is another affair. His romance is the romance he himself projects" (96). As I argue later in this essay, this "romance" constitutes the "unsaid" (122) of the novel because Nick's intimacy with Nash (as a project and projection) is not successfully resolved. On this point, it is notable that James dramatically revised Nick and Nash's "romance." In the January 1889 issue of the *Atlantic Monthly*, for instance, he described his conception of the novel as

> the history of an American aesthete (or possibly an English one) [i.e., Nick], who *conceives a violent admiration* for a French aesthete (a contemporary novelist) [i.e., Nash], and goes to Paris to make his acquaintance; where he finds that his Frenchman is so much more thorough going a specimen of the day than himself, that he is appalled and returns to Philistinism (qtd. in Robert S. Baker, "Gabriel Nash's 'House of Strange Idols': Aestheticism in *The Tragic Muse*," *Texas Studies in Literature and Language* 15 (1973): 151 [my emphasis]).

The absence of all reference to women here—for example, to Julia as Nick's partner, and to Miriam as the novel's principal "object"—endorses my argument that women initially are subordinate to the "violent admiration" prevailing between Nick and Nash. Moreover, this "violence" recurs in Nash's removal from the text, and the narrative's insistence that marriage constitutes its only possible closure.

34. *The Tragic Muse*, 89.

35. Ibid., 86.

36. Ibid., 20.

37. See Alan W. Bellringer, "*The Tragic Muse*: 'The Objective Centre,' " *Journal of American Studies* 4, no. 1–2 (1970): 75–76.

38. Goetz, "The Allegory of Representation in *The Tragic Muse*," 156–64; Hall, "Gabriel Nash: 'Famous Centre' of *The Tragic Muse*," 167–84; Macnaughton, "In Defense of James's *The Tragic Muse*," 5–12.

39. "Nick greeted him and said it was a happy chance—he was uncommonly glad to see him.
"I never come across you—I don't know why," Nick remarked, while the two, smiling, looked each other up and down, like men reunited after a long interval [. . .]

"... But surely we've diverged since the old days. I adore what you burn; you burn what I adore." [. . .]

"How do you know what I adore?" Nicholas Dormer inquired.

"I know well enough what you used to."

"That's more than I do myself; there were so many things."

"Yes, there are many things—many, many; that's what makes life so amusing."

"Do you find it amusing?"

"My dear fellow, *c'est à se tordre!* [it's a scream!] Don't you think so? Ah, it was high time I should meet you—I see. I have an idea you need me."

"Upon my word, I think I do!" Nick said, in a tone which struck his sister and made her wonder still more why, if the gentleman was so important as that, he didn't introduce him" (21–22).

40. *The Tragic Muse*, 385.

41. Ibid., 19.

42. Ibid., 125.

43. Ibid.

44. Ibid., 122.

45. Ibid., 127.

46. Ibid., 125–26.

47. For elaboration on the "paranoid Gothic," see Sedgwick, "Toward the Gothic: Terrorism and Homosexual Panic," *Between Men: English Literature and Male Homosocial Desire* (New York: Columbia University Press, 1985), 83–96, and *Epistemology of the Closet*, 186–87. Sedgwick includes in this tradition Mary Shelley's *Frankenstein* (1818), Ann Radcliffe's *The Italian* (1797), William Godwin's *Things as They Are; or, The Adventures of Caleb Williams* (1794), and James Hogg's *The Private Memoirs and Confessions of a Justified Sinner* (1824). Sedgwick's account of the "paranoid Gothic" has sharpened our understanding of same-sex rivalry and eroticism, but her model tends to simplify the psychic etiology and repercussions of this eroticism, in the process eclipsing or misrepresenting psychoanalytic formulations of desire. I elaborate on the related limitations of "homosocial" arguments in "The Homosexual in the Text," in *The Burdens of Intimacy: Psychoanalysis and Victorian Masculinity* (Chicago: University of Chicago Press, 1999), 224–45.

48. Concerning narrative opacity, the note on the text in the 1978 Penguin edition of *The Tragic Muse* claims that James "minutely revised [the novel] . . . for the New York 'Definitive' Edition of the *Novels and Tales*, published in 1908, making verbal changes in almost every paragraph. These changes are usually, by the introduction of a periphrasis, to make the sentences more allusive and less simple and direct" (6).

49. *The Tragic Muse*, 22, 23, 37, 44, 53, 117, 120, 262, 263, 263, 326.

50. Ibid., 104.

51. Ibid., 372.

52. Ibid., 374.

53. See Susanne Kappeler, *Writing and Reading in Henry James* (New York: Columbia University Press, 1980), 118; and Silverman, "Too Early/Too Late: Subjectivity and the Primal Scene in Henry James," *Novel* 21, no. 2–3 (1988): 147–73. The narrator of *The Sacred Fount*, for example, describes his preoccupation with voyeurism as "my private madness" and a "ridiculous obsession" (118, 72).

54. See esp. chap. 3 of Linda Dowling's valuable study *Hellenism and Homosexuality in Victorian Oxford* (Ithaca: Cornell University Press, 1994).

55. *The Tragic Muse*, 126.

322   PART THREE: LATE VICTORIAN

56. Ibid., 176.

57. Ibid., 166.

58. Ibid., 161.

59. For a different reading of Nick's ontological division, see John L. Kimmey, "*The Tragic Muse* and Its Forerunners," *American Literature* 41 (1970), who argues, with a confidence the novel does not support: "Of course, Nick conquers his double nature and learns 'to be continuous.' He rids himself of his hypocrisy, his fatal 'talent for appearance' " (525–26).

60. *The Tragic Muse*, 177.

61. Ibid., 265.

62. Ibid., 282–83; my emphasis.

63. Ibid., 272, 229.

64. Ibid., 126, 117, 372.

65. I interpret this issue in *The Ruling Passion: British Colonial Allegory and the Paradox of Homosexual Desire* (Durham: Duke University Press, 1995), 72–98, and "The Drama of the Impostor: Dandyism and Its Double," *Cultural Critique* 28 (1994): 29–52.

66. *The Tragic Muse*, 505; my emphasis.

67. Ibid., 505.

68. Ibid., 516.

69. Ibid., 119.

70. Oscar Wilde, *Dorian Gray*, 8.

71. Ibid., 35.

72. Ibid., 245.

73. *The Tragic Muse*, 511.

74. Ibid., 511–12.

75. Ibid., 515. See Hall, "Gabriel Nash: 'Famous Centre' of *The Tragic Muse*," 180.

76. Concerning the "fading" of the beloved, see Roland Barthes, *A Lover's Discourse: Fragments*, trans. Richard Howard (New York: Hill & Wang, 1978), 112: "Fade-out": "Painful ordeal in which the loved being appears to withdraw from all contact, without such enigmatic indifference even being directed against the amorous subject or pronounced to the advantage of anyone else, world or rival." The psychoanalytic significance of *aphanisis* is also important to consider here: According to Lacan, the subject must relinquish "being" for "meaning" in order to grasp its symbolic position (see Lacan, *The Four Fundamental Concepts of Psycho-Analysis*, ed. Jacques-Alain Miller, trans. Alan Sheridan [New York: Norton, 1978], 209–15; and Kaja Silverman, *The Subject of Semiotics* [New York: Oxford University Press, 1983], 168–73).

77. *The Tragic Muse*, 502–3. Wilde discovered an almost identical phenomenon when he seemed to capture the sexual enigma of Shakespeare's *Sonnets*: "Perhaps, by finding perfect expression for a passion, I had exhausted the passion itself. . . . How was it that it had left me? Had I touched upon some secret that my soul desired to conceal? Or was there no permanence in personality?" (Wilde, *The Portrait of Mr. W. H.* (1889), in *The Riddle of Shakespeare's Sonnets*, ed. E. Hubler, et al. [London: Routledge, 1962], 246–47). For interesting accounts of this text's elliptical homosexual meanings, see Dowling, "Imposture and Absence in Wilde's *Portrait of Mr. W. H*," *Victorian Newsletter* 58 (1980), 26–29; Lawrence Danson, "Oscar Wilde, W. H., and the Unspoken Name of Love," *ELH* 58 (1991): 979–1000; and William A. Cohen, "Willie and Wilde: Reading *The Portrait of Mr. W. H*.," in *Displacing Homophobia: Gay Male Perspectives in Literature and Cul-*

ture, ed. Ronald R. Butters, John M. Clum, and Michael Moon (Durham: Duke University Press, 1989), 207–33.

78. *The Tragic Muse*, 518.

79. See Jacqueline Rose, *Sexuality in the Field of Vision* (London: Verso, 1986), 226–27, and Silverman, *The Subject of Semiotics*, 162–67.

80. *The Tragic Muse*, 282; my emphasis.

Bernard Shaw and the Economy
of the Male Self

KATHLEEN MCDOUGALL

CAPITALISM PRIVILEGES THE INDIVIDUAL OVER THE COLLECTIVITY; IT also rationalizes this "selfish" bent by measuring the worth of the individual—as an agent of innovation, progress, and growth—with reference to the collectivity's ultimate well-being. In late nineteenth-century Britain, that phase of science known as "scientific naturalism" established itself as *the* instrument with which to effect and measure progress.[1] It provided an apt "cosmological backcloth" to industrialization and the rise of the bourgeois middle class, and much of its value as such resided in its subordination, within an evolutionary framework, of individual strivings to collective processes.[2]

The increasing authority granted science redefined and, to a certain extent, discredited literature and other artistic pursuits, as Tom Gibbons explains[3]:

> emotional-expressionist views [of art] . . . became increasingly extreme during the course of the nineteenth century mainly as a consequence of the continual and highly impressive advances which were being made in the natural sciences. The more did scientists come to be regarded as possessing a monopoly in the field of fact and objective truth, the more did artists come to be regarded as dealing solely in their alleged opposites, i.e. subjective visions and emotions.[4]

Thus science, viewed as a secular, practical, and public-spirited endeavor, posed a threat to literature, which tended to be placed (or to place itself) at an opposite pole of beauty-, tradition-, and self-worship. A main point of the discussion to follow, centered on Bernard Shaw, is that arguments for the continued importance of literature were always self-defeating in some sense: they took for granted various scientific "truths" that undermined more than they bolstered credibility.[5] Another point is that both camps tended to ground personal worth in sexuality, understood as the way in which the animal core of the self was "managed." A defense of one's work, therefore, frequently involved a defense of a particular sexual bent. In Shaw's case, this often meant opposing the useful sublimator to the useless sensualist; his conviction, however, that it was impossible to escape nature's processes led him to explore various ways in which the relation of intellect to natural impulse might be one of cooperation rather than simply of cooptation.

Because it was lent the glamor of objective truth—as is still the case today, to a certain extent—science in this essay will figure as a primary discourse, a source of "facts" from which views of self and society were elaborated. There is no such thing as a primary discourse, of course, and in fact there was "a constant movement of commonplaces between discourses" in the late nineteenth century.[6] One such commonplace, and a central one for my purposes, is the metaphor of the social organism, which represents a tangle of received ideas associated with various theories, such as cell theory. Rudolf Virchow's *Die Cellularpathologie* (1858) likened the body to a "state in which every cell is a citizen" and disease to "civil war."[7] Perhaps as a result of being endlessly shuttled between texts, the comparison became an equation, a "dead metaphor" that was "a putative source of knowledge about society rather than simply another rhetorical figure for it."[8]

Contributing to the deadening of the social organism metaphor— and giving it its fin-de-siècle, panic-tinged flavor—were the rules supposed to govern its survival. Evolutionary theory, as expounded for example by the very influential Herbert Spencer, dwelt upon the notion of change as ongoing and inevitable, but also proposed a way of coping with nature's chronic restlessness. For Spencer, organisms must evolve by becoming increasingly complex, or else face "dissolution." A stable organism is not static; rather, it is characterized by dynamic tensions internally (between its various parts) and externally (between it and outside forces); these interactions allow it to keep pace with changes in the larger organism to which it belongs. In the sense that everything is always changing, every organism is in a state of flux, but this can direct it along two different paths: what one might call a dynamic instability will allow the organism to adapt, survive, and progress toward further complexity, whereas a static instability leads to dissolution.[9]

This brief overview enables me to focus on the idea of degeneration, which can be linked to the second law of thermodynamics, according to which "although the total quantity of energy remains constant, its quality or 'usefulness' is continually being degraded."[10] This entropic threat exercised many a late-Victorian imagination: energy, at all levels of existence, was believed to be scarce. What was needed to keep degeneration in check was sufficient and properly allocated energy, as prescribed by French author Paul Bourget:

> The individual is the social cell. In order that the organism should perform its functions with energy it is necessary that the organisms composing it should perform their functions with energy, but with a subordinated energy. . . . If the energy of the cells becomes independent, the lesser organisms will likewise cease to subordinate their energy to the total energy and the anarchy which is established constitutes the *decadence* of the whole.[11]

This formulation illustrates the fin-de-siècle "preoccupation with the economy of the body" as well as the tendency to detect everywhere the operation of the same laws.[12] When applied to society, the hierarchical ranking of energy meant that it was crucial that each individual know his or her place and expend energy only as a function of the larger unit[13]; and this meant, in turn, that each individual had to maintain a well-ordered self, with subordinate components such as animal instinct held firmly in check. The saving strategy was to be active as opposed to passive (or dynamic as opposed to static), so as never to offer the forces of regression an opportunity to corrode the self or society, to peel back a layer of civilization and reveal a more primitive state underneath.

The onion model I am evoking here is present in the idea of mind as a hierarchy of faculties, from an animal core to a lately acquired, and fragile, civilized veneer. According to evolutionary psychology, mental disease occurred when the higher faculties were eroded and control was thus relinquished to lower faculties. It was quite commonly assumed that artistic creation was made possible by a relaxation (or failure) of reason and will and a surrender to less evolved mental habits.[14] Thus were brought artistic creation, spiritual yearnings, genius (which required mental activity that was too intense to be healthy), criminal leanings, insanity, sexual perversion, and so on, into the same class. Very often the physical explanation for these manifestations of abnormal mental functioning invoked notions of force or energy. Because of excessive energy spent in one direction and/or because of a hereditarily depleted constitution (i.e., degeneracy), the energy needed to marshall the will in the proper direction was deemed unavailable.

It is important to note that social regeneration, in a universe governed by strict organic laws, can only happen through the body;

each body must contribute to the collective pool of positive heredi-tary traits, hence a preoccupation with hereditary "capital."[15] Or-ganic laws dictate that each person's sexual destiny is so tied up with the social destiny that the vagaries of desire become a liability. A typical pronouncement (which is also a typical example of impe-rialist rhetoric) is made by H. G. Wells, who blithely leaps from sex to social entropy and from individuals to nations:

> the monogamic family, with an entire prohibition of wasted energy, is no doubt the moral ideal, so far as sex is concerned, of the modern mili-tant civilised state. States and nations that fall away from that ideal will inevitably go down before States that maintain it in its integrity.[16]

A frequent objection to masturbation was that it led to "a pointless and prodigal waste of limited and valuable resources," which con-travened the need to conserve the body's supply of energy, for self and country. "Resources" can of course also be understood in a financial sense, to wit "the English colloquialism for having an or-gasm—'to spend.' "[17] In fact, sexual energy (governed by thermo-dynamic rules) and money are inseparable in late nineteenth-century views of sexuality. It has been noted how the sphere of "of-ficial" sexuality (that of marriage) and that of the economy were collapsed one into the other: desire, "the universal solvent" of the sexual organization of bourgeois society, operates in conjunction with money, the "fundamental unit of conversion" of the capitalist economic organization.[18] Thus "the sexual economy of the male became integrated with the monetary economy of capitalism" which, as I have noted, was assimilated to a thermodynamic econ-omy.[19] Because of this conflation, the "lived double articulation of sex in bourgeois capitalist society—that is, expression and repres-sion" could be rendered in various ways.[20] On the one hand, one could opt for consummation or consumption or dissipation, and, on the other, deferral or thrift or conservation. These were the alterna-tives, backed by scientific and economic discourse, available to Shaw as he attempted to address the age-old problem of preserving male bodily integrity.

As a competitor on the marketplace of cultural criticism, Shaw had to lend his works value by making himself the guarantor of their relevance and authority. This meant presenting a self that was energy-efficient and collectivity-minded, as opposed to a marginal-ized other that was parasitical, wasteful of energy, and selfish. As I mention above, Shaw's prevalent strategy was to construct a subli-mated self, the workings of which were often couched in scientific terms. In doing so he was met halfway by bourgeois ideology, which reserved a space for art that transcended scientific truths and their quotidian usefulness. I am referring to a bourgeois aesthetic whose basic function is to "mark the difference between humans and non-humans" or in other words to demonstrate a capacity for "purifying, refining, and sublimating facile impulses and primary needs," namely biological urges as well as "practical urgencies."[21] Given the association of superiority with disinterest, the practicality of scientific discourse, in a sense, detracted from its truth value, and even the most extreme defenders of science, seemingly bent on assigning all social value to science and none at all to any other discourse, could not dismiss art altogether. Max Nordau, for instance, in his *Degeneration* (which appeared in English translation in 1895), attacks modern art on all fronts and declares that "thinkers and investigators" deserve society's "profoundest respect," in contrast to "the poet or artist," whose "enthusiasts . . . are youth and women—i.e., those components of the race in whom the unconscious outweighs consciousness."[22] He hastens to add, however, that "the artist is sometimes placed . . . on a level with . . . the man of science" because "art is equally a source of knowledge."[23] Good art ("moral art" as opposed to the "art of the Aesthetes," one of Nordau's targets) "projects itself into the future, and gives us at least a dream-like idea of the outlines and direction of our future organic developments"; this prophetic art is "the highest mental activity of the human being."[24] Nordau must declare some little corner of art to be pure so as to maintain splits such as cultural/natural and disinterested/interested. In typical bourgeois fashion, he defines himself as mostly practical, and he fantasizes an impractical being who so thoroughly sublimates his impulses as to produce a non-organic, nonutilitarian object whose "ideality akin to rational perfection . . . is the beautiful."[25]

Criticism of Shaw's works often assumes a relationship between his creative self and his sensual self whereby repressed sexuality fuels creativity. According to this repression/expression model, Shaw was to a great extent self-repressed; he was "a virgin until the age of 27," and by his early forties he "was giving up all sex as an ingredient in love."[26] Usually, Shaw's quashing of his own sexual impulses is described in terms of sublimation,[27] as in the following remarks by Michael Holroyd: "he shifted his desires into his literary life. Sexual excitement in him produced an ejaculation of words from which letters were conceived, novels and plays were born."[28] In positing this process critics are aided by Shaw himself, who wrote to Janet Achurch, one of several platonic lovers:

I have become a sort of sublime monster, to whose disembodied heart the consummation of ordinary lives is a mere anti-climax.

Do you know anyone who will buy for twopence a body for which I have no longer any use? I have made tolerable love with it in my time; but now I have found nobler instruments—the imagination of a poet, the heart of a child.[29]

One notes that the same dubious thermodynamic model subtends both Shaw's and the critics' assumption that the energy of repressed physiological impulses can be converted into expressed ideas. Rather than speculating on the actual relationship between Shaw's sexuality and his art, I will explore the link between his own view of this relationship and late nineteenth-century ideas of self, nature, and society. My construction of Shaw locates him at the nexus of various overlapping discourses; I am considering him as a "center of operations" wielding these discourses so as to claim cultural centrality.

Shaw's name for change as *the* principle of existence was the Life Force, a cosmic will seeking through evolution (what he would eventually call Creative Evolution) "to achieve higher and higher organization and completer self-consciousness."[30] As a self-appointed vehicle of the spirit of his age, he deemed himself a promoter of the proper sort of evolutionary change and he set himself against the rank and file who opposed such change out of fear, laziness, and lack of vision.

Shaw defines inferiority primarily in terms of economy of self (rather than gender, social class, and so on). The less one is able to quell selfish, atavistic impulses (in particular sexual ones), the lower one's place in his hierarchy. In his prefatory remarks to *Three Plays for Puritans* (1900), for example, one finds many sexualized and unworthy others. As Holroyd remarks, definitions in this cantankerous preface are very slippery: the argument "is continually being displaced" and "Shaw passes almost unnoticeably from demolishing the genteel assumptions of the sex instinct as shown on the stage," that is, the disguising of sex as romantic love, "to a demolition of the sex instinct itself," which he sees as the prime mover in almost everyone.[31] Shaw bemoans the fact that theatre managers, faced with a diverse audience and wishing to appeal to each of its members, are "flung . . . back on the instinct of sex as the avenue to all hearts."[32] Respectable appearances are maintained, however: in the plays presented the "realistic treatment of the incidents of sex is quite out of the question," and "love is carefully kept off the stage, whilst it is alleged as the motive of all the actions presented to the audience."[33] This audience is composed of a minority of well-to-do types (the blasé and sensual gentleman, the "sporting publican," as well as "the rich Jewish merchant" and his family) and a majority of lower middle-class patrons, mostly women.[34] One segment of the public whose absence is noted by Shaw is "the rich Evangelical merchant and his family,"[35] but he is not exempted from sensuality: "[w]hen he wants sensuality he practises it" and from the theater he demands edification—which makes him somewhat of a hypocrite.[36]

The proletariat, left out of this discussion of theater-goers, is included elsewhere in Shaw's sexualizing of everyone but sublimators like himself, to wit this passage from *Essays in Fabian Socialism* (1889):

> the more you degrade the workers, . . . the more you throw them back, reckless, on the one pleasure and the one human tie left to them—the gratification of their instinct for producing fresh supplies of men . . . [Your] slaves . . . breed like rabbits; and their poverty breeds filth, ugliness, dishonesty, disease, obscenity, drunkenness, and murder.[37]

The problem presented by all these sexualized others is that they cannot effect change, they can only stagnate, or worse, degenerate. The solution to this urgent problem is an integral part of Shaw's socioeconomic program, in which "Property and Promiscuity" (meaning indiscriminate breeding) are yoked together as the twin enemies of progress.[38] Because love, on the whole, is for Shaw "a mere physical appetite" leading to an indulgence in "the brutalities of the sexual instinct," only the injection of a greater cause, that of the amelioration of the race, into human coupling can make it acceptable to him.[39] This is because Shaw's scheme mirrors Spencer's: passivity before natural forces leads to dissolution.[40] The intellect must be alert and the will asserting itself at all times to counteract nature, whose ultimate goal is to diversify and improve, but whose operation in the lazy-minded and self-indulgent results in mediocrity and greater slavery to instinct.[41] Proof of this is civilization's "advanced stage of rottenness."[42] Believing that "the health of society as an organic whole" can only be as sound as the individual organisms composing it, Shaw thought that reproduction should be regulated in such a way as to create a race of unselfish, work-oriented, intellect-driven people.[43] To realize this project he and fellow socialists of the Fabian variety advocated "a highly scientific social organization" and put forward a roster of scientific tools: eugenics, statistics, sociology, political economy, and so on.[44]

According to Shaw there are two ways to serve the Life Force: the physical production of human beings, and the production of ideas for them to inherit. These evolutionary roles correspond (most of the time) to femininity and masculinity, defined through procreation on the one hand, and cerebration and/or creation on the other. They also correspond to two options between which Shaw hesitated in his presentation of self: practicality at the socio-organic level, compatible with an ordinary economy of self; and practicality in the spiritual realm. The latter option is a bid for a position of authority "as a vessel of the Zeitgeist or will,"[45] a "genius . . . selected by Nature to . . . build up an intellectual consciousness of her own instinctive purpose."[46] Calling upon the stereotypes of the truly inspired artist and the diseased artist, Shaw casts himself in the former role (and backs his contentions with evolutionary theory) in the following passage:

There are two sorts of genius in this world. One is produced by the breed throwing forward to the godlike man, exactly as it sometimes throws backward to the apelike. The other is the mere monster produced by an accidental excess of some faculty—musical, muscular, sexual even. . . . I am a genius of the first order.[47]

But there often creeps into Shaw's seemingly sanguine pronouncements an element of mistrust as to his role. In his 1902 preface to *Mrs. Warren's Profession* (1894), for example, Shaw declares himself "convinced that fine art is the subtlest, the most seductive, the most effective instrument of moral propaganda in the world," which suggests that art, because it seduces rather than rationally convinces, might be dangerous in the hands of an ill-intentioned or misguided person.[48] He also suspected that art might be dangerous *for* that person. As he stated in a letter to Achurch (from which I quote at length below), Shaw sometimes feared that the conviction of having talent was a delusion and a symptom of decay. In another letter he dissociates himself from the worthless artist by contending that his writing is the result not of inspiration but of dogged work and hard-acquired craftsmanship, as well as intense involvement in real, prosaic life:

Man & Superman no doubt sounds as if it came from the most exquisite atmosphere of art. As a matter of fact, the mornings I gave to it were followed by afternoons & evenings spent in the committee rooms of a London Borough Council, fighting questions of drainage, paving, lighting, rates, clerk's salaries &c &c &c &c.[49]

Shaw's wavering between the personae of prophet and craftsman, which is paralleled by a wavering between spiritual and physical insemination, to be discussed below, always takes for granted that evolution must be hurried forward one way or the other. The question is whether one functions within or without the social organism, not whether one labors *for* the social organism. Art for art's sake is not an option, in other words, and if Shaw elevated art above other endeavors it was by virtue of its usefulness, which he defended in his response, entitled *The Sanity of Art* (1895), to Nordau's *Degeneration*:

> The worthy artist or craftsman is he who serves the physical and moral senses. . . . The great artist is he who . . . , by supplying works of a higher beauty and a higher interest than have yet been perceived, succeeds . . . in adding this fresh extension of sense to the heritage of the race.[50]

One notes the close similarity between Shaw's argument and Wilde's contention that the critic-artist's sin "increases the experience of the race."[51] Both Wilde and Shaw see art as a dynamic force combatting sameness and stagnation in the physical and the spiritual realms.[52]

An important stimulus to innovation, for Shaw, is love, even though he tends to lump it together with sex and therefore mere physicality. One positive feature of love, he believes, is that it unbalances one, thereby facilitating the absorption of new ideas. In "The Cassone" (an unpublished story written in 1889), the hero Ashton holds that in order to advance intellectually, one must combat common sense with impulses strong enough to overcome it, and that since "no feeling overpowers a man's common sense so effectually as love," one "must keep constantly falling in love" in order to keep "advancing."[53]

A related use of love is the above-mentioned sublimation: in the following passage from a letter to Achurch, Shaw alleges that sublimation has afforded him ecstasy similar to sexual ecstasy, only stronger, "higher," and more long-lasting. This letter articulates various Shavian beliefs about economy of self, including the danger of degeneration and the necessity of "paying" for energy expenditure (Shaw hopes that he has found a way of escaping these processes):

> It may possibly be that my growing certainty that I can be a dramatic poet . . . may be a symptom of decay; but it obviously will not do to

proceed on that assumption. During all these years I have acquired a certain power of work. . . . But ability does not become genius until it has risen to the point at which its keenest states of perception touch on ecstasy, on healthy, self-possessed ecstasy, untouched by mere epileptic or drunken incontinence, or sexual incontinence. Well . . . on the plains of heaven, I was not incontinent; but I was ecstatic. For the moment I got far beyond any former rapture; and there was no rebound, no reaction, no bill to pay: for many days the valleys and plains were still in sight; and I never lost the ground I had gained afterwards . . .

. . . The step up to the plains of heaven was made on your bosom.[54]

Shaw is claiming, in effect, to have become a self-sustaining, closed system—one which defies the second law of thermodynamics—thanks to the boost onto a higher plain provided by the fascinating but unattainable Janet (who was married).

One notices that when love combats common sense it is destabilizing, whereas sublimation leads to a kind of stability. What is common to both of these facets of love is that neither is static—neither represents procreative sex, the conventional and corroding subjection of the self to natural forces. Shaw's strategy is to do away with forms of pleasure enjoyed in a state of passivity in order to achieve, in his new, active state, complete control, inexhaustible energy, and therefore the kind of dynamic, controlled instability, mentioned earlier in connection with Spencer, that attunes one to the world's flux. What is required to reach this state of stability is the strength to withstand the temptation to possess (which amounts to being possessed), and/or a refusal to comply with marriage laws which legitimize possessiveness.[55] In *Man and Superman* (1903), the hero Jack explains the tactics of the artist-in-love to Tavy, himself an artist:

He gets into intimate relations with [women] . . . knowing that they have the power to rouse his deepest creative energies, to rescue him from cold reason, . . . to inspire him, as he calls it. He persuades women that they may do this for their own purpose whilst he really means them to do it for his.[56]

Shaw thus formulated a nonsacrificial scenario whereby the (male) artist serves the cosmic organism without sacrifice of energy or integrity. According to Shaw, however, a refusal to fall prey to the mundane aspects of sexuality does not guarantee complete control. For to be "rescued" from "cold reason" is to trade irrationality for rationality.[57] A large degree of passivity before the Life Force therefore characterizes anyone who is leading a significant existence, such as the "artist-philosopher" of *Man and Superman's* "Epistle Dedicatory" (examples of whom are Bunyan, Blake, Goethe, and Wagner).

So participation in evolution, as an artist, is a submission-inducing process but one that is acceptable nonetheless in that its ultimate aim is to free humanity from nature's material shackles, with the help of great minds that point the way toward a highly conscious and controlled state of existence. But pointing the way does not mean achieving such a state, because in most artists rationality is a small component of the creative process.[58] Inspiration is nature's sanction of the artist's life, but it falls short of the final goal of total awareness, being more involuntary, more instinctual and natural, than it is self-willed. This means that art is an agent of disruption and change, not an end in itself. And this means, in turn, that there is always a sense in which art is sterile. Art is part of a process, not the fruit of a process; in the far-away future of biological perfection and the triumph of mind over matter, in *Back to Methuselah* (1921), art is relegated to a very secondary role in human life, and the same goes for sex.

As well, though the artist's intellectual side strives against blind process and unconscious generation, nature cannot be escaped: it encompasses everything, including the spiritual, and there is no way of contributing to the heightened consciousness of the species without submitting to the laws of nature, selecting a sexual partner, and reproducing. In *Man and Superman,* Shaw is quite literal about the insemination of nature with ideas: it must happen through sexual relations.

But one encounters various difficulties at this juncture of Shaw's thought. For one thing, the mind/matter dialectic is singularly inefficient, as Daniel J. Leary notes: "the Life-Force limits and obstructs itself by this dialectic action with matter, for . . . improvement is retarded because of matter."[59] For another, it is not at all clear just how heredity operates.[60] The conclusion to be drawn from most of the examples of parent/child relationships given by Shaw seems to be that it is to one's intellectual advantage to resemble one's parents as little as possible. Thomas Postlewait comments that in Shaw's plays

> [t]he family bond is a loose one . . . so individual will comes to the fore. Shaw is determined to show that heredity matters less than will power; or, more specifically, that will power is the most significant aspect of heredity. The genius of strong-willed children is to be self-creating.[61]

Granted, Shaw can be understood to advocate a combination of two elements as the best possible circumstances for procreation: first, a strong sexual attraction between the parents (*"alias* Voice of Nature," sanctioning the match) and second, a certain degree of indifference between parents and children.[62] But this tells us nothing about the physical transmission of will: all it tells us is that the child's will, whose relation to the parent's will (or lack thereof) is unclear, should not be interfered with.[63]

Another difficulty regarding Shaw's idea of heredity is that, even if one assumes that intellect and will are transmissible, those who are supposed to pass them on by mating do not possess them to the same degree as people who resist the mating instinct. For an artist faced with Shaw's mother-woman, there is no way to participate in the reproductive process without forsaking his awareness and damaging his integrity as an artist, hence the temptation to step aside. The artist is faced with an impossible choice, between sterility from the point of view of consciousness, on the one hand, and sterility from the point of view of racial continuation, on the other. In the first act of *Man and Superman* Jack tells Tavy that as an artist he "creates new mind as surely as any woman creates new men," and thus plays a vital role in the advancement of the race.[64] This is as expected in the context of Shaw's theory of male creation versus female procreation, as is Ann's assertion, in the final act, that "that sort of man never marries."[65] What is more surprising, given Jack's earlier assertions about the artist serving the Life Force, is his response that the "poetic temperament" is "[b]arren" and that the "Life Force passes it by."[66] Tavy's ideas, apparently, will die with him.

If one considers that Jack's attitudes in the final act are influenced by the play's dream sequence, in which Don Juan speaks of the artist slightingly (because of his slavery to illusion) and of the philosopher as the culmination (so far) of human accomplishments, then it becomes clear why Tavy is now deemed to be overlooked by evolution: the stage of evolution he represents is passing. But what has become of the artist-philosopher of the "Epistle Dedicatory"? One could say that he has been reduced by half as a logical result of having been divided into two parts—Tavy the poet and Jack the philosopher. This strategy dissociates the sensual, selfish, emotional, non-philosophical artist from the ascetic, altruistic, rational, serious artist.

But the result of this strategy, contrary to what one might think, is not a model of safe (noncorroding) yet significant intellectual activity, represented by Jack. For Jack is the one who is sexually sacrificed to nature's evolutionary project by being mated to Ann, who completes him with her vitality, fearlessness, and fertility. Jack aspires to being a pilot of the Life Force, which would require remaining inviolate. The time has not yet come for such piloting, however, and Jack cannot hold out against Ann, even though capitulation means "apostasy, profanation of the sanctuary of [his] soul, violation of [his] manhood," and even though he will "decay like a thing that has served its purpose and is done with . . ."[67] There is a sense in which the philosopher's ideas are just as barren as the artist's. As Holroyd notes, in *Man and Superman* "biological progress must precede intellectual development," and "since Tanner . . . can contribute more to evolutionary advancement through producing children than political handbooks, this is a happy ending."[68] It is a happy ending, that is, if one decides that the union of Ann and Jack will be biologically useful.[69] The acquired characteristics (independence of mind, and so on) that are desirable in Jack will become "disacquired," he seems convinced, if he initiates his own decline as a married man.

So far I have emphasized the aspects of Shaw's thought that denote a great concern for integrity and control. But an economy of self which shelters integrity and ensures control by hoarding energy is not Shaw's only ideal. His "Epistle Dedicatory" contains the following passage:

> This is the true joy in life, the being used for a purpose recognized by yourself as a mighty one; the being thoroughly worn out before you are thrown on the scrap heap; the being a force of Nature instead of a feverish little clod of ailments and grievances complaining that the world will not devote itself to making you happy.[70]

The modifying phrase "recognized by yourself as a mighty one" raises the possibility of doubt and subjects the joyful unconcern for integrity, and the project of disseminating all one's energies, to sanctioning by the self, and thus in a sense invalidates the sentiment expressed. "If one could be sure that it was not all going to waste," Shaw seems to be saying, "what joy to spend one's strength recklessly!"

In effect, that is what his superman does. In *The Perfect Wagnerite* (1898) Shaw describes four possible economies of self. There are "instinctive" people who give free rein to impulse and lay the world to waste, and "stupid, respectful, money-worshipping people" who quell all their instincts. Neither of these kinds of people makes any contribution to humanity. Then there are "the intellectual, moral, talented people who devise and administer States and Churches," members of an aristocracy/meritocracy who are characterized by a healthy equilibrium, spending themselves in a measured way.[71] Lastly, there is the yet unrealized possibility of the hero, prefigured in Wagner's Siegfried,

> a type of the healthy man raised to perfect confidence in his own impulses by an intense and joyous vitality which is above fear, sickliness of conscience, malice, and the makeshift moral crutches of law and order which accompany them.[72]

The hero's economy of self can be defined as a healthy disequilibrium: he does not withhold or misspend his energy (he embraces neither thrift nor deferral), but rather releases all of it because he is certain that it will serve a worthy purpose. He embodies a kind of joyful entropy at the service of evolution. Shaw's hero is free of inner tension because convention has no hold on him—he is completely a child of nature. The constraints of the social organism are inoperative, and this flux-attuned self serves the cosmic organism, not through a sublimation of natural impulse but through a surrender to nature's forces, which when operating outside the money/desire system cannot compromise the self.[73]

Shaw's scripting of his own life, in a present still bound by short-sighted social exigencies, is in a sense less realistic than that of many of his characters' lives. His was a sexless marriage based on friendship, and his intense affairs with other women (Ellen Terry, for example) were by and large cerebral. Confronted with a choice between the rational notion of procreation as a social and cosmic duty (as well as the only means of perpetuating the self) and the fantasy of sublimation as an emancipation from natural processes, Shaw favored, physically as well as rhetorically, a sexual dialectic of denial and energy transformation. He illustrates how warring discourses, competing for a share of the cultural marketplace, are internalized as warring aspirations and desires in the individual.

But Shaw's inconsistencies beckon beyond a focus on discourses and the opportunities they provide for self-construction. In a different context, that of homosexual identity, Jeffrey Weeks argues that Foucauldian analysis fails to consider that, when hailed by a given sexual orientation, "some are able to respond and recognize themselves in the interpellation and others are not."[74] This can be applied to Shaw's resistance to his own heterosexual prescription: the strategy he embraces, according to his own logic, aims at selfishly and unproductively protecting his integrity in the present rather than ensuring an improved human race in the future.[75] In Shaw we see how "the subject's internal apprehension of desire often varies with public testimony and cultural symbolization" and may "testify to acute levels of ambivalence, hostility, even disgust."[76] For reasons which only another critical apparatus could address, he was unable to heed the interpellation of a discourse that sought to create an unproblematic and standardized heterosexuality.

NOTES

1. Barnes and Shapin comment: "naturalism was the ideology of rapidly ascending new professional groups in an industrializing society. Expert laymen, legitimating their authority in terms of the secular ideology of naturalism, competed with and opposed the traditional sacred authority of clerics. And in this they were ultimately sustained by the newly powerful 'bourgeois' groupings whose commercial and industrial activities set them in opposition to the landed interest and its traditional minions" (93).

2. Brian Wynne, "Physics and Psychics: Science, Symbolic Action, and Social Control in Late Victorian England," *Natural Order: Historical Studies of Scientific Culture*, ed. Barry Barnes and Steven Shapin (Beverly Hills: Sage Publications, 1979), 174.

3. See also Heyck 198–208 and Stokes 31.

4. Tom Gibbons, *Rooms in the Darwin Hotel: Studies in English Literary Criticism and Ideas, 1880–1920* (Nedlands: University of Western Australia Press, 1973), 142.

5. It is only with the advent of an unabashedly nonorganic, synthetic self, constructed in defiance of scientific laws by such authors as Conrad, James, and Yeats (and hinted at in Wilde), that this self-defeating mechanism ceases to operate.

6. Greg Myers, "Nineteenth-Century Popularizations of Thermodynamics and the Rhetoric of Social Prophecy," *Victorian Studies* 29 (1985): 63.

7. Quoted in Charles Singer, *A Short History of Science to the Nineteenth Century* (Oxford: Clarendon Press, 1941), 413.

8. Daniel Pick, *Faces of Degeneration: A European Disorder, c. 1848–c. 1918* (Cambridge: Cambridge University Press, 1989), 180.

9. Spencer writes, in *The Principles of Biology*: "survival of the fittest is a maintenance of the moving equilibrium of the functions in presence of outer actions: implying the possession of an equilibrium which is relatively stable in contrast with the unstable equilibrium of those which do not survive" (548).

10. Stephen G. Brush, *The Temperature of History: Phases of Science and Culture in the Nineteenth Century* (New York: Burt Franklin, 1978), 10, see 14.

11. Quoted in Havelock Ellis, "A Note on Paul Bourget," *Views and Reviews: A Selection of Uncollected Articles 1884–1932* (London: Desmond Harmsworth, 1932), 52.

12. Pick, *Faces of Degeneration*, 6.

13. This tendency must be related to two important features of scientific naturalism: the first law of thermodynamics (the law of energy conservation) and the principle of continuity. The latter was not new: within the framework of natural theology, the scientific movement that dominated the first part of the nineteenth

century, it had been seen as a feature of God's magnificently simple design. The acceptance of evolutionary theory, however, coupled with the idea that explanations of phenomena were not valid if they posited "new infusions of external energy into the closed mechanism of nature," resulted in the ruling out of all supernatural causes (Turner 27).

14. Anthropologist Edward B. Tylor, for example, established a parallel between poetic imagination and the myth-making of "primitive" peoples; he wrote of "the poet's gift of throwing [his] mind back into the world's older life" (305). He also wrote of the closeness of "mythic fancy" to the "morbid subjectivity of illness" (306).

15. See Pick 197.

16. H. G. Wells, *H. G. Wells: Early Writings in Science and Science Fiction*, ed. Robert M. Philmus and David Y. Hughes (Berkeley: University of California Press, 1975), 224.

17. Peter Gay, *Education of the Senses* (New York: Oxford University Press, 1984), 317.

18. Jon Stratton, *The Virgin Text: Fiction, Sexuality and Ideology* (Brighton: Harvester Press, 1987), 3.

19. Ibid., 144.

20. Ibid., xi.

21. Pierre Bourdieu, *Distinction: A Social Critique of the Judgement of Taste*, trans. Richard Nice (Cambridge: Harvard University Press, 1984), 491, 176, 54.

22. Max Nordau, *Degeneration* (London: William Heinemann, 1895), 332.

23. Ibid., 333.

24. Ibid., 334.

25. Terry Eagleton, "The Ideology of the Aesthetic," *The Rhetoric of Interpretation and the Interpretation of Rhetoric* (Durham: Duke University Press, 1989), 76.

26. Michael Holroyd, *Bernard Shaw*, 5 vols. (London: Chatto & Windus, 1988), 1 : 310.

27. In a letter to Jules Magny, Shaw explains that he "preserved [his] virginity by mere force of circumstances until [he] was nearer thirty than twenty" because, being "unknown, and shabby, and penniless, and awkward, and at the same time fastidious and proud," he shrank from "attempting a role which requires at least some pocket money and a presentable hat" (*Letters* 1 : 279).

28. Holroyd, 1 : 108.

29. Bernard Shaw, *Collected Letters,* ed. Dan H. Laurence, 4 vols. (New York: Dodd, Mead & Company, 1965–88), 1 : 591.

30. Bernard Shaw, *The Works of Bernard Shaw*, 30 vols. (London: Constable, 1930–32), 10 : 111.

31. Holroyd, 2 : 35.

32. Shaw, *Works*, 9 : xiv.

33. Ibid., 9 : xix.

34. Ibid., 9 : x, xi.

35. One reason for Shaw's dislike of the rich evangelical Englishman is that he remains at an evolutionary stage, once crucial but now obsolete, marked by the quelling of instinct. For Shaw instinct is not all bad, and he despises a man who cannot rise above "the danger and the fear that his acquisitiveness will lead him to theft, his temper to murder, and his affection to debauchery." (*Works* 19 : 33).

36. Shaw, *Works*, 9 : xi.

37. Ibid., 30 : 22.

38. Shaw, *Letters*, 2 : 369.

39. Shaw, *Works*, 19 : 28.

40. H. G. Wells declared that "Shaw had a physiological disgust at vital activities" and that he "detected an element of cruelty . . . in sexual matters" ("Bernard
Shaw by H. G. Wells," *Daily Express*, 3 November 1950; qtd. in Holroyd 2 : 134).

41. In *Back to Methuselah* the last speech is given to Lilith, the incarnation of
the Life Force, who says of her human creations: "let them dread, of all things,
stagnation; for from the moment that I . . . lose hope and faith in them, they are
doomed" (*Works* 16 : 262).

42. Shaw, *Works*, 19 : 24.

43. Marriage, an institution created by "the iron laws by which Society regu-
lates [the] gratification of the sex instinct," represented to Shaw an unhealthy immersion of the self in processes governed by obsolete social laws and mind-
numbing natural laws (*Works* 19 : 28). Evolution, he hoped, would lead away from
duty as defined in terms of "honorable love," marital obligations, filial affection,
and so on, and toward a world in which sexuality would be confined to eugenically-
defined duties (*Works* 10 : 121).

44. Shaw, *Works*, 10 : xix.

45. Shaw, *Letters*, 1 : 228.

46. Shaw, *Works*, 10 : xxii–xxiii.

47. Shaw, *Letters*, 1 : 332.

48. Shaw, *Works*, 7 : 151.

49. Shaw, *Letters*, 2 : 426.

50. Shaw, *Works*, 19 : 328–29.

51. Ibid., 10 : 23.

52. One can gather from his pronouncements on sin as variation and aesthetics
as akin to sexual selection that Wilde thought of homosexuality (as it would come
to be known) as a beneficial (i.e., culturally useful), variation worthy of selection
by nature (see *Works* 1023, 1058). Shaw, on the other hand, considered same-sex
desire to be an aberration that nature tolerated (as society should) but did not regard as useful. In a letter to the editor of *Truth* on the subject of the Cleveland
Street scandal, Shaw called homosexuality an "abnormal appetite" affecting "a
small minority of people" (*Letters* 1 : 231). Elsewhere, writing this time about
Havelock Ellis's *Sexual Inversion*, he characterizes homosexuality as a "morbid
idiosyncrasy" not to be automatically associated with "depravity of character" and
harmless to the population at large (2 : 57).

53. Quoted in Ishrat Lindblad, *Creative Evolution and Shaw's Dramatic Art
with Special Reference to Man and Superman and Back to Methuselah* (Uppsala:
Uppsala University Press, 1971), 71.

54. Shaw, *Letters*, 1 : 625.

55. Another solution, one adopted by Shaw himself, is to marry someone whom
one does not desire. For variations on the theme of a possessive passion's incom-
patibility with artistic and social effectiveness, see Shaw's novels *Love Among the
Artists* (1881) and *An Unsocial Socialist* (1884).

56. Shaw, *Works*, 10 : 24.

57. See Frederick P. W. McDowell, "Heaven, Hell, and Turn-of-the-Century
London," 39.

58. One exception is Ibsen as portrayed in *The Quintessence of Ibsenism*
(1891).

59. Daniel J. Leary, "The Evolutionary Dialectic of Shaw and Teilhard: A Perennial Philosophy," *The Shaw Review* 9 (1966): 15.

60. Shaw was a neo-Lamarckian who adopted many of Samuel Butler's ideas regarding heredity, such as the belief that embryology's recapitulation theory "enabl[es] us to hope that the most prolonged and difficult operations of our minds may yet become instantaneous, or, as we call it, instinctive" (*Works* 16 : xxvii). Shaw despised the theory of natural selection, according to which "Nature is nothing but a casual aggregation of inert and dead matter" (xlii), and which "subjects man to impersonal, statistical laws, operates apart from his will, and thereby deprives him of responsibility and a sense of conscious purpose" (Kagarlitski 66). Neo-Lamarckism, on the other hand, bridges the gap between individual will and racial improvement: "in Shaw's thought long-felt needs accumulate until they affect the genes, and then a 'leap' occurs. The idea is religious, for it is not clear to biologists that desire influences the genes" (Bailey 49).

61. Thomas Postlewait, "Bernard Shaw and Science: The Aesthetics of Causality," *Victorian Science and Victorian Values, Annals of the New York Academy of Sciences*, vol. 360, ed. James Paradis and Postlewait (New York: New York Academy of Sciences, 1981), 349.

62. Shaw, *Works*, 10 : 180.

63. In a letter Shaw wrote that

the best brought-up children . . . are those who have been brought up in a large family, where the parents have had no time to study individual children much, and where the children themselves have knocked one another into some sort of communal conscience without the least sense of duty. . . . Next to them come the children of busy parents, who have lived their own lives frankly before their children as hard as they can, and not bothered about their character or tried experiments in moral abortion (*Letters* 2 : 413).

64. Shaw, *Works*, 10 : 24.

65. Ibid., 10 : 167.

66. Ibid., 10 : 167–68.

67. Ibid., 10 : 166.

68. Holroyd, 2 : 78.

69. The critics differ widely on this point. Holroyd represents the "happy evolutionary ending" point of view. Others hold that Tanner is not the superior person he believes himself to be and that the comedy of *Man and Superman* derives from the deflation of his evolutionary pretentions: "Whatever his initial intention, Shaw has given us . . . , not two irresistible forces, but the snapping-up of a clever young man by a shrewd young woman" (Bentley 17). Still others perceive an unhappy evolutionary ending, defining Jack as someone "developed beyond the generality" and therefore interpreting his capitulation as "a situation which on another scale might well fulfill the conditions of tragedy" (Valency 100).

70. Shaw, *Works*, 10 : xxxiv–xxxv.

71. Ibid., 19 : 201.

72. Ibid., 19 : 225.

73. That desire is the more threatening component is apparent in Shaw's ambivalence toward the idea of being "used" by women (which parallels his partial mistrust of nature's purposes), as expressed in the following contradictory statements, both made in letters to Ellen Terry:

I dread success. To have succeeded is to have finished one's business on earth, like the male spider, who is killed by the female the moment he has succeeded in his courtship. I like a state of continual *becoming*, with a goal in front and not behind. (*Letters* 1 : 645)

I must be *used*, built into the solid fabric of your life . . . and thrown aside when I am used up. It is only when I am being used that I can feel my own existence. . . . All my love affairs end tragically because the women *can't* use me. (676)

74. Jeffrey Weeks, "Discourse, Desire and Sexual Deviance: Some Problems in a History of Homosexuality," *The Making of the Modern Homosexual*, ed. Kenneth Plummer (London: Hutchinson, 1981), 107.

75. Weeks mentions the need to examine "specific family pressures, the educational and labeling processes, the media images that reinforce the identity and the individual shaping of meaning" ("Discourse" 98).

76. Christopher Lane, *The Ruling Passion: British Colonial Allegory and the Paradox of Homosexual Desire* (Durham: Duke University Press, 1995), 7.

Selected Bibliography

Abrams, M. H., et al. *The Norton Anthology of Literature*. Vol. 2, 6th ed., 718–31. New York: W. W. Norton, 1993.

Acton, William. *The Functions and Disorders of the Reproductive Organs*. Philadelphia: Lindsay, 1871.

Adams, James Eli. *Dandies and Desert Saints: Styles of Victorian Manhood*. Ithaca: Cornell University Press, 1995.

Alexander, Boyd. *England's Wealthiest Son: A Study of William Beckford*. London: Centaur Press, 1962.

Anderson, Benedict. *Imagined Communities: Reflections on the Origin and Spread of Nationalism*. London: Verso, 1986.

Archer, William. "Mr. W. S. Gilbert." *St. James Magazine* 49 (1881). Reprinted in *W. S. Gilbert: A Century of Scholarship and Commentary*, edited by John Bush Jones, 17–49. New York: New York University Press, 1970.

Ariosto, Lodovico. *Orlando Furioso*. Translated by Guido Waldman. 1516. New York: Oxford University Press, 1974.

Armstrong, Isobel. *Victorian Poetry: Poetry, Poetics & Politics*. London: Routledge, 1993.

———. *Victorian Scrutinies: Reviews of Poetry 1830–1870*. London: Athlone, 1972.

Armstrong, Nancy. *Desire and Domestic Fiction: A Political History of the Novel*. New York: Oxford University Press, 1987.

Auerbach, Nina. *Our Vampires, Ourselves*. Chicago: University of Chicago Press, 1995.

Augustine. *Confessions*. Translated by R. S. Pine-Coffin. New York: Penguin, 1988.

Bailey, J. O. "Shaw's Life Force and Science Fiction." *The Shaw Review* 16 (1973): 48–58.

Baker, Robert S. "Gabriel Nash's 'House of Strange Idols': Aestheticism in *The Tragic Muse*." *Texas Studies in Literature and Language* 15 (1973): 149–66.

Barham, Richard Harris. *The Newgate Calendar or Malefactors' Bloody Register*. London: T. Werner Laurie, 1932.

———. "The Wondrous Tale of Ikey Solomons" (Berg Collection, New York Public Library), n. p., sh. 6.

Barnes, Barry, and Steven Shapin, eds. *Natural Order: Historical Studies of Scientific Culture*. Beverly Hills: Sage Publications, 1979.

Barrus, Clara. *Whitman and Burroughs: Comrades*. Boston: Houghton Mifflin, 1931.

Barthes, Roland. *A Lover's Discourse: Fragments.* Translated by Richard Howard. New York: Hill & Wang, 1978.

Barton, Anne. *Don Juan.* Cambridge: Cambridge University Press, 1992.

Beckford, William. *The Episodes of Vathek.* Sawtry, Cambs.: Dedalus, 1994.

———. *Vathek and Other Stories.* Edited by Malcolm Jack. London: Penguin, 1993.

———. *Vathek. Three Gothic Novels.* Edited by E. F. Bleiler. New York: Dover, 1966.

Beer, Gillian. *George Eliot.* Bloomington: Indiana University Press, 1986.

Begnal, Michael H. *Joseph Sheridan LeFanu.* Lewisburg: Bucknell University Press, 1971.

Beith, Gilbert. *Edward Carpenter: In Appreciation.* 1931. New York: Haskell House, 1973.

Bellringer, Alan W. "*The Tragic Muse*: 'The Objective Centre.' " *Journal of American Studies* 4, no. 1–2 (1970): 73–89.

Benson, Arthur C. *Walter Pater.* English Men of Letters. New York: Macmillan, 1906.

Benson, Nancy A. "Hero and Narrator in Byron's *Don Juan*: A Piagetian Approach." *Centennial Review* 28–29 (1984–85): 48–57.

Bentley, Eric. "The Theatre." In *George Bernard Shaw's "Man and Superman,"* edited by Harold Bloom, 15–19. New York: Chelsea House Publishers, 1987.

Bersani, Leo. *A Future for Astyanax: Character and Desire in Literature.* Boston: Little, Brown, 1976.

Black, Jeremy. *The British Abroad: The Grand Tour in the Eighteenth Century.* New York: St. Martin's Press, 1992.

Bloom, Harold, and Lionel Trilling, eds. *Romantic Poetry and Prose.* New York: Oxford University Press, 1973.

Bodenheimer, Rosemarie. *The Private Life of Mary Ann Evans.* Ithaca: Cornell University Press, 1994.

Bohstedt, John. "Gender, Household and Community Politics: Women in English Riots, 1790–1810." *Past and Present* 120 (August 1988): 88–122.

Boone, Joseph Alan. "Vacation Cruises; or, The Homoerotics of Orientalism." *PMLA* 110 (January 1995): 89–107.

Booth, Alan. "Food Riots in the North-West of England, 1790–1801." *Past and Present* 77 (1977): 84–107.

Born, Daniel. *The Birth of Liberal Guilt in the English Novel: Charles Dickens to H. G. Wells.* Chapel Hill: University of North Carolina Press, 1995.

Boswell, John. *Christianity, Social Tolerance, and Homosexuality.* Chicago: University of Chicago Press, 1980.

Bourdieu, Pierre. *Distinction: A Social Critique of the Judgement of Taste.* Translated by Richard Nice. Cambridge: Harvard University Press, 1984.

Boyarin, Daniel. *Carnal Israel: Reading Sex in Talmudic Culture.* Berkeley: University of California Press, 1993.

———. *A Radical Jew: Paul and the Politics of Identity.* Berkeley: University of California Press, 1994.

Boyarin, Jonathan. *Storm from Paradise: The Politics of Jewish Memory.* Minneapolis: University of Minnesota Press, 1992.

Brake, Laurel. "The Discourses of Journalism: 'Arnold and Pater' Again—and Wilde." In *Pater in the 1990s*, edited by Laurel Brake and Ian Small, 43–61. Greensboro: ELT Press, 1991.

———. "Judas and the Widow. Thomas Wright and A. C. Benson as Biographers of Walter Pater: The Widow." In *Walter Pater: An Imaginative Sense of Fact*, edited by Philip Dodd, 39–54. London: Frank Cass, 1981.

———. *Subjugated Knowledges: Journalism, Gender and Literature in the Nineteenth Century*. New York: New York University Press, 1994.

Bray, Alan. "Homosexuality and the Signs of Male Friendship in Elizabethan England." *History Workshop Journal* 29 (Spring 1990): 1–19.

———. *Homosexuality in Renaissance England*. London: Gay Men's Press, 1982.

Briggs, Julia. *Night Visitors: The Rise and Fall of the English Ghost Story*. London: Faber, 1977.

Bristow, Joseph. *Effeminate England: Homoerotic Writing After 1885*. New York: Columbia University Press, 1995.

Bruhm, Steven. *Gothic Bodies: The Politics of Pain in Romantic Fiction*. Philadelphia: University of Pennsylvania Press, 1994.

Brush, Stephen G. *The Temperature of History: Phases of Science and Culture in the Nineteenth Century*. New York: Burt Franklin, 1978.

Buckton, Oliver S. "Closet Dramas: Strategies of Secrecy and Disclosure in Four Victorian Autobiographies." Ph.D. dissertation, Cornell, 1992.

———. *Secret Selves: Confession and Same-Sex Desire in Victorian Autobiography*. Chapel Hill: University of North Carolina Press, 1998.

———. " 'An Unnatural State': Gender, 'Perversion,' and Newman's *Apologia Pro Vita Sua*." *Victorian Studies* 35 (Summer 1992): 359–83.

Butler, Judith. *Bodies that Matter: On the Discursive Limits of "Sex."* New York: Routledge, 1993.

———. *Gender Trouble: Feminism and the Subversion of Identity*. New York: Routledge, 1990.

Butler, Marilyn. "The Orientalism of Byron's *Giaour*." In *Byron and the Limits of Fiction*, edited by Bernard Beatty and Vincent Newey, 78–96. Totowa, N.J.: Barnes and Noble Books, 1988.

Byron, Lord George Gordon. *Byron's Letters and Journals*. Edited by Leslie A. Marchand. 12 vols. Cambridge: Harvard University Press, 1973–82.

———. *Byron: The Oxford Authors*, edited by Jerome J. McGann, 378–403. New York: Oxford University Press, 1986.

———. *The Complete Poetical Works*, edited by Jerome J. McGann, 6 vols. Oxford: Clarendon Press, 1980-.

Bythell, Duncan. *The Sweated Trades: Outwork in Nineteenth Century Britain*. London: Batsford Academic, 1978.

Calhoun, Craig. *The Question of Class Struggle*. Chicago: University of Chicago Press, 1982.

Cameron, Sharon. *Thinking in Henry James*. Chicago: University of Chicago Press, 1989.

Carlyle, Thomas. "Characteristics." 1831. In *A Carlyle Reader*, edited by G. B. Tennyson, 67–103. Cambridge: Cambridge University Press, 1984.

———. *Sartor Resartus*. 1833–34. New York: Oxford University Press, 1987.

Carpenter, Edward. *Days with Walt Whitman*. London: George Allen, 1906.

————. *England's Ideal, and Other Papers on Social Subjects*. London: Swan Sonnenschein, 1887.

————. *Homogenic Love*. London: Redundancy Press, n.d.

————. *My Days and Dreams: Being Autobiographical Notes*. London: Allen & Unwin, 1916.

————. *Selected Writings*. Vol 1. In *Sex*, edited by Noel Grieg. London: Gay Men's Press, 1984.

————. *Towards Democracy*. London: Swan Sonnenschein, 1905.

————. *An Unknown People*. London: n.p., 1897.

Carpenter, Mary Wilson. "Representing Apocalypse: Sexual Politics and the Violence of Revelation." In *Postmodern Apocalypse: Theory and Cultural Practice at the End*, edited by Richard Dellamora, 107–35. Philadelphia: University of Pennsylvania Press, 1995.

Cartledge, Paul. "The Importance of Being Dorian: an Onomastic Gloss on the Hellenism of Oscar Wilde." *Hermathena* 147 (1989): 7–15.

Castle, Terry. *Masquerade and Civilization: The Carnivalesque in Eighteenth-Century English Culture and Fiction*. Stanford: Stanford University Press, 1986.

Catullus, Gaius Valerius. *The Poems of Catullus*. Translated by Charles Martin. Baltimore: Johns Hopkins University Press, 1990.

Chambers, J. D. "The Worshipful Company of Framework Knitters (1657–1778)." *Economica* (November 1929): 296–329.

Chambers, Ross. *Room for Maneuver: Reading (the) Oppositional (in) Narrative*. Chicago: University of Chicago Press, 1991.

————. "Poaching and Pastiche: Reproducing the Gay Subculture." *Canadian Review of Comparative Literature/Revue Canadienne de Littérature Comparée* 21, no. 1–2 (1994): 169–92.

Chauncey, George. *Gay New York: Gender, Urban Culture, and the Making of the Gay Male World, 1890–1940*. New York: Harper, 1994.

Childers, Joseph. *Novel Possibilities: Fiction and the Formation of Early Victorian Culture*. Philadelphia: University of Pennsylvania Press, 1995.

Chitty, Susan. *The Beast and the Monk: A Life of Charles Kingsley*. London: Hodder & Stoughton, 1975.

Christensen, Jerome. *Lord Byron's Strength: Romantic Writing and Commercial Society*. Baltimore: Johns Hopkins University Press, 1993.

Church, R. W. *The Oxford Movement. Twelve Years 1833–1845*. London: Macmillan, 1932.

Clement, Catherine. *Synecope: The Philosophy of Rapture*. Translated by Sally O'Driscoll and Deirdre M. Mahoney. Minneapolis: University of Minnesota Press, 1994.

Cohen, Ed. *Talk on the Wilde Side: Toward a Genealogy of a Discourse on Male Sexualities*. New York: Routledge, 1993.

————. "Writing Gone Wilde: Homoerotic Desire in the Closet of Representation." In *Critical Essays on Oscar Wilde*, edited by Regenia Gagnier, 68–87. New York: G. K. Hall, 1991.

Cohen, William A. "Manual Conduct in *Great Expectations*." *ELH* 60, no. 1 (Spring 1993): 217–60.

―――. "Willie and Wilde: Reading *The Portrait of Mr. W. H.*" In *Displacing Homophobia: Gay Male Perspectives in Literature and Culture*, edited by Ronald R. Butters, John M. Clum, and Michael Moon, 207–33. Durham: Duke University Press, 1989.

Colley, Linda. *Britons: Forging the Nation 1707–1837*. New Haven: Yale University Press, 1992.

Colloms, Brenda. *Charles Kingsley: The Lion of Eversley*. London: Constable, 1975.

Cooper, Michael A. "Discipl(in)ing the Master, Mastering the Discipl(in)e: Erotonomies in James' Tales of Literary Life." In *Engendering Men: The Question of Male Feminist Criticism*, edited by Joseph A. Boone and Michael Cadden, 66–83. New York: Routledge, 1990.

Corber, Robert J. "Lesbian and Gay Studies in Today's Academy." *Academe* (September-October 1998): 46–49.

―――. "Representing the 'Unspeakable': William Godwin and the Politics of Homophobia." *Journal of the History of Sexuality* 1, no. 1 (1990): 85–101.

Craft, Christopher. "Alias Bunbury: Desire and Termination in *The Importance of Being Earnest*." *Representations* 31 (Summer 1990): 19–46.

―――. *Another Kind of Love: Male Homosexual Desire in English Discourse, 1850–1920*. Berkeley: University of California Press, 1994.

Creech, James. *Closet Writing / Gay Reading: The Case of Melville's "Pierre."* Chicago: University of Chicago Press, 1993.

Crompton, Louis. *Byron and Greek Love: Homophobia in 19th-Century England*. Berkeley: University of California Press, 1985.

―――. "*Don Leon*, Byron, and Homosexual Law Reform." *Journal of Homosexuality* 8 (1983): 53–71.

Curran, Stuart. "*Adonais* in Context." In *Shelley Revalued*, edited by Kelvin Everest, 165–82. Totowa N.J.: Barnes and Noble Books, 1983.

Curtin, Philip D. *The Image of Africa: British Ideas and Action, 1780–1850*. Madison: University of Wisconsin Press, 1964.

Daffron, Eric. " 'Magnetical Sympathy': Strategies of Power and Resistance in Godwin's *Caleb Williams*." *Criticism* 37, no. 2 (Spring 1995): 213–32.

Dale, Peter Allan. "Oscar Wilde: Crime and the 'Glorious Shapes of Art.' " *Victorian Newsletter* 88 (Fall 1995): 1–5.

Danson, Lawrence. "Oscar Wilde, W. H., and the Unspoken Name of Love." *ELH* 58 (1991): 979–1000.

Dante Alighieri. *The Divine Comedy: Inferno*. Translated and Introduction by Allen Mandelbaum. Berkeley: University of California Press, 1980.

d'Arch Smith, Timothy. *Love in Earnest*. London: Routledge, 1970.

Dark, Sidney, and Rowland Grey. *W. S. Gilbert: His Life and Letters*. 1923. New York: Benjamin Blom, 1972.

Davis, Natalie Zemon. *Society and Culture in Early Modern Europe*. Stanford: Stanford University Press, 1975.

De Lauretis, Teresa. "Habit Changes." *Differences* 6 (Summer-Fall 1994): 296–313.

―――. *The Practice of Love: Lesbian Sexuality and Perverse Desire*. Bloomington: Indiana University Press, 1994.

Dellamora, Richard. "The Androgynous Body in Pater's 'Winckelmann,' " *Browning Institute Studies* 11 (1983): 51–68.

———. *Apocalyptic Overtures: Sexual Politics and The Sense of an Ending.* New Brunswick: Rutgers University Press, 1994.

———. "Critical Impressionism as Anti-Phallogocentric Strategy." In *Pater in the 1990s,* edited by Laurel Brake and Ian Small, 127–42. Greensboro: ELT Press, 1991.

———. *Masculine Desire: The Sexual Politics of Victorian Aestheticism.* Chapel Hill: University of North Carolina Press, 1990.

———. "Victorian Homosexuality in the Prism of Foucault." Review Essay. *Victorian Studies* 38, no. 2 (Winter 1995): 265–72.

"Development." *Punch* 20 September 1890: 135.

Disraeli, Benjamin. *Alroy.* Introduction by Philip Guedalla. London: Peter Davies, 1927.

———. *Letters.* Edited by J. A. W. Gunn, John Matthews, Donald M. Schurman, and M. G. Wiebe. Toronto: University of Toronto Press, 1982.

———. *Whigs and Whiggism: Political Writings.* Edited by William Hutcheon. London: John Murray, 1913.

Disraeli, Isaac. *The Genius of Judaism.* London: Edward Moxon, 1833.

Dollimore, Jonathan. *Sexual Dissidence: Augustine to Wilde, Freud to Foucault.* Oxford: Clarendon Press, 1991.

Donoghue, Denis. *Walter Pater: Lover of Strange Souls.* New York: Knopf, 1995.

Douglas, Mary. *Purity and Danger: An Analysis of Concepts of Pollution and Taboo.* Harmondsworth: Penguin, 1966.

Dowling, Linda. *Hellenism and Homosexuality in Victorian Oxford.* Ithaca: Cornell University Press, 1994.

———. "Imposture and Absence in Wilde's *Portrait of Mr. W. H.*" *Victorian Newsletter* 58 (1980), 26–29.

———. "Ruskin's Pied Beauty and the Constitution of a 'Homosexual' Code." *Victorian Newsletter* 75 (Spring 1989): 1–8.

Drinka, George Frederick, M. D. *The Birth of Neurosis: Myth, Malady and the Victorians.* New York: Simon & Schuster, 1984.

During, Simon. "Literature—Nationalism's Other? The Case for Revision." In *Nation and Narration,* edited by Homi K. Bhabha, 138–153. London: Routledge, 1994.

E. R. "Parallel." *Punch* 19 July 1890: 25.

Eagleton, Terry. "The Ideology of the Aesthetic." In *The Rhetoric of Interpretation and the Interpretation of Rhetoric,* 76–86. Durham: Duke University Press, 1989.

Edelman, Lee. *Homographesis: Essays in Gay Literary and Cultural Theory.* New York: Routledge, 1994.

———. "Seeing Things: Representation, the Scene of Surveillance, and the Spectacle of Gay Male Sex." In *Inside/Out: Lesbian Theories, Gay Theories,* edited by Diana Fuss, 93–116. New York: Routledge, 1991.

Elfenbein, Andrew. *Byron and the Victorians.* Cambridge: Cambridge University Press, 1995.

Eliot, George. *The Mill on the Floss*. 1860. Edited by Gordon S. Haight. Boston: Houghton Mifflin, 1961.

——. *Silas Marner*. 1861. New York: Signet Books, 1960.

Ellis, Edith. *Personal Impressions of Edward Carpenter*. Berkeley Heights, NJ: Free Spirit Press, 1922.

Ellis, Havelock. *My Life*. London: Heinemann, 1940.

——. "A Note on Paul Bourget." In *Views and Reviews: A Selection of Uncollected Articles 1884–1932*, 48–60. London: Desmond Harmsworth, 1932.

Ellmann, Richard. "Henry James Among the Aesthetes." *Proceedings of the British Academy* 69 (1983): 209–28.

——. *Oscar Wilde*. New York: Vintage Books, 1987.

Feldman, David. *Englishmen and Jews: Social Relations and Political Culture, 1840–1914*. New Haven: Yale University Press, 1994.

Fothergill, Brian. *Beckford of Fonthill*. London: Faber, 1979.

Foucault, Michel. *Discipline and Punish: The Birth of the Prison*. Translated by Alan Sheridan. New York: Pantheon, 1977.

——. *The History of Sexuality. Volume 1: An Introduction*. Translated by Robert Hurley. New York: Pantheon, 1978.

——. "Sexuality and Solitude." *On Signs*. Edited by Marshall Blonsky, 365–72. Baltimore: Johns Hopkins University Press, 1985.

——. *The Use of Pleasure*. Vol. 2 of *The History of Sexuality*. Translated by Robert Hurley. New York: Vintage Books, 1986.

Franklin, Caroline. *Byron's Heroines*. Oxford: Clarendon Press, 1992.

Freedman, Jonathan. *Professions of Taste: Henry James, British Aestheticism, and Commodity Culture*. Stanford: Stanford University Press, 1990.

Freud, Sigmund. *Dora: An Analysis of a Case of Hysteria*. New York: Macmillan, 1963.

——. *The Standard Edition of the Complete Psychological Works of Sigmund Freud*. Edited and translated by James Strachey in collaboration with Anna Freud. 24 vols. London: Hogarth Press, 1957–1974.

——. *Three Essays on the Theory of Sexuality*. Translated by James Strachey. New York: Basic Books, 1962.

Funston, Judith E. " 'All Art Is One': Narrative Techniques in Henry James's *Tragic Muse*." *Studies in the Novel* 15 (1983): 353–55.

Fuss, Diana. *Inside/Out: Lesbian Theories, Gay Theories*. New York: Routledge, 1991.

Gagnier, Regenia. *Idylls of the Marketplace: Oscar Wilde and the Victorian Public*. Stanford: Stanford University Press, 1986.

Gallop, Jane. *The Daughter's Seduction: Feminism and Psychoanalysis*. Ithaca: Cornell University Press, 1989.

Gates, Barbara T. "Blue Devils and Green Tea: Sheridan Le Fanu's Haunted Suicides." *Studies in Short Fiction* 24 (1987): 15–23.

Gates, Henry Louis, Jr., ed. *"Race," Writing, and Difference*. Chicago: University of Chicago Press, 1986.

Gay, Peter. *The Bourgeois Experience: Victoria to Freud*. 5 vols. New York: Oxford University Press, 1984–97. Vol. 1, *Education of the Senses*; vol. 2, *The Tender Passion*; vol. 3, *The Cultivation of Hatred*.

Gellner, Ernest. *Nations and Nationalism*. Oxford: Basil Blackwell, 1983.

Gibbons, Tom. *Rooms in the Darwin Hotel: Studies in English Literary Criticism and Ideas, 1880–1920*. Nedlands: University of Western Australia Press, 1973.

Gilbert, Sandra, and Susan Gubar. *The Madwoman in the Attic: The Woman Writer and the Nineteenth-Century Literary Imagination*. New Haven: Yale University Press, 1979.

Gilbert, W. S. *The Bab Ballads*. 1869. Cambridge: Harvard University Press, 1970.

———. *Engaged*. 1877. *Gilbert's Original Plays*. Vol. 2, 39–85. London: Chatto & Windus, 1875.

———. *Topsyturvydom*. 1874. Oxford: Oxford University Press, 1931.

———. *The Wicked World*. 1873. *Gilbert's Original Plays*. Vol. 1, 1–63. London: Chatto & Windus, 1875.

Gilbert, W. S., and Arthur Sullivan. *Patience, or Bunthorne's Bride*. 1881. In *The Complete Plays of Gilbert and Sullivan*, 183–233. New York: Modern Library, 1936.

Gilman, Charlotte Perkins. *The Living of Charlotte Perkins Gilman*. 1935. New York, Arno Press, 1972.

Gilman, Sander. *Disease and Representation: Images of Illness from Madness to AIDS*. Ithaca: Cornell University Press, 1988.

Gilmore, David D. *Manhood in the Making: Cultural Concepts of Masculinity*. New Haven: Yale University Press, 1990.

Gleckner, Robert. *Byron and the Ruins of Paradise*. Baltimore: Johns Hopkins University Press, 1967.

Godwin, William. *Caleb Williams*. Edited by David McCracken. New York: W. W. Norton, 1977.

———. *Cloudesley*. Edited by Maurice Hindle. *Collected Novels and Memoirs of William Godwin*. Vol. 7. London: Pickering & Chatto, 1992.

———. *Deloraine*. Edited by Maurice Hindle. *Collected Novels and Memoirs of William Godwin*. Vol. 8. London: Pickering & Chatto, 1992.

———. *Fleetwood: or, the New Man of Feeling*. 1805. London: Richard Bentley, 1832.

———. *Mandeville: A Tale of the Seventeenth Century*. Edited by Pamela Clemit. *Collected Novels and Memoirs of William Godwin*. Vol. 6. London: Pickering & Chatto, 1992.

———. *Political and Philosophical Writings of William Godwin*. Edited by Mark Philp. 7 vols. London: Pickering & Chatto, 1993.

———. *St. Leon: A Tale of the Sixteenth Century*. Edited by Pamela Clemit. Oxford: Oxford University Press, 1994.

Goetz, William R. "The Allegory of Representation in *The Tragic Muse*." *Journal of Narrative Technique* 8, no. 3 (1978): 151–64.

Gold, Alex, Jr. "It's Only Love: The Politics of Passion in Godwin's *Caleb Williams*." *Texas Studies in Literature and Language* 19, no. 2 (Summer 1977): 135–60.

Goldberg, Jonathan. *Sodometries: Renaissance Texts, Modern Sexualities*. Stanford: Stanford University Press, 1992.

Goldsmith, Steven. *Unbuilding Jerusalem: Apocalypse and Romantic Representation*. Ithaca: Cornell University Press, 1993.

Graham, Peter. *Don Juan and Regency England*. Charlottesville: University of Virginia Press, 1990.

Green, T. H. *Lectures on the Principle of Political Obligation and Other Writings*. Edited by P. Harris and J. Morrow. Cambridge: Cambridge University Press, 1986.

Greenberg, David. *The Construction of Homosexuality*. Chicago: University of Chicago Press, 1988.

Greenday. "Longview." On *Dookie*. New York: Reprise Records, 1994.

Gross, Jonathan. "Byron and the Liberal: Periodical as Political Posture." *Philological Quarterly* 72 (Fall 1993): 471–85.

Grosskurth, Phyllis. *Byron: The Flawed Angel*. New York: Houghton Mifflin, 1997.

———, ed. "Introduction." *The Memoirs of John Addington Symonds: The Secret Homosexual Life of a Leading Nineteenth-Century Man of Letters*, 13–28. New York: Random House, 1984.

Gunter, Susan Elizabeth. "The Russian Connection: Sources for Miriam Rooth of James's *The Tragic Muse*." *South Atlantic Review* 53, no. 2 (1988): 77–91.

Halberstam, Judith. *Skin Shows: Gothic Horror and the Technology of Monsters*. Durham: Duke University Press, 1995.

Hall, Donald E. "On the Making and Unmaking of Monsters: Christian Socialism, Muscular Christianity, and the Metaphorization of Class Conflict." In *Muscular Christianity: Embodying the Victorian Age*, edited by Donald E. Hall, 45–65. Cambridge: Cambridge University Press, 1994.

Hall, Richard. "Henry James: Interpreting an Obsessive Memory." *Journal of Homosexuality* 8, no. 3–4 (1983): 83–97.

Hall, William F. "Gabriel Nash: 'Famous Centre' of *The Tragic Muse*." *Nineteenth-Century Fiction* 21, no. 2 (1966): 167–84.

Halperin, David M. *One Hundred Years of Homosexuality: And Other Essays on Greek Love*. New York: Routledge, 1990.

Hammond, J. L., and Barbara Hammond. *The Skilled Labourer, 1760–1832*. 1919. New York: Augustus M. Kelley, 1967.

Hartley, Allan John. *The Novels of Charles Kingsley: A Christian Social Interpretation*. Folkestone: Hour-Glass Press, 1977.

Hartsock, Mildred E. "Henry James and the Cities of the Plain." *Modern Language Quarterly* 29 (1968): 305–11.

Hazlitt, William. "On Effeminacy of Character." 1822. *Table Talk: Essays on Men and Manners*. London: Oxford University Press, 1933.

Heath, Stephen. "Joan Rivière and the Masquerade." In *Formations of Fantasy*, edited by Victor Burgin, James Donald, and Cora Kaplan, 45–61. New York: Methuen, 1986.

Heyck, T. W. *The Transformation of Intellectual Life in Victorian England*. London: Croom Helm, 1982.

Heyns, Michiel. *Expulsion and the Nineteenth-Century Novel: The Scapegoat in English Realist Fiction*. Oxford: Oxford University Press, 1994.

Hichens, Robert. *The Green Carnation*. 1894. New York: Dover, 1970.

Higgins, Lesley. "Jowett and Pater: Trafficking in Platonic Wares." *Victorian Studies* 37, no. 1 (Fall 1993): 43–72.

Hilliard, David. "UnEnglish and Unmanly: Anglo-Catholicism and Homosexuality." *Victorian Studies* 25 (Winter 1982): 181–210.

Hoad, T. F., ed., *The Concise Oxford Dictionary of English Etymology*. Oxford: Clarendon Press, 1986.

Hoagwood, Terence. *Byron's Dialectic: Skepticism and the Critique of Culture*. Lewisburg: Bucknell University Press, 1983.

Hobhouse, J. C. *A Journey through Albania and Other Provinces of Turkey in Europe and Asia, to Constantinople, During the Years 1809 and 1810*. Philadelphia: M. Carey, 1817.

Hogle, Jerrold. *Shelley's Process*. New York: Oxford University Press, 1988.

Hollander, Anne. *Seeing through Clothes*. New York: Viking, 1975.

Holmes, Richard. *Shelley: The Pursuit*. London: Penguin, 1974.

Holroyd, Michael. *Bernard Shaw*. 5 vols. London: Chatto & Windus, 1988.

Home Office Papers. Series 40/1 and 42/119. Public Records Office, Kew.

Horace. *Ars Poetica*. In *Critical Theory Since Plato*, edited by Hazard Adams, rev. ed., 68–74. New York: Harcourt, Brace, Jovanovich, 1992.

Howe, Joseph W. *Excessive Venery, Masturbation, and Continence*. 1887. New York: Arno Press, 1974.

Hudson, Nicholas. "From 'Nation' to 'Race': The Origin of Racial Classification in Eighteenth-Century Thought." *Eighteenth-Century Studies* 29 (1996): 247–64.

Hudson, Pat. *Regions and Industries: A Perspective on the Industrial Revolution in Britain*. Cambridge: Cambridge University Press, 1989.

Hughes, Thomas. *Thomas Brown's School Days*. New York: A. L. Burt, 1900.

Hume, David. *Selected Essays*, edited by Stephen Copley and Andrew Edgar. Oxford: Oxford University Press, 1993.

Hunt, Leigh. *Lord Byron and Some of His Contemporaries*. London: Henry Colburn, 1828.

[Hutchinson, Charles Edward.] *Boy Worship*. Oxford: priv. pub., 1880.

Hyde, H. Montgomery. *The Cleveland Street Scandal*. New York: Coward, 1976.

———. *The Other Love: An Historical and Contemporary Survey of Homosexuality in Britain*. London: Heinemann, 1970.

———, ed. *The Trials of Oscar Wilde*. London: William Hodge, 1948.

Inman, Billie Andrew. "Estrangement and Connection: Walter Pater, Benjamin Jowett, and William M. Hardinge." In *Pater in the 1990s*, edited by Laurel Brake and Ian Small, 1–20. Greensboro: ELT Press, 1991.

———. *Walter Pater and His Reading: 1874–1877*. New York: Garland, 1990.

———. *Walter Pater's Readings: A Bibliography of His Library Borrowings*. New York: Garland, 1981.

James, Henry. "Preface to *Roderick Hudson*." 1874. Harmondsworth: Penguin, 1986.

———. "Preface to *The Tragic Muse*." In *The Art of the Novel: Critical Prefaces*, edited by Richard P. Blackmur, 79–97. New York: Scribner's, 1934.

———. *The Sacred Fount*. Edited by Leon Edel. 1901. London: Hart-Davis, 1959.

———. *The Tragic Muse*. 1889; 1890. Harmondsworth: Penguin, 1978.

Jenkyns, Richard. "Recline and Fall." Review of *The Stranger Wilde: Interpreting Oscar* by Gary Schmigdall. *The New Republic* 211 (16 May 1994): 38–42.

Jordan, Frank, ed. *The English Romantic Poets*. 4th edition. New York: Garland, 1988.

Kagarlitski, Julius. "Bernard Shaw and Science Fiction: Why Raise the Question?" *The Shaw Review* 16 (1973): 59–66.

Kamen, Henry. "The Secret of the Inquisition." *New York Review of Books* (1 February 1996): 4–6.

Kappeler, Susanne. *Writing and Reading in Henry James*. New York: Columbia University Press, 1980.

Kaufmann, David. *George Eliot and Judaism: An Attempt to Appreciate "Daniel Deronda."* Translated by J. W. Ferrier. 1888. New York: Haskell House, 1970.

Kingsley, Charles. *Charles Kingsley: His Letters and Memories of His Life*. Edited by F. E. Kingsley. 2 vols. New York: Fred De Fau, 1899.

———. "The Poetry of Sacred and Legendary Art," *Fraser's* 39 (1849): 283–98.

———. *Westward Ho!* 1855. Everyman's Library. London: Dent, 1925.

———. "What, Then, Does Dr. Newman Mean?" 1864. In *Newman's "Apologia Pro Vita Sua": The Two Versions of 1864 & 1865 Preceded by Newman's and Kingsley's Pamphlets*. Introduction by Wilfred Ward. London: Oxford University Press, 1931.

———. *Yeast*. 1849. New York: Fred De Fau, 1899.

Kristeva, Julia. *Desire in Language*. Translated by Leon Roudiez. New York: Columbia University Press, 1982.

———. *Pouvoirs de l'horreur: essai sur l'abjection*. Paris: Éditions du Seuil, 1983.

———. *Powers of Horror: An Essay on Abjection*. Translated by Leon S. Roudiez. New York: Columbia University Press, 1982.

Kroeber, Karl. *Ecological Literary Criticism: Romantic Imagining and the Biology of Mind*. New York: Columbia University Press, 1994.

Lacan, Jacques. *Écrits: A Selection*. Translated by Alan Sheridan. New York: W. W. Norton, 1977.

———. *The Four Fundamental Concepts of Psycho-Analysis*. Edited by Jacques-Alain Miller. Translated by Alan Sheridan. New York: W. W. Norton, 1978.

———. *The Seminar of Jacques Lacan, Book II: The Ego in Freud's Theory and in the Technique of Psychoanalysis, 1954–1955*. Edited by Jacques-Alain Miller. Translated by Sylvana Tomaselli. New York: Cambridge University Press, 1988.

Lane, Christopher. *The Burdens of Intimacy: Psychoanalysis and Victorian Masculinity*. Chicago: University of Chicago Press, 1999.

———. "The Drama of the Impostor: Dandyism and Its Double." *Cultural Critique* 28 (1994): 29–52.

———. *The Ruling Passion: British Colonial Allegory and the Paradox of Homosexual Desire*. Durham: Duke University Press, 1995.

Lang, Cecil Y. "Narcissus Jilted: Byron, *Don Juan*, and the Biographical Imperative." In *Historical Studies and Literary Criticism*, edited by Jerome J. McGann, 143–79. Madison: University of Wisconsin Press, 1985.

Laqueur, Thomas. *Making Sex: Body and Gender from the Greeks to Freud*. Cambridge: Harvard University Press, 1990.

Lavater, Johan. *Essays on Physiognomy*. Translated by Thomas Holcroft. London: William Tegg, 1869.

Lawler, Donald L. "A Note on the Texts." In *The Picture of Dorian Gray*, x–xiii. New York: W. W. Norton, 1988.

Lears, T. J. Jackson. *No Place of Grace: Antimodernism and the Transformation of American Culture, 1880–1920*. New York: Pantheon Books, 1981.

Leeds Mercury 25 April 1812.

Leary, Daniel J. "The Evolutionary Dialectic of Shaw and Teilhard: A Perennial Philosophy." *The Shaw Review* 9 (1966): 15–34.

Le Fanu, Joseph Sheridan. "Carmilla." In *Best Ghost Stories of J. S. Le Fanu*, 274–339. New York: Dover, 1964.

———. "Green Tea." In *Best Ghost Stories of J. S. Le Fanu*, 178–207. New York: Dover, 1964.

Leighton, Angela. "Deconstructive Criticism and Shelley's *Adonais*." In *Shelley Revalued*, edited by Kelvin Everest, 147–64. Totowa, N.J.: Barnes and Noble Books, 1983.

Lillo, George. *The London Merchant*. Edited by William H. McBurney. Lincoln: University of Nebraska Press, 1965.

Lindblad, Ishrat. *Creative Evolution and Shaw's Dramatic Art with Special Reference to "Man and Superman" and "Back to Methuselah."* Uppsala: Uppsala University Press, 1971.

Little, Douglas. "Byron and the Eunuch Muse." *Keats-Shelley Journal* 25 (1976): 24–25.

Litvak, Joseph. *Caught in the Act: Theatricality in the Nineteenth-Century English Novel*. Berkeley: University of California Press, 1992.

Lloyd, Genevieve. *The Man of Reason: "Male" and "Female" in Western Philosophy*. Minneapolis: University of Minnesota Press, 1984.

Lock, John. *A Man of Sorrow*. New York: Nelson, 1965.

Looby, Christopher. " 'The Roots of the Orchis, the Iuli of Chestnuts': The Odor of Male Solitude." In *Solitary Pleasures: The Historical, Literary, and Artistic Discourses of Autoeroticism*, edited by Paula Bennett and Vernon A. Rosario II, 163–88. New York: Routledge, 1995.

Lovell, Ernest. *His Very Self and Voice*. New York: MacMillan, 1954.

Lynch, Deidre. " 'Beating the Track of the Alphabet': Samuel Johnson, Tourism, and the ABCs of Modern Authority." *ELH* 57 (1990): 357–405.

Mackenzie, Henry. *The Man of Feeling*. Edited by Brian Vickers. London: Oxford University Press, 1970.

Macnaughton, W. R. "In Defense of James's *The Tragic Muse*." *The Henry James Review* 7, no. 1 (1985): 5–12.

Mallock, W. H. *The New Republic: Culture, Faith and Philosophy in an English Country House*. 1877. Leicester: Chatto & Windus, 1881.

Manning, Peter J. *Byron and His Fictions*. Detroit: Wayne State University Press, 1978.

———. *Reading Romantics: Texts and Contexts*. New York: Oxford University Press, 1990.

Marchand, Leslie. *Byron: A Portrait*. Chicago: University of Chicago Press, 1972.

———. "Narrator and Narration in *Don Juan*." *Keats-Shelley Journal* 25 (1976): 26–42.

Marcus, Steven. *The Other Victorians*. New York: Humanities Press, 1965.

Marks, Elaine. *Marrano as Metaphor: The Jewish Presence in French Writing*. New York: Columbia University Press, 1996.

Marlowe, Christopher. *Edward the Second*. Edited by W. Moelwyn Merchant. Reprint, 1967. New York: W. W. Norton, 1994.

Marshall, Peter H. *William Godwin*. New Haven: Yale University Press, 1984.

Marshall, William H. *The Structure of Byron's Major Poems*. Philadelphia: University of Pennsylvania Press, 1962.

Martin, Philip W. *Byron: A Poet before His Public*. Cambridge: Cambridge University Press, 1982.

Martin, Robert Bernard. *The Dust of Combat: A Life of Charles Kingsley*. London: Faber & Faber, 1959.

———. *Gerard Manley Hopkins: A Very Private Life*. New York: Putnam's, 1991.

Martin, Robert K. "The 'High Felicity' of Comradeship: A New Reading of *Roderick Hudson*." *American Literary Realism* 11 (1978): 100–8.

Mason, Michael. *The Making of Victorian Sexuality*. New York: Oxford University Press, 1994.

McClintock, Anne. *Imperial Leather: Race, Gender, and Sexuality in the Colonial Contest*. New York: Routledge, 1995.

McCormack, W. J. *Sheridan Le Fanu and Victorian Ireland*. Oxford: Clarendon Press, 1980.

McCracken, Scott. "Writing the Body: Edward Carpenter, George Gissing and Late-Nineteenth-Century Realism." In *Edward Carpenter and Late Victorian Radicalism*, edited by Tony Brown, 178–200. London: Frank Cass, 1990.

McDowell, Frederick P. W. "Heaven, Hell, and Turn-of-the-Century London." In *George Bernard Shaw's "Man and Superman,"* edited by Harold Bloom, 35–47. New York: Chelsea House, 1987.

McGann, Jerome J. *Don Juan in Context*. Chicago: University of Chicago Press, 1976.

———. *Fiery Dust: Byron's Poetic Development*. Chicago: University of Chicago Press, 1968.

McKeon, Michael. "Historicizing Patriarchy: The Emergence of Gender Difference in England, 1660–1760." *Eighteenth-Century Studies* 28 (1995): 295–322.

Mellor, George. "To Thomas Ellis." 30 November 1812. [Sir Joseph] Radcliffe Papers. Document 126/127a. Leeds District Archives.

Meyer, Eric. " 'I Know Thee Not, I Loathe Thy Race': Romantic Orientalism in the Eye of the Other." *ELH* 58 (1991): 657–99.

Michasiw, Kim Ian. "The Social Other: *Don Juan* and the Genesis of the Self." *Mosaic* 22, no. 2 (Spring 1989): 29–48.

Mill, John Stuart. *Essays on Literature and Society*. Edited by J. B. Schneewind. New York: Collier, 1965.

Miller, D. A. *Bringing out Roland Barthes*. Berkeley: University of California Press, 1992.

Milton, John. *Paradise Lost. Complete Poems and Major Prose.* Edited by Merritt Y. Hughes, 173–469. New York: Odyssey Press, 1957.

Monsman, Gerald. "Introduction." In *Gaston de Latour: The Revised Text,* xvii–xlvi. Greensboro: ELT Press, 1995.

———. *Walter Pater's Art of Autobiography.* New Haven: Yale University Press, 1983.

Moon, Michael. "A Small Boy and Others: Sexual Disorientation in Henry James, Kenneth Anger, and David Lynch." In *Comparative American Identities: Race, Sex, and Nationality in the Modern Text,* edited by Hortense Spillers, 141–56. New York: Routledge, 1991.

Moore, Doris Langley. *The Late Lord Byron: Posthumous Dramas.* Philadelphia: Lippincott's, 1957.

Morgan, Thaïs. "Mixed Metaphor, Mixed Gender: Swinburne and the Victorian Critics." *The Victorian Newsletter* 73 (Spring 1988): 16–19.

———. "Reimagining Masculinity in Victorian Criticism: Swinburne and Pater." *Victorian Studies* 36, no. 3 (Spring 1993): 315–32.

Morning Chronicle 1814.

Mosse, George L. *Nationalism and Sexuality: Respectability and Abnormal Sexuality in Modern Europe.* New York: Howard Fertig, 1985.

Myers, Greg. "Nineteenth-Century Popularizations of Thermodynamics and the Rhetoric of Social Prophecy." *Victorian Studies* 29 (1985): 35–66.

Nehemas, Alexander, and Paul Woodruff. *Plato: The Symposium.* Indianapolis: Hackett Publishing Co., 1989.

Nelson, Claudia. *Boys Will Be Girls: The Feminine Ethic and British Children's Fiction, 1857–1917.* New Brunswick: Rutgers University Press, 1990.

Newman, Jay. "The Gilbertianism of *Patience.*" *Dalhousie Review* 65, no. 2 (Summer 1985): 263–82.

Newman, John Henry. *Loss and Gain: The Story of a Convert.* 1848. Edited by Alan G. Hill. Oxford: Oxford University Press, 1986.

Nixon, Jude. *Gerard Manley Hopkins and his Contemporaries.* New York: Garland, 1994.

Nordau, Max. *Degeneration.* London: William Heinemann, 1895.

Norton, Rictor. *Mother Clap's Molly House: The Gay Subculture in England 1700–1830.* London: Gay Men's Press, 1992.

Nunokawa, Jeff. *The Afterlife of Property: Domestic Security and the Victorian Novel.* Princeton: Princeton University Press, 1994.

Oliver, J. W. *The Life of William Beckford.* London: Oxford University Press, 1932.

Owens, Craig. "Outlaws: Gay Men in Feminism." In *Men in Feminism,* edited by Alice Jardine and Paul Smith, 219–32. New York: Routledge, 1989.

"Parallel." *Punch* 19 July 1890: 25.

Parker, David. "The Narrator of *Don Juan.*" *Ariel* 5, no. 1 (1974): 49–58.

Parsons, E. C. *Memorials and Correspondence.* Leeds: T. Walker, 1849.

Parsons, Edward. *History of Leeds.* 2 vols. Leeds: Frederick Hobson, 1834.

Pateman, Carole. *The Sexual Contract.* Stanford: Stanford University Press, 1988.

Pater, Walter. "The Aesthetic Life." Harvard University Library. bMS Eng 1150: 1–39.

———. "Aesthetic Poetry," "Postscript (Romanticism)," and "A Novel by Mr. Oscar Wilde." In *Selected Writings of Walter Pater*, edited by Harold Bloom, 190–98, 208–23, 263–66. New York: Columbia University Press, 1974.

———. "Diaphaneitè." *Miscellaneous Studies*. Vol. 8. The Library Edition of the Works, 247–54. London: Macmillan, 1910.

———. *Gaston de Latour: The Revised Text*. Edited by Gerald Monsman. Greensboro: ELT Press, 1995.

———. *Imaginary Portraits*. Edited by Eugene J. Brzenk. New York: Harper, 1964.

———. *Letters of Walter Pater*. Edited by Lawrence Evans. Oxford: Clarendon Press, 1970.

———. *Marius the Epicurean*. 2 vols., 2d ed. London: Macmillan, 1885.

———. *Plato and Platonism*. Vol. 6. The Library Edition of the Works. London: Macmillan, 1910.

———. *The Renaissance: Studies in Art and Poetry*. The 1893 Text. Edited by Donald L. Hill. Berkeley: University of California Press, 1980.

Paxton, Nancy. *George Eliot and Herbert Spencer*. Princeton: Princeton University Press, 1991.

Pearson, Hesketh. *Gilbert: His Life and Strife*. London: Methuen, 1957.

Peel, Frank. *The Risings of the Luddites*. 4th Edition. London: Cass, 1968.

———. *Spen Valley: Past and Present*. Heckmondwike: Senior & Company, 1893.

Pelham, Camden. *The Chronicles of Crime; or, The New Newgate Calendar*. 2 vols. London: Miles, 1887.

Penzoldt, Peter. *The Supernatural in Fiction*. New York: Humanities Press, 1965.

Pick, Daniel. *Faces of Degeneration: A European Disorder, c. 1848–c. 1918*. Cambridge: Cambridge University Press, 1989.

Pinchbeck, Ivy. *Women Workers and the Industrial Revolution, 1750–1850*. 1930. London: Cass, 1969.

Plato. *The Collected Dialogues of Plato*. Edited by Edith Hamilton and Huntington Cairns, 99–122, 475–574. Princeton: Princeton University Press, 1961.

Plummer, Kenneth, ed. *The Making of the Modern Homosexual*. New York: Barnes & Noble, 1980.

Poovey, Mary. *Making a Social Body: British Cultural Formation 1830–1864*. Chicago: University of Chicago Press, 1995.

Postlewait, Thomas. "Bernard Shaw and Science: The Aesthetics of Causality." In *Victorian Science and Victorian Values, Annals of the New York Academy of Sciences*, vol. 360, edited by James Paradis and Thomas Postlewait, 319–58. New York: New York Academy of Sciences, 1981.

Potkay, Adam. "Beckford's Heaven of Boys." *Raritan* 13 (Summer 1993): 73–86.

Potts, Alex. "Beautiful Bodies and Dying Heroes: Images of Ideal Manhood in the French Revolution." *History Workshop Journal* 30 (Fall 1990): 1–21.

———. *Flesh and the Ideal: Winckelmann and the Origins of Art History*. New Haven: Yale University Press, 1994.

Powder. Directed by Victor Salva. Performed by Mary Steenburgen, Sean Patrick, Lance Henriksen, and Jeff Goldblum. Hollywood Pictures, 1995.

Powers, Lyall H. "James' *The Tragic Muse—Ave Atque Vale.*" *PMLA* 73 (1958): 270–74.

Pratt, Mary Louise. *Imperial Eyes: Travel Writing and Transculturation.* London: Routledge, 1992.

Probyn, Elspeth. *Sexing the Self: Gendered Positions in Cultural Studies.* London: Routledge, 1993.

Ragussis, Michael. *Figures of Conversion: "The Jewish Question" and English National Identity.* Durham: Duke University Press, 1995.

Randall, Adrian. *Before the Luddites: Custom, Community, and Machinery in the English Woolen Industry, 1776–1809.* Cambridge: Cambridge University Press, 1991.

———. "The Shearmen and the Wiltshire Outrages of 1802: Trade Unionism and Industrial Violence." *Social History* 7 (1982): 283–304.

Reade, Brian. *Sexual Heretics: Male Homosexuality in English Literature from 1850 to 1900.* London: Routledge & Kegan Paul, 1970.

Reid, Robert. *Land of Lost Content: The Luddite Revolt, 1812.* London: Heinemann, 1986.

Reiman, Donald, ed. *The Romantics Reviewed: Contemporary Reviews of British Romantic Writers.* 5 vols. New York: Garland, 1972.

Ridenour, George. "The Mode of Byron's *Don Juan.*" *PMLA* 79, no. 4 (1964): 442–46.

———. *The Style of Don Juan.* London: Hamden, 1969.

Ridley, Jane. *Young Disraeli: 1804–1846.* New York: Crown, 1995.

Rieff, Philip. "The Impossible Culture: Wilde as a Modern Prophet." *Salmagundi* 58–59 (Fall 1982-Winter 1983): 406–26.

Rivière, Joan. "Womanliness as a Masquerade." In *Formations of Fantasy*, edited by Victor Burgin, James Donald, and Cora Kaplan, 35–44. London: Methuen, 1986.

Rivers, W. C. *Walt Whitman's Anomaly.* London: George Allen, 1913.

Rose, Jacqueline. *Sexuality in the Field of Vision.* London: Verso, 1986.

Ross, Robert. "Mr. Benson's 'Pater.' " In *Masques and Phases*, 125–34. London: Humphreys, 1909.

Rotundo, E. Anthony. *American Manhood: Transformations in Masculinity from the Revolution to the Modern Era.* New York: Basic Books, 1993.

Rousseau, G. S. "The Pursuit of Homosexuality in the Eighteenth Century: 'Utterly Confused Category' and/or Rich Repository." In *'Tis Nature's Fault: Unauthorized Sexuality during the Enlightenment*, edited by Robert Purks Maccubbin, 132–68. New York: Cambridge University Press, 1987.

Rowbotham, Sheila, and Jeffrey Weeks. *Socialism and the New Life: The Personal and Sexual Politics of Edward Carpenter and Havelock Ellis.* London: Pluto Press, 1977.

Ruskin, John. *Sesame and Lilies.* 1865. New York: Chelsea House Publishers, 1983.

Rutherford, Andrew, ed. *Byron: The Critical Heritage.* New York: Barnes & Noble, 1970.

———. *Byron: A Critical Study.* Stanford: Stanford University Press, 1965.

Ryals, Clyde De L. "The Concept of Becoming in *Marius the Epicurean.*" *Nineteenth-Century Literature* 43, no. 2 (September 1988): 157–74.

Sacks, Peter. *The English Elegy.* Baltimore: Johns Hopkins University Press, 1985.

Said, Edward W. *Beginnings: Intention and Method.* New York: Columbia University Press, 1985.

———. *Culture and Imperialism.* New York: Vintage, 1994.

———. "On Repetition." In *The Literature of Fact*, edited by Angus Fletcher, 135–58. Selected Papers from the English Institute. New York: Columbia University Press, 1976.

———. *Orientalism.* New York: Vintage, 1978.

Sale, Kirkpatrick. *Rebels against the Future: The Luddites and Their War on the Industrial Revolution: Lessons for the Computer Age.* Reading: Addison-Wesley, 1995.

Scarry, Elaine. *The Body in Pain: The Making and Unmaking of the World.* New York: Oxford University Press, 1987.

Schmidgall, Gary. *The Stranger Wilde: Interpreting Oscar.* New York: Dutton, 1994.

Schwarz, Daniel R. *Disraeli's Fiction.* London: Methuen, 1979.

Sedgwick, Eve Kosofsky. *Between Men: English Literature and Male Homosocial Desire.* New York: Columbia University Press, 1985.

———. *Epistemology of the Closet.* Berkeley: University of California Press, 1990.

Seiler, R. M., ed. *Walter Pater: A Life Remembered.* Calgary, Alberta: University of Calgary Press, 1987.

———. *Walter Pater: The Critical Heritage.* Boston: Routledge, 1980.

Semmel, Bernard. *George Eliot and the Politics of National Inheritance.* New York: Oxford University Press, 1994.

Shakespeare, William. *Romeo and Juliet*, edited by J. A. Bryant, Jr. New York: Signet, 1964.

Shaw, Bernard. *Collected Letters.* Edited by Dan H. Laurence. 4 vols. New York: Dodd, Mead & Company, 1965–88.

———. *The Works of Bernard Shaw.* 30 vols. London: Constable, 1930–32.

Shelley, Percy Bysshe. *The Complete Works of Percy Bysshe Shelley.* Edited by Roger Ingpen and Walter E. Peck. 10 vols. New York: Scribner's, 1926–30.

———. "A Discourse on the Manners of the Ancient Greeks Relative to the Subject of Love." In *Shelley's Prose or the Trumpet of a Prophecy*, edited by David Lee Clark, 216–23. Albuquerque: University of New Mexico Press, 1954.

———. *Letters of Percy Bysshe Shelley.* Edited by Frederick L. Jones. 2 vols. Oxford Clarendon Press, 1964.

———. *Shelley's Poetry and Prose.* Edited by Donald H. Reiman and Sharon B. Powers. A Norton Critical Edition. New York: W. W. Norton, 1977.

Shively, Charley, ed. *Calamus Lovers: Walt Whitman's Working-Class Comerados.* San Francisco: Gay Sunshine Press, 1987.

Showalter, Elaine. "The Female Tradition." In *Feminisms: An Anthology of Literary Theory and Criticism*, edited by Robyn R. Warhol and Diane Price Hendl, 269–99. New Brunswick: Rutgers University Press, 1991.

———. *Sexual Anarchy: Gender and Culture at the Fin de Siècle*. New York: Penguin, 1990.

Shuter, William F. "Pater's Reshuffled Text." *Nineteenth-Century Literature* 43 (March 1989): 500–525.

Siegal, Lee. "The Gay Science: Queer Theory, Literature, and the Sexualization of Everything." *The New Republic* 219, no. 19 (9 November 1998): 30–42.

Silverman, Kaja. *The Acoustic Mirror: The Female Voice in Psychoanalysis and Cinema*. Bloomington: Indiana University Press, 1988.

———. *Male Subjectivity at the Margins*. New York: Routledge, 1992.

———. *The Subject of Semiotics*. New York: Oxford University Press, 1983.

———. "Too Early/Too Late: Subjectivity and the Primal Scene in Henry James." *Novel* 21, no. 2–3 (1988): 147–73.

Simon, Henry W., ed. *The Victor Book of the Opera*. 13th ed. New York: Simon & Schuster, 1976.

Sinfield, Alan. *The Wilde Century: Effeminacy, Oscar Wilde and the Queer Moment*. New York: Columbia University Press, 1994.

Singer, Charles. *A Short History of Science to the Nineteenth Century*. Oxford: Clarendon Press, 1941.

Smith, Bruce R. *Homosexual Desire in Shakespeare's England: A Cultural Poetics*. Chicago: University of Chicago Press, 1991.

Smith, F. B. "Labouchere's Amendment to the Criminal Law Amendment Bill." *Historical Studies* 17 (October 1976): 165–73.

Spencer, Herbert. *The Principles of Biology*. Vol. 1. New York: D. Appleton, 1904.

Spenser, Edmund. *The Fairie Queene*. Edited by Thomas P. Roche, Jr., and C. Patrick O'Donnell, Jr. Harmondsworth: Penguin, 1978.

St. Clair, William. *The Godwins and the Shelleys: A Biography of a Family*. New York: W. W. Norton, 1989.

———. *Lord Elgin and the Marbles*. London: Oxford University Press, 1967.

———. *That Greece Might Still Be Free: The Philhellenes in the War of Independence*. London: Oxford University Press, 1972.

St. John-Stevas, Norman. *Obscenity and the Law*. London: Secker & Warburg, 1956.

Stearns, Peter N. *Be a Man! Males in Modern Society*. 2d ed. New York and London: Holmes & Meier, 1990.

Steffan, T. G., E. Steffan, and W. W. Pratt, eds. *Lord Byron: Don Juan*. London: Penguin, 1957.

Sterne, Laurence. *A Sentimental Journey Through France and Italy*. Edited by Ian Jack. 1768. New York: Oxford University Press, 1984.

Stewart, R. W. *Disraeli's Novels Reviewed, 1826–1968*. Metuchen, NJ: Scarecrow Press, 1975.

Stoddardt, Helen. " 'The Precautions of Nervous People Are Infectious': Sheridan Le Fanu's Symptomatic Gothic." *Modern Language Review* 86 (1991): 19–34.

Stokes, John. *In the Nineties*. Chicago: University of Chicago Press, 1989.

Stowe, Harriet Beecher. *Lady Byron Vindicated*. London: Sampson Low, 1870.

Stratton, Jon. *The Virgin Text: Fiction, Sexuality and Ideology*. Brighton: Harvester Press, 1987.

Sussman, Herbert. "Masculinity Transformed: Appropriation in Walter Pater's Early Writing." In *Victorian Masculinities: Manhood and Masculine Poetics in Early Victorian Literature and Art*, 173–202. New York: Cambridge University Press, 1995.

Sutherland, John. "King of the Tories." *New York Times Book Review* 30 April 1995: 28.

Sutton, Max Keith. *W. S. Gilbert*. Boston: Twayne, 1975.

Sykes, D. F. E. *Ben o' Bill's, The Luddite*. London: Simpkin, Marshall & Company, 1898.

———. *History of the Colne Valley*. Slaithwaite: F. Walker, 1906.

Symonds, John Addington. *The Letters of John Addington Symonds*. 3 vols. Edited by Herbert Schueller and Robert Peters. Detroit: Wayne State University Press, 1969.

———. *A Problem in Greek Ethics*. In *Male Love*, edited by John Lauritsen, 1–73. New York: Pagan Press, 1983.

———. *A Problem in Modern Ethics*. In *Male Love*, edited by John Lauritsen, 75–113. New York: Pagan Press, 1983.

Tasso, Torquato. *Jerusalem Regained*. Translated by Edward Fairfax. Introduction by Roberto Weiss. 1580. Carbondale: Southern Illinois University Press, 1962.

Tennyson, Alfred. *The Poems of Tennyson*. Edited by Christopher Ricks. London: Longman Group, 1969.

Terdiman, Richard. *Discourse/Counter-Discourse: The Theory and Practice of Symbolic Resistance in Nineteenth-Century France*. Ithaca: Cornell University Press, 1985.

Theweleit, Klaus. *Male Fantasies*. Minneapolis: University of Minnesota Press, 1989.

Thomis, Malcolm I. *The Luddites: Machine-Breaking in Regency England*. Hamden: Archon, 1970.

Thomis, Malcolm, and Jennifer Grimmett. *Women in Protest, 1800–1850*. New York: St. Martin's, 1982.

Thompson, E. P. *Customs in Common*. 1991. Harmondsworth: Penguin, 1993.

———. *The Making of the English Working Class*. 1962. Harmondsworth: Penguin, 1972.

———. "The Moral Economy of the English Crowd in the Eighteenth Century." *Past and Present* 50 (1971): 76–136.

Thorslev, Peter. *The Byronic Hero*. Minneapolis: University of Minnesota Press, 1982.

Traubel, Horace, ed. *With Walt Whitman in Camden*. Vol. 4. Edited by Sculley Bradley; vol. 5 edited by Gertrude Traubel; vol. 6 edited by Gertrude Traubel and William White; vol. 7 edited by Jeanne Chapman and Robert MacIsaac. Boston: Small, Maynard, 1906 (v.1). New York: D. Appleton (v.2). New York: M. Kennerley (v.3). Philadelphia: U of Pennsylvania P, 1964 (v.4–5). Carbondale: Southern Illinios University Press, 1982–92 (v.6–7).

Treasury Solicitor's Papers 11/813, Public Records Office.

Trumbach, Randolph. "London's Sapphists: From Three Sexes to Four Genders in the Making of Modern Culture." In *Body Guards: The Cultural Politics of Gender Ambiguity*, edited by Julia Epstein and Kristina Straub, 112–41. New York: Routledge, 1991.

———. "London's Sodomites: Homosexual Behavior and Western Culture in the 18th Century." *Journal of Social History* 2, no. 1 (1977): 15–18.

Tsuzuki, Chushichi. *Edward Carpenter 1844–1929, Prophet of Human Fellowship*. Cambridge: Cambridge University Press, 1980.

Turner, Frank Miller. *Between Science and Religion: The Reaction to Scientific Naturalism in Late Victorian England*. New Haven: Yale University Press, 1974.

Tylor, Edward B. *The Origins of Culture*. Gloucester: Peter Smith, 1970.

Uglow, Jennifer. *George Eliot*. New York: Pantheon Books, 1987.

Valency, Maurice. "*Man and Superman*." In *George Bernard Shaw's "Man and Superman*," edited by Harold Bloom, 75–104. New York: Chelsea House, 1987.

Vance, Norman. *The Sinews of the Spirit: The Ideal of Christian Manliness in Victorian Literature and Religious Thought*. Cambridge: Cambridge University Press, 1985.

Vicinus, Martha. *Independent Women: Work and Community for Single Women, 1850–1920*. Chicago: University of Chicago Press, 1985.

———. *The Industrial Muse: A Study of Nineteenth-Century British Working-Class Literature*. New York: Barnes & Noble, 1974.

Virchow, Rudolph. *Die Cellularpathologie*. Berlin: A. Hirschwald, 1858.

Virgil. *The Aeneid*. Translated by Robert Fitzgerald. New York: Random, 1981.

Viswanathan, Gauri. "Raymond Williams and British Colonialism." *Yale Journal of Criticism* 4 (Spring 1991): 47–66.

Vital, Anthony. "Byron and the Regency: The Great World in *Don Juan*." *Bulletin of Research in the Humanities*. Vol. 79. New York: Public Library, 1976.

Von Eckardt, Wolf, Sander L. Gilman, and J. Edward Chamberlin. *Oscar Wilde's London: A Scrapbook of Vices and Virtues, 1880–1900*. New York: Anchor Press, 1987.

Waldron, Randall. "Whitman as the Nazarene: An Unpublished Drawing." *Walt Whitman Quarterly Review* 7, no. 4 (1990): 192–193.

Walker, George. *The Costume of Yorkshire*. London: Bensley, 1814.

Walkowitz, Judith. *Prostitution and Victorian Society*. New York: Cambridge University Press, 1982.

Waller, Gregory A. *The Living and the Undead: From Stoker's "Dracula" to Ramero's "Dawn of the Dead*." Urbana: University of Illinois Press, 1986.

Walpole, Horace. *Horace Walpole's Correspondence*. Edited by W. S. Lewis. 48 vols. New Haven: Yale University Press, 1937–82.

Waters, Lindsay. "The 'Desultory Rhyme' of *Don Juan*: Byron, Pulci and the Improvisatory Style." *ELH* 45 (1978): 429–42.

Watkins, Daniel P. *Social Relations in Byron's "Easter Tales*." Rutherford: Associated University Press, 1987.

Weeks, Jeffrey. *Against Nature: Essays on History, Sexuality and Identity*. London: Rivers Oram, 1991.

———. *Coming Out: Homosexual Politics in Britain from the Nineteenth Century to the Present*. 2d ed. London: Quartet Books, 1990.

———. "Discourse, Desire and Sexual Deviance: Some Problems in a History of Homosexuality." In *The Making of the Modern Homosexual*, edited by Kenneth Plummer, 87–111. London: Hutchinson, 1981.

———. "Inverts, Perverts, and Mary-Annes: Male Prostitution and the Regulation of Homosexuality in England in the Nineteenth and Early Twentieth Centuries." *Journal of Homosexuality* 6 (Fall 1980-Winter 1981): 113–34.

———. "Movements of Affirmation: Sexual Meanings and Homosexual Identities." *Radical History Review* 20 (Summer/Spring 1979): 164–79.

———. *Sex, Politics and Society: The Regulation of Sexuality Since 1800*. 2d ed. London: Longman, 1981.

———. *Sexuality and Its Discontents: Meanings, Myths, and Modern Sexualities*. London: Routledge, 1985.

Weiner, Marc A. *Richard Wagner and the Anti-Semitic Imagination*. Lincoln: University of Nebraska Press, 1995.

Weintraub, Stanley. *Disraeli: A Biography*. New York: Truman Talley Books, 1993.

Wells, H. G. *H. G. Wells: Early Writings in Science and Science Fiction*. Edited by Robert M. Philmus and David Y. Hughes. Berkeley: University of California Press, 1975.

White, Norman. *Hopkins: A Literary Biography*. Oxford: Clarendon Press, 1992.

Whitman, Walt. *Leaves of Grass, Comprehensive Reader's Edition*. Edited by Harold W. Blodgett and Sculley Bradley. New York: New York University Press, 1965.

———. *Prose Works 1892*. Edited by Floyd Stovall. 2 vols. New York: New York University Press, 1963–64.

Wihl, Gary. "Novels as Theories in a Liberal Society." In *Constructive Criticism: The Human Sciences in the Age of Theory*, edited by Martin Kreiswirth and Thomas Carmichael, 101–13. Toronto: University of Toronto Press, 1995.

Wilde, Oscar. *The Artist as Critic: Critical Writings of Oscar Wilde*. Edited by Richard Ellmann, 340–408. Chicago: University of Chicago Press, 1982.

———. *The Complete Works of Oscar Wilde*. New York: Harper & Row, 1989.

———. *Letters of Oscar Wilde*. Edited by Rupert Hart-Davis. New York: Oxford University Press, 1962.

———. *Oscar Wilde's Oxford Notebooks*. Edited by Philip E. Smith and Michael S. Helfand. New York: Oxford University Press, 1989.

———. *The Portrait of Mr. W. H.* In *The Riddle of Shakespeare's Sonnets*, edited by E. Hubler, et al., 246–47. 1889. London: Routledge, 1962.

———. *The Picture of Dorian Gray*. Edited by Donald L. Lawler. A Norton Critical Edition. New York: W. W. Norton, 1988.

———. *The Picture of Dorian Gray*. 1890, revised 1891. Harmondsworth: Penguin, 1982.

———. *Teleny: A Novel Attributed to Oscar Wilde*. Edited by Winston Heyland. 1893. San Francisco: Gay Sunshine Press, 1984.

———. *Works of Oscar Wilde: Poems*. Vol. 1, Sunflower Edition. Edited by Richard Le Gallienne, 64–79, 219–43. New York: Lamb Publishing, 1909.

Williams, Carolyn. "Utopia, Limited: Nationalism, Empire and Parody in the Comic Operas of Gilbert and Sullivan. In *Cultural Politics at the "Fin de Siècle,"* edited by Sally Ledger and Scott McCracken, 221–47. Cambridge: Cambridge University Press, 1995.

Winckelmann, John Joachim. *History of Ancient Art*. Translated by G. Henry Lodge. 4 vols. New York: Ungar, 1968.

Winwar, Frances. *Oscar Wilde and the Yellow Nineties*. New York: Harper, 1941.

Wolfson, Susan J. " 'Their She Condition': Cross-Dressing and the Politics of Gender in *Don Juan*." In *Recent Romantic Revisionary Poetry Criticism*, 267–89. New Brunswick: Rutgers University Press, 1993.

Wollstonecraft, Mary. *A Vindication of the Rights of Woman*. Edited by Miriam Brody. 1792. London: Penguin, 1985.

Woolf, Virginia. *Mrs. Dalloway*. 1925. New York: Harcourt, Brace, Jovanovich, 1953.

Wright, Thomas. *The Life of Walter Pater*. 2 vols. London: Everett, 1907.

Wynne, Brian. "Physics and Psychics: Science, Symbolic Action, and Social Control in Late Victorian England." In *Natural Order: Historical Studies of Scientific Culture*, edited by Barry Barnes and Steven Shapin, 167–86. Beverly Hills: Sage Publications, 1979.

List of Contributors

KEVIN BINFIELD is Assistant Professor of English at Murray State University. He is interested in working-class authors of the eighteenth and nineteenth centuries. He has published articles on William Cobbett, Percy Bysshe Shelley, and Joanna Southcott and is currently finishing a book, under contract with Johns Hopkins University Press, on the writings of the Luddite movement.

WILLIAM D. BREWER is Professor of English at Appalachian State University. He received his A.B. from Harvard University (*magna cum laude*) in 1977 and his M.A. and Ph.D. in English literature from the University of Virginia in 1979 and 1985, respectively. He is a member of the Keats-Shelley Association, the Modern Language Association, the North American Society for the Study of Romanticism, and the John Clare Society. His previous publications include *The Shelley-Byron Conversation* (University Press of Florida, 1994), and articles in *Papers on Language and Literature*, *Philological Quarterly*, *Keats-Shelley Journal*, and *Southern Humanities Review*. He has also edited *New Essays on Lord Byron* (Contemporary Research Press, forthcoming).

ERIC DAFFRON is Assistant Professor of English at Mississippi University for Women. In addition to having written articles on William Godwin, Mary Shelley, and Jane Austen, he is completing a book manuscript entitled "Romantic Doubles: Sex and Sympathy in British Gothic Literature, 1790–1830.

ANDRÉ L. DECUIR is Assistant Professor of English at Muskingum College and specializes in Victorian literature. He has published and presented papers on George Eliot, Mary Shelley, Thomas Hardy, Charlotte Brontë, and Elizabeth Gaskell; Stephen King and the aesthetics of horror fiction has become a growing scholarly interest.

ELIZABETH DELL is a Ph.D. candidate at the University of Texas, Austin. Her dissertation, titled "When Mammy Left Missus: Confederate Women, Cultural Loss, and the Modern South," concentrates on Southern women diarists, investigating the autobiographical form and its relation to the culturally constructed Southern lady. She has edited two recently published books, a biography on an eighteenth-century Russian historian and a work on Central Texas anthropology. She has also presented papers focusing on issues of masculine identity, race, and gender in the works of Emily Brontë, Elizabeth Barrett Browning, and Mary Chesnut.

RICHARD DELLAMORA lives in Toronto and teaches in the departments of English and Cultural Studies at Trent University. In 1998–1999, he was affiliated as a Guggenheim fellow with New York University, where he was writing a book to be entitled Jews, Sodomites, and Irishmen. He is the editor of *Victorian Sexual Dissidence* (University of Chicago Press, 1999), co-editor, with Daniel Fischlin, of *The Work of Opera* (Columbia University Press, 1997) and the author of *Apocalyptic Overtures: Sexual Politics and the Sense of an Ending* (Rutgers Univ. Press, 1994) and *Masculine Desire: The Sexual Politics of Victorian Aestheticism* (Univ. of North Carolina Press, 1990).

DENNIS DENISOFF is Assistant Professor at the University of Waterloo, Ontario. He is completing a book on gender and portraiture in Victorian literature. He has published, or has forthcoming, various articles on gender, sexuality, and aesthetics in nineteenth- and twentieth-century literature. He is the editor of *Queeries: An Anthology of Gay Male Prose* (Arsenal, 1993) and co-editor of *Perennial Decay: On the Aesthetics and Politics of Decadence* (University of Pennsylvania Press, 1999).

LAURA FASICK is Associate Professor of English at Moorhead State University. She has published articles on eighteenth- and nineteenth-century authors in such journals as *Nineteenth-Century Literature, Victorian Newsletter, English Literature in Transition, Essays in Literature, South Atlantic Review*, and *Dickens Studies Annual*. She is the author of *Vessels of Meaning: Women's Bodies, Gender Norms, and Class Bias from Richardson to Lawrence* (Northern Illinois University Press, 1997).

FREDERICK GREENE received his Ph.D. from the University of California, Santa Barbara, in June 1996. His dissertation, titled "Subversions of Pastoral: Queer Theory, Abjection, and the Politics of Arcadia," deals with the function of queer theory in providing a discourse and means for interpreting pastoral's denaturalizing, allegorical, and ironic poetics. He presently lives in Hollywood and is doing freelance work for film and television.

JONATHAN GROSS is Associate Professor of English at DePaul University and Director of the M.A. in English program. He is the editor of *Byron's "Corbeau Blanc": The Life and Letters of Lady Melbourne, 1751–1818* (Houston: Rice University Press, 1997) and has written on Byron's politics and Hazlitt's *Liber Amoris* for *Philological Quarterly* and *Studies in English Literature*. He has also contributed to *British Romanticism: An Encyclopedia* and *The Columbia History of British Poetry*.

DONALD E. HALL is Professor and Associate Chair of English at California State Univeristy, Northridge. He is the editor of *Muscular Christianity: Embodying the Victorian Age* (Cambridge University Press, 1994), the co-editor of *RePresenting Bisexualities: Subjects and Cultures of Fluid Desire* (New York University Press, 1996), and the author of *Fixing Patriarchy: Feminism and Mid-Victorian Male Novelists* (New York University Press, 1996). He is currently working on a book entitled "The Ties That Bind: Victorian Classifications and Postmodern Crises."

CHRISTOPHER LANE is Associate Professor of English at Emory University. He is the author of *The Ruling Passion: British Colonial Allegory and the Paradox of Homosexual Desire* (Duke University Press, 1995) and *The Burdens of Intimacy: Psychoanalysis and Victorian Masculinity* (University of Chicago Press, 1999), as well as editor of *The Psychoanalysis of Race* (Columbia University Press, 1998).

JAY LOSEY is Associate Professor of English and Director of Graduate Studies at Baylor University. He has published articles on nineteenth- and twentieth-century authors in such journals as *English Literature in Transition, Conradiana, James Joyce Quarterly*, and the *Journal of European Studies*. He is presently at work on a book-length study of literary epiphany in the nineteenth and twentieth century.

KATHLEEN MCDOUGALL received her Ph.D. at the University of Toronto in 1995. Her thesis, titled "Sexuality and Creativity in the 1890s: Economy of Self in the Social Organism," deals with four fin-de-siècle authors: Oscar Wilde, Bernard Shaw, H.G. Wells, and

Joseph Conrad. The thesis explores the ways in which these writers represent the ideal male self and how their representations demonstrate an engagement with scientific naturalism and other nineteenth-century discourses. She is a co-author of "Semiotic Play at McDonald's: Food, Fakes, and Fun," published in *Recherche semiotique/Semiotic Inquiry* 14 (1994) and recently published an article on Oscar Wilde in *Victorian Review* 23 (1997).

WILLIAM A. PANNAPACKER received his Ph.D. in the History of American Civilization at Harvard University in 1999. He is now a lecturer in the Department of History and Literature at Harvard, where he specializes in American cultural studies. He has published numerous articles in this field and is currently revising his dissertation on Anglo-American authorial identities for publication.

Acknowledgments

THE EDITORS ARE GRATEFUL TO THE FOLLOWING FOR PERMISSION TO reproduce copyright material: Duke University Press for Christopher Lane's essay, "The Impossibility of Seduction in Henry James's *Roderick Hudson* and *The Tragic Muse*," which originally appeared in *American Literature*, 68:4 (Winter 1996), pp. 739–64. Copyright 1996. Duke University Press. All rights reserved. Reprinted with permission. The Society of Authors on behalf of the Bernard Shaw Estate for extracts from Bernard Shaw's *Collected Letters: 1874–1897* and *Collected Letters 1898–1910*. The Director of Leisure Services, Sheffield City Council for photographs of Edward Carpenter in his late twenties, of Carpenter with John Johnston and George Merrill, and of Carpenter aged 43. The editors of *European Romantic Review* for Jonathan David Gross's essay " 'One Half What I Should Say': Byron's Gay Narrator in *Don Juan*," 9:3 (Summer 1998): 323–350. We are grateful to the Working Class Movement Library for supplying us with a photograph of the original print of *The Leader of the Luddites* and to Emory University for permission to use an illustration from George Walker's *The Costume of Yorkshire*. The Graduate School of Appalachian State University supplied funds to pay for reproductions of the Edward Carpenter photographs. Jay Losey expresses appreciation to Christine Pye and Robin Rhea Fennelly for their editorial assistance and to Elizabeth and their children, Dylan and Clare, for their abiding love.

Index